Alym Amlani, CPA, CA

Paul Davis, MBA, LL.D.

PRESENTING AND MODELING BUSINESS DATA

BETA3 EDITION AUGUST 2025

Cover by Luna Design, Buenos Aires

ISBN: Paperback: 978-1-7380436-2-0

TERRITORIAL ACKNOWLEDGMENT

This book was entirely written and researched on the ancestral territories of the First Nations in what is today known as Canada. Both authors teach, and Paul lives, at the University of British Columbia on the unceded territory of the *xʷməθkʷəy̓əm* (Musqueam) people. For thousands of years, they have sought to walk gently on this land. We honor their deep connection to the land, water and resources of the Point Grey Peninsula.

Author Alym lives, and also teaches, on the unceded territories of the *Semyome (*Semiahmoo), *q̓íc̓əy̓* (Katzie), and qʷaƛ̓ən (Kwantlen) First Nations, who have cared for and stewarded the land for thousands of years.

We honor their histories, their cultures, and their ongoing contributions to this region. It is important that we reflect on the legacy of colonization and affirm our commitment to respectful relationships with Indigenous communities. We sincerely express our gratitude for the opportunity to meet, learn, study, teach and write on their lands.

ACKNOWLEDGMENTS

A huge THANK YOU to Erin Majid for providing valuable feedback on the Excel dashboard section of this book, and to Alina McGuinness for her review and feedback on Solver methodology. Our student research assistants Stefanija Kovacevic and Ruby Petchsang reviewed several sections of the book and made valuable suggestions, corrections and contributions.

LINKS

For eBook users who receive the .pdf version: this book contains many links to online files. Although they may appear to be "clickable," sometimes the format causes them to be truncated. If an error message appears after clicking on a link, please try instead copying the entire link into a browser; the problem should then be resolved.

FEEDBACK

We are always open to, and very grateful for, feedback about any aspect of this book, which is continuously monitored, corrected, and updated. It would not be what it is without the contributions of many students who have sent us corrections, requests, and suggestions during its embryonic phase.

Please email pauldavisca@gmail.com to:

(1) send corrections, complaints, or suggestions.
(2) request a zip file of the downloadable Excel source files.
(3) order a paperback copy.

BY THE SAME AUTHORS

Information Systems for accountants, 4th edition. 2025, published by Kendall Hunt.

ChatGPT Ate My Homework: What educators need to know about generative AI. Canadian edition published in July 2025, available direct from the authors or from Lulu Press, https://www.lulu.com/shop/alym-amlani-and-paul-davis/chatgpt-ate-my-homework-what-educators-need-to-know-about-gen-ai-canadian-edition/paperback/product-dy6dnyr.html

ChatGPT Ate My Homework: American Edition published in July 2025.

O Chatgpt Comeu Minha Lição de Casa: O que os educadores precisam saber sobre IA generativa Portuguese/Brazilian edition also published in July 2025.

COMING SOON

With Professor Seni Hazzan of Hult International Business School, *International Business Strategies for Growth Markets: Creating Sustainable, Entrepreneurial Expansion.* Published by Routledge, it will be available from Amazon in October 2025.

Contents

PREFACE

In the 1980s I (Paul) lived in Indonesia, in central Java. While studying the national language, Bahasa Indonesia, I learned the fascinating idiom of local greetings. When Javanese locals meet, two of the most common expressions, both rhetorical, are "Dari mana?" and "Mau ke mana?" Literally, "Where are you coming from?" and "Where are you going?"

Almost half a century later, as an accountancy student, I reflected on those questions and realized that they express the very essence of the courses about data and its uses. Audit and accountancy are all about "Where are we coming from and where are we today?" Into the mix introduce "Where are we going?" which addresses budgeting and forecasting. Descriptive and diagnostic analytics satisfy questions about where we've been and where we are; predictive analytics, including regression and other tools, help us understand where we might be going, while visualizations enable us to present our findings clearly and cogently.

At the center of it all is the art of storytelling. It's featured in every facet of human existence. Storytelling is enshrined in every great culture—for example Ping Shu is an essential element of Chinese cultural identity.

In Indigenous cultures in what is now Canada, storytelling has a sacred nature. Storytellers must often be specially trained and given special rights; they are the trusted knowledge keepers of society. They hold and share the values that keep communities together, connecting generations, ancestors, past, present, and future. Stories reinforce cultural identity, bolster resilience in the face of adversity, and inspire today's youngsters to continue values and traditions exemplified by the heroes and heroines of yesterday's legends. Today, in business, stories are used to share complex information and facilitate comprehension; this is but a continuation of an educational effort practiced for thousands of years by Indigenous narratives. Storytelling draws its strength from truth and insight; as you work to draw out the deeper aspects of financial data, you are becoming part of an immutable tradition that was established here long before the arrival of the first European settlers.

As languages die and literature is lost, stories live on to preserve the wisdom and spirit of our forebears. Not convinced? Think about these areas of modern endeavor:

- *Religion.* Every major world religion, without exception, is based on a story. The Quran, the Bible, the Tipitaka, the Bhagavad-Gita, the Guru Granth Sahib, the Book of Mormon—the list is almost endless. Most such books not only contain stories but also predictions of the future.
- *Politics.* "Vote for me, this is what I've done! And I'm going to do that." Successful politicians are among the world's greatest storytellers; when you come to study abuses of data and visualization, you might be surprised to see how often the culprits are also politicians.
- *Literature, including poetry.* Almost every famous and widely read book in the world is a story. And every great author is a phenomenal storyteller. JK Rowling, Fyodor Dostoevsky, Ernest Hemingway, Charles Dickens—an endless list. Some timeless authors like George Orwell partially earned fame by their accurate predictions of the future.

- *Music.* Many great songs tell a story, but even classical compositions are often based on legends. Rimsky-Korsakov's Scheherazade may be the best-known, but Tchaikovsky's 1812 Overture is based on actual history; every opera ever written is a narrative.
- *Law.* Every legal case, civil or criminal, and every investigation is about getting to the bottom of the story. What happened? The determination of each case prescribes what is going to happen.
- *Medicine.* What is the patient's history? What is their status (diagnosis)? What is going to happen (prognosis)?
- *Military Life.* Every commander wakes up to a daily briefing (what has happened, what is the current situation?) then plans for the day ahead (what do we do next?).
- *Relationships.* How do you get to know a person, make decisions about the future you might have with them? You listen to their stories, evaluate the source and the content, and think about what a future with them might be like.

We could go on, and on, and on … instead let's get to business. We will first look at the data we have, see or acquire. We will think critically about whether we are handling it correctly. Next, we will look at how it might be presented visually, then move on to various mathematical treatments. We will explore together how to compile and evaluate data, how to portray it, what tools are available for those processes, and what predictions we can make from it. We'll learn how to establish the facts, tell the story, and look into the future. All using data. What could be more interesting than that?

We hope you will enjoy learning from this book as much as we have enjoyed writing it. And, we hope this is not the only book you will read while studying data visualization. Stephen Few is a leading author in the field; he has published several seminal works. We highly recommend the three books listed in the "References" section.

VANCOUVER, B.C., AUGUST 2025

Alym Amlani
Paul Davis

PART I. VISUALIZING BUSINESS DATA

1. CRITICAL THINKING, DATA QUALITY, BIASES, AND LOGICAL ERRORS

Introduction

A challenge[1]

Imagine yourself in a classroom. The teacher writes three large numbers on the whiteboard and tells you that their sequence conforms to a rule. Your task is simply to determine what the rule is by guessing triplets of numbers. After you make each attempt, you'll either receive a check mark if your sequence conforms, or a cross if it doesn't.

The numbers are:

2 — 4 — 6

While we can't replicate the experiment here because you are reading a book, try this instead. Take a blank piece of paper and write down the five sequences you think you might try as you attempt to identify the rule.

If you are like most of our students, you will probably have attempts resembling the ones below:

TABLE 1: Sequential guesses to test a theory

4 — 6 — 8	✓
5 — 10 — 15	✓
10 — 14 — 18	✓
3 — 2 — 1	X
10 —100 — 999	✓

[1] The original publication of this test was by British psychologist Peter Cathcart Wason (1960), who was a pioneer in the study of reasoning.

Typically, in our classes it takes a few minutes (and many guesses) before someone has figured out the rule. It's not a very complex rule, it is simply that each successive number must be higher than the last. But the rule itself is not what's important, it's the nature of the attempts made to discover it.

It was only on the <u>fourth</u> attempt that this student tried something they thought was likely to be wrong, to move closer to knowing the rule. In each of the three previous attempts, they attempted to write down a sequence that would be correct, to test their latest belief about the rule.

In 4–6–8, they tested whether the numbers had to rise in increments of two, and whether they had to be even numbers. Although the attempt had a positive result, it did not prove either theory.

In 5–10–15, they tested whether the numbers needed to grow in equal increments, and this time whether they had to be even numbers. All they succeeded in learning, however, was that the even number aspect was not required.

10–14–18 achieved nothing. The student already knew that the numbers could be odd or even but was still assuming that the increments had to be the same.

It was only with 3–2–1 that the student finally tested whether incrementation was required at all—and learned that without incrementation, the rule was not satisfied.

At this point, students will often correctly guess the rule. It's only when we identify *incorrect* triplets that we truly learn something. So why do most people guess triplets that fit the pattern? The answer is confirmation bias. Not only do we look for information to confirm our views positively, we tend to interpret anything ambiguous in a way that also confirms what we already believe (Darley & Gross, 1983). We'll spend much more time studying biases shortly.

For example, if the first proposed sequence had been 6–4–2, and it was marked incorrect, the student would already have guessed that there was no rule about even numbers. And from the fact that the incorrect sequence descended, they could safely have concluded that some sort of ascendency was required. It's a fair bet that as a second attempt, this student would have tried an ascending sequence with non-matching increments, including odd numbers, and would have discerned the rule after two attempts.

This chapter will be all about assumptions, beliefs, testing data and arriving efficiently at correct conclusions. We'll look carefully at all sorts of fallacies and failings, to better prepare ourselves for making conclusions supported by our data. We'll be travelling on a path towards a result—arriving at, and communicating, a conclusion based on data. The journey is beset with tricks, traps and trash just waiting to lead the unwary down the wrong path.

To achieve the best results from our analysis, we want to start with good data, we want to continue with best practices in processing the data, and end with top notch interpretation and presentation. Critical thought asks the enquiring mind to evaluate each of these areas, which can be summarized as inputs, processes and outputs (including presentation). In the following pages we will engage in a great deal of metacognition—thinking about thinking.

The data sets may be large, indeed vast; the consequences of a conclusion may be earth-shattering. Nonetheless the process of following these steps remains the same and the potential failings along the way do not change.

Quality of data

Consider the source

Stories about numbers begin with data. Here, too, our suspicion must also begin.

Data divide into two principal types: primary data, which are original, untouched numbers or observations directly gathered by researchers, and secondary data, which have already gone through treatments so that they can be included in publications such as websites, books or articles (Creswell & Creswell, 2018). Often, however, data are presented which bear neither of these features; they are supposed "facts" repeated by people with an interest in drawing conclusions from them.

There's an adage attributed to William Mellin, an IBM programmer who worked in the 1950s and 1960s. Garbage in, garbage out. GIGO is today regarded as a fundamental principle of computing. Before starting our analysis, we must pause and think about data quality. How were they collected? By whom, and in what circumstances? When were they collected (how old, or dated, are they)? Why are these data important (if they are)? What methods were used and how were they applied? Did the people collecting the data have any vested interest in the outcome? What is/was the geographical scope? Who is presenting the data, and can they be trusted? Statisticians generally agree that there are at least five key aspects of data quality: accuracy, completeness, reliability, relevance and timeliness; different authors add further characteristics, such as uniqueness and validity, but always include the first five. Detailed breakdowns can reach 20 or more individual aspects (for example Bryman, 2016).

A sad but compelling illustration of data which vary according to the source is estimation of casualties in the Ukraine-Russia war. In August 2023, a Turkish news website, Hurseda Haber (hurseda.net), reported that to date, 157,000 Ukrainian soldiers had died in the conflict. The site went on to claim that Russian losses were 18,000 (Grass Factcheck, 2023). Yet in December 2022, Mykhailo Podolyak, a senior advisor to the Ukrainian government, was putting official losses at 10,000 to 13,000 (Maishman & Lukiv, 2022). Shortly before that, Russian defense minister Sergei Shoigu had given out a startlingly precise number of Russian military deaths at 5,937 (Reuters, 2022). On February 2, 2023, the New York Times boldly claimed that at least 200,000 Russian soldiers had died in the conflict (Cooper et al, 2023). Meanwhile in one of the first independent analyses of Russian losses conducted in Germany, put the current figure at around 50,000 in July, 2023 (The Associated Press, 2023).

While these numbers were not produced simultaneously, they are close enough in time to make us think that they can't all be right. Going back to the Turkish claim, it emerges that the website said the numbers came from research by the Israeli intelligence agency, Mossad. Really? Is it likely that Mossad would share its research with a Turkish journalist?

We invite you to look at each of these calculations and consider them critically. What do you conclude about the quality of the data and their sources?

Quite besides reviewing numbers with suspicion, there are often great clues that data are in fact unreliable. You will often see these words in American news stories—"an official spoke on condition of anonymity." This could be code for "no one actually wants to take responsibility for the accuracy of these figures" but it could equally mean "we don't want to tell you where we got these numbers from." How reliable are data that no one wants to own?

A well-known test for evaluating the objective reliability of data is the colorfully named CRAAP test, originally created at the University of California (Blakeslee, 2004). The acronym recalls the application of five questions:

- Currency—how recent are the data?
- Relevance—does the data truly relate to the research topic?
- Authority—if in a publication, is it respected? If there's an author, are they an expert?
- Accuracy—does the source give good evidence for its assertions?
- Purpose—does the source have an intention?

You have surely noticed the pervasiveness of data analysis in the world of politics. The pursuit of political polling, prediction and analysis provides vast numbers of instances of data which are unreliable. Election data might well be thought of as the ultimate in data collection, but only if the election is conducted in a free, fair and unforced manner. A stunning example is the Syrian presidential election in 2021. Incumbent president Bashar al-Assad "won" the election with a resounding 95% of votes. But there's a problem—due to a civil war, displacement of population and the fact that ballots were only available in areas under government control, only about 10 million people were truly able to vote, another 8 million were displaced or in areas where no voting could take place (Associated Press, 2021). Yet according to official results Assad received over 13 million votes. Voter turnout was over 130% (Reuters, 2021)!

History is replete with examples of research results compiled by organizations with a vested interest in the outcome. Here are just a few you will easily recognize:

- Lung cancer "research" compiled for cigarette manufacturers (Harris, 2008).
- Intelligence "research" compiled for racist organizations (Croizet, 2012).
- Health benefits "research" on margarine compiled for the dairy industry (Warwick, 2020).
- Fuel emissions "research" compiled for auto manufacturers (EPA, 2024).
- Sexual health "research" carried out for vendors of nutritional supplements (Bruno, 2022).

Do we have all the data we need?

In May 2019, journalist Clare Hennig posted the following grim news on the CBC news website:

> *Motorcyclist deaths in B.C. spike 50% in a year*
>
> Last year saw 51 deaths across the province—higher than any other year over the past decade and a 50 per cent increase compared to 2017, when 34 motorcyclists died (Hennig, 2019).

Clare's colleague Moira Wyton posted another article on the subject in May 2023:

> *String of motorcycle deaths in B.C. spurs calls for improved road repairs, safety standards*

> At least six motorcyclists have died so far this year, the same as this time in 2021... Motorcycles account for about four per cent of ICBC-insured vehicles, but make up about 14 per cent of crash claims ... Each year, there are about 2,200 crashes resulting in around 1,500 injuries and 40 deaths (Wyton, 2023-a).

Ms. Wyton didn't leave it there. On June 1, 2023, she posted a similar article:

> *Rise in motorcyclist deaths prompts calls for enhanced safety training.* 6 motorcyclists have died so far this year in B.C. (Wyton, 2023-b).

A close reading of the second article, which focuses on a rider who died after riding into a large pothole, shows that the other five fatalities had nothing to do with the condition of the road—at least half were caused by collisions with other vehicles. In effect the call for action, to improve road conditions by fixing potholes, is based on a single event! How many other riders died or were injured because of road defects? We have no idea.

The bulk of additional reporting in these two articles consisted of speculation and calls for various actions, and no one would dispute that any initiative which reduces accidental deaths could be worthwhile. However, there were no data offered in these articles which supported the conclusions or calls for action contained within them. They illustrate several data shortcomings which can lead to invalid conclusions.

In the first article, it was wisely noted that multiple factors could lead to an increase in deaths. An expert obliquely drew attention to the possibility that an increased number of riders could be a factor, pointing to the increase in the price of fuel. If indeed the number of riders had grown by 50% in 2018, or even the number of miles travelled by the same number of motorcycles had increased by that amount, that could fully explain the "spike." The data would be much more meaningful if supplemented by statistics on these and other factors. Was there a significant change in the weather that year? Were there any "outlier" factors such as many fatalities in a single accident? How exactly did those accidents occur, and was there any change in the pattern from the previous year? If we were analyzing data from the following year, we might even have to consider that at least one of the riders was fatally shot while riding his dirt bike!

A more compelling statistic, not cited in the article, is that on average there are about 300 traffic fatalities in British Columbia each year, and while only 4% of vehicles are motorcycles, they account for over 13% of deaths associated with road traffic accidents. From that we could conclude, carefully, that if you are in a motor vehicle accident, and your vehicle is a motorcycle, you are over three times more likely to die. What call to action would flow from that?

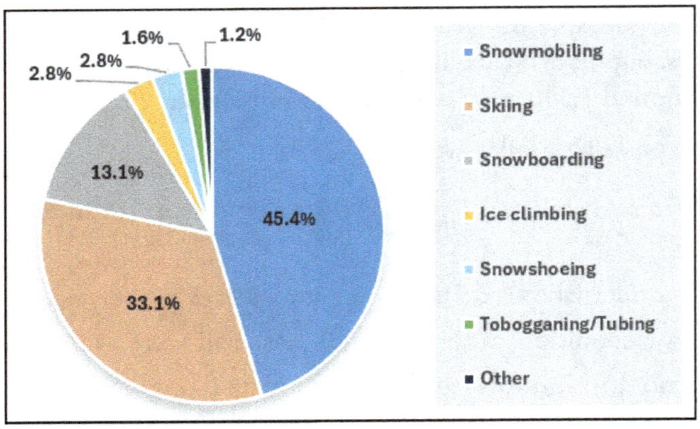

FIGURE 1: Winter sports deaths

The British Columbia Coroners' Service published this chart after the 2017/18 winter sports season (British Columbia Coroners Service, n.d.). Imagine that your teenage son wants to buy a motorcycle, while you are against the idea. He points out that you encourage him to go snowboarding every winter, and that 13.1% of winter sports deaths occur on snowboards. That's almost the same percentage as motorcyclists who die in road traffic accidents. Is he making a good case? What data are being omitted, that would allow you to evaluate the comparison correctly?

Our discussion of the above examples has illustrated several different types of questions that must be asked to determine if relevant numbers are missing, with the first two being especially important.

- If a dramatic percentage is reported, ask what the absolute numbers are. A change from 2 to 3 is a 50% increase but could be insignificant in context.
- If a big number is reported, ask about the percentage change. A budget increase of a million dollars sounds impressive but is insignificant if the overall budget is $100 million and inflation is 2%.
- Where there is a call to action, ask whether it is supported by all the data, or only some part of them.
- Always consider contextual and parallel comparisons. A 50% increase in skiing accidents might be a cause for concern, but if the snow was particularly good and there was a 60% increase in ticket sales, it's *an improvement*. An inflation rate of 7% this year might not look great, but compared to 14% last year it's fantastic!
- Think about the possibility of unusual factors. In the second week of June 2021 the B.C. Coroners' Service was receiving an average of 227 reports of death per week. The normal number of reports for June should have been 975, but the actual number was around 1,100, a sudden increase of more than 10%. The difference was entirely caused by the "heat dome" which sat over Vancouver for four days in the last week. The Guardian newspaper in the UK dramatically reported that sudden deaths in B.C. exhibited a 195% increase over normal years. The numbers are sad and dramatic, but in no sense represent a sustained change of any significance. A rare event caused a sudden spike, but without acknowledging its influence, any conclusions drawn from the percentages could be highly misleading.

What can we not know?

Former U.S. Secretary of Defense Donald Rumsfeld famously said in a 2002 speech:

> Reports that say something hasn't happened are always interesting to me, because as we know, there are *known knowns*; there are things we know we know. We also know there are *known unknowns;* we know there are some things we do not know. But there are also *unknown unknowns;* the ones we don't know we don't know.

Secretary Rumsfeld encapsulated, in the last two concepts, the difficulties of the area of unknowable statistics.

This is comparable to learning a new skill or trade. When you start an accounting degree or diploma course, for example, you may have a general idea that there is something called "depreciation." Maybe you've owned a car or truck that went steadily down in value. But until you take a course that delves into detail, you don't know that you didn't know anything about the several different ways depreciation can be calculated, let alone the complexities created by the difference between depreciation and the CRA's Capital Cost Allowance (CCA).

It is not difficult to find published statistical declarations that are severely open to question if one thinks about the difficulties of obtaining data, or even of getting honest answers from survey subjects.

For example:

- *Studyfinds*, a New York-based research organization, reports that 34% of adults still snuggle with a stuffed animal, blanket, or other anxiety-reducing item of sentimental value, based on a survey of 2,000 adults. But how many other people do this, but didn't admit to it through embarrassment?
- *The Massachusetts Male Aging Study* in 1994 concluded that 52 percent of men suffer some form of erectile dysfunction. The real number is probably higher due to the number of men who didn't want to admit it to the researchers!
- *Time Magazine* in 2015 published the results of a study finding that over a 15-year period, involving several question sessions, 20% of young men and 10% of young women reported stealing something in the past year. Most people who commit petty crimes find a justification for them—denial would result in a lower figure than the actual statistic.

At least *Time* included one short paragraph which qualified the results: "One potential issue with the study is that stealing was self-reported, so actual numbers *could* be higher."

That's exactly right. Any time a researcher seeks to obtain data on a subject which people are likely to find embarrassing, a subject where exaggeration is common, or a subject about which people are likely to lie, the reported numbers are likely to be low. It requires a very adept design to include questions which will verify the data or suggest how wrong they may be. For example, respondents to a survey might be asked "Have you ever lied on a resume?" For obvious reasons some people might answer no when the truth is yes. A follow-up question might ask the same respondents to estimate how often people in general lie on resumes; respondents giving a high-level response to the second question after answering no to the first might be indicating indirectly what they were reluctant to say directly. There are lots of possible variations on this theme, for example asking people whether they have ever driven under the influence of alcohol, or whether they have ever stolen from a store.

Researchers have cleverly developed several techniques for obtaining correct responses to embarrassing questions. These range from using forgiving wording and context manipulation, to the ballot box method, where answers are submitted in a manner like electoral voting. The key in most is to allow the subject to maintain privacy and anonymity (Cleave, 2021).

When we encounter survey data on such subjects, an important step is to review the methodology section of the report, if there is one. Well-performed statistical surveys always include a section on how the data were collected, margin-of-error calculations, and caveats. The data become more useful if a secondary source is compared; for example, if a survey concludes based on consumer surveys (as one did some years ago) that one in seven adult Americans use food banks. The number is likely to be understated; even as it stands, it implies that at least 37 million Americans were using food banks. Good confirmatory evidence would be food bank usage statistics obtained from the food banks themselves, added up, and compared to the statistics reported by users.

Whenever we encounter that uncomfortable feeling that there are unknown unknowns at play, we must think carefully about conducting further research to identify and evaluate them.

Problems in Data-Driven Decision-Making

The commonest problems in data-driven decision-making are:

- Sampling Errors
- Interpretive biases
- Reasoning fallacies
- False causal conclusions

Sampling errors

One of the greatest challenges in research—whether you're a scientist, or an accountant—is trying to characterize a larger population by looking at a subset of it. For example, auditors will look at a sample of transactions to determine if the financial transactions are not materially misstated. The sample we select must be representative of the wider population otherwise we will arrive at incorrect conclusions in our analysis.

Sampling errors come in many forms. We will present the ones that are most relevant to business and accounting analysis.

Selection bias

Imagine that you work for a forensic auditing practice (a specialized group of accountants who look for evidence of crimes on behalf of their clients). A client, with a large staff, is concerned about fraudulent expense claims and asks for your help. On an initial review you find that although most people in the company can claim expenses, junior claims average only about $100 a month, while some senior managers claim several thousand dollars each month. You decide that you will provide the most value to your client if you perform a detailed examination of the managers' claims and look for tell-tale differences between managers who claim large amounts and those who don't.

You have just made a sampling bias error. By concentrating on the large claims, which might turn out to be largely legitimate because managers are diligently visiting and entertaining valuable clients, your work will completely miss any widespread problem amongst junior employees, even though the total value of petty fraud might be much greater than occasional false claims by seniors.

The term *selection bias* is a header for a broad range of problems which can occur when researchers make poor choices in survey methodology. There are whole books written about selection bias just in single fields (for example Berger, 2007); here we will describe the main types and provide some entertaining examples.

Most worthwhile research questions will seek knowledge about some factor pertaining to a large group of people or things, but it will not be cost-effective or even possible to ask everyone or test everything. Instead, some form of sampling must be used, and the results from the sample will hopefully be capable of extrapolation to the population of interest. There are several hurdles along the track even after we have found a suitable group from which to draw our sample—we must ensure that our sample is truly random, yet representative; we must make sure that what, or when, we ask, does not skew the outcome in some way.

Imagine that you, and a group of friends, are shown several videos of a collision between two cars, shot from different angles. Each person is then asked "about how fast were the cars going when they …?) The last word in the sentence is different for each person, however. People in your group who are given the word "contacted" will give lower estimates than those who hear "smashed." This was the result of a famous experiment by researchers Loftus and Palmer (1974), half a century ago. They showed that humans are poor at estimating speed, so they are more suggestible when new information is introduced after they observe an event. By changing just one word, the researchers found that they could affect how people remembered and interpreted the event. This reveals how easily memories can be influenced by the way questions are asked.

When we want to extrapolate results from a sample, we must be sure to obtain results which can be reliably extended to the entire population.

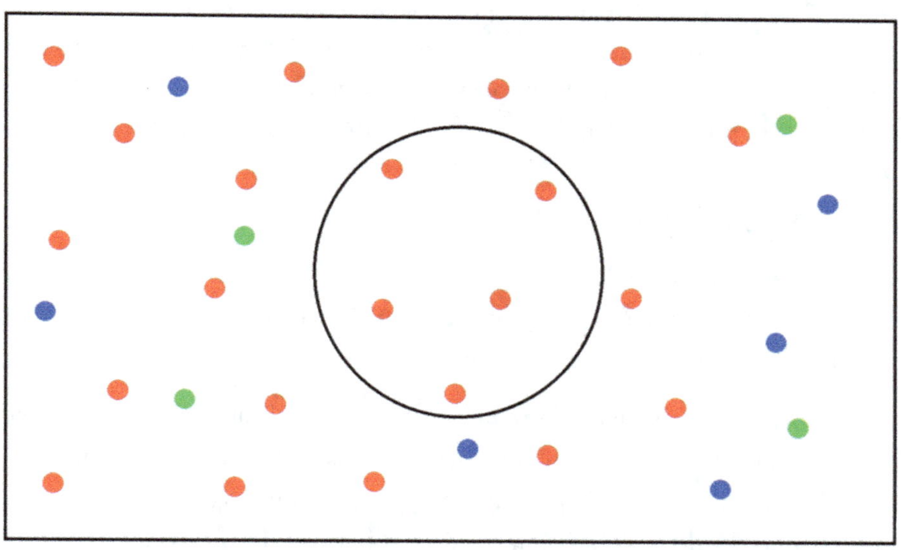

FIGURE 2: The sample is not representative of the population

You are invited on stage by a performer who is holding a black bag of snooker balls. You are asked to say, without looking, how many different colors are in the bag, and permitted to take out five balls for examination. As it happens, there are many more red balls than others in the bag, and you happen to pull out five red balls. You conclude that all the balls must be red and give the answer "One." Your sample, as you will readily conclude, was not large enough. If you had continued to pull out balls, sooner or later you would have seen the other two colors.

Sampling bias is a problem any time that some members of the population who should be surveyed are less likely to be included than others. For example, we might want to study the incidence of depression among students in a university program. There are 500 students registered in the program; we figure that 100 would be a pretty good sample and we visit two classrooms, each with 50 students attending. The problem: students suffering from depression *might* be more likely to miss class, or more likely to register for online sessions. By selecting our sample from an unrepresentative group within the population, we have shot our results in the foot at the first opportunity!

If a survey must be submitted online, which is increasingly common, it automatically filters out anyone who doesn't have access to a computer, anyone with a computer who doesn't have internet access, and anyone who has a computer and internet access but doesn't know how to use it. This may be acceptable, or not, depending on the purpose of the exercise. Imagine that you are advising a Canadian manufacturer of solar-powered water filtration systems, which is exploring the potential market in West Africa. The country of Niger has very significant water purity issues; it is selected for an online survey of potential customers. Unfortunately, only 10–15% of the population has internet access, and it is mainly limited to larger urban populations. Such a survey would produce results about the opinions of wealthy, urban residents, but largely exclude the potentially more valuable ideas of the people who most need the product.

A shameful example of selection bias based on prejudice is to be found in Canada's historical census data. In many years, Indigenous populations were undercounted or misclassified, resulting in misallocation of resources and skewed representation. Some Indigenous people were classified as "other" or even "non-resident" in early censuses. These biases had profound implications for healthcare in Indigenous communities (Smylie & Firestone, 2016).

Hasty generalization error

The *hasty generalization error* (a.k.a. the law of small numbers) occurs in many fields. It happens when people generalize about the population from a sample that is too small. If I were to flip a coin five times, and it were to land heads each time, *it does not follow that the coin will always land heads!*

The Davis family history provides a delightful example of hasty generalization. For at least four generations we have been dog lovers—almost every family unit (and there were many) had a succession of dogs, usually carefully researching the right breed and successfully picking out a pet which fits right in. Yet no family in the line of succession since the Second World War has even considered having a Pekingese for a pet, because of a family legend.

> In the 1940s Great-Aunt Beryl had a Pekingese. One day she bent down to pet it, but it misunderstood the gesture, sprung up and bit through her top lip! When it tasted the blood, it gave in to canine instinct

FIGURE 3: Pekingese

and hung on for dear life. She had to go to hospital, with the dog attached, to have it anaesthetized and removed. Or so the story goes. We suspect it has grown and become more sensational in the telling. But everyone in the family knows the tale, and no-one would even think of having a "Peke" join the family. The oft-expressed conclusion is that Pekes are vicious little creatures, and we don't understand why anybody would keep one.

Yet if you read up on the advantages and disadvantages of the breed, nowhere will you find any reference to them being nasty or vicious. In fact, their good points include that the Pekingese are one of the most dignified, confident, and independent of the toy breeds; are calm and quiet indoors and don't need much exercise; are polite with strangers and usually accepting of other animals (Welton, n.d.).

What are the downsides of having a "Peke"? The same sources suggest that snorting, snuffling, wheezing, loud snoring, shedding and flatulence are the main issues. Nowhere is there any mention of inbred viciousness. In fact, this sounds like a great breed for an old lady who might not want to do much walking but needs affection and enjoys caring for her pet.

Four generations of the Davis family have succumbed to a hasty generalization based on an exaggerated tale about just one dog!

We are particularly vulnerable to this misimpression if there is an emotional aspect to the subject. Hasty generalizations are societally dangerous, as they often lead to misinformed stereotyping. This can lead to unethical, unfair prejudice against a person or group.

At the start of his 2015 election campaign, President Donald Trump delivered a speech containing a stunning example of hasty generalization.

> When Mexico sends its people, they're not sending their best. They're sending people that have lots of problems, and they're bringing those problems with us. They're bringing drugs. They're bringing crime. They're rapists. And some, I assume, are good people (Phillips, 2017).

Based on a few examples of which he had heard, Trump leapt to the faulty conclusion that crime among Mexican immigrants is at a significant level. In fact, better quality published research tends to show that first-generation immigrants from Mexico commit crimes less frequently than home-born Americans.

Insensitivity to sample size

The fallacy based on insensitivity to sample size was first researched and published by two Israeli psychologists, Daniel Kahneman and Amos Tversky in 1972. They described an experiment where people were asked to estimate the probability of a group of people being an average of over six feet tall. The suggested group sizes were 10,000 and 1000. The estimates were remarkably similar. Almost all their subjects failed to consider the higher possibility of an anomaly (a high average height) in a small sample.

We mention with pride that Dr. Kahneman was a Professor of Psychology at UBC from 1978 to 1986, before moving on to Berkeley then Princeton.

If you flip a fair (unbiased) coin 10 times, there is a strong possibility that you will have an imbalance in the results, more heads than tails or *vice versa*. As the number of flips grows larger, the imbalance between heads and tails becomes smaller. While you have a 48% chance of 6 heads and 4 tails, the chances of 600 heads and 400 tails in 1,000 flips are infinitesimally small. Insensitivity to sample size in this experiment could lead you to conclude after 10 flips that a fair coin will land heads up 60% of the time. That seems obviously wrong, doesn't it?

Why does this matter in accounting, finance or business? Take the example of stock market investments. Large financial institutions employ highly trained, well-equipped professionals to manage their positions; meanwhile, any member of the public can sign up on their mobile phone and play in the exact same markets. On any given day, either the retail investor or the institutional professional can lose money, because there is a certain element of luck. Based on a small sample or a small number of trades, it would be easy to find places where the retail investor did as well as the professional, or even better. But in the long run, the more skilled, better-equipped financial institution will always win out.

Cherry picking

Sampling bias is not necessarily deliberate, though it can be if the researcher has an agenda, in which case it may also be a type named *cherry picking*. If you are conducting a customer satisfaction survey for a particular model of car, and survey only people who have owned one for three years or more, you are likely to hear mainly positive comments. But this says nothing about the opinion of the people who bought one and sold it within three years, or who test-drove the model and decided not to buy one at all.

Cherry picking is very common in politics. An extreme example occurred in February 2015, when Senator James Inhofe brought a snowball onto the floor of the Senate. Inhofe was the author of a 2012 book entitled *The Greatest Hoax: How the Global Warming Conspiracy Threatens Your Future*. Throwing the snowball to a page, he sought to underline how very cold it was outside. But 2015 turned out to be the hottest year, globally, ever recorded. Until 2016 (Leber, 2018).

Voluntary response bias

Also known as *volunteer bias*, it is found wherever subjects who choose to contribute their opinions are significantly different from those who do not participate. It can occur for example in medical settings, where patients who are positive and proactive about their treatment may participate and offer encouraging reviews, while those who are negative, very ill, or resigned to their illness, may not want to be involved.

Internet review sites, and sites which contain reviews (such as Google Maps or restaurant booking sites) are a common example of biased sampling. It is a well-known human factor that people with a complaint are more likely to voice disapproval than people who are happy are likely to voice approval (Zendesk, 2013). This is known as *negativity bias*, and may be caused in part by negative experiences evoking stronger emotions than positive ones. Reputation management professionals argue that customers who have had a bad experience are

2–3x more likely to write an angry review, than customers who had a great experience are likely to post a positive comment (Reputation Builder, n.d.).

The "star ratings" or similar categorizations of facilities or businesses are not only likely to have a heavy preponderance of criticism. They also reflect only the views of a population that has access to the internet. The results may not reflect the views of customers who did not have a strong motivation to publish their opinion, or those that don't use electronic means to book their reservations or make their choices.

You might have visited the site www.ratemyprofessors.com. When you read the list of reviews, you will probably notice that even most teachers who you like and rate highly seem to have several negative comments. That said, if you find a teacher who has only good reviews, they are probably VERY good indeed! If you contribute to the site, do you rate all your teachers, or just the ones of whom you have a strong opinion? For most people, the answer is the latter.[2]

Convenience sampling

Convenience sampling occurs when the researcher fails to find a representative sample, substituting one which is easily available. A study on travelling to campus might be conducted in a live classroom, thus missing all the students not attending that day, but they might be the ones with most difficulty in travelling. This type of bias can be very subtle. For example, a study of "the university experience" might be thought most compelling if third- and fourth-year students are surveyed, as they have the most time in higher education. But what about the students who dropped out in the first or second year? Their opinions would seem very relevant, but they would be completely missed.

Psychology departments are particularly prone to this danger. A class of psychology students is a particularly convenient sample for the professor; but they may be there because they need class credit for their degree, definitely not because they are representative of the wider population, even of university students in the same year.

Non-response bias

Non-response bias occurs any time participants can decline involvement. The reality is that in almost all opinion-type surveys, people are more likely to participate if they have the time, and even more likely to participate if they have time (Groves, 2009) and a strong opinion.[3] If you want to know how people feel about working in a particular building, trying to survey those who turn up at the last minute for work will be very difficult if they're in a rush to get to the office. Yet their opinions are just as valid, and may be more informative, than people who are 15 minutes early and have time to answer your questions at the door.

---

[2] We know this will tempt you to visit the site, if you haven't already. For an example of a teacher with a universally positive rating look at the reports for Alina McGuinness. And we couldn't resist noting the "teddy bear vibes" ascribed to one Alym Amlani by a doting student!

[3] This is known as the *leverage-salience* or *leverage-saliency* theory of participation. (Groves, Singer & Corning, 2000).

Attrition bias and survivorship bias

Attrition bias occurs when the subjects being studied drop out while the study is still continuing. It occurs for example in clinical trials; there may be a difference between subjects who stay for the entire period and those who leave early. In a ten-year study of accounting careers in Canada, some professionals may move to another country or change jobs, reducing the representativeness of data gathered later in the period. Any conclusion based on the reports for the lifetime of the survey must be careful not to generalize to the entire population after these people have left the sample. A sub-category of attrition bias is named *survivorship bias*, and specifically refers to studies where participants die before the study period has ended; the people who have died are not represented in the sample. This is common in medical research. Misreporting of the results may be increased because those who survive may correlate strongly to those who obtain positive benefits from the treatment.

Attrition and survivorship bias are distinguishable from censoring, discussed next. In attrition bias, subjects leave before the study period is complete. In censoring, subjects have data which is not recognized because they were created before or after the study period.

Right and left censoring

Censoring in general, in statistics, refers to a problem where the value of what is being measured or observed is not fully known. In data analysis it mainly refers to time series studies, illustrated by the following example.

Imagine that you work for the consultancy arm of an accounting firm. A client asks for help in analyzing motivation and productivity and wants you to focus on on-time attendance. Being an office-based client, it has standard working hours from 9 a.m. to 5 p.m. All the 100 employees work in a single office, which is serviced by a single elevator to its 22nd floor location (no one takes the stairs!). You decide to physically monitor arrival times to ensure good quality data, arrive at 8 am, and carefully record the arrival time of each employee. On the day you choose, there are no absences for illness or vacation. The following are the tabulated data you collect.

TABLE 2: Employee arrival times

Arrival time	Employee Count	Minutes Early/Late
8:00 to 8:30 am	5	-45
8:31 to 8:50 am	2	-19.5
8:51 to 8:59 am	63	-5
9:00 am	1	0
9:01 to 9:10 am	6	+4.5
9:11 to 9:30 am	3	+20.5
9:31 to 10:00 am	10	+45.5
TOTAL	**90**	
Weighted Average		**-0.39**

You might be tempted to report to the client that there is no apparent issue with timely arrival, which bodes well for motivation. The average employee is 0.39 minutes early for work. After breaking the times into equally spaced segments, you might even create a histogram which demonstrates a normal distribution for the data. But there's a problem—the total employee count is 90. When did the other 10 arrive?

Assume that eight of them are very keen, early birds, who arrived between 4 and 5 a.m. to get a great start on the day. Another two like to beat the urban traffic and are in the office just before 7:30. Those employees' data are *left censored*, because they accomplished the observed behavior *before the study started.* With their data included, the weighted average attendance would show an even earlier average arrival (24 minutes early).

Now make the contrary assumption. The remaining ten employees all showed up after 10 a.m., more than an hour late and in two instances after lunch! With these data added, the average employee is now quite seriously late for work. In this case the data are *right censored*, because the latest employees arrived after the study concluded.

The simple assumption based on the data demonstrates several points which we are exploring. Even using the censored data, the conclusion that there is no problem is based on use of the mean, which suggests there is no issue—but look again at the employee count. 19 employees, or over 20% of the sample, arrived late for work. In this situation it is a very poor conclusion that good motivation can be assumed based on arrival times.

Left censoring, then, occurs when there are data points lower than our starting value (earliest time), but they are not included in the analysis.

Right censoring is the opposite. There are data points above the highest value shown (and thus to the right of the chart).

Left censoring is commonly found in studies of the first time that something occurs. An insurer offering dental coverage might try to calculate the average age at which wisdom teeth "come in" (*i.e.,* present in the mouth). Knowing that the normal age range for presentation is 17–25, the company follows a group of 17-year-olds for eight years to determine the percentage of people who suffer from the problem, and when it starts. The results will be left-censored, because patients (and there will be some) who developed their wisdom teeth before 17 have been ignored. They are also likely to be right censored for patients who develop the problem late.

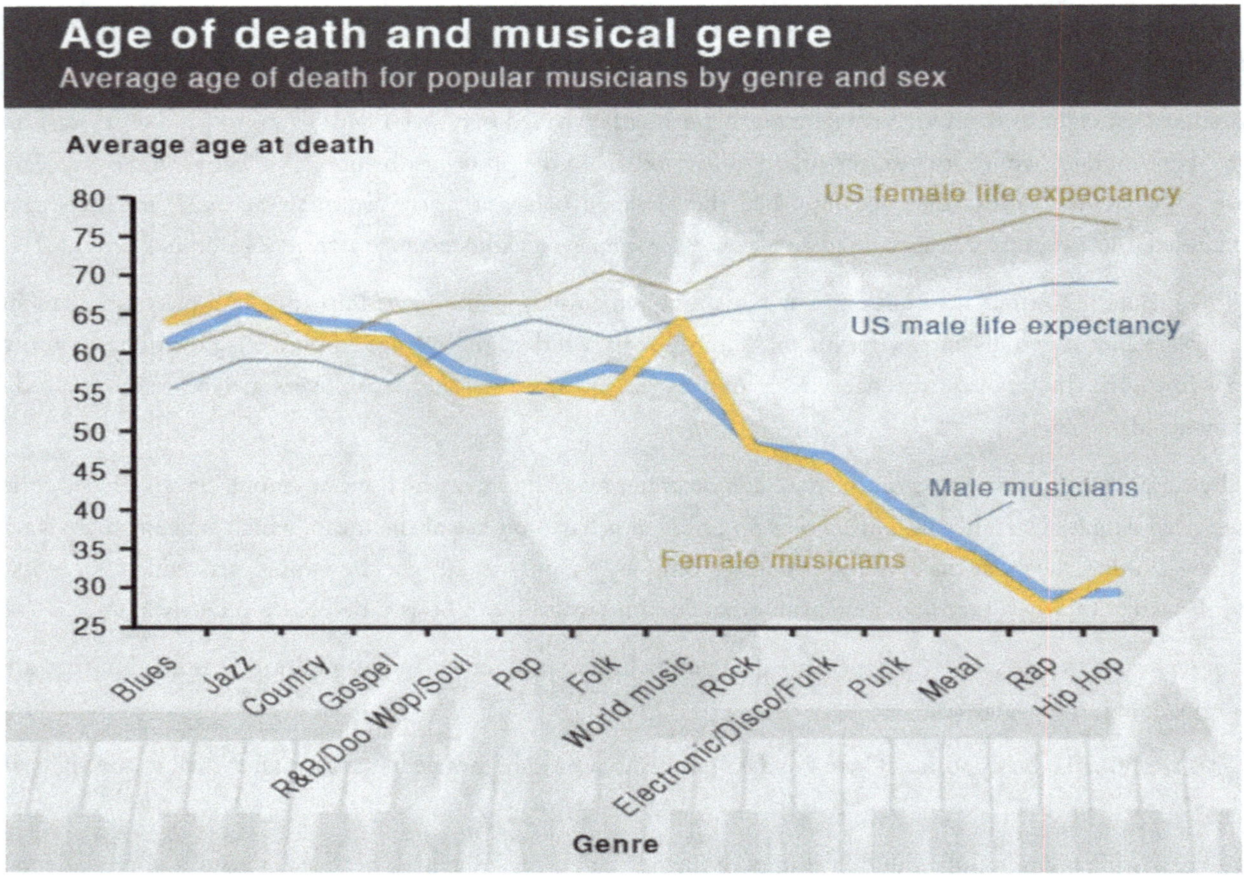

FIGURE 4: Deaths by musical genre

Right censoring gets a lot more airtime in statistical literature, partly because it is more prevalent and possibly also because there are some colorful examples available. One very well-known example is dubbed by Bergstrom & West "The Mortal Danger of Musicianship (2020)." They recount the tale of a 2015 graph which compared average death rates for male and female musicians playing various genres (Kenny, 2015). The researcher seemed to conclude that life expectancy was significantly lower for musicians involved in rap or hip-hop, compared to blues and gospel, for example. We suppose the idea was made more credible by the aggressive, pro-violence lyrics used in some rap music, and by reporting of some high-profile murders of rap and hip-hop stars. The true problem with the study and the chart produced, however, was that some musical genres have been around for nearly a century, meaning lots of practitioners have had the chance to die at a ripe old age, while rap and hip-hop were relatively new to the scene (they became popular only in the early and late 1970s respectively. Most rap and hip-hop artists were still alive; the ones who had died, died young.

Although the reasoning process was flawed, the conclusion may not have been totally incorrect. Approximately half of all deaths of top hip hop musicians who died prior to 2020 were murdered, and half of the murders remain unsolved.

In less dramatic fields, medical, anthropological and educational research are prone to right censoring; it should not be assumed that it is necessarily a bad thing, provided it is recognized. Testing the effectiveness of vaccines is a great example of necessary right censoring; suppose there is a new vaccine for a given disease, and it is given to 1,000 infants before their first birthday. Complete data on the effectiveness of the vaccine would require the researcher to wait approximately 100 years, until the last subject died (having contracted the disease or not). Clearly the developers, users and patients involved with the drug will want data long before that.

In biological and anthropological research, the availability of funding is often a limiting issue. Even when the 100-year potential human lifespan is not the outer margin, a researcher may receive funding, for example, for a three- or four- year study (maybe to coincide with postgraduate studies). If a study is commenced of a population of hamsters, which live for an average of four years and a maximum of seven (the world record), whatever is being studied may not have occurred for all the subjects which outlive the study.

It's not only death, however, that limits the right-hand boundary of the time axis. You might be interested to know at what average (mean) age children in different societies learn to read. Most children in most societies have acquired some reading ability by the age of 8, so you cut off your study at that age. Are your calculations valid? No, because you have no data on late bloomers—in some of your subject populations there may be reasons some folks learn to read at 20, 30, or even 70. These datapoints are outside your chart, so you have no idea where they are. Of course, in this case you might question whether the mean is the best measure (likely median would be a better comparator).

Interval censoring, which may have less dramatic effects on analysis, occurs when measurements are taken at intervals instead of continuously. If you were surveying the length of time trucking companies keep new cabs after purchase, you might call the manufacturer's customers every December to ask if they still have their vehicle. You would learn which truckers had disposed of their purchase during the previous year. You would then know that the disposals had occurred at some point in the previous year, but not exactly when. Your results would only be indicative of a range of years, not months. When considering the risks relating to interval sampling, it is necessary to determine the level of accuracy required.

Censoring, attrition and survivorship in one study

Consider the case of a 40-year long national study of stroke victims. The researchers design an outline as follows:

- Recruit 1000 people aged 30 who agree to participate in a yearly survey.
- Contact them every year for 40 years and determine if they have had a stroke.
- After 40 years, compile the results.

Left censoring occurs immediately, because the selection of participants has excluded people who might have a stroke before their 30th birthday. It's rare, but it does happen.

During the 40 years, some participants lose interest and stop responding. This introduces *attrition bias.*

During the 40 years, some of the participants die. According to the latest Statistics Canada reports, 93% of people aged 30 will live to be 70. 7% of our participants dying will introduce *survivorship bias.* This doesn't mean, however, that there is 7% survivorship bias, because some people who die might have been in the attrition group first.

Finally, we stop studying when everyone reaches 70. But after that age, people will still have strokes—in fact, they become progressively *more* likely to have one. We have right censored the data by ceasing to collect it before their lives are over.

Some exercises in finding bias

Here are some examples of critical thinking through "results." In most cases they are fictional, though they are all based on examples we have seen in real life.

> We have made an exhaustive study and concluded definitively that penguins cannot fly. Over a 6-month period we observed the behavior of over 50,000 penguins at a colony in Antarctica. Not one ever got airborne, though all were excellent swimmers, and most were competent at walking on ice and snow.

There are 18 species of penguins living in many distinct parts of the world. The observers studied only one. The study ran for only six months. What if the penguins huddled down on the land for those two seasons but went flying around at other times of year (they don't, but this study did not prove that). Was the study conducted only in daylight? What if penguins flew only at night? If you studied barn owls by day, you would conclude that they are flightless. But really, they fly only at night!

By saying "concluded definitively," the announcement suggests that *confirmation bias* may be implicated—did the researchers start with a belief that penguins can't fly? *Sampling bias* is invoked, observing a single colony could not possibly produce data which are generalizable to all penguins in the world. Given the cost of travel to all the places where penguins are found, *convenience sampling* has certainly occurred. Reaching a definitive conclusion based on only one sample is also a *hasty generalization.*

> Customer satisfaction is at an all-time high for Toyota Yaris owners. Of 10,000 families surveyed, all had owned their Yaris for five years or more. Over 97% reported complete satisfaction with their vehicle.

What about all the former owners who sold their vehicle within the first five years. Were they satisfied?

The research suffers *selection bias,* because it includes only families who have owned for five years or more. *Attrition bias* has also occurred, as people who disposed of their car during the survey period are excluded. If the survey was conducted by or for Toyota or a dealership, there may be *confirmation bias* which could have affected the actual study design—it was always destined to produce the result which was obtained.

> B.C. Stats invites you to take the B.C. Demographic Survey. *We can only fix what we can see.* However, we also recognize and respect people's right to privacy, especially about their identity. That's why we're asking people to fill out the voluntary B.C. Demographic Survey, rather than conducting a mandatory census or asking for this information when people access services. Scan the QR code. Open the camera on your mobile device and point it at the QR code to access the survey.

Words almost fail us. This survey dropped into our mailbox while we were writing this chapter! It's completely voluntary, meaning that results from the survey will be utterly invalid for extrapolation to the population.

Selection bias has occurred because the explanatory text is written only in English (page 2 says it is available in 15 languages online), but even so the ability to respond is limited to people who have enough English to understand the lengthy request in the first place.

The survey suffers from *volunteer bias*, in that people who feel strongly about the subject may be particularly motivated to respond. It is at risk of *non-response bias*, because its voluntary nature means that many people may ignore the request for a litany of reasons, from not caring to distrust of the government. It suffers from a subcategory of *selection bias* called *digital divide bias* because only people with access to, and familiarity with, the technology can complete it. The very people whose views are most important are the most likely to be excluded. When the government asks questions, a further problem which we have not yet discussed is known as *authority bias*, which invalidates results when respondents, fearing scrutiny or consequences, express false support for policy or programs.

Americans overwhelmingly support the Second Amendment. In a random sample of 30,000 people in America's largest cities, Los Angeles, New York, and Houston, over 85% said they supported gun ownership and 75% owned at least one firearm.

Sampling bias is clear, as only three cities have been surveyed. They may not represent the views of the population across America, or in rural settings or smaller towns. By choosing cities where people are relatively wealthy, the survey has introduced selection bias and potentially excluded several demographic groups. We do not know why these cities were chosen, but there is a strong hint of *convenience sampling. Hasty generalization* has occurred, because the conclusion of overwhelming support is premature based on only three cities.

AI bias

While not new, *AI bias* has relatively recently become a hot topic. It is a dangerous phenomenon, in which a misleading conclusion (output) is based on either a fault with the assumptions which went into the development of an algorithm, or a bias in the training data. Inherent biases in the training datasets may be dangerous, but also the sampling within the data may be biased. We say it is dangerous, because the most prominent examples of AI bias tend to be those which perpetuate racial and gender stereotypes. They may cause decisions and practices which are prejudicial to groups within the population. For example, Amazon in 2014 famously developed a hiring algorithm based on ten years of previous statistics; it favored male applicants (Gonzelez, 2018).

In earlier sections, we have seen just some of the biases which affect human thinking. If one or some of those biases are incorporated into models by their designers, they can form part of the machine outputs. Similarly, if the computer providing AI outputs is trained on a biased dataset, the biases in the dataset will affect the outputs.

Cathy O'Neil is an influential writer on this subject. In her cleverly named book *Weapons of Math Destruction*, she develops the theme. Policing algorithms, she points out, identify high crime areas based on historical data. If it disproportionately targets certain communities, the program will continue to send more police to them, which creates a feedback loop which perpetuates the bias.

This is an advanced development of the GIGO principle (garbage in, garbage out). Hiring data which contains a disproportionate number of men may teach AI to favor men over women when it filters job applications. People affected by such discrimination are powerless in the face of massive computing power to react effectively, raising ethical concerns about fairness and justice (O'Neil, 2016).

Berkson's paradox

Berkson's paradox occurs when we look at only a subset of a population, causing us to see an apparent negative correlation, where seeing the full population would reveal that they are either independent, or positively correlated.

Suppose you're on your favorite dating app, trying to find a date. As you're swiping through profiles, you have two main criteria:

- *Attractiveness:* how good-looking the person is to you
- *Intelligence:* how smart they appear to be based on their bio or what you can gather from their profile.

For the sake of this discussion, assume you score each of the above criteria on a scale of 1–10. In the general population, attractiveness and intelligence *are not correlated.* For example, if we look at the wider population, suppose there is an equal mix of people who are:

- High in both attractiveness and intelligence (you score them both > 8)
- Low in both attractiveness and intelligence (you score them both < 2)
- High in one but low in the other (e.g. 2 for intelligence and 9 for attractiveness)

Let's look at 100 possible candidates who are representative of the greater population:

- 25 are high in both attractiveness and intelligence
- 25 are low in both attractiveness and intelligence
- 50 are mixed (high in one, low in the other)

Now, you're not willing to date just anyone—for the sake of this discussion, let's say you'll swipe right (interested) on anyone with an attractiveness score ≥ 7, regardless of their intelligence or anyone with an intelligence score ≥ 7, regardless of their attractiveness. From the 100 people (above), in your pool of 75 selected / potential matches, 25 are attractive but not intelligent and 25 are intelligent but not attractive. Since you've excluded the 25 people who were low on both traits, it starts to feel like people can be attractive or intelligent, but not both. Who's left? People who are attractive but not intelligent, and people who are intelligent but not attractive. This will give the illusion to you that attractiveness and intelligence are *negatively correlated*—it seems as though when someone is high on one trait, they are low on the other. But that's because your selection process biased the population you examined.

Cognitive biases

Not only may there be problems with our sample, but once we have data to work on, we may consciously or unconsciously misinterpret it. In the next sections we will look at groups of errors which we may make when trying to apply our data to interpret or make decisions about the population of interest.

Cognitive biases arise because our brains seek to be efficient as they are asked to process large amounts of information. They constantly seek to simplify decision-making; in doing so, they can distort our perceptions, cause us to misinterpret data, and affect our reasoning. Understanding the role of biases is critical to professional decision-making especially when data analysis is called for in matters of business and finance.

Anchoring

Anchoring refers to the form of cognitive bias where a person's estimate or perception of a value is affected by the prior positioning of a number in their mind. Especially when people have limited knowledge or are unsure of their beliefs, they can attach undue importance to the first number which they see or hear, whether it is accurate or not.

Employers and recruiters often ask for your current salary when you're interviewing for a new job. Imagine that you have recently qualified as a CPA and are approaching a new firm. It's prepared to pay up to $100,000 per year for good junior recruits. In the interview, though, you disclose that you're currently receiving $60,000 for your work. Your current salary anchors the negotiation; the new firm might only offer $70,000, knowing that will still be attractive to you.

Auditors must be very careful to avoid anchoring when performing valuations. For example, inventory valuation typically starts from a number provided by management. If management provides an initial figure of $10 million, but the audit work produces a total of $6.5 million, the auditor may doubt their own judgment and augment the value based on management's assertion. This would result in a negative adjustment which is smaller than should have been applied.

Anchoring is deliberately and pervasively used in retail sales. A modest car stickered at $40,000 looks more reasonable when placed in the showroom next to a $300,000 Aston Martin. Outdoor market traders often have a patter which starts "I'm not going to charge you $20. I'm not even going to charge you $10. Who wants one for $5?" Even if the new-fangled potato peeler is a cheap plastic product worth at most $3, it looks like a bargain at $5 after the anchoring effect of the $20 starting statement. You may have noticed that when you visit a "big box store" like Costco, you typically see very expensive televisions near the entrance; once you visit the TV department, all the other models look inexpensive by comparison. The $15 bag of candy looks very reasonable compared to the $3,500 TV.

Anchoring bias can operate in areas where large numbers are involved and stakes are high, such as house and building valuations. Awareness of the risk of anchoring is important to accountants and auditors, who are relied on for objective assessment and effective challenges to assumptions and assertions. Adjustments must reflect verifiable data, not psychologically influenced opinions.

Confirmation bias

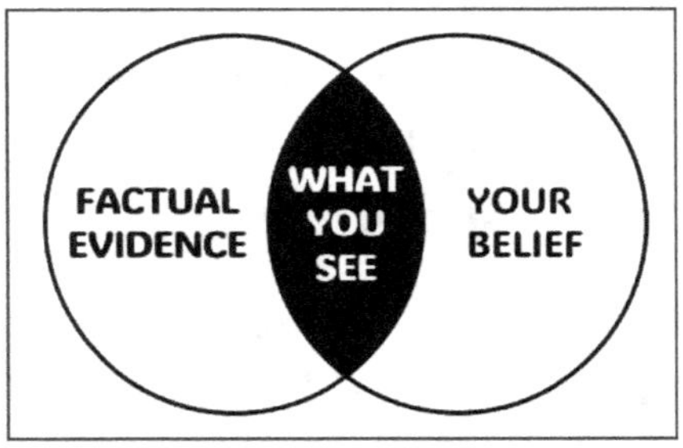

FIGURE 5: Confirmation bias Venn diagram

Confirmation bias is another bane of legal life but intrudes into countless other areas too. People in general tend to seek out, or give disproportionate attention to, information that confirms what they believe. This can occur over a long period as people continually recognize evidence that supports an opinion, or in a short interaction. Police officers are notorious for clinging onto a belief in the guilt of a person while disregarding evidence of innocence; doctors can easily fall into the trap of making an early diagnosis then disregarding factors that point to a different problem. If your friend tells you that their brother is a jerk, then you meet him, you are more likely to notice behaviors that confirm the label than those that would suggest he's actually a decent person.

Confirmation bias is sometimes referred to as *selective perception.*

Confirmation bias has recently become more important than ever before in the context of polarized elections and social media engagement. Few can have failed to notice the increasing extremity of American politics as fervent supporters of the two main parties seek out and believe "evidence" which confirms their political leanings. The world of social media is fueled by algorithms which track the engagement of users, showing them more and more content which aligns with what they have already seen. This reinforces their existing beliefs while reducing their exposure to other perspectives or opinions.

One clue that can signal involvement of confirmation bias is conflictual use of the words "always" or "never." This is also referred to as *awfulization*, a term invented by psychologist Albert Ellis (1962). It refers to a tendency to view things in a very negative way, to the extent of *catastrophizing.* (It has an opposite, too, named *wonderfulization*).

In heated arguments in personal relationships, you will often hear one party say, "You're always late" or "You never pay me any attention." When someone is late driving to an apartment, they may complain that "We've caught every red light." An opinion has been formed, and each recurrance confirms the belief. The four times out of five that the person is not late, or the six days of the week when they give lots of attention, are disregarded in favor of the probative instance, even though it is much less frequent than the desirable behavior. You almost certainly didn't stop at every traffic light, but your heightened sensitivity to delay causes you to overemphasize the reds and forget the greens.

In business, there are amazing examples of failure due to confirmation bias. One of the most famous is the demise of Blockbuster. At the millennium it had thousands of stores and dominated the DVD rental service, in person and by mail. As digital streaming emerged, management ignored the threats from Netflix and other services, even declining the opportunity to buy Netflix at an early stage. They focused on data showing customer loyalty and interpreted it (wrongly) as evidence that people preferred to rent videos, looking back at their lengthy record of success and believing it would continue indefinitely. They gave too much weight to pass success and ignored the evidence that customer preferences were changing. Blockbuster was forced into bankruptcy in 2010.

Halo effect

In this process, an impression based on a single characteristic or observation influences judgments or assessments of traits that may be unrelated. The initial first impression (whether positive or negative) forms a "halo" around the person, leading us subconsciously to make other evaluations that are equally positive or negative. For example, the first time you see someone you may notice that they are very intelligent. This may lead you to believe that they are also kind or honest, even though you have no experience of them having these qualities. Many years ago, author Paul made exactly this mistake, hiring a consultant who had an extraordinary knowledge of card processing technology and entrusting him with management of a company bank account and his own expense card with a high limit. He turned out to be a career fraudster with a criminal record for deceiving other financial institutions. The company was vindicated in a 2008 court judgment, but the defendant then became bankrupt, and the company was unable to collect the debt (Aeropay Ltd & Anor v Bentolila, 2008).

The halo effect is closely related to the *law of first impressions*, or *primacy effect*. The adage "You never get a second chance to make a first impression" draws from this effect and explains in part why we pay careful attention to our wardrobe and grooming when going to a job interview or clean our teeth with special care before a first date. When positive traits are identified first, overall assessments are very likely to be more favorable over a long period. If as a child you are bitten on your first encounter with a dog, you are significantly less likely to trust other dogs for your whole life.

Status quo bias

FIGURE 6: *Status quo* bias

Status quo bias is the tendency to keep things the way they are, or keep doing the same thing, giving insufficient weight to the possible advantage of making a change. Our life experience is likely to be that this effect grows stronger as we age, even though we are gaining experience that should take us in the other direction. Status quo bias can be driven by several underlying psychological factors (Blanchar, 2016; Kahneman, Knetsch & Thaler, 1991; Van Putten & Van Dijk, 2010). The term *status quo* bias is not very old, first used in a 1988 article by Samuelson and Zeckhauser.

As the power and availability of computerized accounting systems has grown, many businesses and public practices have had to deal with status quo bias. A proposal to replace a "tried and true" set of manual procedures with new, machine-oriented processes may meet with strong resistance not only from older accountants but also from management at the highest levels. Some caution is merited; a wholesale refusal to modernize can be harmful, inefficient, and even lead to loss of competitive advantage.

Cognitive dissonance, first described only in 1957, is the discomfort people feel when they believe or do two things that are inconsistent (Festinger, 1957). For example, a person may believe that being slim is important for health reasons yet overeat restaurant food on weekends. If a person must think about a choice between two courses of action, one of which is difficult to reconcile with another belief, they will choose the option that does not cause the feeling of discomfort. Similarly, after making a choice once, humans are more likely to make the same choice again, even if it is demonstrably not the best choice. Does this perhaps explain why so many people stay in troubled relationships or marriages? Does it explain why many people, after a divorce at least partially based on cultural differences, marry into the same culture again?

Loss aversion is a human tendency to focus more on what could be lost by making a change than what could be gained. Do you know someone who has played the same lottery numbers for years and years, never winning? If you do, try pointing out to them how much they will save by not buying further lottery tickets. They will tell you that they dare not stop, for they are sure that their numbers will come up as soon as they do. Many families turn down career opportunities, or stay in expensive cities, to keep their children in the same school and with the same friends. Although there are excellent psychological reasons for making this choice, those children, if consulted, will invariably focus on the friends they would lose, rather than the new ones they might make. They argue in favor of the status quo to address their fear of loss.

Alym, who is a passionate hockey fan and ardent follower of the Vancouver Canucks, provides another compelling example. Imagine that you won a ticket to see the final game of the Stanley Cup, and your team was playing. While you are standing in line to enter the arena, a stranger offers you $1,000 for your seat. Most people would turn it down. Yet, the same person if asked whether they would **pay** $1,000 for a seat at the game, would say no. We overvalue what we have, in comparison to what we don't.

Mere exposure effect occurs when people develop a preference for things for no other reason than that they are familiar with them. The fact that they've always done things a certain way drives them to express a preference for the status quo. There may be no logical reason for the preference; the repeated exposure alone increases preference. If you hear a song several times you may like it more; if you've seen a face many times you may feel more comfortable with the person, even if you don't consciously recall meeting them. We often don't realize how strongly mere familiarity shapes our preferences.

You may well know someone who has never flown in an airplane but drives long distances across Canada or another large country, spending days at the wheel and taking disproportionate risks. They may have a fear of flying—but the more likely reason is the tendency to keep doing things in the familiar way. Do you know folks who go on their annual holidays to the same place every year?

Sunk cost fallacy may be the most expensive and irrational driver of status quo bias. This is the tendency to focus on the time, work or money that has already gone into a project, justifying continuation along the same course. In a stunning example of this, a client of the second author was recently at a decision point in a long-running lawsuit. The value of the action was around $18 million, and approximately $8 million had already been expended with a very expensive law firm that had achieved little result. As the matter neared trial, the existing firm wanted $2 million to prepare for trial and a further $3 million to conduct it. An alternative firm, much more expert in the exact area of law, offered to take over the entire suit for a fixed fee of $1.5 million. Incredibly, the client elected to stay with the under-achieving, $5 million proposition instead of switching up and saving $3.5 million in fees by doing so. The client's only justification was to point to the past investment in the existing provider.

At a less dramatic level, counsellors treating gambling addiction regularly encounter problem gamblers who attempt to justify continuing to bet, rationalizing on the amount of money already lost.

If you have a look around apps on your mobile phone which help you make everyday purchases, you may be amazed at how many there are which exploit the status quo bias. On Amazon, you will regularly be presented with "buy it again" options. Tim Hortons offers easy-tap opportunities to re-order "recent" and "favorite" choices. While these are convenient and quick, they also exploit the status quo bias to increase sales—if your regular breakfast is coffee and an apple fritter, you are more likely than not to buy another apple fritter even on a morning when you are thirsty but not hungry.

Heuristics and decision errors

A heuristic is a shortcut that people might use to simplify a complex decision. While heuristics *can* be useful, because they save time, they can also lead to errors because they rely on only some information and exclude other relevant considerations.

Imagine that you are a risk manager in a bank and are called into a meeting to discuss a large loan requested by a property developer. In the last week, you have met with four other clients in similar businesses, all requesting relaxation of payment terms due to a slow-down in the market for new properties. The most readily available information in your mind is the financial difficulties of those clients, and you may approach the new request too skeptically, bringing up the state of the market long before you consider the actual financial health, sales pipeline or plans of the new customer.

The following are the commonest heuristics encountered in business.

Availability heuristic

Responses to questions which are incorrect, but flow from readily accessible information in the human mind, suffer from the *availability heuristic.* Try answering these questions quickly then compare the first answer which came to your mind with those in text box. If you get them all right, you are likely to do well on a quiz show under pressure!

- What is the capital of New York State?
- What is the capital of Illinois?
- What do cows drink?
- Which is safer, travelling by car or by airplane?
- In any given year, are more people killed by shark attacks or by parts falling off airplanes?
- In Europe, which farm animal kills more farmers than any other?
- In Africa, which is the most dangerous creature?
- What is the capital of Brazil?
- What is the capital of British Columbia?

Several factors can influence this heuristic. Among the most common are *recency* (you are more likely to recall something you heard or read about recently), *sensationalism* (press reports of dramatic events increase their presence in our minds) and *unavailability of information*. The above list contains examples of all three.

Albany
Springfield
Water
By airplane
Parts of airplanes (30x more likely)
Sheep
Mosquito
Brasilia
Victoria

Default effect

FIGURE 7: Netflix.ca subscription plans: Pre-selected premium service

The above is the landing page for new subscribers who visit Netflix.ca. Notice how the checkbox for Premium service—the highest price—is pre-selected. A new subscriber who wants a less expensive service must make a conscious decision to click on a different plan. This is the default effect in action.

Water, it is often said, always takes the easiest course downhill. This is also a human tendency.

Life is full of choices. However, the easiest choice is most often to accept what is most immediately at hand—what we've always done, or the first option presented. Modern software provides many examples of this and is often purposely built to encourage users to simplify their lives (at least in the short term) by accepting defaults when there are other options. The science behind this is known as *nudge theory* and there is a whole area of academic study and politics which has developed around it (Thaler & Sunstein, 2008).

When you open Microsoft Word to type a document, what is your next step? For most people, it's to start typing. This is a demonstration of the default effect. On your ribbon there are many options to choose fonts, font sizes, colors and a variety of other effects. But a whole set of default selections has already been made for you. Perhaps graphic designers and other specially trained people think first about font selection before they start putting their thoughts on paper, but that's the exception. Most users, if they think about visual effects at all, do so late in the process of building their document.

The default effect is heavily exploited by sales and marketing professionals, who strive to make their product or brand the one chosen unthinkingly by consumers. It takes great awareness to rid yourself of the tendency to accept the default and consider other available options. With this effort made, however, you may be surprised at how often you make a choice which is not the most obvious; sometimes the default option is just totally unsuitable.

A statistical example of the result of the default effect is shown in the medical field of organ donation. Some countries, for example the United Kingdom, have a default where willingness to donate organs is assumed unless you opt out; other countries (including Canada and the United States) assume unwillingness unless you opt in. The requirement in the latter to make an active choice to donate results in a lower availability of donated organs.

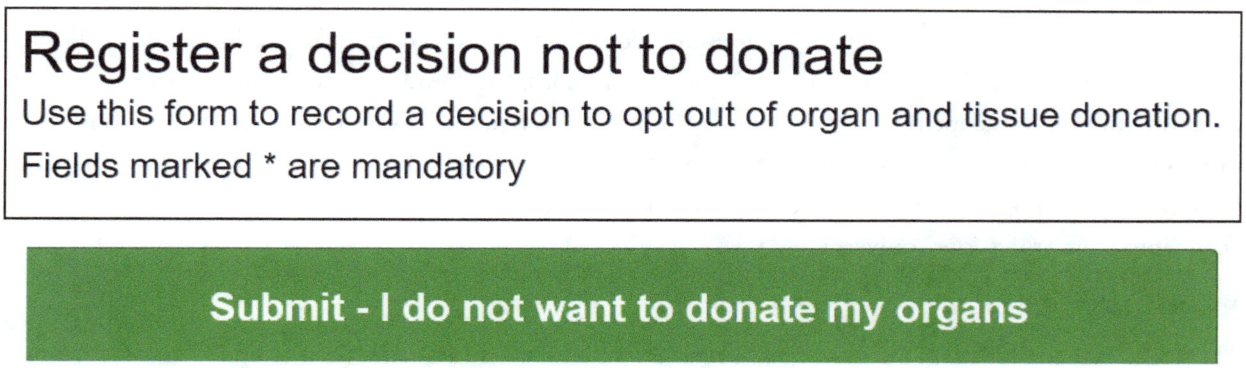

FIGURE 8: U.K. National Health – a requirement to opt out

U.K. residents are presumed to permit donation unless they opt out

(NHS Blood & Transplant, n.d.)

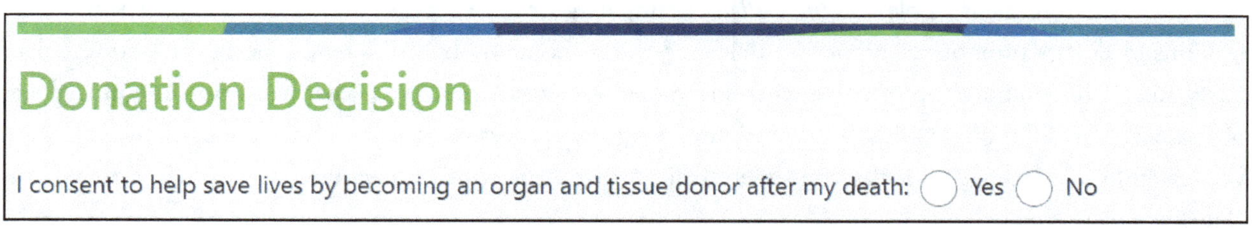

FIGURE 9: British Columbia – a requirement to opt in

British Columbia requires an affirmative decision to opt in (B.C. Transplant, n.d.)

Instrument default

Instrument Default is rather like the default effect. It refers to the tendency of humans to select a familiar tool for a new use, even when a little research would reveal that it is a misfit for the task. There is an old saying that if your only tool is a hammer, everything looks like a nail.

As we age, we become more and more familiar with tools, software and devices which we use over and over again. Governments and regulators are not immune to such tendencies, often viewing newly developed equipment as inferior in the face of overwhelming evidence to the contrary. An excellent example in the aviation industry is the snail's-pace acceptance of GPS technology for instrument landings (where the pilots can't see the ground until the last few seconds) even in the face of overwhelming evidence of their reliability. While regulators, the senior echelons of which were largely staffed by retired airline pilots, dilly-dallied over certifying the procedures, accidents continued to occur which would have been avoided with the use of GPS devices costing under $5,000.

Similarly, the rapid evolution of AI tools which is taking place as we write is separating professionals, universities and others who are willing to use new tools from those who try not to adapt. The pace of this separation is increasing exponentially—don't be left behind!

The best antidote to instrument default is continuing education. As an accounting professional you will become familiar with several tools like Excel, maybe Intuit QuickBooks, Sage products and the like. These are all great programs and can be adapted to use in many businesses and activities. However, new apps come along all the time, and you should stay constantly on the lookout for new technology which will help you do your job better. Introductory training is usually free of charge and sufficient for you to evaluate whether it's time to put a new arrow into your professional quiver.

Repetition error

The Latin name of this argument is *Argumentum ad Nauseam.* Its idiomatic translation is “argument to the point of exhaustion,” though strictly translated it means "argument until feeling sickness.” The premise is that if something is repeated enough, that makes it true—or at least it will convince an audience that it is true. It is widely used by politicians, salespeople and religious leaders.

A well-known example is Apple's *Think Different* campaign. Over the course of five years, Apple spent tens of millions of dollars promoting the notion that everything about Apple is different. The slogan permeated its advertising, presentations, product launches and more. Sometimes, however, what was being announced was not radical or revolutionary—just an evolution of a camera, processor or utility. Still, the constant repetition was carefully engineered to make consumers believe that Apple and innovation are virtually synonymous (Francis, n.d.).

US President Donald Trump is a master of this technique. In almost every speech he makes, he invokes repetition with subtleties of timing and tone to tremendous effect on his followers. Here are just three sentences from his January 6 speech denying the validity of the presidential election:

> The weak Republicans, and that's it. I really believe it. I think I'm going to use the term, the weak Republicans. You got a lot of them, and you got a lot of great ones, but you got a lot of weak ones.

In 43 words, those weak Republicans appear three times. They must exist (and it's apparently all their fault). Who could doubt the existence of those weak Republicans after hearing that from their trusted leader? A few moments later he surpassed that performance with these words:

> Over 8,000 ballots in Pennsylvania were cast by people whose names and dates of birth match individuals who died in 2020 and prior to the election. Think of that. Dead people! Lots of dead people, thousands. And some dead people actually requested an application.

Those dead people make four appearances in five sentences. Who could doubt that dead folk were casting their votes?

Problems in data interpretation

Averages

One of the most frequently abused terms in statistical misrepresentations is "average." From the most basic statistics courses you might have learned that there are three types of average: mean, median and mode. Semantically, it can be argued that they are not "averages" at all – the less contentions phraseology is *measures of central tendency*. Erroneous impressions are often created by use of an inappropriate type, use of averaging where it is inappropriate, or using the term *average* without specifying which type is being used (Newbold, Carlson & Thorne, 2013).

The *mean* is calculated by summing all the numbers in a dataset and dividing by the number of values. It is highly sensitive to being influenced by extreme values, known as outliers.

The *median*" value represents the central number in a dataset. If all the numbers are arranged in order, the median is the middle number if the number of values is odd, or the average of the two middle values if the number of values is even.

The *mode* is the number which appears most frequently. There can be more than one mode in a dataset. Consider the following series of values, produced by the HR department of a professional firm. It shows the number of years worked prior to leaving, for resignations in a one year period.

```
1, 1, 1, 1, 1, 2, 5, 10, 14, 25, 25, 25, 25, 25, 26, 27, 30, 30
         MEAN 15.2     MEDIAN 19.5     MODES 1, 25
```

Training new employees is a significant expense, is recovered over an extended period when skilled staff stay with the firm. A report on "average" length of stay will produce very different insights, depending on

If we look at the mean, we see that the "average" employee stays with the company for 15.2 years. Based on this, we might conclude that the cost of training employees could be spread over the 15+ years of expected employment.

Even better if we look at the median. Now, those costs can be spread over nearly 20 years.

The two modes, however, tell a different story. 5 of the employees who left, out of a total of 18, stayed only one year. A significant investment in their training was quickly lost. The second mode, 25, shows another five people departing at that stage in their careers. The modes give insight into two problems which need to be addressed but were obscured by the mean and median. How could the company avoid the fast attrition of newly qualified people, and why did so many very experienced people depart after exactly 25 years?

Both problems related to issues with the compensation schemes for professional employees. Competitor companies were paying higher salaries and offering desirable geographical mobility to recently qualified candidates, as soon as they had their certificates. The company might usefully have employed some form of bonding to ensure that they were repaid the training costs if employees stayed just long enough to qualify. The 25-year point marked the vesting of share options; employees who passed their 25th anniversary suddenly became wealthy enough to retire and many did. To keep these key staff members, the company needed to offer better incentives for them to continue working, and for the future perhaps reconsider its share option planning so that it did not have such a damaging outcome for the company.

Other examples from financial contexts include average housing prices, where Canada-wide statistics using a mean calculation are unduly influenced by Vancouver and Toronto, and mean salary calculations in a company where the CEO's income as a large multiple of others.

However, there are many practical uses of averages. For example, airlines need to know with considerable precision what the weight of an aircraft will be when it takes off and lands, to ensure sufficient runway length and fuel loading. While a few airlines weigh each passenger (typically for small aircraft flights between islands with short runways), most use the number of adult males, adult females and children, multiplied by an industry-standard mean weight (in 2021, it was adjusted upwards in the United States as population weights are increasing). In general, though, the most important use of averages is to measure change over time in comparable populations.

The mean, which is the type which most listeners imagine is being used when they hear "average," may not be the best measure for any group where there are significant outliers. Outliers are values within a dataset which are significantly higher or lower than most of the others. They tend to pull the arithmetical mean towards them, particularly in small populations. Wherever outliers cause this phenomenon, the median is likely to be a better indicator of the middle of the range, or the typical measure.

In *Naked Statistics,* Charles Whelan (2013) gives this example:

> Imagine ten middle-class people each earning $35,000 per year. Bill Gates walks in with an income of $1 billion. Now the average income ("mean") of the group jumps to roughly $91 million—yet none of the original ten became richer.

It is also inappropriate to use the mean when the population surveyed contains diverse groups. A popular demonstration is the analysis of divorce statistics (Luellen, 2018). The U.S. Bureau of Labor Statistics published data that showed an "average" divorce rate of 43.1%; that might be very discouraging for anyone contemplating marriage; however, if you were aged 35–40 and had a college degree, the likelihood of divorce is only 13.4%. What value is a calculation of the weight of the "average" (mean) dog? There are breeds that weigh 2 kilos and some that reach over 100 kilos—world record holder Zorba the mastiff weighed 150 kilos!

Using the term "average" without specifying the type is common in advertising and promotional media. The well-known recruitment website glassdoor.com reports that a graduate engineer in Dubai can expect an average salary of 9,000 dirhams (about $3,300 CAD) per month. Yet its competitor indeed.com reports that the average salary is 5,549 dirhams per month, while salaryexplorer.com says that 5,140 dirhams is the average starting salary, but the maximum is over 39,100 per month. It's impossible to make any sense of these numbers, all purporting to report "average" salaries. Are the numbers means, medians, or even modes? There is no way to know. The best we can probably do is suggest that a starter is likely to earn around 5,000 to 6,000 dirhams per month, and that perhaps Glassdoor's average might be a mean heavily influenced by outliers in the 40K range. We might wonder what an "average engineer" is, in any event!

Base rate

The base rate itself is the most fundamental probability of an event happening across a whole population. It quantifies what "normally happens"—the statistic we should establish and consider, before any new evidence is added. Imagine that you are called onto stage in a live show, and the performer has two bags of balls. You are blindfolded, the performer pulls a ball out of one bag, then when the blindfold is removed, you are asked to guess which bag it came from. The base rate, without any additional information, is a 50% chance of the ball coming from either bag.

Base rate neglect describes what happens when people ignore statistical probability (what typically happens), in favor of an opinion based on a specific case or cases. It is often found in investment decisions, personal hopes and expectations, medical opinions and legal analyses.

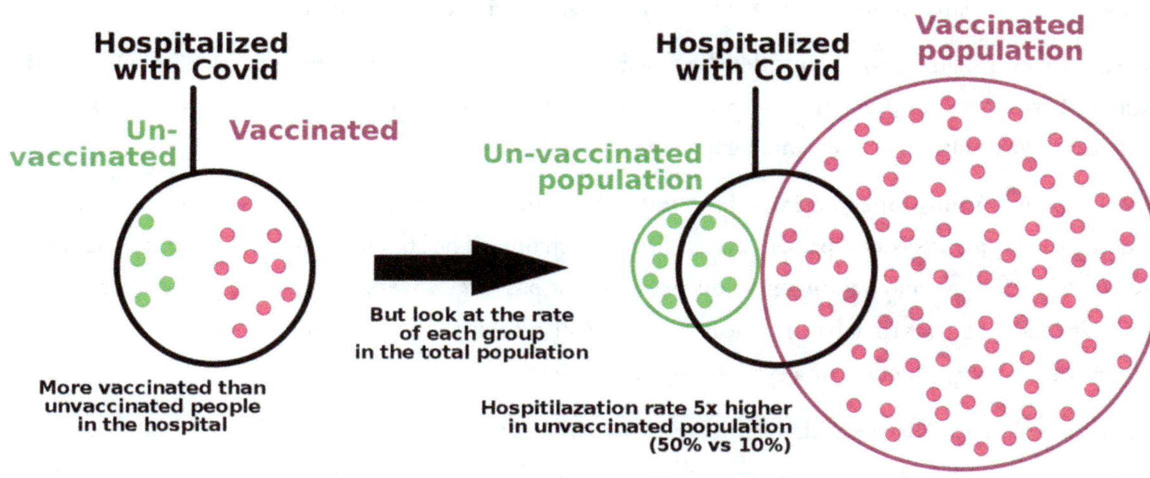

FIGURE 10: COVID base rate

The above diagram was posted, improved and reposted on Twitter in 2021 by Marc Rummy, who had recently graduated from high school (Marcrummy, 2021). If you looked at the percentages of vaccination rates in people hospitalized with COVID, you might conclude that the vaccine was not effective. But that ignores the base rate—the relative percentages of people in the population who are vaccinated.

Tversky and Kahneman (1973) describe an experiment which neatly demonstrates base rate neglect.

> Tom W. is of high intelligence, although lacking in true creativity. He has a need for order and clarity, and for neat and tidy systems in which every detail finds its appropriate place. His writing is rather dull and mechanical, occasionally enlivened by somewhat corny puns and by flashes of imagination of the sci-fi type. He has a strong drive for competence. He seems to feel little sympathy for other people and does not enjoy interacting with others. Self-centered, he nonetheless has a deep moral sense.[4]

The researchers demonstrated a close match between similarity judgments and likelihood judgments; participants tended to assign a high likelihood of Tom W being a student in a particular field based on stereotypes rather than the true numbers of students in each field.

Now a personal example. In August 2024, Paul's son Daniel flew his first solo (take-off and landing without an instructor in the plane). Paul, as most parents would, worried deeply about the flight's outcome, even though virtually all properly trained pilots complete their first solo without incident. Instructors only allow trainees to go solo when they are fully prepared, on days when conditions are good. Focusing on the rare possibility of a crash is a classic base rate neglect.

Another real-world story shows how base rate neglect can lead consultants astray. Some years ago, a small city-state introduced a new bus fare system involving prepaid cards and cash collection boxes. Drivers were no longer involved in enforcement, and there were no other employees to collect fares. Early research found that on an average journey, about 10% of passengers were not paying the fare at all. Suggested theories were that the avoidance might be by students, low-income residents, or immigrant communities who did not understand the rules. The authority began to consider measures to fight the perceived fare avoidance.

The analysts, however, had failed to consider the base rate. This was a country with an exceedingly law-abiding population and strong social pressure to conform. The country had draconian laws against dishonesty which made it unattractive to cheat for even small gains.

The authority then commissioned an interview study of apparent fare evaders and discovered the real reason; with the new cash payment system, passengers couldn't get change. The standard fare was 75 cents; the smallest banknote was $1. After overpaying for three journeys, honest passengers were simply taking the fourth without paying and rationalizing that they hadn't cheated the transit system at all. The solution was neither education nor penalties, but the introduction of a system to provide change.

Base rate neglect can lead to very damaging results in forensic auditing and credit card fraud detection. Transactions with certain characteristics may be flagged as having a high risk (say 75%) of fraud. However, if auditors fail to consider that the company or industry has a very low rate of fraud (the base rate), they can prematurely jump to unnecessary investigations or even accusations. Accountants and lawyers examining

---

[4] Naturally most people choose professional actor, ignoring the fact that bank workers outnumber professional actors many times over. Ignoring the base rate—the ratio of bankers to actors—leads to the false conclusion that he is more likely to be an actor. Despite his thespian talents, he is much more likely to be a bank employee.

potential frauds should always try to establish the base rate and plan their work based on assumptions modified to take account of "what usually happens."

Here are some additional examples of base rate neglect and its consequences.

- A company has produced strong earnings and growth for several years. However, in the last financial year it incurred a loss, for the first time. The nervous investor may conclude that the company is headed downhill and decide to sell their shares. However, downturns can be temporary or caused by unique events (such as a pandemic); the decision to sell is, without further analysis, a knee-jerk reaction driven by the base rate fallacy.
- Yale Law School has rejected, over the last decade, 94% of applicants. Yet a top, high-performing student at a top undergraduate school may well believe that they will beat the statistics and be admitted. The expectation of an offer relies on the base rate fallacy; even with good undergraduate standing, the odds overwhelmingly indicate that a rejection is the most likely outcome (not that this should stop anyone from applying—someone gets in!).
- The unending debate with vaccine opponents since the COVID pandemic started has provided plenty of fuel for exploring this concept. Even vaccinated people catch COVID, and some require hospitalization. In a city with an 80% vaccinated rate, it would not be uncommon for most hospital admissions to be of vaccinated people. Does this tell us that the vaccine is ineffective? No, of course not. At its logical extreme, in a city with a 100% vaccination rate, 100% of admissions would be vaccinated. Any argument that the vaccine is ineffective ignores majority of the vaccinated population who were not admitted to hospital.

Base rate neglect is of particular interest to prosecuting and defense lawyers, where it is often referred to as the *prosecutor's fallacy*. The name flows from the frequent misuse of statistics, tainted with base rate fallacy, in criminal trials. There are many real examples (such as the O.J. Simpson trial) but a hypothetical example will suffice.

An expert witness is called to testify about DNA matching after a serious crime. After explaining some technicalities, they inform the court and jury that "the odds of this not being the defendant's DNA are approximately one in a million." While that might sound like beyond reasonable doubt—enough to convict—here's the problem—the offence was committed in New York City, which has a population of nearly nine million. Logically, not accounting for other people who might have been in the city on the date of the offense, there are eight other people who could have committed it. That *does* sound like reasonable doubt, and other evidence will certainly be needed to establish guilt.

Publication bias

Publication bias is a persistent problem in academic and scientific literature. Studies which find something positive, new, or interesting, are much more interesting to editors than those that confirm a belief or negate a theory. As a result, the former are much more likely to be published, creating a misimpression of the weight of evidence in favor of a particular outcome. Then, the situation is compounded when literature reviews count or summarize previously published works (Rothstein, Sutton & Borenstein, 2005).

Bayes' theorem

Bayes' theorem is not a separate problem, but a remedy for base rate neglect. It shows us how to figure out a revised probability, using new information, but without ignoring the base rate. The broader coverage of Bayes' theorem is a mathematical method of calculating probability, based on what we already know about the statistics of "conditions" that might be related to the event. It kicks in when we know at least two probabilities; it is particularly useful when examining something with a possibility of false positives or negatives.[5]

Bayes' theorem is that *new* evidence should not determine what we believe standing alone; it should, rather, update what we already knew before considering it. Going back to the two bags of balls we mentioned in the previous section, you now learn that each bag contains 100 balls. Bag 1 contains 95 red balls and 5 yellow; bag 2 contains 95 yellow balls and 5 red. The ball in the performer's hand is red—if you guess that it came from bag 1, Bayes' theorem tells us there is a 95% chance that you are right.

Bayes' theorem forms the basis of machine learning. Every time you type terms into a search engine like Google or Yahoo, the items listed in response are calculated using Bayes' theorem to figure out what you are *probably* seeking, based on what other people have searched for using the same terms.

Some basic terminology should be defined. We'll use the example of disease testing to illustrate.

You take a test COVID test. At the time, in the general population 200 out of every 100,000 have the disease. The test comes back positive. You shouldn't panic yet—the test is only 99% accurate for positive tests, that is, it wrongly reads positive 1% of the time. This test has a 1% *false positive rate.* You want to know the chances that you actually have the disease. The test also misses the disease in 30% of people who have it. It has a **30%** *false negative rate.*

Reporting the results of a Bayesian analysis may use a *null hypothesis.* This is a statement, to be tested, like "I do not have the disease." In this disease example, the base rate was 200/100000 (0.2%). We want to recalculate the likelihood of having the disease, based on the new evidence (the test).

Incorrect rejection of a null hypothesis (i.e. saying you have the disease, when you don't) is a false positive. It's also known as a *type I error.* Where the null hypothesis is accepted, but it should not have been, this is a *type II error.* An easy way to remember this is that in type I an innocent person is convicted, while in type II, a guilty person is acquitted.

---

[5] The English Reverend Thomas Bayes managed to balance his clerical duties with some serious attention to statistics and philosophy. He died in 1761, with his *Essay towards solving a Problem in the Doctrine of Chances* unpublished. His work might have been lost, but luckily his family gave his papers to another minister, Richard Price, who wrote an introduction, edited the text, and focused on one of two solutions proposed by Bayes. According to modern rules of attribution, we should perhaps be talking about the Bayes-Price theorem, but nearly three centuries of usage have firmly cemented Bayes' credit and relegated Reverend Price to the footnotes.

A convenient way to calculate the Bayesian probabilities is to tabulate the statistics into a *confusion matrix.* It is constructed by positioning the hypothesis along the top, and the new evidence down the side. This creates the four possible combinations; also, we can populate the bottom row with the known statistic (200 people have COVID, therefore 99,800 don't, and the total is 100,000). We can also populate the left column for the known positive (140, because the false negative rate is 30% therefore 60). Then the false positive rate (1%) gives us the number of people out of the remaining 99,800 people who don't have COVID but test positive—998. The remaining blank is the number of people who don't have COVID and test negative, which must be 98,802.

TABLE 3: COVID correct and false positives and negatives

	Have COVID	Don't have COVID	Total
Tests Positive	140	998	1,138
Tests Negative	60	98,802	98,862
Total	**200**	**99,800**	**100,000**

With the table complete, we can now ascertain what percentage of people who test positive really do have COVID. The answer is 140/1,138, or 12.3%.

Another way to visualize the analysis is to draw a rectangle containing the population, and mark off the numbers that are relevant to the calculation. This example is borrowed from the 3Blue1Brown channel on YouTube, an excellent resource devoted to explaining mathematical theory (2015).

Steve, a hypothetical person in the example, is very shy and withdrawn, meek and tidy, with a need for order and structure and a passion for detail. Is it more likely that he is a librarian or a farmer? When this question was presented in a study, 84% of people chose librarian (Kahneman & Tversky, 1972). Kahneman and Tversky point out that this is illogical, because it fails to consider that farmers outnumber librarians by 20 to 1. This ratio is remarkably consistent: in mid-2025 we looked at Statistics Canada employment data and read that Canada has approximately 10,000 professional librarians and about 200,000 farmers.

Assume we believe that 40% of librarians would fit the description of Steve, and 10% of farmers would fit the description. What are the odds that a person randomly drawn from the population, who had Steve's characteristics, would be a librarian? The following picture shows the population of 210 people, 10 librarians and 200 farmers.

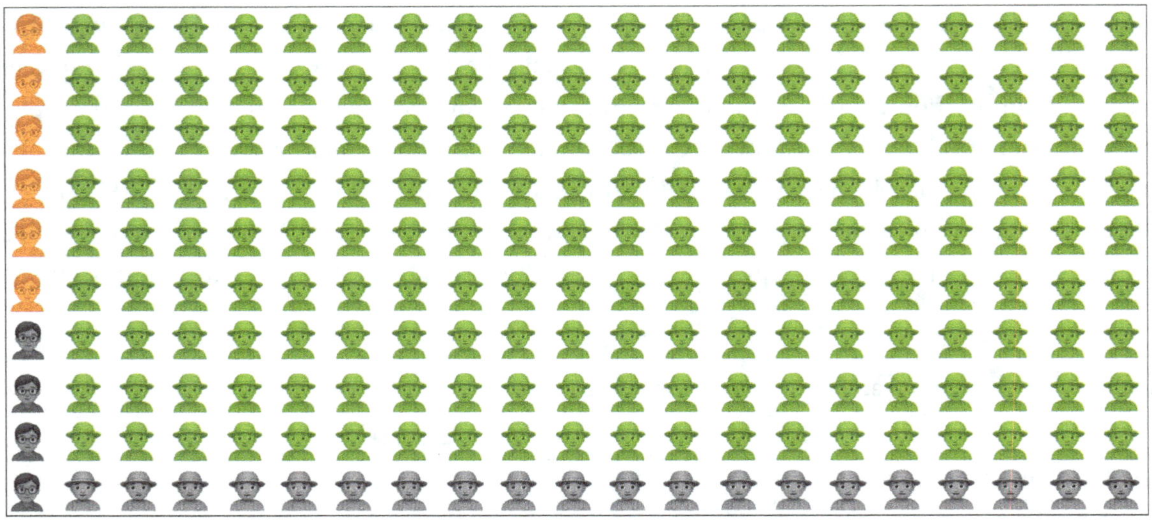

FIGURE 11: 10 Librarians and 200 Farmers

On the left are 10 librarians. The bottom four, in gray, are those with Steve's characteristics. On the right are 200 farmers. The 20 farmers in the bottom row have Steve's characteristics.

If we randomly draw a person with Steve's characteristics, the probability of him being a librarian is 4 / 24, or 16.67%. The probability of him being a farmer, on the other hand, is 20/24, or 83.33%.

This final belief after weighing the evidence is known as the posterior probability.

This logic can be applied to an infinite number of situations. Consider this question:

> The city of Manchester, in England, has two famous soccer teams, United and City. United are however much more popular than City, supported by 70% of residents. The other 30% support City. Attendance is different too: 80% of United fans have been to at least one game this season, while only 50% of City fans have done so. If a random selection is made of one person from the city, and they have attended a game recently, what is the probability that they are a United fan?

If we drew a similar picture to the "farmers and librarians" above, assuming the total population to be 100, there would be 70 United fans on the left, and 30 City fans on the right. Out of them, 56 of the United fans would be marked for game attendance, but only 15 of the City. We can now solve the question: the total number of fans who attended a game is 71, 56 of them being United fans. So, the probability of our selection being a United fan is 56/71.

Mathematically, the theorem is expressed as follows:

$$P(A|B) = P(B|A)P(A)/P(B)$$

On the left side of the equation, P, the conditional probability, is the probability of A happening, if B is true. The vertical line (or pipe symbol) in the equation means "given that," so P(A|B) is interpreted as "the probability of A, given that B is true. A is the hypothesis, while B is the new evidence. Note that conditional probabilities are *not* reversible. The probability of being pregnant if you are a female aged 15–50 cannot be inverted to know the probability of being a female if you are pregnant.

On the right side, P(B|A) is the converse—the probability of A happening if B is true. P(A) is the independent probability of A, and P(B) is the independent probability of B.

Last, we should revisit the concept of *priors*. In our example, the prior probability of having COVID was 200 in 100,000. However, if this prior changes based on new information, the calculation changes. If you have several of the symptoms of COVID, the base rate would not be the percentage of the population who have COVID, but the percentage of the population who have COVID symptoms and have COVID—certainly a much higher percentage.

Appeals

The philosophy of persuasion takes us back to the teachings of Aristotle, who more than two millennia ago wrote that there are four fundamental techniques for convincing an audience to believe the speaker. They are Ethos, Pathos, Logos (which he grouped) and Kairos, which he mentioned but did not include in the first group. Ethos relies on credibility, which might be established by education or experience; Pathos appeals to human emotion, and Logos appeals to logic. Kairos is more fleeting—it calls upon the audience to "seize the moment" which may not last (for example, persuading people to fit snow tires to their cars immediately after a heavy snowfall).

There is quite a long list of "appeals"—false calls on logic to establish a claim. Some examples:

- *Appeal to Authority / Appeal to Accomplishment.* These closely related claims point to the power or abilities of a third party as evidence of the correctness of that person's beliefs or statements. "Professor X told us in class that ..., so it must be true." No! Even professors occasionally make mistakes! In a public accounting practice, a great deal of deference is often paid to senior partners and managers. While their opinions are valuable, skeptical thinking is part of the duty of junior staff and they should not be tempted to rely on seniors' opinions solely based on their status.
- *Appeal to Common Belief* is also known as *Appeal to the Masses* or the *Bandwagon Fallacy.* "Oxford and Cambridge are the best universities in the world. Everybody knows that." There are many problems with this appeal—first, it is likely that not everyone does know that, and second, just because everyone believes it, that doesn't make it true! Common beliefs can be the product of propaganda, religious indoctrination, plain mass ignorance or the failure of science to arrive (yet) at a demonstration of the truth. Even if everyone does "know" something or is doing something, that doesn't mean it's right for you. "Everyone" might be watching *Dallas* and want to know who killed JR—but you don't have to like the show, and you certainly don't have to watch it. In audit work, there are many examples of procedures which are widely used and commonly understood to be reliable. This does not excuse the auditor from skeptical enquiry. For example, experts are often employed to provide valuations of complex assets like shopping malls or financial instruments. Just because an estimate comes from a recognized expert used by many firms, however, does not mean that it must be accepted without question. The auditor should review the data relied on, examine key assumptions, and especially ensure that there is no conflict of interest when management has potential reasons for overvaluing assets.

- *Appeal to Common Sense.* Also known as the *argument from incredulity*, this appeal suggests that something must be correct because it is difficult or impossible to imagine that the opposite might be true. In the summer of 2023, we had a great example in British Columbia with a record season of wildfires. It's common sense that this was caused by global warming, right? There are some problems with this apparently obvious analysis, not least that global temperatures have truly only increased by about 2° Fahrenheit, or 1° Celsius, since 1880! Surely the analysis of global and local weather patterns, unassociated human behavior and surface conditions requires a much more sophisticated analysis before we conclude that the change in temperature is the direct cause of the devastating wildfires we have seen. Some areas have had continued increases of far more than the global average, while some have seen no change at all. It requires far more than "common sense" to understand what's really happening.
- *Appeal to Consequences.* Also known as *wishful thinking*. There are two forms of this appeal, positive and negative. In both cases, the listener is asked to believe a statement based on the outcome of that belief. In the positive form, the argument is "If X is true, Y will follow. Y is desirable. Therefore, X must be true." If God exists, good people will go to heaven. Therefore, God must exist. For the negative form, substitute "undesirable" and therefore X must be false.
- *Appeal to Emotion.* This complex fallacy illogically invokes a potential emotional feeling (sadness, guilt, fear) that will result if the argument being advanced is not accepted. When stopped for speeding, you might say to the officer "If you give me a ticket my father will be really angry." Dad's reaction has no logical connection to your guilt or reasoning as to why you should be fined or let off—but the officer may be persuaded by imagining the suffering you will feel at the hands of your father.
- *Appeal to Ignorance.* An opinion is argued to be factual because the opposite has not been proven or cannot be proven. This appeal is particularly prevalent in religious arguments, in forms "God must exist because no one has proved that He doesn't."
- *Appeal to Nature.* "The more water you drink, the healthier you'll be." (Because it's natural, right?). Well, no, if you drink too much water you can become very ill with "overhydration" (in Europe it's sometimes referred to as "water poisoning").
- *Appeal to Ridicule.* In this manipulative device, the proponent of a proposition states that the opposite view is ridiculous or laughable to enhance the acceptability of their own view.

Reasoning fallacies

The hot hand and gambler's fallacies

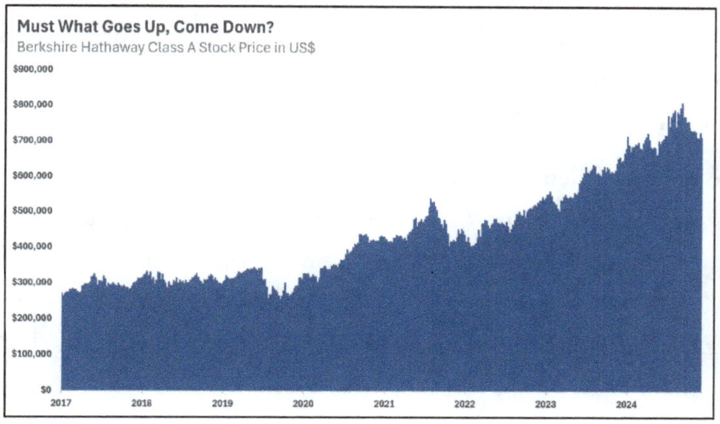

FIGURE 12: Berkshire Hathaway stock price

This pair of errors is particularly interesting because both are widely observable, yet they are in direct opposition to each other. In investment markets, sufferers from the *gambler's fallacy* believe that "what goes up, must come down." They think that a sustained upward run *must* reverse and that at some point, things *must* go the other way. We've emphasized *must* here – this is the precise nature of the fallacy.

Reversion to the mean, the tendency of spikes or troughs to reverse towards a more moderate position, is well documented, but it doesn't always apply.

We've shown the eight year performance of the world's most expensive stock, Berkshire Hathaway. A sufferer from gambler's fallacy who short-sold the stock throughout the period would have lost millions of dollars!

Hot hand believers think that a sustained upward run is an indicator that things will continue that way for at least the next while. They would have done well on Berkshire Hathaway. Complex analyses of stock and market performances indicate that neither belief is necessarily true—the fact that the market is rising is neither a reliable indicator that it will next turn downwards or continue upwards. Far too many external factors determine the actual next movement. Overall, however, retail investors as a group generally misjudge the timing and either sell too quickly in a rising market or sell too late in a falling market.

FIGURE 13: Yuanhe Deluxe roulette wheel

Neither fallacy is inevitably correct. Let's treat this mathematically, not emotionally. Consider a conventional roulette wheel,[6] and assume that it is honestly constructed.[7] Each time the wheel spins and the ball is released (only one is released, ignore the second ball in the picture), there are 18 possibilities of a red number, 18 of a black number, and two of a green number (0 or 00). The colors of the numbers do NOT correspond to odd and even, as some red numbers are odd, and some are even. We can calculate, however, that the odds of the ball falling into a red slot on each spin are 18/38, or 9/19. The same for black.

Now consider that on the last seven spins, the ball has fallen into a black slot. What are the odds that a red number will come up next time? The answer remains the same, 9/19. Yet believers in the gambler's fallacy will say that after seven black numbers, there is a much higher likelihood of a red number. Mathematically this is based on the calculation that the odds of 8 black numbers in a row are $(9/19)^{8}$, or 1/394—but that is NOT the same thing. If we start now, the odds of the NEXT 8 numbers being black are 1/394; but as we've already had 7 blacks, the odds of the next one being black remain 9/19.

Conversely and equally illogically, a believer in the *hot hand fallacy* will note the unlikely run of seven black numbers and conclude that another black number is the most likely outcome.

The logic is slightly different for a deck of 52 cards, where half are red, and half are black. On drawing one card at random, the odds are 26/52 of either color. But if that card is kept out of the pack and a second card is drawn, the odds are now different; if the first card was red, there is a slightly higher chance of a black for the second card because its odds are now 26/51, whereas red is 25/51. Ultimately when 51 cards have been drawn, there will be a 100% probability that the final card is a particular color (the color of which only 25 have been drawn so far). If the first six cards drawn are all black, the statistical odds of the next one being red are significantly higher than for black—the gambler's fallacy becomes correct, while the hot hand fallacy fails.

Regression fallacy

Regression to the mean describes the fact that most things, including sports performances, human characteristics and medical situations, tend to move back towards the average (mean) after extreme performances, statistics, or situations. A person suffers from *regression fallacy* when they naively assume that an exceptional situation will continue. This is the opposite of the hot hand fallacy. A sports team which has an exceptional season, far exceeding expectations in one season, will usually fall back into the pack in the following season. Extremely tall parents may breed even taller children, but it is more likely that their children will be somewhere between the parents' height and the mean. This was the example studied by Sir Francis Galton in 1885, when he published the first paper on the subject.

---

[6] The picture is the Yuanhe Deluxe Roulette Wheel, available from Amazon.ca. https://www.amazon.ca/Yuanhe-Casino-Deluxe-Glossy-Roulette/dp/B09KZGC3LQ/

[7] European roulette wheels typically have 37 numbers, whereas the house is given a greater edge in North America where there are typically 38. The calculations here use the 38-pocket wheel.

English premier league team Leicester City provide a compelling example. In the 2015–16 season they finished in top place, labeled by Forbes Magazine as a "once in a lifetime footballing miracle." Their best previous performance ever was to come second in 1928–29. The following year they finished in the lower half of the table, a much more familiar position for them.

The fallacy is made more credible by the fact that humans tend to respond to abnormal situations when they are at their peak. Sales of lottery tickets rocket upwards when the prize is abnormally high; this is entirely illogical (on the assumption that winning say $300 million would have about the same effect on your life as winning $600 million). The odds of winning the big prize are far higher when the value is lower and there is no excitement. Yet the queues to buy tickets get far longer as zeroes are added to the prize pot. If sports betting is your thing, you might turn a decent profit betting that a team will NOT win a second league title after an outstanding performance.

Semmelweis effect

Dr. Ignaz Semmelweis discovered, nearly 200 years ago, that children's mortality rates dropped by 90% when physicians disinfected their hands between patients, especially after performing autopsies. This was two decades before germ theory was promulgated. The discovery saved many lives, but his colleagues rejected his theory that doctors could transmit disease from one person to another, some even believing that a gentleman's hands could not carry disease (Holmes, 1861).

That's all it is. The *Semmelweis effect* is the tendency to reject new evidence because it conflicts with something that you believe. You will quickly recognize its corollary in confirmation bias—accepting only the evidence that confirms what you believe.

False conclusions about causation

Data by themselves consist only of facts and figures. When humans approach data, however, they use thought processes to discern meaning. One avenue of inquiry may be causal—can the data tell us *why* something happened, rather than just *what* happened. As accountants we are deeply interested in what data can tell us about *why* something happened. Over the last half decade, however, mathematicians and statisticians engaged in an almost existential debate about whether "cause" could be a term of science; for many years students were not allowed to use the word "cause" but only "relation" or "association" (Pearl & MacKenzie, 2018). Thankfully the debate is over, and the rule no longer exists!

We should not be too quick to conclude that one event is the cause of another. Here we explore three of the most common mistakes made in the pursuit of causal explanations.

Post hoc, ergo propter hoc

Translated from Latin, *post hoc, ergo propter hoc* means "after this, therefore on account of this." It is the assumption that because one thing happens after another, and appears to have a connection, the first was the cause of the second. Writers on this subject commonly refer to the whole concept as a fallacy; however, the fallacy lies in believing in the attribution of the cause. It can be true that one event following another indicates a likely cause. On a city street, government workers remove all the trees. Shortly thereafter, internet speeds increase at all the houses alongside. Residents conclude that the trees had been interfering with signals, and that the improvement was caused by removing the trees. In fact, the utility company upgraded its signal at the same time, and the trees had no effect whatsoever.

Some other examples:

- On January 30, the World Health Organization declared COVID-19 to be a Public Health Emergency of International Concern. The next day my father died in the hospital, which was overwhelmed with COVID cases. My father must have died of COVID. (In fact, he died of heart failure.)
- 65 million years ago, a massive asteroid between 6 and 9 miles wide hit the earth. Shortly afterwards, ¾ of the plant and animal species on earth became extinct. The impact of the asteroid must have caused the extinction of the dinosaurs. (This is still the subject of great scientific debate (Editors, 2023); other possibilities are volcanic activity, climate change, or biological competition.)
- On February 9, 1986, Halley's comet reached the closest point in its orbit to the sun. The number of volcanic eruptions in the world steadily increased from 1984 to 1986, then decreased from the peak for the next four years. Volcanic eruptions must be caused by the passage of the comet.
- Brazilian footballer Pele famously attributed a decline in his play to giving away a favorite shirt to a fan. Legend has it that he was given another shirt by a friend, who told him it was the same one. His performance then improved.

In each of these instances, the conclusion *may* be true. The error is in the assumption that it *must* be true, and indeed the words "must be" are a red flag for this error having intruded into the reasoning process. The antidote is to consider the possibility of other reasons for what was observed.

Spurious correlations

Data can show us correlations, which are important clues in the search for causality. However, correlation alone does not prove causality. Tyler Vigen, a former law student and now a partner at Boston Consulting Group, has made great sport of this concept on his website https://tylervigen.com/spurious-correlations. The site is well worth a visit, some of the obviously impossible explanations have extremely high statistical correlations. Here is just one.

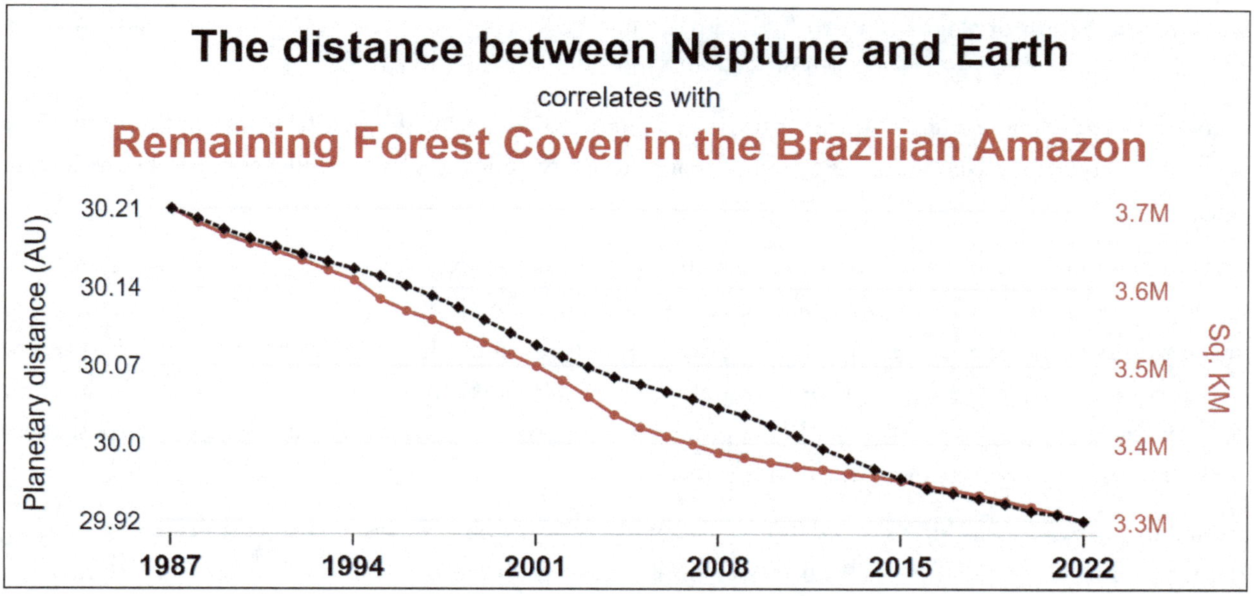

FIGURE 14: Spurious correlation

Illogical connections

British stand-up comedian Eddie Izzard had a routine that included this statement:

> Those Egyptians were lucky people. Not only did they see the pyramids going up, but they got to see the dodo and the mammoth. These are three things we will never see!

It is true that the Egyptians who started construction of the Great Pyramids lived around 2550 B.C. (Handwerk, 2023). Equally, it is true that the dodo bird became extinct in the late 1600s (Encyclopaedia Britannica, n.d.). And the last woolly mammoths survived until around 1650 BC, 7,500 years after most of their relatives (Cannon, 2024). We hope the fallacy of this statement is obvious! The pyramids were built in northern Africa; the dodos were on the island of Mauritius, a practically unreachable destination at that time, and the mammoths roamed on Wrangel Island, остров врангеля, in the Arctic Sea off the coast of Russia.

Izzard established one set of facts but concluded something quite illogical from them. While the fallacy in this statement is easy to detect, there are occasions when the connection looks very logical but is demonstrably false with proper analysis.

Goodhart's law

Bergstrom and West (2020), who we mentioned earlier, recount the city of Hanoi's misconceived plan to remove a plague of rats. The city hired ratcatchers and paid a bounty for rats' tails—resulting in people slicing tails off the rats but leaving them alive to breed more rats with more tails, importing more rats, and breeding rats in cages to harvest the tails. What is this phenomenon called?

Meet Professor Charles Goodhart, MBE, FBA. Born in 1936, his distinguished career included military service, employment at the Bank of England, and a professorship at the London School of Economics. In 1975 he wrote a paper titled "Problems of Monetary Management: the UK Experience." In a footnote he quipped "Whenever a government seeks to rely on a previously observed statistical regularity for control purposes, that regularity will collapse." Anthropologist Marilyn Strathern, simplifying in her paper *Improving Ratings*, said "When a Measure becomes a Target, it Ceases to be a Good Measure."

Goodhart's law demonstrates how data can be misinterpreted or misused when false assumptions are made about causality. While Goodhart was thinking about monetary policy, his law extends far beyond banking and finance.

His law is in our faces, on our phones, every day. If you haven't watched a video on TikTok or YouTube shorts, or "liked" something on Facebook, you are in a very small minority in your class. Each time you do this, you are contributing to the measurement of popularity of whatever you just liked. Because there is no initial review of content on social media sites—anyone can post to Facebook, LinkedIn, TikTok or YouTube—the sites rely on peer review to generate statistics which decide which are better than others and consequently post them more prominently or recommend them to more users.

Even if businesses ask customers to post honest reviews, they are gaming the system because they are influencing the metric for business purposes. If businesses employ click factories to inflate their reputation by providing false reviews, they are acting dishonestly and misleading customers. In both instances Goodhart's law is in operation, because the ratings which result have become influenced by the fact that they are being produced.

Financial accounting encounters the law regularly. At the time of preparing annual financial statements, management are often motivated to meet specific targets or benchmarks, to earn bonuses, promotions, or other advantages. The metrics could be sales, costs, profits, turnover, improvements, or a long list of others. So-called creative accounting (a euphemism for "cooking the books"), such as moving expenses or recognizing revenues in the wrong period, can skew the numbers so that the accounts are no longer fair or accurate measurements. The financial statements are then no longer representative of management's performance.

There are many examples in academia. During your course of university study, did you register in a course where a certain number of points or marks were awarded each class merely for "participation"? Was one of the ways to earn those participation marks, to ask a question of the lecturer? The intent is clear—the professor wants students to be more engaged, pay more attention, and become better educated. When the students learn, as they inevitably will, that asking a question is an easy way to gain those points, the questions become contrived and ungenuine. Worse, the marking of the course, a form of assessment, becomes invalid because the students are *gaming the system for marks*. Not only students can play these games but also, if the professors are rated based on the exam performance of their students, faculty will be tempted to "teach to the exam" instead of attempting to provide a comprehensive course. Colleges and universities themselves may adjust class sizes or acceptance rates to boost their national or international rankings (Bergstrom& West, 2020).

American professor Donald Campbell first presented his thoughts on the education system in 1971, questioning the value of standardized testing. There are subtle differences in his approach which has led some academics to consider Campbell's Law to differ slightly from Goodhart's law. However, they have a great deal in common and seem just to have been considered in different contexts. Campbell's actual statement was "The more any quantitative social indicator is used for social decision-making, the more subject it will be to corruption pressures and the more apt it will be to distort and corrupt the social processes it is intended to monitor."

Could a mistake of this nature be made on a national level? In 2022, the Indian government's University Grants Commission[8] published new regulations regarding the minimum standards for the award of a Ph.D. degree. This was necessary because of a horrendous mistake that had far-reaching unintended and far-reaching consequences.

Prior to the change, it was a national requirement to obtain a Ph.D. that the candidate must have published a research paper in a peer-reviewed journal. Tens of thousands of Ph.D. candidates every year were frantically searching for a topic and a reputable journal that would publish it. The consequences were two-fold:

- Research topic selection came to be based not on the need for research, but the likelihood of finding a publisher; and
- An industry of *predatory journals*[9] sprang up—also known as fraudulent, deceptive or pseudo-journals, they falsely claimed peer reviewing standards, secretly charged authors to publish their work, lied about membership of their editorial boards, or otherwise violated the ethics of scholarship.[10]

Search engines are another example. The companies who build and run the platforms want to maintain credibility and market share by providing realistic, valuable results to users. People and companies who want to come out on top of the search listings, however, scour the world for information on how to do so—which has led to another massive industry, SEO or *search engine optimization*. This is not a small business—being on the first page of Google, or even in the top four or five entries, can be the difference between life and death of an enterprise. SEO is the systematic exploitation of Goodhart's law.

In summary, Goodhart's law is pervasive in many fields including accounting, education and finance. When a measure becomes the goal, its integrity and meaning can quickly become questionable.

Change Blindness

Later in this book, we will devote attention to the construction of dashboards, which are built to give key information, conveniently, for the user. To absorb and interpret what they see, people need to give attention: they can only take in so much at once. If they are presented with too much information, or their focus is diverted to one area, they can become blind to other events. In presenting actionable data, it is critically important not to overwhelm the user.

Blindness to change comes in two common forms, "continuity" blindness and "inattention" or "inattentional" blindness. You will often completely fail to notice a significant change, or discontinuity, while watching a human interaction or movie, or even looking at a picture. If you are distracted by one activity or question, you may completely fail to see something even though you look at it. Some of the most important research on

---

[8] Not only India suffered from this problem. It has also been a serious issue, for example, in China.

[9] The term "predatory publishers" is credited to Jeffrey Beall, a University of Colorado librarian. For five years he published "Beall's List," of predatory publishers, but it has been taken down from the internet.

[10] For an excellent list of characteristics of predatory journals please visit Elmore & Weston (2020).

change blindness has been conducted by Professor Ron Rensink and his colleagues at the University of British Columbia (Rensink, O'Regan & Clark, 1997).

Continuity blindness is the failure to notice that something which you have just seen, has changed, or the failure to notice a change as it happens. In the movie Spider-Man, the hero saves Mary-Jane from attackers by throwing them through a glass window. Moments later an iconic kiss takes place as he hangs upside-down. Yet the window is undamaged. The 1959 movie *Ben Hur,* thought to be one of the greatest motion pictures of all time, has an astonishing number of such bloopers (Evans, 2012). Changes in a visual scene can be completely unnoticed if the observer's attention is not specifically directed to the change (Levin & Simons, 2000).

Inattentional blindness is the failure to notice something that should be obvious, due to concentration on something else. A famous example of this is the 1999 experiment "The Invisible Gorilla" (Simons, 2010). Participants are instructed to watch a video showing people passing basketballs between them and given the difficult task of counting the number of passes by players wearing white. Part-way through, a gorilla walks onto the screen from one side, pauses to face the viewer, pounds its chest, then exits on the other side. Most subjects don't see the gorilla at all, until the video is shown again, and they are told to look for it.

Inattentional blindness is the cause of over 700 vehicle crashes, and more than seven deaths, per day in the United States (National Safety Council, 2018). A great deal of research convincingly demonstrates people's lack of understanding of their own limitations. Just listening to a phone call reduces attention on driving by more than a third; other activities like texting, programming a GPS or applying makeup are even more debilitating that using the phone (National Safety Council, 2020).

This human tendency lies at the very heart of the magician's art. A successful practitioner will develop their skills using misdirection to focus the audience's attention on some aspect or aspects of the show. In effect, the magician controls what you see and what you don't see. It is only in this century, however, that academic, scientific attention has been turned onto the study of cognitive errors in the context of magic (Kuhn, 2019; Kuhn, Amlani & Rensink, 2008).

Remedies

As accountants, we have a professional duty to use structured analysis and avoid false conclusions. We know that fallacies can spoil our work when we rush to answers without applying logical, data-driven analysis; the antidotes then must invoke careful, unrushed, grounded analysis.

When seeking to learn from data, it is important to give attention to the precise questions which are asked. We have already stressed the importance of professional skepticism, and the use of accurate data gathered using unbiased methods. We should always attempt to apply logic, not emotion, and we should never hesitate to consider the views of others, especially those more expert than ourselves.

There are three steps which will aid greatly in using data for causal analysis.

Critical evaluation techniques

Edler and Paul in their seminal (2012) book on intellectual thinking lay out what they consider to be the nine most essential factors required to evaluate thinking. By inference, they also lay out the tests that should be applied to a question before an attempt is made to answer it using data. Their nine elements are as follow:

- *Clarity*—can the conclusion be understood, and the meaning discerned?
- *Accuracy*—is the analysis free of errors and distortions?
- *Precision*—is the conclusion sufficiently specific or exact?
- *Relevance*—is the conclusion relevant to the question under discussion?
- *Depth*—has the analysis addressed the complexities of the issue?
- *Breadth*—has the analysis considered the issue from a broad perspective, and examined the possibility of other points of view?
- *Logic*—does the conclusion follow from the evidence and the analysis?
- *Significance*—does the conclusion express the most important issues, or rank them correctly?
- *Fairness*—is the process fair in context, and considerate of the thinking of others?

Data cleaning

So far, we have concentrated on evaluating data, with presentations by others. There is another dimension to this discussion, which is the question of what to do when given data with a requirement to produce analysis and/or visualization(s). One outstanding scholar in this field is Dr Thomas C Redman, sometimes nicknamed "the Data Doc." He is the President of consulting company Data Quality Solutions, and has published several outstanding books and articles on data quality and cleaning (for example Redman, 2023). The "Redman Workflow" is widely recognized as a standard model for evaluation of data quality (Redman, 2015).

Redman suggests that when presented with new data, the first question is to evaluate where it came from. If created using a first-rate data quality program, then it can be trusted; many datasets however will not qualify, therefore a cautious and skeptical approach must be taken. If the data are not pristine, then cleaning is the next step.

At first sight, there is no substitute for simply "eyeballing" the dataset and taking the time to understand what is there, what you would expect to see, and most of all what is missing. Redman suggests manually reviewing a small random sample (he says, maybe 1,000 records) and evaluating the number of obvious errors, then correcting them. The results of this exercise will dictate what needs to be done with the remaining records, which can be a long process if performed manually. If there are lots of missing entries, for example, there are automatic processes which can be used to impute values to the missing areas (for example, PANDAS in Python, MICE in R).

Redman goes on to address the issue of data integration—using more than one dataset in generating results. There are three key processes which must be done well:

- *Identification*—ensuring that people or objects in one dataset are correctly matched with the same names in others.

- *Alignment of units of measure*—ensuring that a dataset with values in euros, for example, is not integrated with a dataset where the values are in dollars.
- *De-Duplication*—making sure that the same data are not repeated two or more times.

One last key point must be emphasized here: whatever steps you take to clean data, all must be thoroughly documented. If you are working for example in PowerQuery, this is done for you; but if you undertake manual manipulation of your data, then a comprehensive diary of what was done must be created for posterity. Tomorrow you may recall what you did, but after 50 tasks two years from now, you will almost certainly not. Other users of the data you have cleaned must be able to understand fully what was done.

Apply Mills' methods

The brilliant English philosopher and politician John Stuart Mill (1806–1873) made great contributions to scientific methodology as well as feminist theory. He lends his name to the five *Mills' methods* which are the bedrock of causal analysis.

- The *method of agreement* suggests that we search for something that is present on all occasions when a specific event occurs. Imagine that on a given day, an urban hospital incurs a sudden influx of emergency patients suffering from inhalation of noxious fumes. A comparison of medical records shows that although they came from 20 different families, they all lived in the same building. The method of agreement strongly indicates that the source of the fumes is to be found in the building.
- The *method of difference* leads us to find a cause by examining all the circumstances of a repeated event, then identifying the only one that is different. It is suggested by a true story—on January 1, 2019, all the male members of the Paul's family fell seriously ill with symptoms of food poisoning. Only mum remained well and could thankfully care for the others. On New Year's Eve, the family had shared a pizza; but in the evening, the males ate oysters from a seafood buffet while mum chose salmon. The method of difference strongly suggests that oysters were the cause of the food poisoning.
- The *joint method* combines the method of agreement and the method of difference, to produce a stronger result. Imagine that in the example given for the method of agreement, the common factor was that all sufferers had taken the same bus route home. Establishing that none of the passengers on the 5 pm and 6 pm bus fell ill, but those on the 5:30 and 6:30 did, and that the same vehicle plied the half-hourly route, would point to the specific bus rather than the bus route as being causative.
- The *method of concomitant variation* suggests that if something you observe varies in proportion to a potential cause, there *might* be causality. It provides a basis to investigate further. Suppose you suffer from anxiety to different degrees on different days. You notice that it's always worse on weekends, when you don't go to work. You look at your coffee consumption, and observe that on weekdays, you grab one quick cup on your way out of the door, but on Saturday and Sunday you linger over breakfast and usually drink two or even three cups. Concomitant variation suggests that the extra coffee *may* be causing the greater anxiety.
- The *method of residues* says that when we have several factors and several effects, if we conclude that all the factors except one cause all the effects except one, we may conclude that the exceptional factor is the cause of the exceptional effect. Here is an example.

You are asked to assess the effects of ongoing training programs on productivity of workers in a factory. You conclude that there are three factors which greatly influence productivity: working conditions, workload, and training. To assess the effect of the training, you look at the productivity scores of the workers then subtract numbers for the known influence of working conditions and workload, which will differ from person to person. What is left is an estimate of the productivity which can be specifically connected to training. Training has been isolated or left as a residue.

Table of Common Data Production and Interpretation Errors

TABLE 4: Common errors

Name	Definition	Example
	SAMPLING ERRORS	
Selection Bias	Excluding some members of a population so that the sample becomes unrepresentative	Conducting a survey on internet access only in towns and cities.
Hasty Generalization	Drawing a conclusion before receiving enough data.	Family avoiding Pekingese dogs because one member was once bitten by one.
Insensitivity to Sample Size	Failing to consider the higher probability of an anomaly in a smaller sample	Concluding that a coin is not "fair" because it lands heads three times and tails seven times in ten flips.
Cherry Picking	Selecting only data that proves your point.	Politician points to one cold winter day as evidence that global warming is a myth.
Voluntary Response Bias	Drawing conclusions based on data offered by subjects.	Online review platform dominated by reports by dissatisfied customers.
Convenience Sampling	Using a convenient sample when not representing whole population	Surveying students present in a class about their commuting difficulties.
Non-Response Bias	Where subjects have the option not to respond to questions.	Survey of students given during exam season when some are too busy to make time.
Attrition Bias	When participants drop out of a study before it ends.	Medical study where healthier participants stay longer in treatment.
Survivorship Bias	Drawing conclusions from subjects who survive for period of study, ignoring those who die.	Study of start-up companies that stays connected only with successful ones.
Right and Left Censoring	Drawing conclusions from what happened during the survey but ignoring events before or after the period.	Study of battery lives ignoring batteries still working at end of study period.
AI Bias	Relying on a conclusion from an AI program which has been trained on a biased dataset.	Facial recognition software in a security setting is trained mainly on local people. Foreigners are misidentified as security threats at a higher rate.
Berkson's Paradox	Selecting data in a biased manner, resulting in a misperception of negative correlation	Believing that attractive people on a dating app are less intelligent due to selection criteria.
	COGNITIVE BIASES	
Anchoring	Relying too heavily on the first piece of information received.	Job applicant discloses salary, which influences offer from prospective employer.
Confirmation Bias	Searching for, interpreting and relying on evidence which confirms a belief.	Employer makes initial assessment of employee's competency then ignores subsequent evidence

Name	Definition	Example
Halo Effect	Perception of one positive trait obscures evidence of negatives.	A consultant is hired based on knowledge, and company fails to notice ongoing fraud.
Status Quo Biases	Generally, resisting change in favor of things remaining the same.	Firm refuses to upgrade to automated accounting and relies on outdated manual processes.
Mere Exposure Effect	Developing a preference based only on repeated exposure.	Accounting firm holds its Christmas party in the same hotel every year, not exploring other options
Sunk Cost Fallacy	Continuing a course of action because of past investment, even when it would be more prudent to change or stop.	Company continues to support a failing product based on R&D investment.
Loss Aversion	Focus on potential loss instead of considering gains.	Holding on to stock of a failing company even though it is likely to fall further.
Cognitive Dissonance	Creating justifications that reduce discomfort caused by conflict with belief.	Buying a gasoline car on the basis that it's on sale, when you're a deep believer in global warming risk
HEURISTICS		
Availability Heuristic	Making decisions based on the most immediately available information.	Fearing air travel more than car travel because of publicity around airline disasters.
Default Effect	Accepting pre-set options because it's easier than making changes	Continuing with a pre-checked box to pay for checked baggage, instead of exploring price without baggage.
Instrument Default	Relying on familiar tools or procedures when better ones become available.	Auditors using outdated software and failing to learn new tools.
Repetition Error	Accepting truth of a statement because of number of times it has been said	Politician talking about voter fraud over and over despite lack of evidence.
INTERPRETATION ERRORS		
Averages	Failure to recognize different forms of average—mean, median, mode	HR department relies on mean length of service, influenced by outliers, failing to recognize a problem with high number of early departures
Base Rate Neglect	Failing to consider statistical reality in favor of anecdotal evidence.	Worrying about possibility of a plane crash, ignoring fact that most flights are safely completed.
Publication Bias	Ratio of positive to negative studies published does not reflect totality of data	Over-publication of clinical trials showing positive results for patients results in false perception of efficacy of drug.
Appeals	Illogical references to supposedly authoritative supports for argument.	Arguing that life must exist on other planets because no-one has proved that it doesn't.
REASONING FALLACIES		
Hot Hand, Gambler's Fallacy	Illogical belief that the next event in a sequence is determined by past events	Believing that a stock in the market will rise today because it has risen each day of the last 10. Or believing that because it has risen, it must eventually fall.
Regression Fallacy	Assumption that an exceptional situation will continue.	Believing that a sports team will top the league again this year, because it had an exceptional season last year.
Semmelweis Effect	Tendency to reject new evidence because it conflicts with belief.	Doctors refusing to believe that hand-washing reduces patient infections because they are "gentlemen."
CAUSATION ERRORS		
Post Hoc, Ergo Propter Hoc	Believing that because outcome B occurred after event A, A caused B	Concluding that babies are made by visiting a maternity clothing store.
Spurious Correlation	Concluding that there is a relationship between A and B because they have statistical similarity	Concluding that the number of drivers killed in railway collisions is related to US crude oil imports from Norway.

Name	Definition	Example
Illogical Connections	Believing that two things are connected because they happened at the same time or in the same place.	Believing that the ancient Egyptians who built the pyramids were able to see woolly mammoths because they lived at the same time.
Goodhart's Law	When something is studied or quantified and the subjects are aware, the subjects change behavior because they are aware of the study.	Company accountants moving expenses or recognizing revenue in the wrong period to enhance performance results.
PERCEPTUAL ERRORS		
Continuity Blindness	Failure to notice a change in something just seen or under observation.	Window is undamaged in the scene following one in which a person is thrown through it.
Inattentional Blindness	Failure to see one thing because of concentration on another.	Motor vehicle crashes caused by drivers reading text messages.

Multiple Choice Questions for Chapter 1

1. In 2019, CBC News reported that the previous year saw 51 motorcyclist deaths in British Columbia—a 50% increase over 2017. What should we conclude from these statistics?
    a. Motorcycling is becoming more popular due to the increase in fuel prices.
    b. Motorcycling is becoming more dangerous due to the condition of the roads.
    c. If there was no change in fuel price or road condition, there must have been 50% more riders on the roads to account for the change.
    d. There aren't enough data to conclude anything.
2. Donald Trump in his 2015 election campaign delivered this speech: "When Mexico sends its people, they're not sending their best. They're sending people that have lots of problems, and they're bringing those problems with us. They're bringing drugs. They're bringing crime. They're rapists. And some, I assume, are good people." This is an example of:
    a. the Hot Hand fallacy.
    b. sampling bias.
    c. the appeal to common belief.
    d. the hasty generalization error.
3. A university lecturer wants to know about the incidence of depression among students. A live class is selected as a sample and a survey is conducted by a show of hands in response to questions about depression. The professor has committed the error of:
    a. convenience sampling.
    b. voluntary response bias.
    c. hasty generalization error.
    d. the law of small numbers.
4. In an expensive lawsuit, the defendant is running low on money but has a very pricey lawyer. It is apparent that the lawyer is not doing a good job, regardless of the price. The defendant decides to stay with the expensive lawyer because otherwise, all the money already spent will be wasted. This is an example of:
    a. the gambler's fallacy.
    b. the sunk cost fallacy.
    c. the hot hand fallacy.
    d. cherry picking.
5. "Oxford and Cambridge are the best universities in the world. Everyone knows that." This is an example of:
    a. the appeal to common sense
    b. the appeal to common belief
    c. the appeal to authority
    d. the appeal to incredulity.
6. Try to pronounce the word "silk" three times quickly. What do cows drink? If you answer "milk" this is an example of:
    a. the appeal to ridicule.
    b. the availability heuristic.
    c. confirmation blindness.
    d. inattentional blindness.

7. Confirmation bias is also known as
    a. selective perception.
    b. continuity blindness.
    c. the default effect.
    d. nudge theory.
8. The national lottery prize this week is at more than $600 million, which is almost exactly double the usual size. As a result, many more people are buying tickets. People buying twice as many tickets as usual are suffering from
    a. repetition error.
    b. Semmelweis effect.
    c. status quo bias.
    d. base rate fallacy.
9. 65 million years ago, a massive asteroid between 6 and 9 miles wide hit the earth. Shortly afterwards, ¾ of the plant and animal species on earth became extinct. The impact of the asteroid must have caused the extinction of the dinosaurs. Which Latin maxim expresses this unsupported conclusion?
    a. *Per arduum ad astra.*
    b. *Semper paratus.*
    c. *Expecto Patronum.*
    d. *Post hoc, ergo propter hoc.*
10. According to Edler and Paul, which of the following is NOT an essential factor in the intellectual thinking process?
    a. Clarity.
    b. Precision.
    c. Economy.
    d. Fairness.
11. Google works hard to keep the details of its search algorithm secret to avoid the effects of
    a. Goodhart's law.
    b. Bayes' theorem.
    c. sampling bias.
    d. right censoring.
12. Selection bias is a problem which would not exist but for
    a. the difficulty of examining large populations.
    b. the prevalence of social media.
    c. the tendency of participants to lose interest in long term studies.
    d. using computer algorithms to randomly select participants in studies.
13. Online rating sites which are open to everyone to contribute are likely to suffer from
    a. attrition bias.
    b. non-response bias.
    c. volunteer bias.
    d. survivorship bias.
14. A study which runs over time but comes to an end before the full course of events being studied has run for all participants is at risk of suffering from:
    a. right censoring.

   b. selection bias.
   c. left censoring.
   d. Berkson's paradox.
15. A car dealership decides to award bonuses based on the number of cars sold by each salesperson. After a year, it is surprised to learn that car sales have risen by 40% but profits have slumped by 15%. This demonstrates the operation of:
   a. Murphy's law.
   b. Finagle's law.
   c. Goodhart's law.
   d. The friendship paradox.
16. Berkson's paradox partially explains:
   a. positive correlations between positive factors.
   b. negative correlations between negative factors.
   c. counterintuitive negative correlations.
   d. the tendency for werewolves to howl during a full moon.

2. TYPES OF CHARTS, AND VISUAL DISTORTIONS

Why is it important to create high quality visualizations? We work better with visual representations than tables of numbers and facts. With a picture, we can take meanings and insights on board with less work. That is, of course, provided they are well and accurately constructed.

According to IBM, visual displays "communicate complex data relationships and data-driven insights in a way that is easy to understand" (IBM, n.d.). That condenses the purpose into a single phrase, but it is rather broad. The *Harvard Business Review* is more granular, suggesting that there are four key purposes: idea generation, idea illustration, visual discovery, and "everyday data viz." Author Scott Berinato draws from this the very sensible suggestion that before deciding what kind of visualizations to create, we should determine the purpose of our work (Berinato, 2016).

In this chapter we are going to concentrate on *charts*, which are just one type of visualization—there are also maps, infographics, graphs, diagrams, word clouds, and more. The words chart and graph are often used interchangeably, but there is a difference. A chart is any visual representation of data, while a graph is a mathematical diagram that depicts two or more variables in a relationship. Complicating things, it's fine to call a graph a line chart, usually there is no distinction. However, while you can call a pie chart a pie graph, people might look at you strangely as this is not the normal usage.

For business professionals, visual tools, especially charts and graphs, enable us to summarize large amounts of data in a digestible form, drawing insights and from there, making decisions and building strategies. If they are badly designed, they can mislead viewers, deliver false messages, and cause bad decisions.

To illustrate some potential uses of visualization, we present next an alphabetically sorted list of the populations of the world's countries, captured from worldometer.com. By the time this was printed, it was already out of date—world population is growing every moment. You can watch the number increase in real-time at https://www.worldometers.info/world-population/.

TABLE 5: World population by country

COUNTRY	POPULATION	COUNTRY	POPULATION	COUNTRY	POPULATION	COUNTRY	POPULATION
Afghanistan	42,239,854	Ecuador	18,190,484	Lithuania	2,718,352	Saint Pierre & Miquelon	5,840
Albania	2,832,439	Egypt	112,716,598	Luxembourg	654,768	Samoa	225,681
Algeria	45,606,480	El Salvador	6,364,943	Macao	704,149	San Marino	33,642
American Samoa	43,914	Equatorial Guinea	1,714,671	Madagascar	30,325,732	Sao Tome & Principe	231,856
Andorra	80,088	Eritrea	3,748,901	Malawi	20,931,751	Saudi Arabia	36,947,025
Angola	36,684,202	Estonia	1,322,765	Malaysia	34,308,525	Senegal	17,763,163
Anguilla	15,899	Eswatini	1,210,822	Maldives	521,021	Serbia	7,149,077
Antigua and Barbuda	94,298	Ethiopia	126,527,060	Mali	23,293,698	Seychelles	107,660
Argentina	45,773,884	Faeroe Islands	53,270	Malta	535,064	Sierra Leone	8,791,092
Armenia	2,777,970	Falkland Islands	3,791	Marshall Islands	41,996	Singapore	6,014,723
Aruba	106,277	Fiji	936,375	Martinique	366,981	Sint Maarten	44,222
Australia	26,439,111	Finland	5,545,475	Mauritania	4,862,989	Slovakia	5,795,199
Austria	8,958,960	France	64,756,584	Mauritius	1,300,557	Slovenia	2,119,675
Azerbaijan	10,412,651	French Guiana	312,155	Mayotte	335,995	Solomon Islands	740,424
Bahamas	412,623	French Polynesia	308,872	Mexico	128,455,567	Somalia	18,143,378
Bahrain	1,485,509	Gabon	2,436,566	Micronesia	544,321	South Africa	60,414,495
Bangladesh	172,954,319	Gambia	2,773,168	Moldova	3,435,931	South Korea	51,784,059
Barbados	281,995	Georgia	3,728,282	Monaco	36,297	South Sudan	11,088,796
Belarus	9,498,238	Germany	83,294,633	Mongolia	3,447,157	Spain	47,519,628
Belgium	11,686,140	Ghana	34,121,985	Montenegro	626,485	Sri Lanka	21,893,579
Belize	410,825	Gibraltar	32,688	Montserrat	4,386	St. Vincent & Grenadines	103,698
Benin	13,712,828	Greece	10,341,277	Morocco	37,840,044	State of Palestine	5,371,230
Bermuda	64,069	Greenland	56,643	Mozambique	33,897,354	Sudan	48,109,006
Bhutan	787,424	Grenada	126,183	Myanmar	54,577,997	Suriname	623,236
Bolivia	12,388,571	Guadeloupe	395,839	Namibia	2,604,172	Sweden	10,612,086
Bosnia and Herzegovina	3,210,847	Guam	172,952	Nauru	12,780	Switzerland	8,796,669
Botswana	2,675,352	Guatemala	18,092,026	Nepal	30,896,590	Syria	23,227,014
Brazil	216,422,446	Guinea	14,190,612	Netherlands	17,618,299	Taiwan	23,923,276
British Virgin Islands	31,538	Guinea-Bissau	2,150,842	New Caledonia	292,991	Tajikistan	10,143,543
Brunei	452,524	Guyana	813,834	New Zealand	5,228,100	Tanzania	67,438,106
Bulgaria	6,687,717	Haiti	11,724,763	Nicaragua	7,046,310	Thailand	71,801,279
Burkina Faso	23,251,485	Holy See	518	Niger	27,202,843	Timor-Leste	1,360,596
Burundi	13,238,559	Honduras	10,593,798	Nigeria	223,804,632	Togo	9,053,799
Cabo Verde	598,682	Hong Kong	7,491,609	Niue	1,935	Tokelau	1,893
Cambodia	16,944,826	Hungary	10,156,239	North Korea	26,160,821	Tonga	107,773
Cameroon	28,647,293	Iceland	375,318	North Macedonia	2,085,679	Trinidad and Tobago	1,534,937
Canada	38,781,291	India	1,428,627,663	Northern Mariana Islands	49,796	Tunisia	12,458,223
Caribbean Netherlands	27,148	Indonesia	277,534,122	Norway	5,474,360	Turkey	85,816,199
Cayman Islands	69,310	Iran	89,172,767	Oman	4,644,384	Turkmenistan	6,516,100
Central African Republic	5,742,315	Iraq	45,504,560	Pakistan	240,485,658	Turks and Caicos	46,062
Chad	18,278,568	Ireland	5,056,935	Palau	18,058	Tuvalu	11,396
Chile	19,629,590	Isle of Man	84,710	Panama	4,468,087	U.S. Virgin Islands	98,750
China	1,425,671,352	Israel	9,174,520	Papua New Guinea	10,329,931	Uganda	48,582,334
Colombia	52,085,168	Italy	58,870,762	Paraguay	6,861,524	Ukraine	36,744,634
Comoros	852,075	Jamaica	2,825,544	Peru	34,352,719	United Arab Emirates	9,516,871
Congo	6,106,869	Japan	123,294,513	Philippines	117,337,368	United Kingdom	67,736,802
Cook Islands	17,044	Jordan	11,337,052	Poland	41,026,067	Uruguay	3,423,108
Costa Rica	5,212,173	Kazakhstan	19,606,633	Portugal	10,247,605	USA	339,996,563
Côte d'Ivoire	28,873,034	Kenya	55,100,586	Puerto Rico	3,260,314	Uzbekistan	35,163,944
Croatia	4,008,617	Kiribati	133,515	Qatar	2,716,391	Vanuatu	334,506
Cuba	11,194,449	Kuwait	4,310,108	Réunion	981,796	Venezuela	28,838,499
Curaçao	192,077	Kyrgyzstan	6,735,347	Romania	19,892,812	Vietnam	98,858,950
Cyprus	1,260,138	Laos	7,633,779	Russia	144,444,359	Wallis & Futuna	11,502
Czech Republic (Czechia)	10,495,295	Latvia	1,830,211	Rwanda	14,094,683	Western Sahara	587,259
Denmark	5,910,913	Lebanon	5,353,930	Saint Barthelemy	10,994	Yemen	34,449,825
Djibouti	1,136,455	Lesotho	2,330,318	Saint Helena	5,314	Zambia	20,569,737
Dominica	73,040	Liberia	5,418,377	Saint Kitts & Nevis	47,755	Zimbabwe	16,665,409
Dominican Republic	11,332,972	Libya	6,888,388	Saint Lucia	180,251		
DR Congo	102,262,808	Liechtenstein	39,584	Saint Martin	32,077		

This is a lot of data. We may be interested in asking some questions.

What are the countries with the highest and lowest populations?

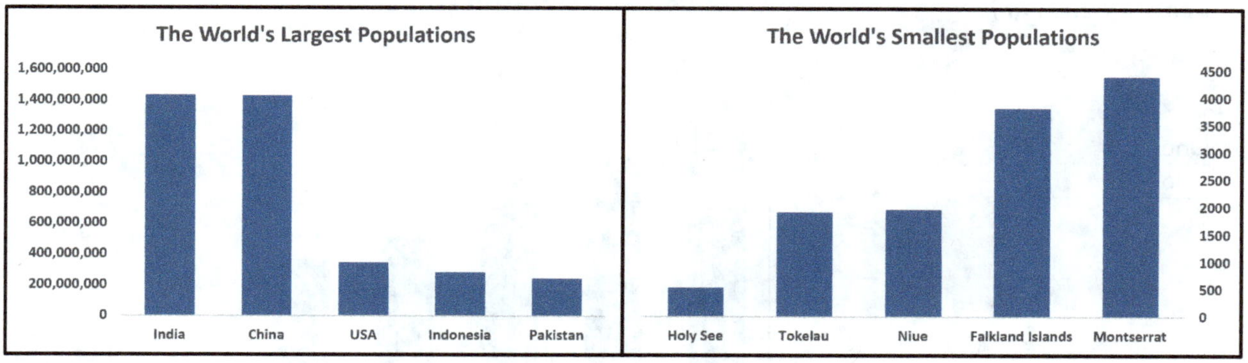

FIGURE 15: World's largest and smallest populations

A pair of column charts might answer this call. However, we've already ventured into the area of visual trickery—can you see how easy it would be to conclude that the population of Montserrat is bigger than that of India or China? We have honestly shown the scales on the left—0 to 4.5 thousand in the smaller places, and 0 to 1.6 billion in the larger, but it takes a little work by the viewer to figure that out. The right-hand chart does however show how much smaller the Holy See's population is than Tokelau, the next smallest number. In the left-hand chart, some perspective is given on the US population relative to China and India, which dwarf it. It's also easy to see how the Chinese and Indian populations are closely similar. In the next chapter, we'll spend more time examining how people see things.

Our plan is take you through a survey of the principal chart types which you need to know and understand. We'll look at lots of examples, continuing the theme of thinking critically about what you see. We'll illustrate with examples from the business world and highlight some common abuses and problems to be avoided. First, though, let's make sure we understand the basic terminology.

Visualization Terminology

Many data visualizations employ a chart of some type. "Visualization" and "chart" are not pure synonyms—a chart is just one type of visualization.

In his leading (2019) work *How Charts Lie*, scholar Alberto Cairo invokes an analogy from the building trade by referring to the non-data elements which comprise a chart as *scaffolding*—he is referring to "titles, legends, scales, bylines, sources *etc.*" He would not have been wrong if he had used such terms as "skeleton" or "bones" instead.

Professor Cairo goes on to talk about "visual encodings." He says that "Charts are always built with symbols—usually, but not always, geometric." These encodings are typically altered in some way—color, size, position—to depict the data they represent. A longer bar represents something of which there are more than depicted by the short bar, for example.

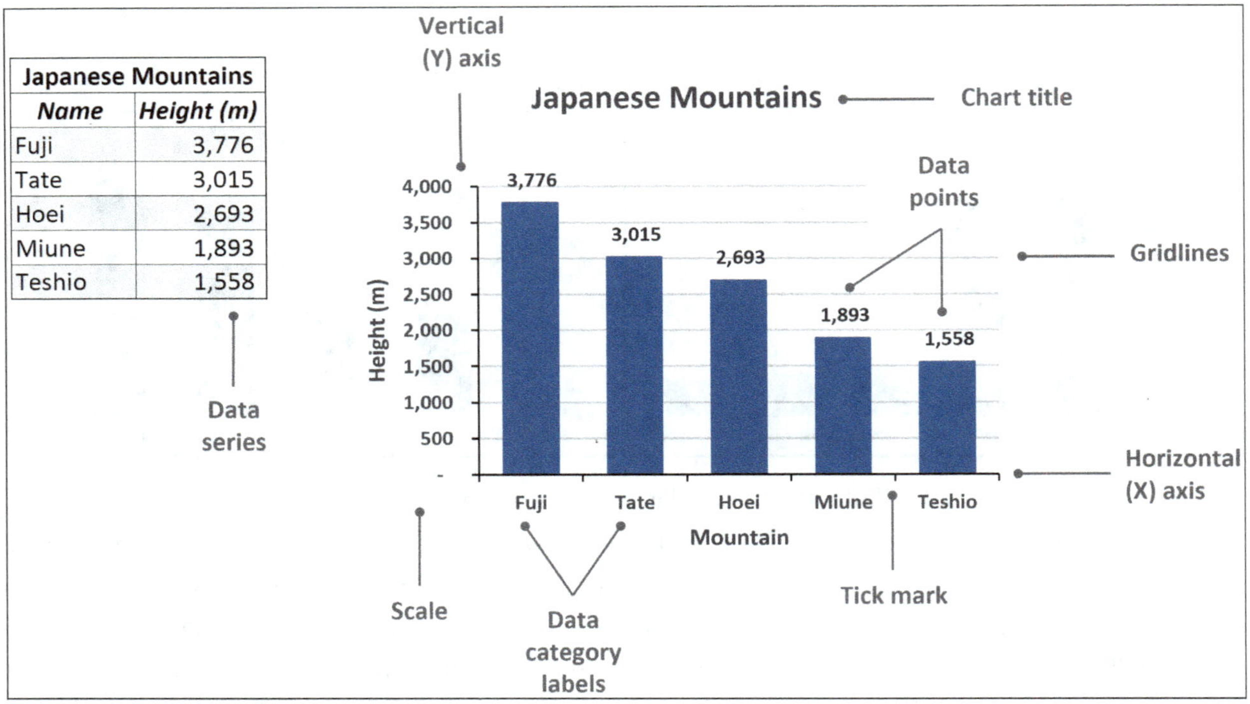

FIGURE 16: Visual encodings

Charts for Categorical Data

Bar charts

Definition and purpose

Bar charts are used for categorical data. One variable requires a simple bar chart. Two or more need clustered or stacked bats. Relative percentages are shown in a 100% stacked bar chart.

In a bar chart, horizontal rectangles allow comparison of measurements using their length. Their best use is to compare counts of items or concepts. Using time in bar charts is permissible if you are counting, for example showing the number of years various pets can be expected to live. But if a time series is implicated, such as showing stock prices over several years, a column or line chart is the best If the labels which identify the data are long, a bar chart is the best choice because the start of the bars can move across the page to accommodate. Bar charts are very like column charts, in which the bars are vertical—in fact you may even see the term "vertical bar chart" used. You won't see "horizontal column chart" though!

In accounting and business, bar charts are particularly useful for comparing quantities, costs and revenues. They work well for expenses, headcounts and aged accounts receivable. To illustrate this, and some variations, we've created a fictional table of aged A/R for a company.

TABLE 6: Aged accounts receivable

Age (days)	Vixen Inc	Walrus News	Xyner Corp	Yummy Foods	Zeldo Ltd	TOTAL
0-30	850	3,000	4,000	2,000	3,500	13,350
31-60	1,000	1,500	2,500	1,800	2,200	9,000
61-90	2,000	1,200	900	800	1,100	6,000
90+	5,000	750	790	900	800	8,240
TOTAL	8,850	6,450	8,190	5,500	7,600	36,590

Appearance

It's not very difficult to look at this tiny table and see totals, compare them, imagine what cash flow might be like for the next while. In a typical business, however, there might be many more debtors and more complex calculations, meaning that a mere glance at a table is unlike to reveal insights.

Who owes the most? A bar chart gives us an easy visual comparison. We've added data labels to inform on the amounts, but the main feature is the bar lengths—Vixen is immediately identifiable as the longest bar, thus the largest debtor.

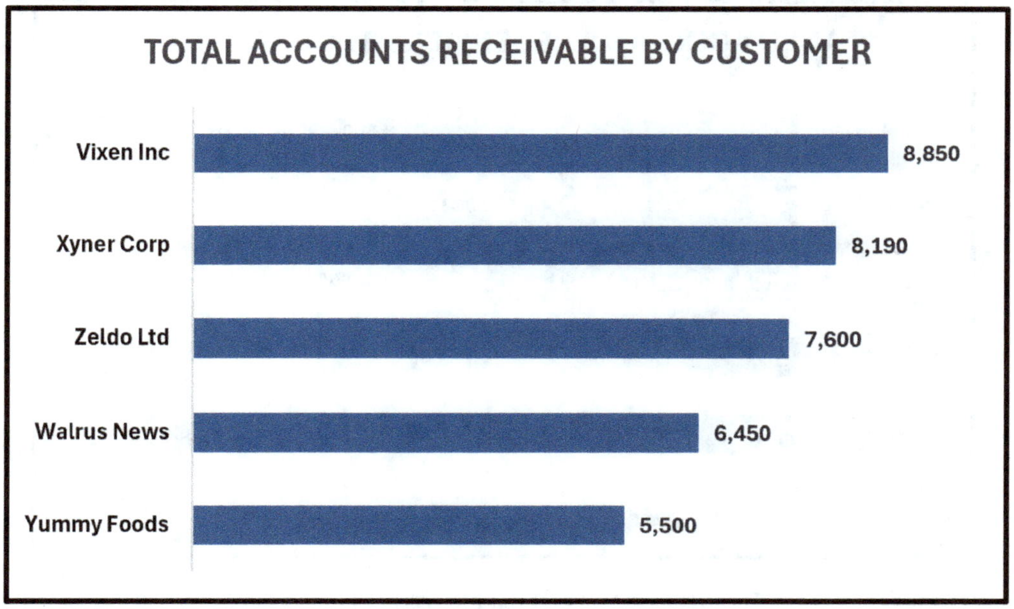

FIGURE 17: Simple ranking of Accounts Receivable, by customer

There are two common enhancements to the simple bar chart, which enable us to see the make-up of totals, or see groups with common characteristics. First, a *clustered bar chart* allows us to show groups of counts. In this case we've left a scale on the bottom, to avoid clutter (about which, more later). This chart helps us see the components of the receivables, with progressive darkness of the blues drawing attention to the oldest debt, but loses the element of overall comparability.

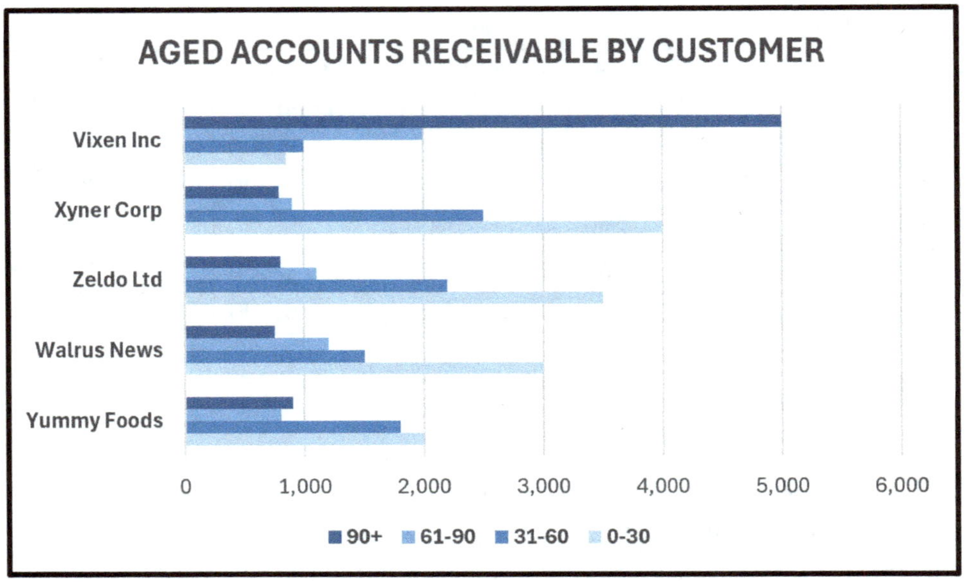

FIGURE 18: Clustered bar chart for all customers

A *stacked bar chart* depicts totals and uses color effectively to show components within them. In this case, we can see for each total, what proportion of the debt is current and what proportions are from older periods.

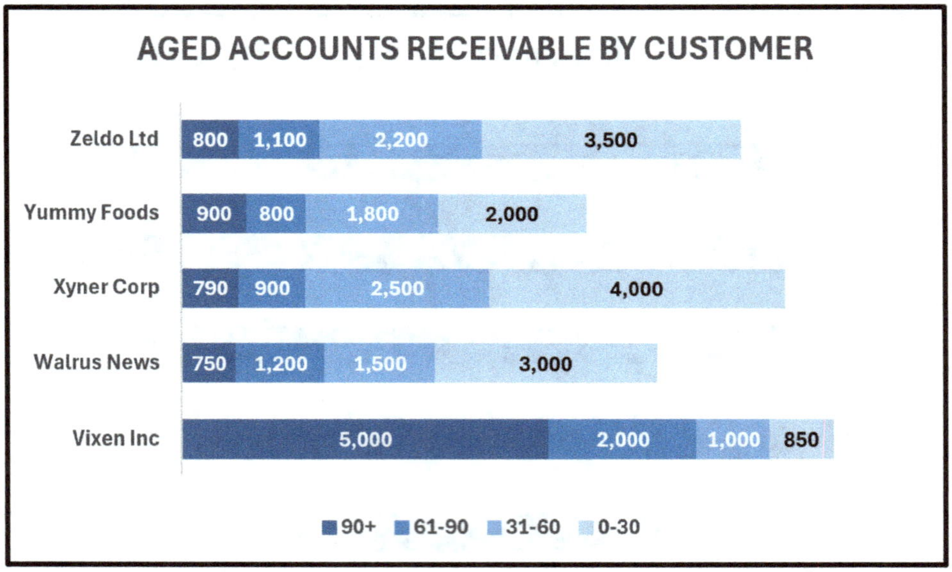

FIGURE 19: Stacked bar chart for all customers

The overall length of the bar gives us the total, but we can make comparisons between components both within individual customer accounts and between the customers. Although the same data are visible in the table and all these charts, far and away the easiest interpretation is from the stacked bar chart – what is going on with Vixen? They have an extremely large debt more than 90 days old, and progressively smaller amounts due more recently, possibly because they are ordering less. Are they going out of business, or having their own cash flow problems? This is certainly worth investigating – an *actionable insight* made clear by the visualization.

Best practices

THE PRINCIPLE OF PROPORTIONAL INK

In 2016, Bergstrom and West coined the phrase "the principle of proportional ink." They have written, recorded and taught extensively on topics related to misleading data. Their basic rule states:

> When a shaded region is used to represent a numerical value, the area of that shaded region should be directly proportional to the corresponding value.

Violations of this principle can occur in just about any type of chart which attempts to depict relative measurements; it is an extremely useful principle to keep in mind to as we consider many different chart types.

CONSISTENT SCALING

It's important to use consistent scaling. If the intervals on the axes are not equally spaced, this can exaggerate or downplay differences, which misleads viewers. An inconsistent scale might be one which has intervals of 1, then 10, then 100 (1,2,3,10,20,30,100,200,300).

KEEP BARS APART AND CONSISTENT

Bar widths should always be kept the same, as different widths can confuse viewers who will seek to find meaning in them. Too many bars, groups that are too large, overcrowding, all need to be avoided.

BASELINES

Bar chart baseline values (the Y axis) should always be 0. This rule is shared with column charts, so when we get to them in the next section, we'll show its potential abuse there.

Column charts

Definition and purpose

A column chart uses vertical bars to depict values of categorical data. It's sometime called a vertical bar chart. The height of each column is proportional to the value. Quantified values are on the Y axis, while categories are on the X axis. Alongside line charts, column charts can be good choice to show a time series. There are variations with clusters and stacks, just like bars, which we've just seen.

Appearance and best practices

Retail Therapy Central is a fictitious department store that's been in town for nearly 100 years. It has always been successful and had a good December season. However, overall sales figures are dropping, and the Board convenes a strategy meeting to plan for the next year. Over 50% of the store's annual profits are generated in the month of December, so it's critical to get the mix of products and store layout right.

As head of finance, you are asked to make a presentation to the Board that will help it get started. The CEO, while giving you the job, say's "It's obvious that Christmas is the season when men buy perfume and families buy toys. Beauty and toys are the key departments: we need to build up their performance to stay in business."

TABLE 7: Department store sales

Department	Sales ($)
Groceries	91,000
Electronics	78,000
Home Goods	52,000
Clothing	45,000
Beauty	41,000
Toys	36,000

You run the numbers and arrive at this summary. You can see immediately that the CEO's ideas are outdated and wish to start your presentation with a clear, non-controversial delivery of this news. A column chart is a great choice for this simple message.

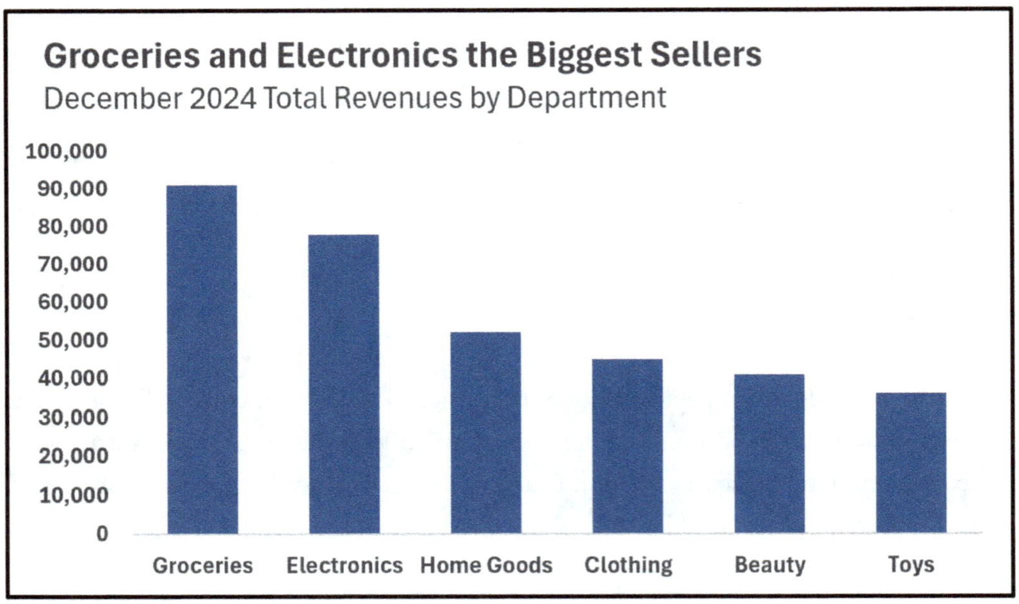

FIGURE 20: Department store December sales

Everything the Board can learn from this chart they can also determine from the table—but it takes a lot more work. In a second, the viewer can see that groceries and electronics lead the way—this is reinforced by the title, but the column lengths tell the real story. The CEO's ideas about Beauty and Toys being the way to go is graphically debunked by the size of the columns, reinforced by the title and their positioning last in order.

Why do you think this is? What has happened in the retail economy in 2024 to push groceries to the top of the list, and toys to the very bottom? Spoiler: it's probably the case that there's a recession under way, so more of people's budgets go to essential items like food—and most kids now want cool electronic gadgets, not traditional toys. In one chart, you have all the tools you need to generate this discussion and guide the Board to data-driven decisions about December 2025.

When building a column chart, the best practices are much the same as for bar charts. Clear axes with consistent scaling are important; categorial values are usually sorted in order, to make ranking and comparison easy. If times or dates are involved, they read from left to right, earliest first. Color can be sparingly used to highlight important insights, if they are not obvious. If the precise numbers are important, data labels instead of a scale are useful for the viewer. The Y-axis should not be distorted, truncated or manipulated so that viewers are misled. Finally, as we'll see in the next chapter, 3-D effects distort perception and make column charts very hard to understand. Stay tuned for more about this.

Misuse and abuse

The British Columbia General Election of 2024 was hotly contested between two leadings parties. If you have any political leanings in this debate, please put them aside and understand that here, we are merely going to demonstrate the way that statistics can be abused to portray "reality" in distorted ways. The following two charts are purely based on the official B.C. government statistics about the election—the NDP had 944,463 votes, while the Conservatives had 911,142. Just over 8% of the vote went to the Green Party, but that did not translate into 8% of the seats in the provincial parliament (Elections B.C., 2024).

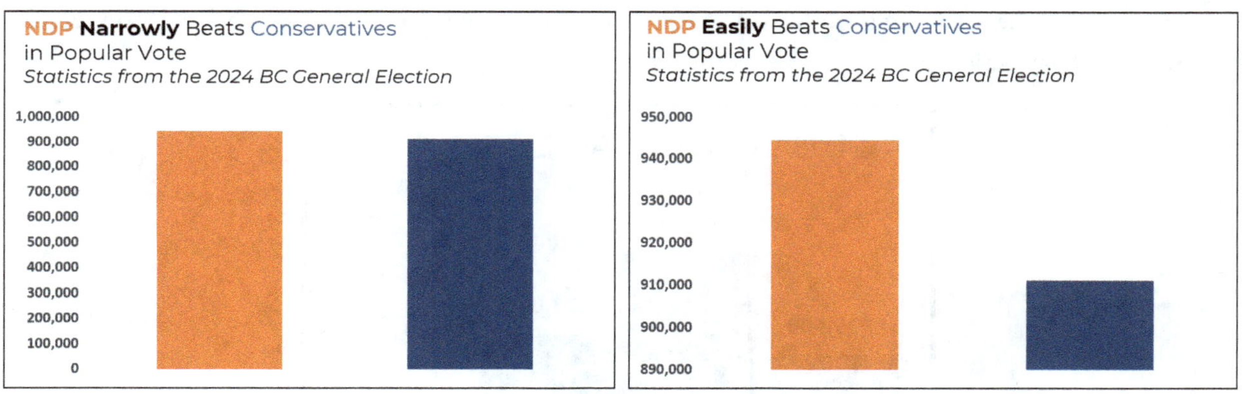

FIGURE 21: British Columbia General Election results

The same statistics underly both these charts. There is only one difference in the headers—the left-hand chart says the NDP won "narrowly," while the right-hand chart says they won easily. If you read across from the top of each column to the scale, you will get the same numbers from the axis. But the designer has played a trick in the right-hand chart; look at the lowest number on the Y (vertical) axis. The scale starts at 890,000, which massively exaggerates the difference by excluding the first 890,000 votes for each party. NDP voters outnumbered Conservatives by only 3.6%.

In the left-hand chart, the NDP bar is 3.6% taller than the Conservative bar, which is clear and accurate. But the over-wide bars risk creating an incorrect perception, if their relative areas bars become disproportionate. Fortunately, humans are better at perceiving and assessing relative lengths than areas, so this is a lesser problem (Cleveland & McGill, 1984).

Y-axis manipulation is by far the most common abuse of column charts that we see. Other sins include overcrowding with too many categories, inappropriate groups or sorting, cherry-picking data, and ignoring accessibility by using very small fonts or similar colors. All these are best avoided.

Histograms

Definition and purpose

A histogram depicts the distribution of *continuous* data which are grouped into bins, also known as intervals, thus making the data quasi-categorical.

ach bin is represented by a column, the height of which corresponds to the number on the Y axis. The bins are usually placed together without gaps, though this is not mandatory.

The purpose of a histogram is to help understand the distribution of data. Is it "normal," is the distribution skewed (left or right—data which is skewed right has the "long tail" on the right, and the highest point to the left of center). Right skew is also known as positive skew. Histograms also reveal if data have more than one mode, or other unusual characteristics such as outlier groups.

Appearance and best practices

An example from the accounting world is an Aged Receivables histogram, like the one below. Here each bin represents a 30 day period, and there is very little skewness.

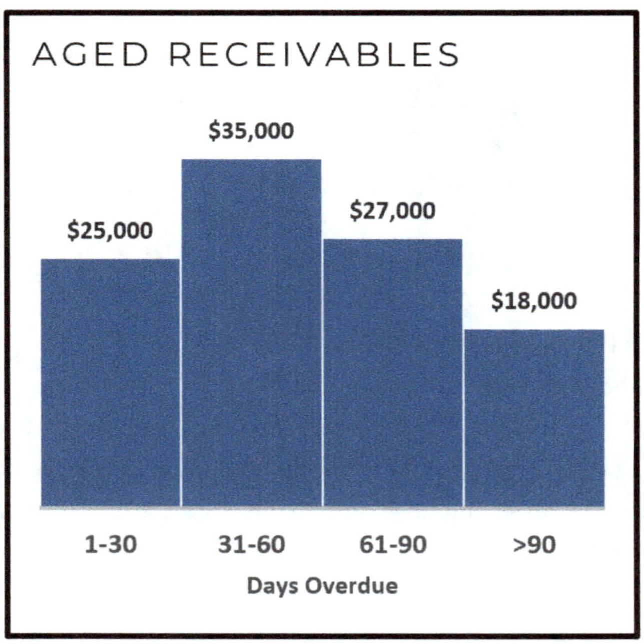

FIGURE 22: Aged accounts receivable histogram

Misuse and abuse

As histograms have much in common with column charts, many of the potential abuses are the same, such as truncated axes. However, bin treatment can also be abused—too few, too many, inappropriate sizes, or varying sizes without explanation (for example, 0–2,3–5,6–8,9–20).

Be careful not to select a histogram when there is no need, sometimes a simple column chart is preferable.

Pie charts

Definition and purpose

Pie charts depict categorical data. They are sometimes appropriate when there is one dominant category but quickly become ineffective if there are similar or many slices.

A pie chart is a circle, divided into slices depicting percentages and proportions. Each slice is a category; the slices add up to 360°, representing the whole pie, or 100% of the population. They satisfy the requirements of proportional ink, but there are also perceptual problems. Humans tend to focus on areas, rather than angles, while their ability to compare lengths is stronger than either. In business, pie charts are popularly used to depict the proportions of a group such as contributions to revenue of departments, relative expenses, or market share.

Appearance and best practices

Model	Units Sold
Model Y	1,160,000
Model 3	518,072
Cybertruck	38,965
Model X	19,855
Model S	12,426

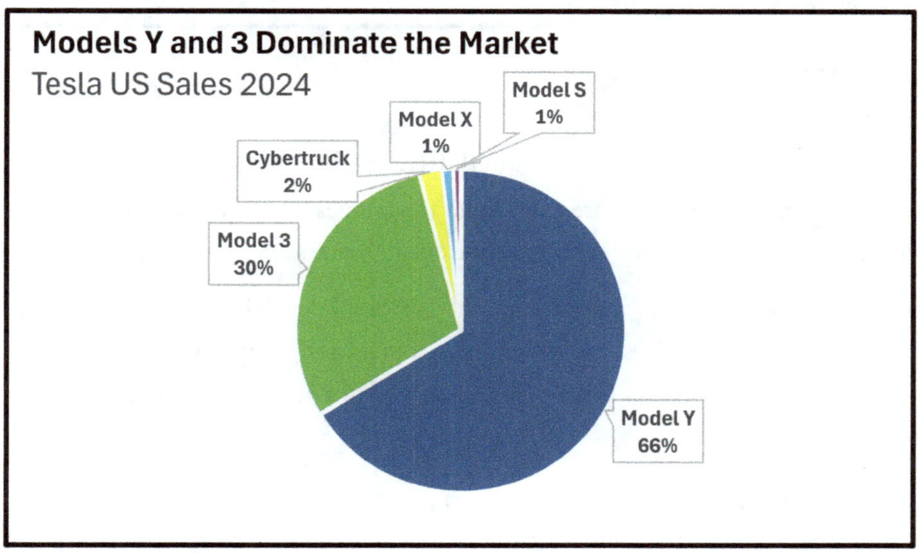

FIGURE 23: Tesla US sales 2024

Where there are most five or six slices, pie charts can be effective, especially to show dominance as in this depiction of Tesla's sales by model. Even without the percentages, the relative contributions to company sales are readily apparent. Use of proportions, as here, is more appropriate for pie charts, and the logical order is to start at 12 o'clock with the largest pie and rotate clockwise. Clear labels are very important, otherwise the immediate impact of the chart is lost. A very important rule for pie charts is, however—don't use too many of them!

Misuse and abuse

Pie charts are capable of evoking strong emotional reactions. Walt Hickey wrote in 2013 that "The pie chart is easily the worst way to convey information ever developed in the history of data visualization." Because they appear simple and convincing, they are easily susceptible of manipulation. Cole Nussbaumer Knaflic, a thought leader in data visualization, has a section in her 2015 book headed "Pie charts are evil."

Here is what happens when there are too many categories or colors (or both):

Model	Units Sold
Silverado	560,264
Equinox	207,730
Trax	200,689
Malibu	117,319
Traverse	105,835
Tahoe	105,147
Trailblazer	104,398
Colorado	98,012
Blazer	52,576
Suburban	44,398
Express	44,221
Corvette	33,330
Equinox EV	28,874
Blazer EV	23,115
Bolt	8,627
Camaro	5,859
Low Cab	5,409

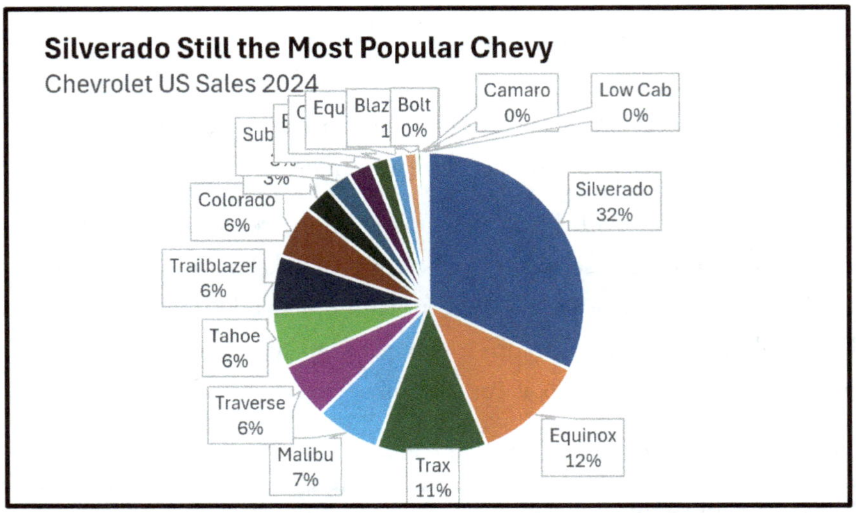

FIGURE 24: Chevrolet U.S sales 2024

Although the designer has used the same techniques as for Tesla earlier, it is impossible to read most of the chart's data or to assess the size of the various models' sales from the pie slices.

Pulling out a segment of a chart can make it look bigger than other pieces, even if it is smaller. Intending to keep the number of slices small, designers sometimes group several small categories and call them "other"—what is in there? Consider this small dataset, which is a proposed budget for a company.

TABLE 8: Company budget

Category	Budget Share
Salaries	40%
Operations	35%
Marketing	15%
Research & Development	10%

Imagine that someone in R&D is jealous of the marketing budget and wants to make it look excessive. At 15%, it looks reasonable in the table. But they draw this visualization in Excel, avoiding making any key point in the title:

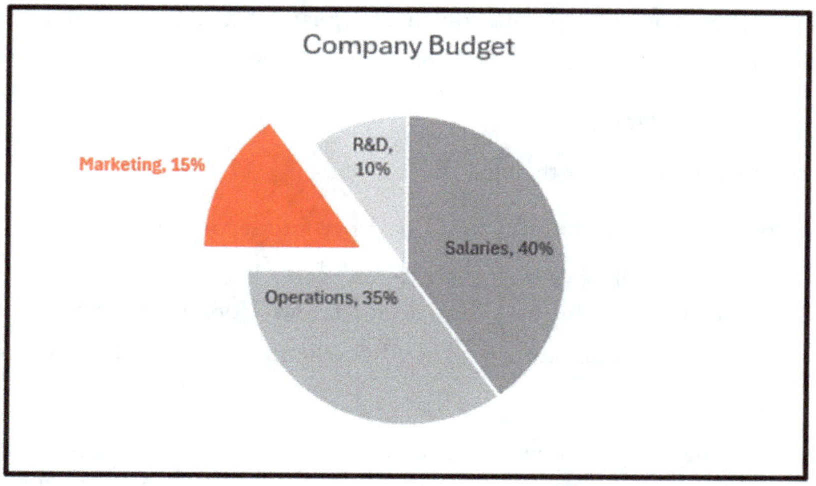

FIGURE 25: Pulled pie slice

This apparently simple chart exploits human perception by drawing focus onto the pulled-out portion, suggesting that it's dominant, then adding to the effect with a brighter color. The viewer may associate a distinct color with importance, even if the numbers haven't changed. Humans, as we mentioned, have trouble comparing angles, so it's hard to judge the relationship of marketing to the other elements. The conclusion that R&D intend, that the company is spending too much on marketing, is induced rather than statistically proven.

Other abuses of pie charts include using them for non-proportional data (like trends over time), omitting categories or percentages, and sorting in random order. Pie charts are particularly difficult to compare side-by-side.

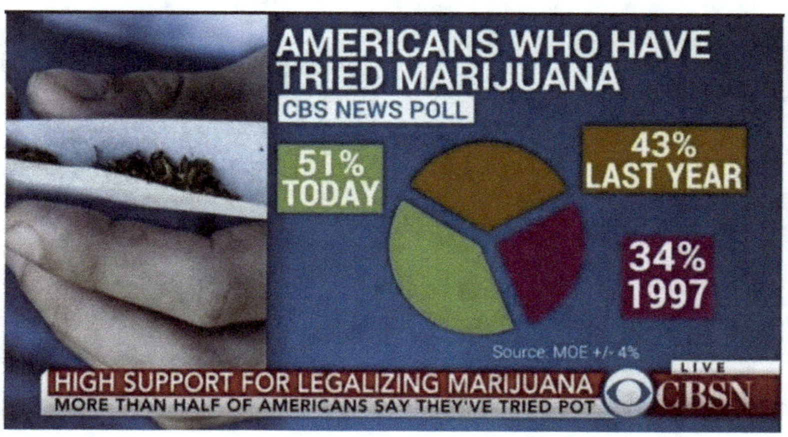

FIGURE 26: 128% Pie Chart (Source: https://www.painting-with-numbers.com/blog/getting-high-on-bad-data-visualization/)

The prize for most inane abuse, however, must go to the charts which don't add up to 100%.

The chart at left is one of many famous misuses of pie charts, in this case the slices adding up to 128%.

Donut (doughnut) charts

Definition and purpose

A donut chart depicts proportions of a population in a circular format. It's similar to a pie chart, with the difference that a hole is created in the center. While pie charts have slices, donut charts have segments.

Appearance and best practices

Consider the following text, then look at the table.

Tourists visiting the city of Vancouver for less than 27 days pay four separate taxes. The province takes 8% sales tax, adds a municipal tax of 3%, and a special events tax of 2.5% to pay for building a new stadium for the FIFA World Cup. Then, they are also hit with federal Goods and Services Tax of 5%, but it is also levied on top of the provincial taxes, so the actual rate is 5.68%. Altogether, taxes add 19.1975% to the cost of renting a room.

That's complicated, if all you want to know is which government is taking the tourism dollars! Does a table help? At least it analyzes the elements, but it's still difficult to assess the relative take. Now look at the donut chart—thanks to the use of color, the provincial taxes are in the blue group and the federal GST is readily perceived as just over a quarter of the tax burden.

B.C. Short Term Lease Taxes		
Tax	**Share**	**Rate**
PST	41.72%	8.00%
MRDT	15.65%	3.00%
SET	13.04%	2.50%
GST	29.60%	5.68%
TOTAL	100.00%	19.175%

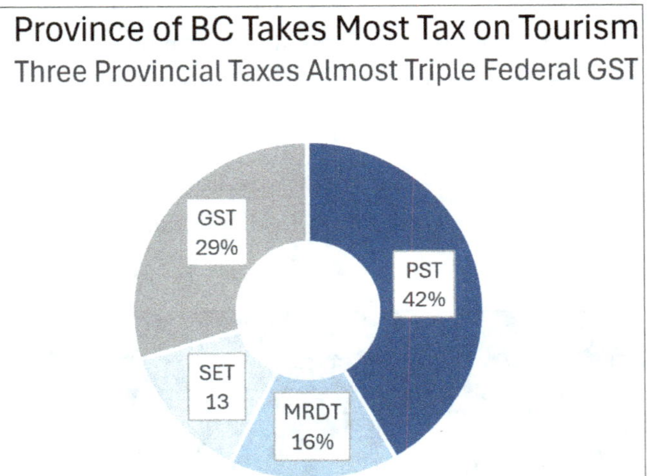

FIGURE 27: Provincial tax donut chart

This could have been achieved with a simple pie chart, but the designer chose to create a central area for the labels, reducing the overall size required and reducing outside clutter. This is good use of space on compact displays like cellphone dashboards, reducing visual clutter and obviating the need for an external key. Other best practices for donut charts are just like those for pies, so we won't repeat them.

Misuse and abuse

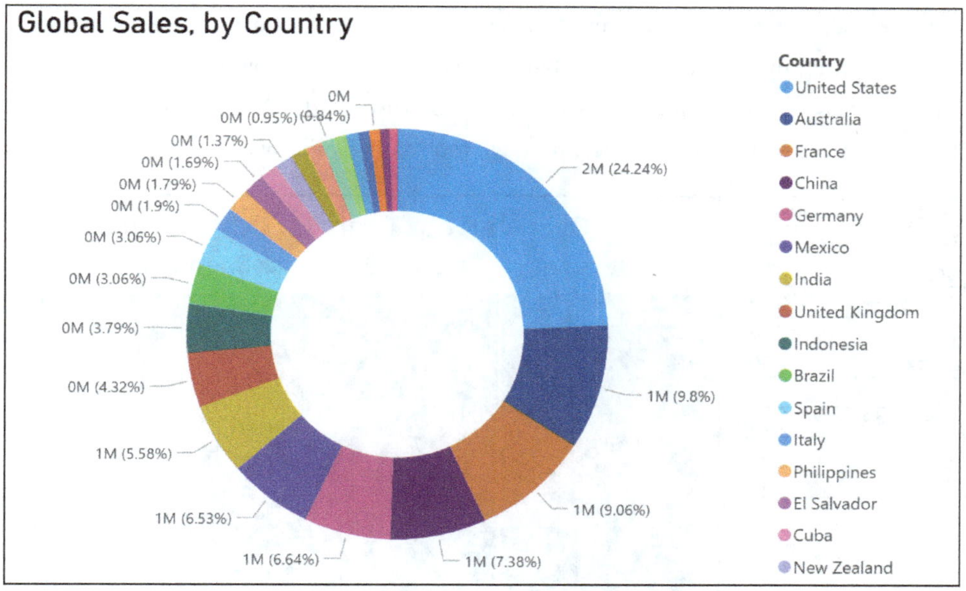

FIGURE 28: Overcrowded donut chart

This donut chart was produced in Power BI, using world sales data for a multinational corporation. It is obviously "too busy" and inappropriate as (except for the largest few countries on the list of total sales) it conveys little useful information. And the designer has completely wasted the main feature, the hole, by leaving it blank serving no useful purpose!

Tree maps

Definition and Purpose

Tree maps display categorical data within a rectangle, relating area to category values. Smaller rectangles can be nested into the larger ones to show hierarchical structures. It may not be visually obvious why tree maps have this name, as they don't look anything like a tree. They are said to resemble a tree's structure, where the largest rectangle (the entire map) is the root, then branches are smaller rectangles with subcategories, and leaves sit within them. [11]

Tree maps can be useful in cases where space is constrained, for example on dashboards. In business, they can show statistics like market share across competitors, sales by product category, or resource allocation. It's important to have sufficient identifying information on the map but trying to add too much can result in truncation or over-complexity.

---

[11] The history of the tree map is mathematically fascinating, though far beyond scope here. It is the modern successor to the **mosaic plot** which had been around for decades when Professor Ben Shneiderman at the University of Maryland in the 1990s developed algorithms to produce logical tree maps.

Appearance and best practices

The authors of the Tableau reference library (Tableau, n.d.) state that a good tree map will have distinct numerical values, a distinct hierarchy, no more than 3–4 labeled tiles, an obvious highest level, and no negative values (it is hard to imagine how a negative value could be displayed). A poor tree map, they say, will look cluttered with too many categories and labels, and have too many similar values.

Category	Product	Sales
Beverages	Tea	300
Beverages	Coffee	200
Beverages	Chocolate	100
Sandwiches	Turkey	550
Sandwiches	Chicken	450
Sandwiches	Egg	350
Snacks	Chocolate	105
Snacks	Chips	85
Snacks	Jellies	50

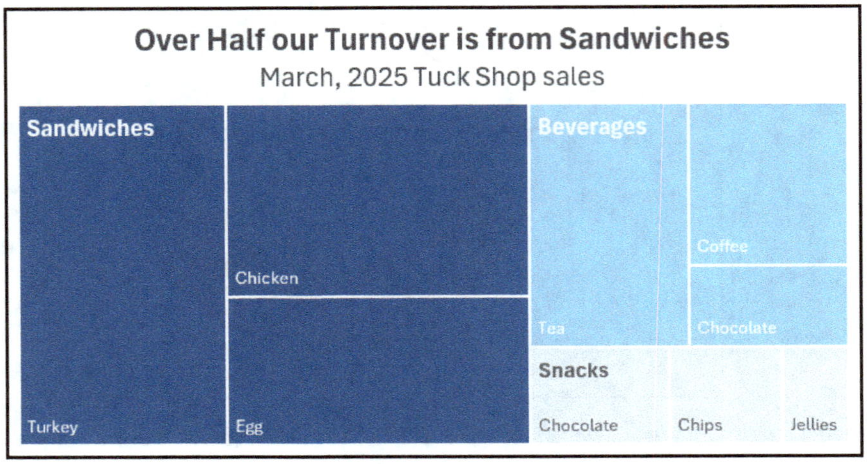

FIGURE 29: Tableau tree map

While it can be difficult to calculate precise values from a tree map, relative contributions to the whole are easy to assess. In the above example, three product categories can be compared, but then individual products within those categories are also represented. Excel's ability to produce tree maps is exceptional. The largest categories will always be shown on the left, with gradual diminution as we move to the right.

Misuse and abuse

The map of Algerian exports, presented next, purports to use the nesting concept, using colors to group sub-categories—but note how it falls foul of almost all Tableau's rules.

What did Algeria Export in 2021 (The Observatory of Economic Complexity, 2021)?

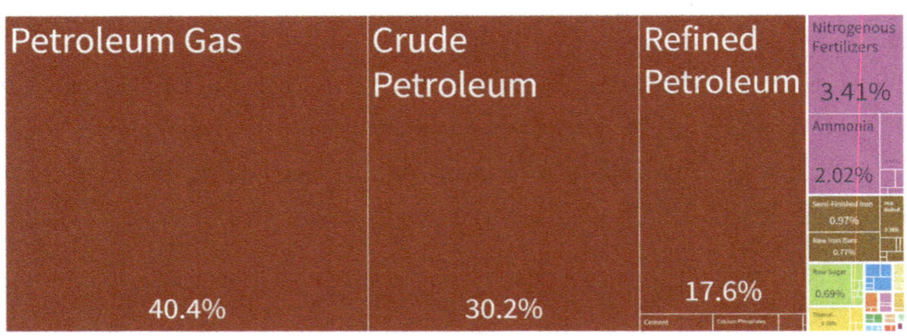

FIGURE 30: Algerian exports 2021

It's obvious with only a bit of mental arithmetic that petroleum products are the lion's share of exports—88.2 percent. But we got to that number by adding the three percentages, not by assessing that the brown area is

88.2 percent of the complete rectangle. Look at the "Ammonia" rectangle in the purple area to the right—again mental arithmetic on the figure will quickly inform that ammonia is 1/50 of the export value—but if the number weren't there, could we have concluded that from the size of the rectangle? Now go down to the bottom right and see if you can learn anything at all from the tree map without a magnifying glass.

Heatmaps

Definition and purpose

Heatmaps use intensity, or darkness, of color to represent ranges of values on a two-dimensional diagram. Although an actual map may be used, as will be demonstrated below, this is not a necessity; a heatmap can simply be a frame. For example, a webpage may be heat mapped to show where more and less users click. Areas of the human body or brain, the surface area of an object, times of day or aspects of weather can all be heat mapped.

Heatmaps allow the viewer to identify the areas of higher, medium or lower intensity of the measured activity. They are also known as proportional symbol maps or hot spot maps.

Appearance and best practices

The most common type of heat map is known as a *choropleth,* a thematic map with shaded or patterned areas becoming more intense, or darker, to reflect the magnitude of a variable. A choropleth is typically used to display demographic data like population density, unemployment, or house prices.

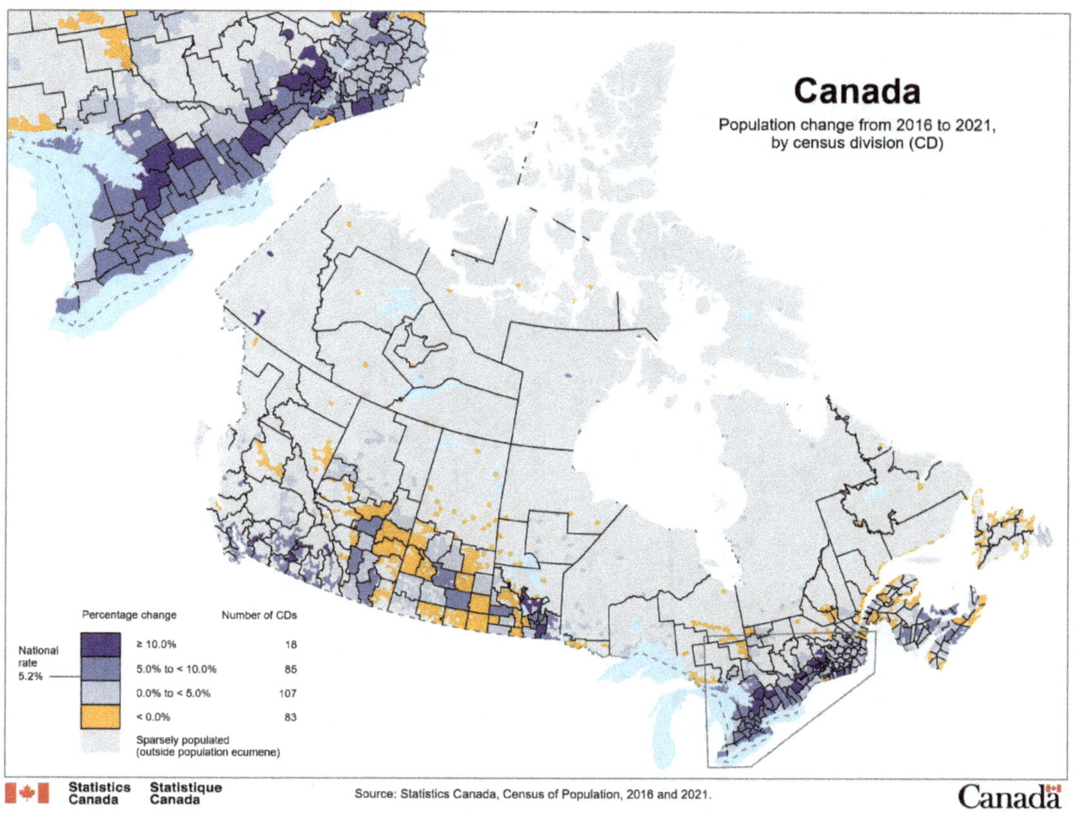

FIGURE 31: 2016-2021 population change in Canada

This choropleth uses a range of colors to demonstrate the rate of population change. Areas of increase use shades of purple; decrease is indicated by the bright orange. The pattern is striking; population is increasing in the areas of eastern and western Canada close to the U.S. border, but decreasing across the north and in many prairie areas. There are several key points to note.

For population increases, distinct *shades* of purple are used; their increasing intensity depicts higher ranges in the continuum. Here the areas have boundaries; in the absence of boundaries, gradual progressions of shades can be used. A map without division into areas, with gradual color changes, is known as an *isopleth*.

As you might expect, there is a substantial list of best practices that apply to the creation of heatmaps, such as the requirement for equal ranges in the color continuum. One of the most important, however, is that in the selection of colors, due consideration must be given to cultural associations. We will go more deeply into this below. Meanwhile, however, it is also important that not too many colors be chosen, similar shades be avoided, and that scales be kept consistent. It's best so far as possible to let the shades and colors tell their own story, giving sufficient data for the viewer to understand, but avoiding overloading the area with supplementary data.

Bubble maps

Bubble maps use bubble dimensions to demonstrate geographical distributions. They are popular in depictions of epidemiological and election data.

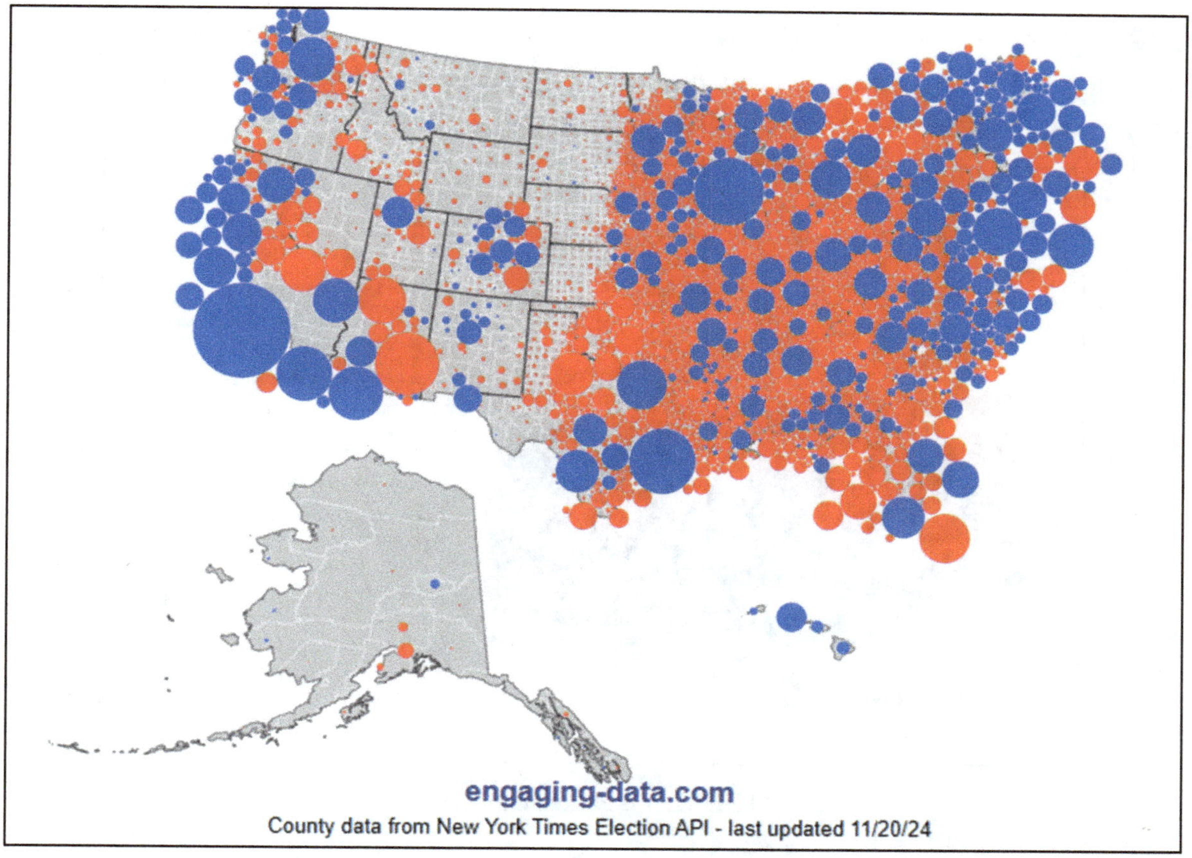

FIGURE 32: Bubble map (Engaging Data, 2023)

Some conclusions that can be drawn from the map are for example that Alaska is dominantly Republican while Hawaii is entirely Democratic, and that there is overwhelming support for Democrats on the West Coast while the Republican party finds its supporters more in rural areas than in large urban centers.

Packed circle charts

Definition and purpose

Packed circle charts use circles to depict categorical quantities. There is no positional meaning to the location of each colored circle. The concept Is similar to a bar chart, except that the bars are circular. Many categorical measurements, such the 20 countries in the example below, can be packed into a small space without a long list or horizontal extension; text can be placed inside the larger bubbles.

Packed circles can be used when there is no strict order to the data points, or there is no need for a numerical scale, when the relationship between categories is more important than exact values. Where there are large numbers of values, a column or bar chart might become too crowded or difficult to read. They also introduce the possibility of using color to add a secondary variable or grouping.

Appearance and best practices

When using a packed circle chart, it is important again to pay attention to the principle of proportional ink, which has been achieved in this example (Fractalytics, n.d.).

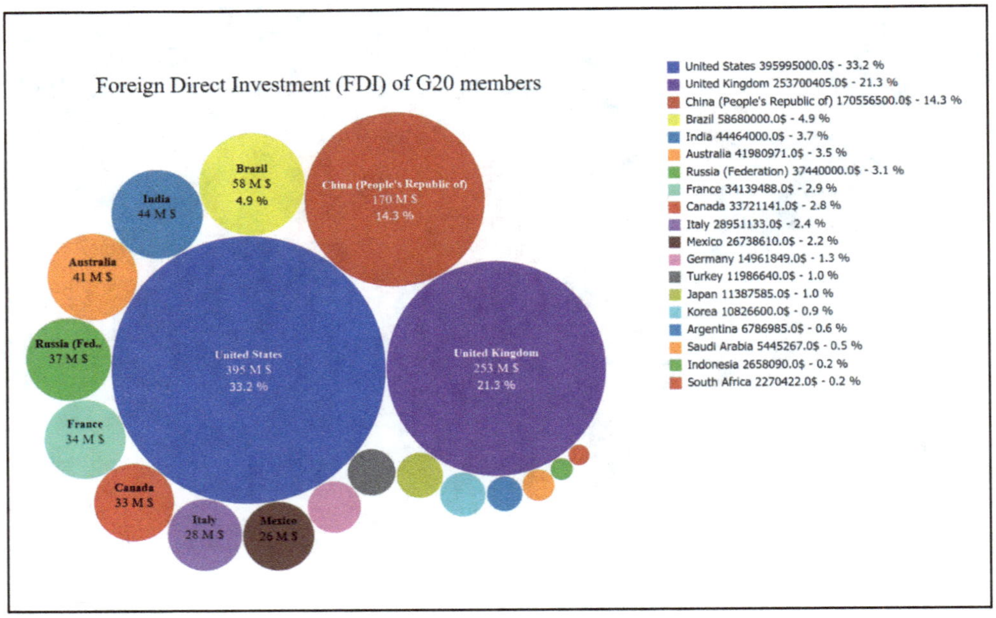

FIGURE 33: Packed circle chart

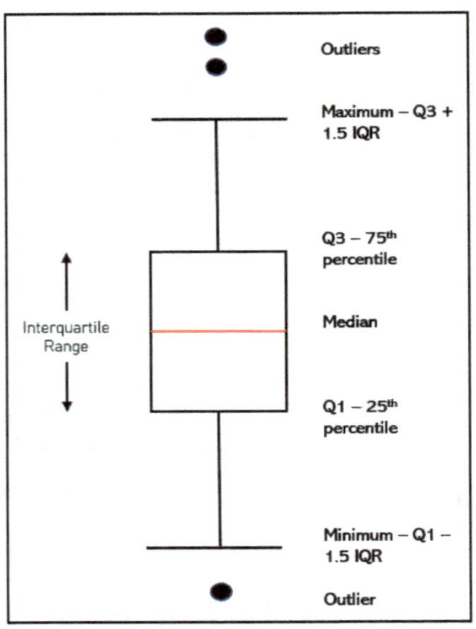

FIGURE 34: Boxplot

Boxplots

Boxplots are used to depict the *distribution* of categorical data. They give a visual impression of the range and central tendency of data, show whether the data are skewed, and indicate the presence of outliners – extreme values outside the normal range.

Typically shown beside a numerical scale, a boxplot depicts the median value inside a box which represents the "middle half" of the data—all values from the 25th percentile to the 75th. The distance between the two percentiles is known as the *interquartile range* (IQR). That range is multiplied by 1.5 and added to the top of the box and subtracted from the bottom, to give a minimum and maximum value for *normal range*. Outliers are depicted as datapoints outside of the normal range.

We often add numerical datapoints to boxplots.

Charts for Depicting Change

Line charts

Definition and purpose

Line charts are used to show change over time, with time periods equally spaced along the X axis. A line chart is a graph which shows the progression of *continuous* data points connected by a line. The X axis is most often time, though it can also be other measurements which progress at fixed intervals, such as fuel inputs to an engine (in which case the measured output on the Y axis might be power).

The main purpose of line charts is to illustrate trends. In business, they are used to show performance metrics like sales, expenses, profits or account balance. In Excel, some chart types allow the addition of a trendline, which does not usually connect datapoints but plots the generalized direction of the datapoints, enabling extrapolation if there is an identifiable trend.

Appearance and best practices

If the trend, the direction of change over a period, is the most important object of study, then line charts are preferred. It's important to have clear titles and labels which tell the viewer what they are looking at.

TABLE 9: Revenue, Expenses and Profit

Month	Revenue	Expenses	Profit
Jan	5,000	3,000	2,000
Feb	5,200	3,200	2,000
Mar	5,400	3,300	2,100
Apr	5,800	3,400	2,400
May	6,000	3,600	2,400
Jun	6,200	3,800	2,400
Jul	6,400	4,000	2,400
Aug	6,600	4,200	2,400
Sep	6,800	4,400	2,400
Oct	7,200	4,500	2,700
Nov	7,500	4,700	2,800
Dec	7,800	5,000	2,800

Although a little work looking at the above figures reveals the upward trend, it's not easy to see just how steep it is, how it varies over time, or how the line items relate to each other. Captured in a line chart, however, all these things are easily apparent.

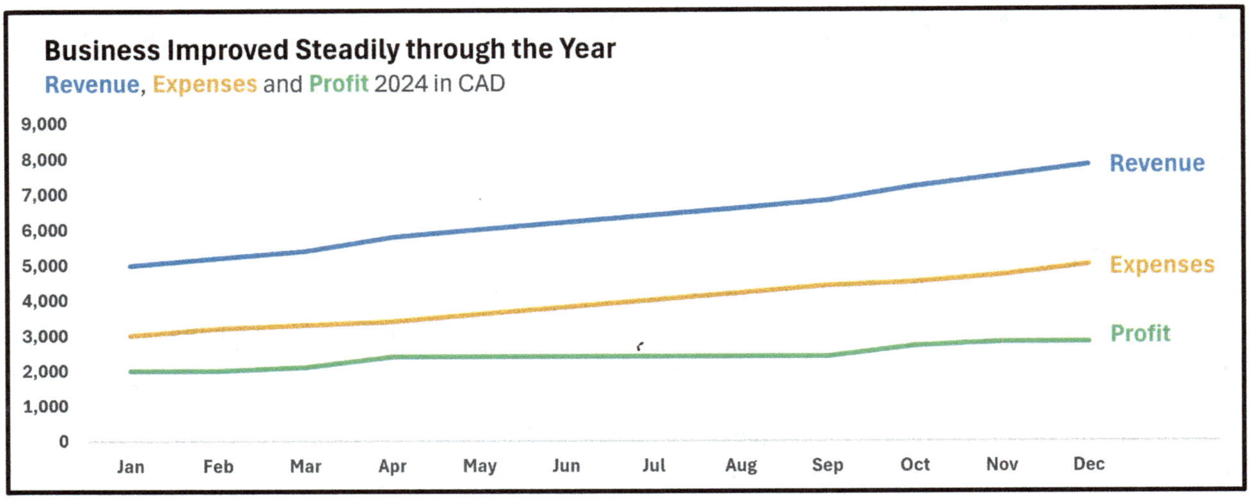

FIGURE 35: Revenue & profits line chart

Here is a chart showing the effect of wildfires in summer 2023. Note the effective use of gray lines for prior years, then bright red for the current year, to emphasize the key point—the dramatic rise in the current year figures for hectares burned, compared to all recent years.

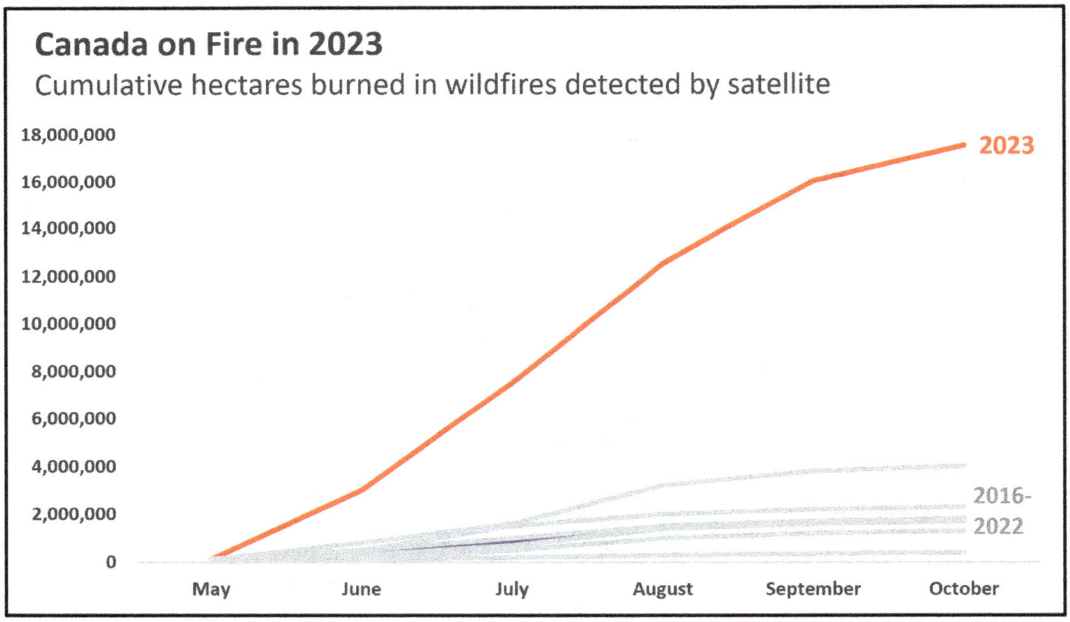

FIGURE 36: Wildfires in 2023

Line charts start to lose their effectiveness if there are too many lines, which make them difficult for the viewer to interpret. A good general rule is to limit them to five lines. In most cases, intervals on both axes should be uniform and proportionate, though there is an exception when dealing with exponential growth, where logarithmic scales become more appropriate. As we just saw with the wildland fires graph, use of modest amounts of color to highlight trends is an excellent practice.

Scaling is a critical concept in considering the clarity of line charts, which makes it important for us to understand logarithmic scales.

LOGARITHMIC SCALES

Logarithmic ("log") scales solve the axis problem, for both column and line charts, when exponential growth is achieved and we want to show ratios, or relationships from one period to the next.

Imagine a start-up company with what appears to be an impressive growth pattern for its second year of operations: having reached $10,000 in sales by January, it proceeds to double its sales in every month. Profits look good too, as they increase at a strong pace.

Month	Sales	Profit
Jan	$ 10,000	$ 5,000
Feb	$ 20,000	$ 10,000
Mar	$ 40,000	$ 20,000
Apr	$ 80,000	$ 40,000
May	$ 160,000	$ 80,000
Jun	$ 320,000	$ 160,000
Jul	$ 640,000	$ 320,000
Aug	$ 1,280,000	$ 640,000
Sep	$ 2,560,000	$ 1,280,000
Oct	$ 5,120,000	$ 2,560,000
Nov	$ 10,240,000	$ 5,120,000
Dec	$ 20,480,000	$ 10,240,000

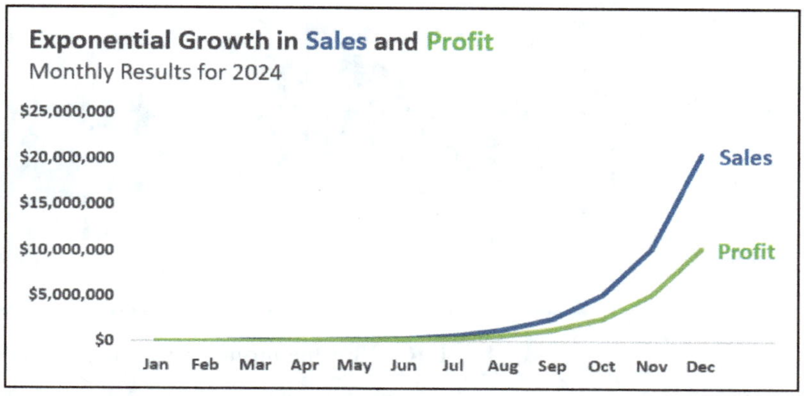

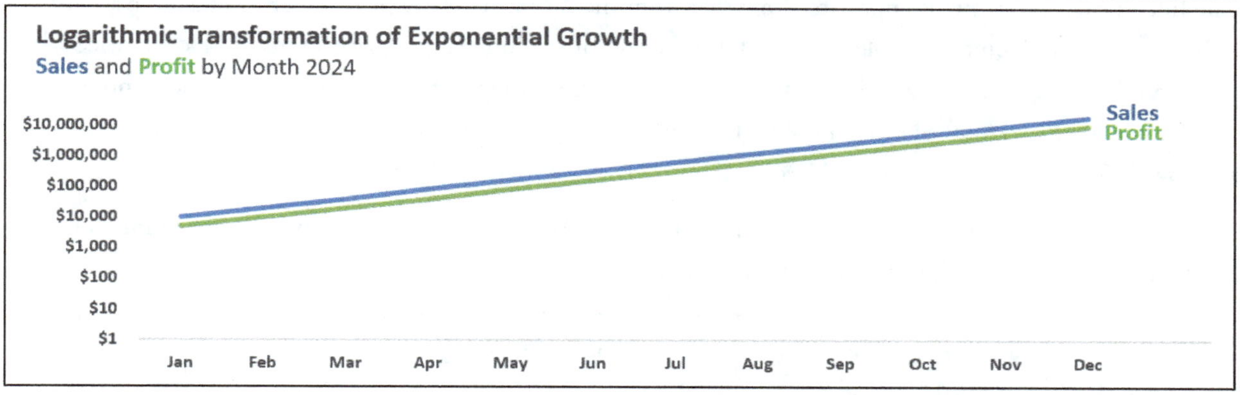

FIGURE 37: Logarithmic scales

After tabulating the results in Excel, we first created a line chart. At first sight, it looks impressive—every month, the company is doubling its sales. Is this true growth? It is—the logarithmic scale shows that the rate of growth is consistent even as the numbers become very large.

You might be curious as to why the baseline value in the logarithmic scale is $1. While there are other rare variations, most logarithmic scales use the concept of Base 10—values are equally spaced according to powers of 10. 10^0 is 1, 10^1 is 10, and so on.

Misuse and abuse

A line chart which covers a time series can be manipulated if the base line is not set at 0. It is accentuated if the area below the line is shaded. The next chart shows movements in the crude oil price for the month of July 2025.

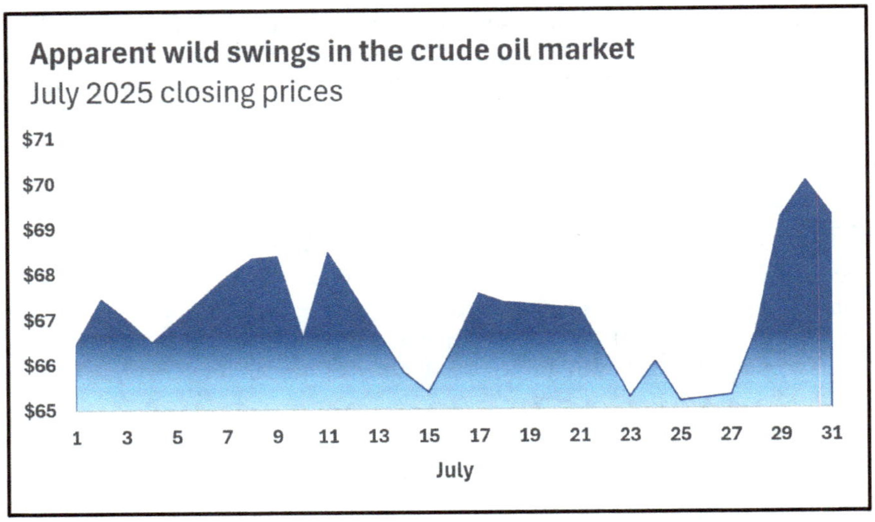

FIGURE 38: One month movements in crude oil price

The filled peaks and troughs appear to show that from the 2nd to the 4th of July, the price had almost halved, only to recover and almost double by the 8th. By the end of the month, the price seems to be over twice what it was 30 days earlier. But wait—look again at the numbers on the right. The Y axis starts at $65 and goes up to $71. The total difference between the highest and lowest points on the axis is $6, and between the high and low $$5—a difference of around 7%.

Here, believe it or not, is the exact same chart with the Y (price) axis starting at 0. It looks like a much less interesting day on the trading floor, wouldn't you agree?

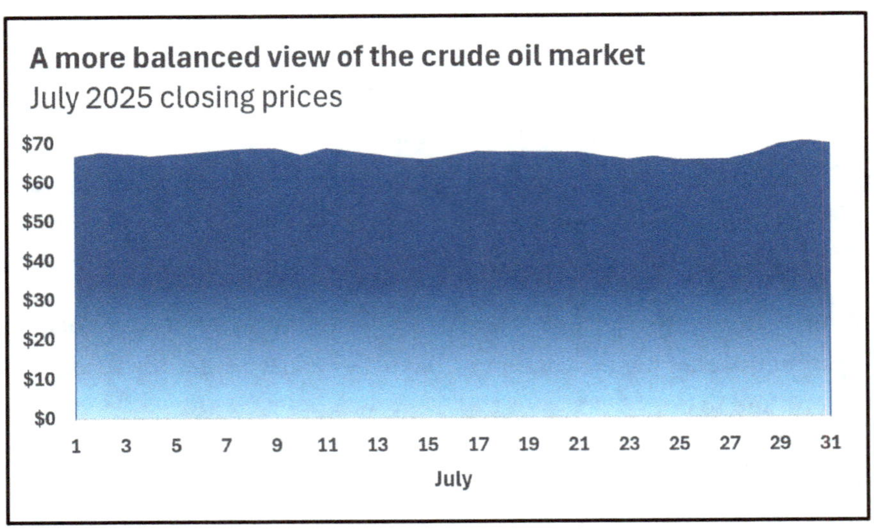

FIGURE 39: Full scale oil price movements

We learn from looking at these charts that we must always carefully examine their construction and determine whether what we see reflects what truly happened. Finance sites are very fond of restricting axes to exaggerate price movements, for they drive investor interest and consequent fees. The clue that jiggery-pokery is afoot is often that whoever is showing the chart has an agenda to shape public perception. In other cases there is no such agenda – it just makes for better news if there are higher peaks and deeper troughs.

Truncated axes are the most common distortions which we encounter. Inconsistent intervals on either axis can create misleading impressions, while overloading the graph with too many lines, too much color, or too many elements can create confusion. Cherry picking, only including some of the data, is a rare sin which causes charts to be produced which reflect their underlying data—but the dataset itself is not honest.

Waterfall charts

Definition and purpose

Waterfall charts show the cumulative progress of a sequence of positive and negative values, from a starting value and ending with their result. They are also known as bridge charts, because of their distinctive shape. They show changes over time. The viewer can see how each individual factor contributes to the overall change.

Waterfall charts are a staple product of the business consulting world and were once claimed as a sort of "trade secret" of McKinsey & Company (Rasiel, 1999). Today, however, they are widely available in software packages including Excel.

Appearance and best practices

Category	Amount	Cumulative
2024 Cash Flow	500,000	500,000
+ Product A	120,000	620,000
- Product B	(80,000)	540,000
New Markets	100,000	640,000
Increased Costs	(150,000)	490,000
Rebates	(50,000)	440,000
2025 Cash Flow	440,000	440,000

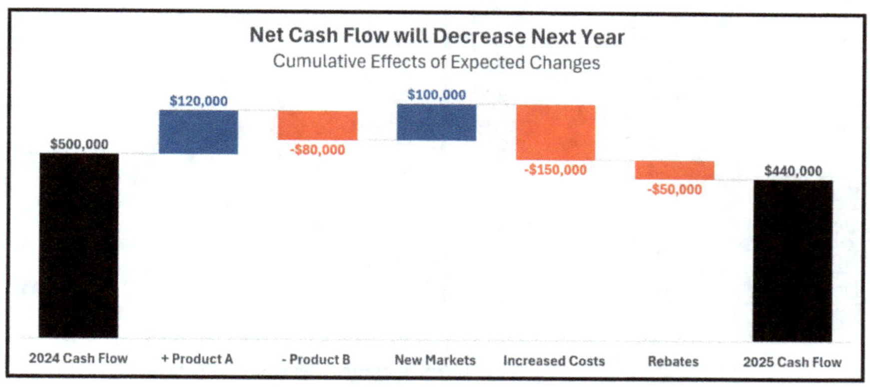

FIGURE 40: Waterfall chart

This demonstration shows the components of a change in cash flow. As each element of the change is added or subtracted, the net effect is shown, with blue blocks indicating positive changes and red for negative.

Best practices for waterfall charts start with clearly stating what the chart is intended to show. The start and end points must be readily identifiable. Positive and negative contributions are always shown in different colors. The width of columns should be uniform, and their height proportionate. If there is a logical sequence to the columns, they should occur in order (as for example during a year). While there is lots of space in a bridge chart, avoid the temptation to fill it with clutter.

Misuse and abuse

Leaving out data, or manipulating the order in which they are presented, can mislead viewers. Some colors are naturally associated with positive effects (green or blue) or negative effects (red), and viewers should not be misled by reversing their roles. Although waterfall charts are impressive, their overuse in circumstances where simpler charts would do the job is best avoided.

Charts for Relationships between Variables

Scatter plots

Definition and purpose

Scatter plots are used to display the relationship between two variables. Each is placed on one axis. Looking at the positions of coordinates, the viewer gains a quick sense of whether there is a correlation or trend, and/or whether there are clusters. They can easily spot outliers. We should beware of forming definite conclusions too quickly—a further examination of statistical measures like correlation coefficients helps quantify relationships and confirm the visual impression. We must always remember, also, that correlation does not prove causation, though it can be important evidence.

Appearance and best practices

Month	Av_Temp	Sales MXN-bn
Jan	13.2	36.48
Feb	14.5	42.56
Mar	16.5	48.64
Apr	18	54.72
May	18	60.8
Jun	18	60.8
Jul	17	54.72
Aug	17.5	54.72
Sep	17	48.64
Oct	15.5	42.56
Nov	13.5	42.56
Dec	14.4	60.8

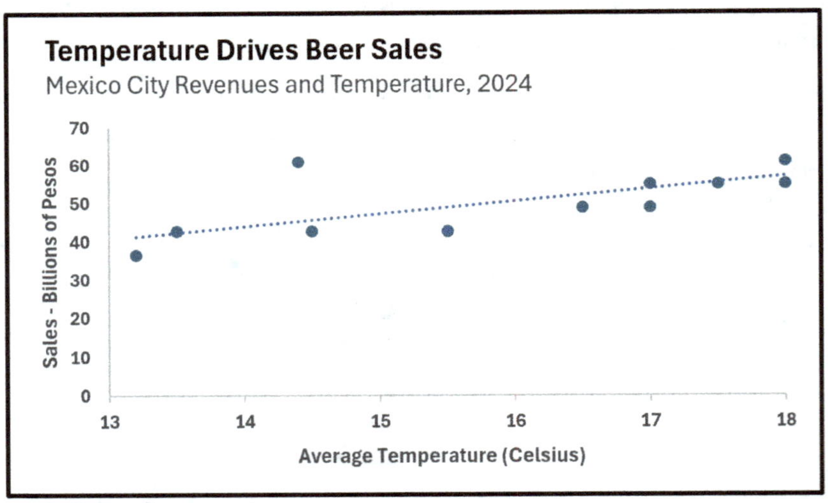

FIGURE 41: Mexico City beer sales

While the dataset for beer sales in Mexico City is not complex, it is not easy to see the relationship between temperature and sales. However, from the scatterplot it is readily apparent that there is a linear, positive relationship; as it gets warmer, sales go up. It is also easy to detect the outlier, the one month in which sales were very high, but the temperature was relatively low. No surprise that it's December, when people filled their fridges ready for family gatherings in the holiday season.

Note carefully that this is NOT a time series, even though months are given in the original table. The two variables are sales and average temperature.

Scatterplots can reveal differences that are not at all apparent from tables of data. The most famous illustration is known as Anscombe's Quartet (Anscombe, 1973). The demonstration starts with the question of whether four datasets are similar:

A

Mean X	9
Var X	11
Mean Y	7.50
Var Y	4.125
Corr XY	0.816
Lin Reg Line	y = 3.00 + 0.500x
Co D Lin Reg	0.67

B

Mean X	9
Var X	11
Mean Y	7.50
Var Y	4.125
Corr XY	0.816
Lin Reg Line	y = 3.00 + 0.500x
Co D Lin Reg	0.67

C

Mean X	9
Var X	11
Mean Y	7.50
Var Y	4.125
Corr XY	0.816
Lin Reg Line	y = 3.00 + 0.500x
Co D Lin Reg	0.67

D

Mean X	9
Var X	11
Mean Y	7.50
Var Y	4.125
Corr XY	0.816
Lin Reg Line	y = 3.00 + 0.500x
Co D Lin Reg	0.67

FIGURE 42: Anscombe's quartet data

They all have precisely the same numbers in exactly the same boxes. But converted to charts, the truth comes out:

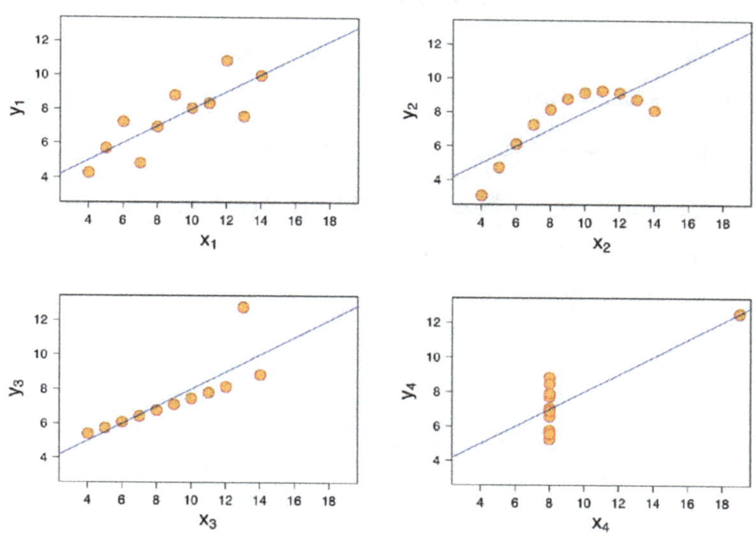

FIGURE 43: Anscombe's quartet plots[12]

[12] Anscombe's Quartet plots by Schutz, based on data from Francis Anscombe (1973), *Graphs in Statistical Analysis, The American Statistician*, 27(1), 17–21. Licensed under CC BY-SA 3.0.

Misuse and abuse

Scatterplots should be simply constructed and easy to understand. Many of the abuses that occur result from poor treatment of the underlying data.

For example, *overplotting* describes the practice of putting too many datapoints onto a chart, so that they overlap and obscure the meaning. Missing axis titles or units can confuse the viewer or render the chart meaningless. Cherry-picking data is a no-no, as usual. Another undesirable practice is known as *overfitting*, which describes using overly complex trendlines which aren't a real relationship.

The commonest errors you are likely to see, however, are an implication that correlation equals causation, and inappropriate use of data that are not continuous. There are very occasional instances where categorical data can be depicted on a scatterplot, but this almost always applied where categories are substituted with numerical values.

Bubble charts

Definition and purpose

A bubble chart is an extension of the scatter plot, permitting depiction of more than two variables. Each data point is plotted against two axes, X and Y, but then a third dimension is added using the size of the bubble. Some bubble charts add a fourth dimension by using color. A typical business use is analysis of market segments, where X is used for market size, Y for profitability, and the bubble size is adjusted for market share. Bubble charts can be used very dramatically in animated presentations.[13]

An additional attraction of bubble charts is that they *can* depict negative values, as bubbles can be placed to the left of the vertical axis or below the horizontal.

Appearance and best practices

The chart below, borrowed from a popular blog (Ricks, 2021), displays all four capabilities being deployed at once.

---

[13] Bergstrom and West quite rightly praise the work and skills of the late Professor Hans Rosling, a Swedish doctor and researcher. His illustrious career included studies in Sweden and India, work as a District Medical Officer in Mozambique, and a 20-year study of konzo, a rare disease found in Africa. He founded the Gapminder Foundation, learned sword swallowing (which he demonstrated in TEDx talks), and presented talks on urbanization and health for the BBC. Amazingly, he was dyslexic. Some of his astoundingly energetic talks can be found on YouTube, and you are encouraged to watch him demonstrate mastery of the animated bubble chart (Rosling, 2010).

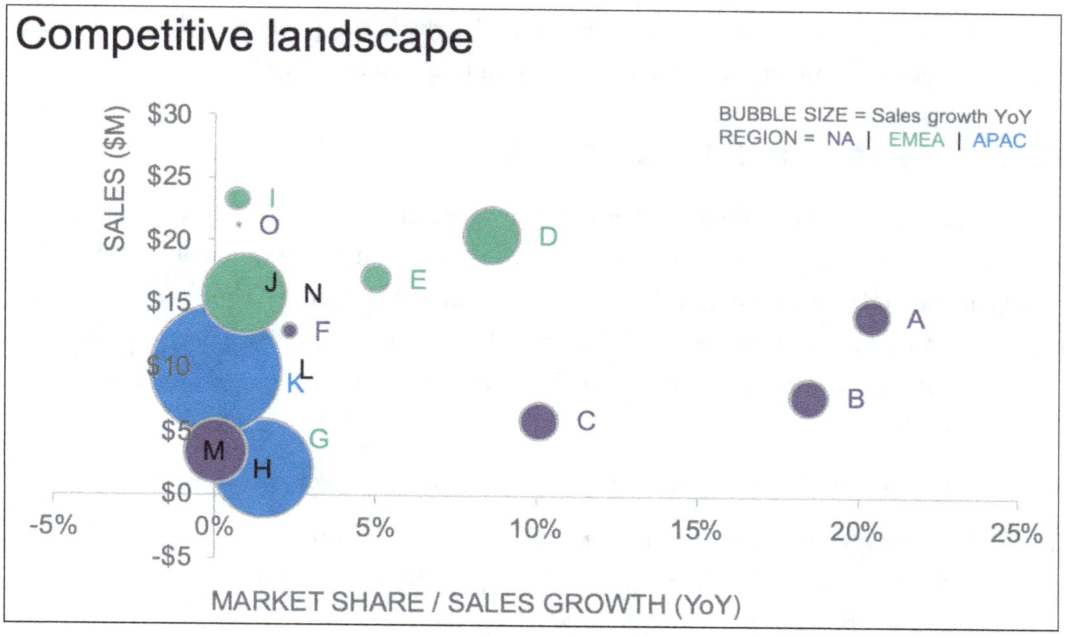

FIGURE 44: Bubble chart

You will often need to incorporate the use of transparency so that all bubbles can be seen. It is easy to forget that one bubble might sit entirely inside a larger bubble and become invisible if all bubbles are opaque. Note how in the above chart, the bubbles make the Y axis values difficult to read.

It's also important to consider whether the correct variables have been chosen for the axes; the two most important should almost always be assigned to the X and Y axes.

Very careful thought is required before deciding to use a bubble chart in a presentation. Putting a complex chart up on a screen asks a lot of the viewers: as in many instances above, they are often much more likely to be able to discern small differences between bars than bubbles. It is difficult to assess relative sizes of areas. More than most other charts, the strategic inclusion of text—words—is often critical to effective use of the bubble chart.

Misuse and abuse

A common mistake made by bubble chart creators is to ignore the principle of proportional ink and use the radius or diameter of bubbles to portray relationships, instead of making sure that the areas of the bubbles reflect the data. That results in the relative areas of the bubbles being incorrect; for example if I have one car and you have two, using the relative radius of bubbles would create an area of (pr^2) 3.14 x 0.5^2 = 0.785 for my circle, and 3.14 x 1^2 = 3.14 for yours, or an area ratio of 4:1—visually conveying the impression that you have four cars while I have one (Kosara, 2019).

Because bubble charts are complex, it's easy to overwhelm the viewer. An overemphasis on large bubbles can cause overestimation of their importance, while too many bubbles, or too many overlaps, can clutter the chart and make it unreadable. Overuse of colors, or non-intuitive color schemes, can overwhelm the viewer. Data context is important; its omission can undermine effectiveness. If you are using a bubble chart, consider the audience; you are the audience to understand a visual interpretation of multi-dimensional data. With the availability of powerful graphics tools, it's tempting to add stylistic components such as 3D effects or other aesthetic elements, but these are ineffective and usually simply complicate the chart.

Chart types for business data

You will already have gathered that there is a bewildering variety of available chart types. Some programs allow you to visualize your data in any available chart type, regardless of whether they are suitable. Others, like Tableau, a widely used analysis and visualization tool, perform more evaluation of the data and allow access only to chart types which are *suitable* for the data selected. When you design your chart, it is standard practice to look at a few different options and choose that most suitable. However, there are some ground rules which will help you narrow down the options.

One way of narrowing down the options is to think through a series of decisions, as follow:

1. Am I displaying what happens over time, or a comparison of categories.
    - With rare exceptions, time series will be displayed horizontally (with the earliest time at the left). Line and column charts work for time series.
    - Comparisons of categories are best displayed vertically. Here, line charts don't work, but there are many variations on bar charts, vertical bubbles and waterfall which can be appropriate.
    - Occasionally, charts with a circular orientation may work. As we've continually stressed these should largely be avoided, but they can work where there are very few categories to be compared, such as a pie chart showing "our" percentage of the world market.
2. What am I trying to show?
    - As above, time series will be horizontal in orientation and include bars, lollipops, dots or lines.
    - If you are trying to show a comparison of categorical data, ranking categories, or showing a pattern, horizontal bars and their variations (such as lollipops or barbells) will work.
    - Part-to-whole comparisons are best achieved by stacked bars or, on rare occasions, the dreaded pie.
    - Variance analysis can also be vertical or horizontal, depending on whether there is a time component. Here, it's important to design the chart so that numbers and variances can be shown on both sides of the relevant axis.
    - Contribution analysis, showing how a total value is built up by components, is best depicted by a waterfall chart—if horizontal (over time) it is also known as a bridge chart.
    - Correlation of two variables is best shown by a scatter plot.
    - A portfolio analysis—if there are three variables, use a bubble chart.

The best book we have ever read about creating charts for business is Scott Berinato's *Good Charts*, published by the prestigious Harvard Business Review Press. We highly recommend this book if you are interested in further developing your understanding of chart psychology and creation; further, he calls in aid (at p.93 of the 2023 edition) a chart typology developed by Andrew Abela, which employs flow-chart methodology to lead to a conclusion on chart selection (eforebrahim, 2022). While there are several chart types missing (most notably actual tables), this is a very useful chart for showing the process of selection.

The following table lists the principal business and accounting data types, with a suggestion of the appropriate chart types to consider.

TABLE 10: Data types and suitable charts

Type of Data`	Chart Type
Accounts payable by vendor	Clustered Bar Chart, Stacked Bar Chart
Aged Accounts Receivable	Column Chart, Heatmap
Accruals and prepayments	Column Chart, Heatmap
Audit sample	Scatter Plot, Heatmap
Bank reconciliation discrepancies	Bar Chart, Line Chart
Break-even analysis	Line Chart
Budget allocation across departments	Stacked Bar or Column Chart, Treemap
Budget vs. actual expenses	Clustered Bar or Column Chart
Cash flow trends	Line Chart
Comparison of sales channels	Clustered Bar or Column Chart
Cost of goods sold (COGS) trends	Line Chart, Waterfall Chart
Customer churn rates	Line Chart, Heatmap
Customer satisfaction scores	Bar Chart, Column Chart
Customer segmentation by demographics	Packed Bubble Chart
Deferred revenue balances	Bar or Column Chart, Waterfall Chart
Dividend payments over time	Line Chart, Column Chart
Employee headcount over time	Line Chart, Waterfall Chart
Employee turnover by department	Bar Chart, Heatmap
Energy usage by department	Clustered Column Chart, Heatmap
Expense breakdown by category	Donut Chart, Pie Chart, Treemap
Expense claims by employee	Stacked Bar Chart, Pie Chart
Financial ratios (e.g., ROA, ROE)	Scatter Plot
Fixed assets and depreciation	Line Chart, Waterfall Chart
Forecast vs. actual revenue	Clustered Column Chart
Fraud detection patterns	Heatmap
General ledger account balances	Bar Chart, Column Chart
Hierarchical data (e.g., company structure)	Treemap, Organizational Chart
Inventory levels by location	Clustered Bar or Column Chart
Inventory turnover ratios	Bar Chart, Line Chart
Loan portfolio performance	Scatter Plot, Bubble Chart
Loan repayment schedules	Waterfall Chart, Line Chart
Market share by competitor	Pie Chart, Packed Bubble Chart, Treemap
Marketing campaign performance	Bar Chart, Line Chart
Net income comparison by period	Column Chart, Line Chart
Net profit contribution by region	Heatmap, Bubble Chart, Bubble Map

Operating expenses by category	Bar Chart, Pie Chart
Overhead allocation by product line	Stacked Bar Chart, Heatmap
Payroll costs by employee type	Pie Chart, Column Chart
Production output by factory	Bar Chart, Column Chart, Treemap
Profit and loss by department	Stacked Bar Chart, Heatmap
Profit margins for products	Stacked Bar or Column Chart
Revenue growth by client	Bar Chart, Line Chart
Sales by product or category	Bar Chart, Column Chart
Segment profitability analysis	Heatmap, Treemap
Shareholder equity changes	Waterfall Chart, Stacked Bar Chart
Stock price movements	Line Chart
Tax liability breakdown	Column Chart, Pie Chart
Tax liability by jurisdiction	Column Chart, Bubble Map
Trends in revenue over time	Line Chart
Trial balance visualization	Bar Chart, Treemap
Website traffic sources	Pie Chart, Packed Bubble Chart, Treemap

Conclusion

In this chapter, we've worked through a list of the main chart types used for presenting business and accounting data. You will certainly have gained the impression, though, that having chosen the right chart type, the job is not finished.

In the next chapter, we'll move to considering the principles of chart design, showing how elements like color, labeling and layout can add to, or detract from, your message. You need to choose the right chart type, then add thoughtful design.

Multiple Choice Questions for Chapter 2

1. Humans are generally visually better at perceiving:
    a. lengths.
    b. areas.
    c. angles.
    d. circumferences.
2. A tree map shows:
    a. a group of rectangles proportional to the data count in each category.
    b. the relationships between various branches of a business and the central enterprise (trunk).
    c. different sized fruits hanging on a bush in proportion to the numbers depicted.
    d. the number of trees per acre in a city environment.
3. Which of the following statements is correct for bar charts?
    a. Bars on a log scale should start at 1, while bars on a linear scale should start at 0.
    b. Bars on a linear scale should start at 1, while bars on a log scale should start at 0.
    c. You should never waste ink and paper by having the Y axis start at 0 when all the bars are at least 100 long.
    d. Three-dimensional bar charts convey more information than two dimensional charts.
4. When creating a bubble map, which of the following should you consider?
    a. Size and overlap of the bubbles.
    b. Color scheme for different categories.
    c. Scale and geographic accuracy.
    d. All the above.
5. What is the main shortcoming of heatmaps?
    a. They are only effective when combined with interactive tools.
    b. They are limited to showing numeric data.
    c. They cannot be used to display large datasets.
    d. Color gradients may cause misinterpretation of values.
6. If you want to display a hierarchical data relationship, which would be the best visualization?
    a. Bar chart.
    b. Line chart.
    c. Scatter plot.
    d. Tree map.
7. What is a common problem with using logarithmic scales in charts?
    a. For non-technical audiences, they are difficult to interpret.
    b. They distort the relationship between two points.
    c. They do not represent zero values correctly.
    d. They exaggerate small differences.
8. Anscombe's quartet demonstrates that:
    a. visualizations can reveal differences that are not apparent from data.
    b. data can reveal differences that are not apparent from visualizations.
    c. tables of data always have unique elements for different datasets.

9. Time series data are strongly communicated using:
    a. box plots.
    b. bar and line charts.
    c. tree maps.
    d. pie charts.
10. "Visualization" is a synonym for "chart."
    a. True.
    b. False.
11. Histograms differ from categorical bar charts because
    a. they contain tick marks.
    b. they depict quantitative data for a range of values.
    c. they cannot be used for categorical data.
12. The interquartile range:
    a. is used to calculate "normal range."
    b. is established by dividing the normal range by 4.
    c. is the precise range of values that does not contain any outliers.
    d. has the median at its exact center.
13. According to the Harvard Business Review, three of the key purposes of data visualization are:
    a. idea generation, idea illustration and visual discovery.
    b. idea illustration, visual discovery and visual analysis.
    c. Visual discovery, visual analysis and visual generation.

3. DESIGN PRINCIPLES

Introduction to Design Principles

The central purpose of any visualization is to communicate to the viewer. The designer of a chart, graphic, poster or other medium can command attention and ensure that the viewer sees the most important information first. Logical structuring of the information in the visualization reduces cognitive load—the amount of work the viewer must do to understand the message. When a viewer sees a chart, they don't look at the elements sequentially as they do with a printed page. Instead, they see first whatever has most prominence, with "change" and "difference" being the dominant features. If you are using a chart to make a point, make sure that the initial impression from the chart is in line with that goal.

Because we want to reduce load, we want to create clean, uncluttered designs. Never feel that all the space must be used—white space has an important role in improving utility and directing focus. Because communication of ideas leads to decision-making, a host of tools including fonts, colors, and patterns give us the chance to evoke emotions, build trust, and guide the viewer. As we consider potential viewers, we must be aware of accessibility issues, ensuring that we don't make elements too small, crowded, or inaccessible to visually challenged viewers including those suffering from color-blindness. We must be careful not to mislead or perpetuate biases, breach professional ethics, or offend cultural values.

FIGURE 45: Read this first

The popular "You will read this first" poster, shown at left, uses a psychological concept known as *attention manipulation.* The designer has established a *visual hierarchy,* using the individual presentations of elements to establish the order in which they are viewed. The largest element, in white type on black, is read first by most people because it "stands out." Then, the reader tends to continue reading down wards, only switching conscious effort to the text at the top after reading the three other lines .

Advertisers and politicians make great use of this, and a consequence of the effect known as the von Restorff effect. Hedwig von Restorff, a German scientist, first documented the *isolation effect* which causes consumers to remember text or imagery that stands out in a picture, better than they remember information that's in the background. This visualization is openly intended to manipulate the memory and actions of the reader.

Take 10 seconds and count the number of letter Fs in this sentence:

First and foremost, cream of wheat leaves you feeling fuller than any other type of cereal.

Now count the Fs in this sentence:

First and foremost, cream of wheat leaves you feeling fuller than any other type of cereal.

Then in this one:

First and foremost, cream of wheat leaves you feeling fuller than any other type of cereal.

When presented to adult classes or at conferences, the most common response to the first question is 4. However, nearly everyone gets it right if they are shown the second and third versions. Why? The data visualization has exploited first color, then font, to make the data easier to process.

Core Design Principles

Pre-attentive attributes

As a visualization designer, you have a deep interest in using the psychological tools at your disposal to make sure that your audience gets your point and pays attention to exactly what you want them to understand.

> "The important thing," says Cole Knaflic, "about iconic memory is that it is tuned to a set of pre-attentive attributes." It is those attributes which we address when designing visualizations.

Newcomers to this field are often surprised by the range of techniques that are available.

If you asked almost any group of people, from first graders to doctors, "how do you see?" you would be most likely to hear a very quick answer, "with my eyes." *This is only partially true*. You need eyes to see—but what you perceive and how you process the images that are conveyed all happens in the brain. Imagine yourself driving a car and approaching an intersection. The green light changes to amber, then to red. The eyes pick up the change, hold it for a split-second in **iconic memory**, which lasts only for a fraction of a second, whereupon it is quickly conveyed to the brain for processing. You stop the vehicle. Researchers on iconic memory and perception theorize that these processes, particularly those that flow from changes in the scene, became highly developed at an early stage in human evolution, to ensure that predators in the distance are quickly noticed.

The nature of **short-term memory** explains why large amounts of information should not be included in a visualization. We can only process a few items of information at any one time; presenting too much incurs the risk of cognitive overload.

Use of pre-attentive attributes lies at the heart of focusing attention. They are many in number and vary according to the medium in which they are used. Before reading on, please look at this page and the previous, and see how many examples have already been used in this chapter. Don't look at the footnote until you think you've found them all.[14]

Although size and position have some relevance to information on charts, graphs and maps, most of the scholarship and rules relate to color. That is where we will focus our attention here.

Three dimensions and perspective

Many software packages enable the user to create three-dimensional versions of common charts. Mostly, this is an example of "cool" software being presented to the market without any real consideration of visualization value. The principle of proportional ink provides a complete answer to any argument for utility, except in the limited case where a bar chart must be used but there are two independent variables to capture.

Month	Revenues
Jan	4,600
Feb	4,800
Mar	4,900
Apr	4,950
May	4,990
Jun	5,010

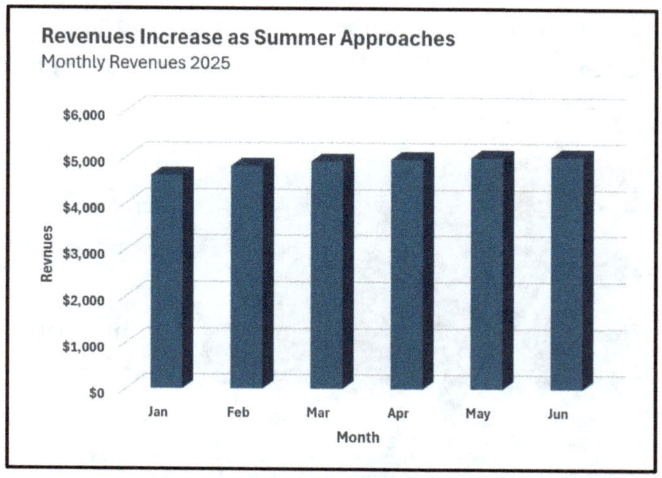

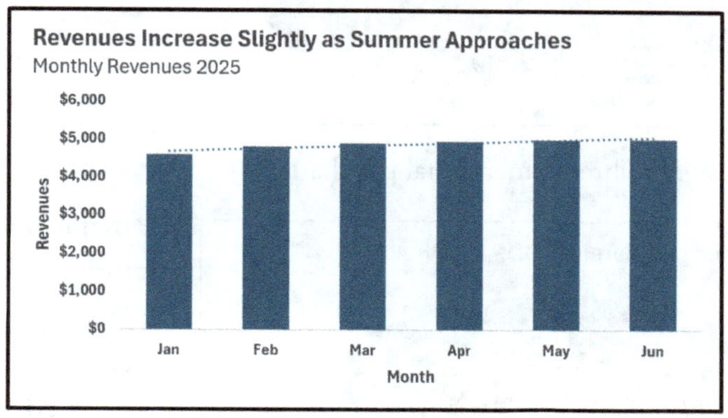

FIGURE 46: 3D and 2D revenue charts

[14] You might have found these: highlighting (iconic memory); text size (predators in the distance); italicization (*This is only partially true*); **bolding** (**iconic memory**); enclosure (the quote from Knaflic); isolation (predators in the distance); enclosure ("The important thing"); Underlining (Don't look at the footnote); color (predators in the distance).

Above you can see a tiny dataset representing business revenues, and first a column chart in 3D. Because the bars are spaced apart, we get a full extra side and an end cap on each bar—the difficulties of comparing areas rather than lengths are compounded now by the addition of the side and cap—the amount of ink consumed by each cap being almost identical for the last four months, regardless of the differences in values.

The addition of grid lines is an implicit admission that it will be harder to read values from this chart. But does it help? The correct position in which to read the value is the front edge of each bar at the top. But it's difficult to see, and the natural tendency is to use the back edge which is higher. Try to read the June revenue from the chart. It sure looks like it might be $4,700 or $4,800. It's $5,010.

Now look at the second chart, which uses simple columns. The best feature of this chart is the addition of the trendline, which shows the upward slope. The precise values in the last four months are still not easy to read, but we can see the trend, and the disappearance of the trend line just over the June column hints that the revenue has just exceeded $5,000. The 3D presentation added absolutely nothing for the viewer.

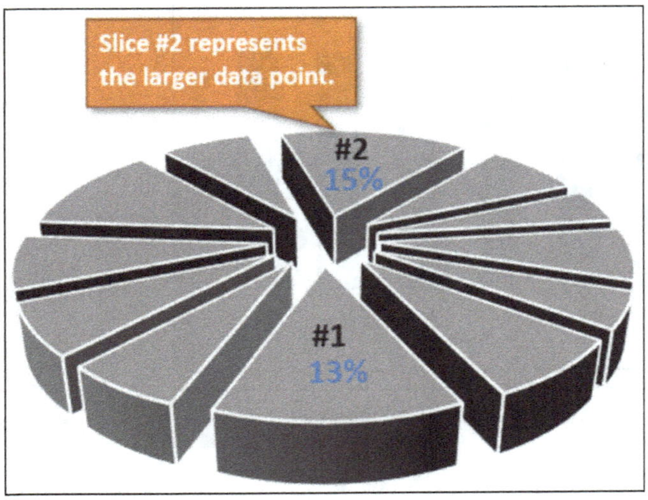

FIGURE 47: Three-dimensional pie chart

Three-dimensional pie charts are even more deceptive. The chart shown here is a compelling demonstration of the problem with perspective (Acampora, 2023). It's a great visualization to show here in that it conveys a single piece of disinformation very convincingly. The larger angle and therefore the larger percentage belongs to slice #2, but it is relegated to the back and therefore looks smaller.

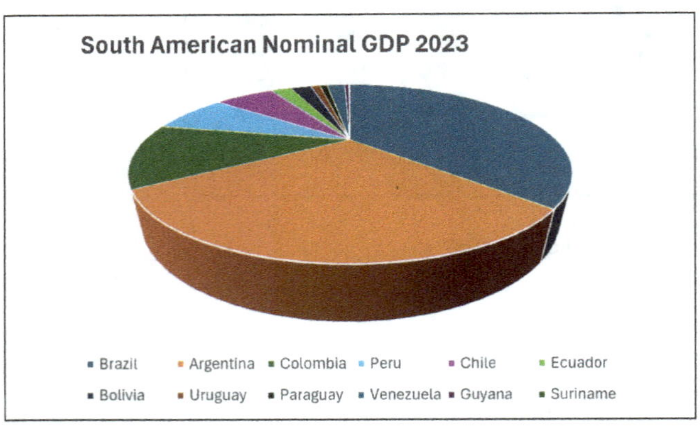

FIGURE 48: Multicolored 3D pie chart

Flattening the perspective can create further confusion. This chart is a three-dimensional depiction of nominal GDP (2023) for Latin American countries. Which country has the largest nominal GDP? Argentina, in orange, dominates the forefront, with all the other countries receding into the background. The effect of total dominance is highly enhanced by the addition of the rim, which serves no useful purpose whatsoever. You might be surprised to learn that Brazil's percentage of the continent's GDP, at 37%, is more than one-fifth larger than Argentina's at around 29%.

There is a serious conflict between the aims of software designers, who present us with increasingly clever and easy ways to produce graphics from our data, and data visualization professionals who repeatedly point out the tricks and traps to which viewers are exposed by the misuse of these depictions. Isometric drawing of charts (in which the two horizontal axes are drawn at 30° angles) are great for cityscapes and architects—they further confuse and contort three-dimensional charts which already have their own problems.

Gestalt principles

FIGURE 49: Dalmatian dog

Gestalt[15] *psychology*, developed in the early 20th century by three German scientists, describes the tendency of the human mind to perceive whole objects, rather than as their individual elements. Look at the box to the left. What do you see? A collection of dots, or a dalmatian?

The gestalt principles of perception develop out of this theory and attempt to categorize visual and auditory processes in response to stimuli (like visual data). There are six (some academics say seven) principles, often called "laws," of great interest to visualization designers.

The law of closure enabled you to see the Dalmatian dog, above. If we see a disparate group of elements, our mind tends to fill in the missing parts and perceive a familiar object. It's used in many well-known logos. Here are a few you may have seen.

FIGURE 50: Closure logos

[15] Many English speakers have difficulty pronouncing this word. It is depicted phonetically as gəˈSHtält, which is not much help for most people! The G is hard, like in "Good," not like in "Giraffe." The s is pronounced as sh, like in sheet. The a with an umlaut accent is pronounced like a double a, "aah." Imagine it written as "geshtaalt" and you will probably get it right.

FIGURE 51: Proximate stars

The law of proximity states that when we look at several objects, we tend to perceive those close together as being part of a group. Look at the picture to the left. Do you see twelve stars, or two triangular formations of stars?

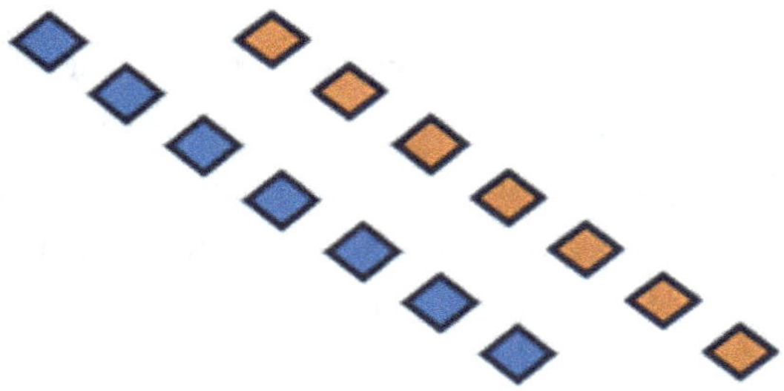

FIGURE 52: Rows of diamonds

The law of similarity explains why images with common features appear to be grouped together. When you look at this picture, do you see 14 diamonds or two rows of seven diamonds?

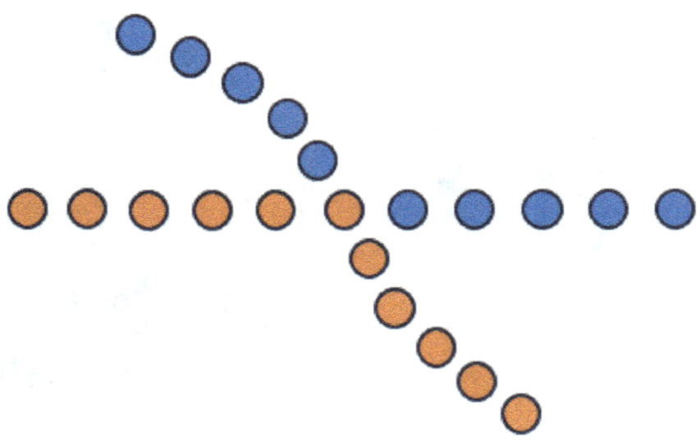

FIGURE 53: Continuous lines

The law of continuity explains that we tend to see things in smooth, logical paths. When you look at the diagram to the left, do you see a straight line running from left to right? Even though it changes color, this is a smoother pattern than the change of course of the like-colored symbols as they dip down at the half-way point.

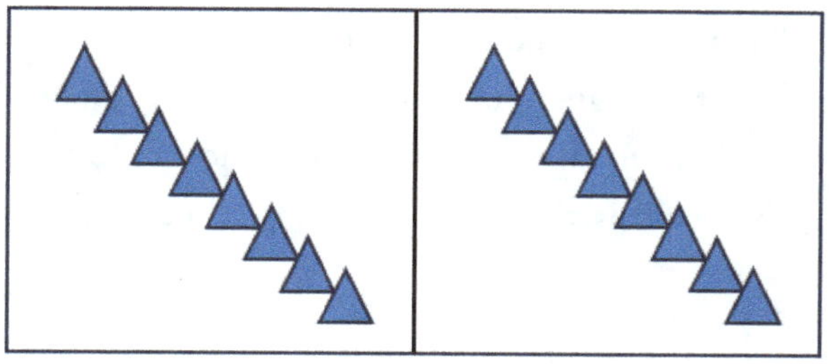

FIGURE 54: Common regions

The law of enclosure (also known as the *common region principle)* describes how we perceive a separation among groups of objects when they are separated by a barrier such as a frame. This principle is used by well-known social media sites such as Pinterest and Facebook. A simpler example is shown at left—all the symbols are identical, but they are perceived as two groups because each set has a box around them.

The *law of connection* is illustrated by this pair of figures, depicting the exact same data. When objects are connected, the relationship is more easily perceived.

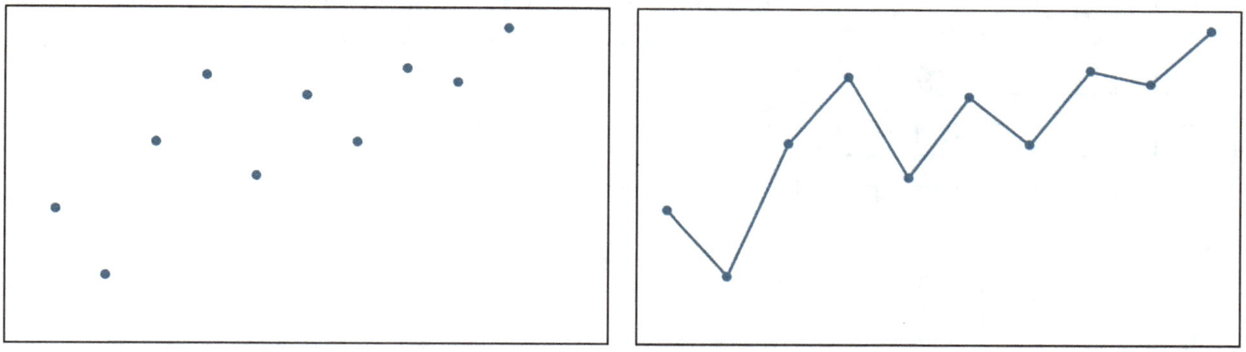

FIGURE 55: Connected dots

The above six law/principles are the most accepted by various authors. There are three more that sometimes make an appearance in discussions of gestalt perception.

FIGURE 56: Figure / Ground

The *figure/ground principle* deals with folks' instinctive tendency to perceive objects as either being in the background or foreground. Several factors can play into this: contrast (lighter objects tend to appear as figures, darker tend to fade into background); size (larger images look closer); and separation (when we see one object physically distant from all the others, we are more likely to perceive that object as the foreground feature). The famous artist MC Escher exploited this principle to create many of his "trick" drawings.

Is the drawing at the left one vase, or two faces? What did you see first?

FIGURE 57: Olympic Rings: a registered trademark of the International Olympic Committee

The *law of prägnanz* (a German word meaning "good figure") suggests that when confronted with a set of ambiguous or complex objects, the brain will simplify the interpretation. The Olympic rings symbol provides an example: this diagram is a complex set of partial circles and loops, but we see five interlocking rings.

FIGURE 58: Focal point

Finally, the *focal point principle* suggests that any object which stands out visually will have first claim on the viewer's attention. We saw this with the "YOU WILL READ THIS FIRST" illustration above; another example is in the picture to the left.

Clutter and simplification

Clutter is a well-studied psychological phenomenon, mostly in the context of people who retain or hoard vast quantities of useless objects in an untidy fashion. This precisely describes the problem with many charts too; the more unnecessary features or objects are placed in a chart, the harder it is for the viewer to process the information. You'll recall that *cognitive load* is used to describe the amount of work a human is being required to do using *working memory*.

There is a direct analogy in computing; if you ask your computer to run too many heavy programs at the same time, it will slow down, make mistakes, or even crash. Good visualization design asks the question of every piece of scaffolding and every *data object*, whether it is necessary and whether the manner of its depiction is making life easier, or more difficult, for the viewer.

A data object is a unit representing something which is counted or depicted. For example, a customer, product, transaction or service.

Considering clutter brings up the more general topic of simplification. As a general proposition, "less is more," but there are times when there is a quantity of information that must be on the visualization. This calls for the exercise of judgment. We can't make everything simple.

Alignment is critical. We simply should not make charts with elements that look haphazard or untidy. We should always ensure that pictorial elements line up vertically and horizontally, and give due consideration to text—should it be left-aligned, right-aligned, centered or justified? Fortunately design software allows these decisions to be tested at the stroke of a key or the click of a mouse. Gridlines and rulers are almost universally available to help tidy positioning of elements but should rarely be left in the final product.

Cole Knaflic, in her brilliant textbook *Storytelling with Data (2015)*, devotes just one paragraph to *diagonal components*. In sum, she says "don't." She says that diagonal elements look messy and are harder to read; she quotes a 2005 study by Wigdor and Balakrishnan which found that 45-degree rotated text was, on average, read 52% slower than horizontal text. This may overstate the case, as with time series sometimes it's necessary to have many dates on the Y axis and if they are full dates, they would take too much space if vertical. 45-degree test running upward left to right is still significantly easier to read than vertical text.[16]

Knaflic also makes a powerful case for more use of white space. Again summarizing, she says that we should "use more of it and don't be afraid." Silence can be powerful in a verbal presentation; white space can speak volumes in visual presentation.

We are going to borrow from Knaflic one more time in this chapter. She identifies six major steps to be used in de-cluttering charts.

1. Remove chart borders—there is no need for a frame (we don't always agree—and we use frames in this book).
2. Remove gridlines, or at least lighten them if the audience really needs them.
3. Remove data markers. For example, if you've joined the dots, there is no reason for the dots to remain. The line will tell the story.
4. Clean up axis labels—there is no need for trailing zeroes on money values (200.00), or for repetitive $ or other currency symbols. Reduce months and days to three-letter abbreviations, everyone knows what they mean.
5. Label data directly—don't make the viewer go looking for a key to know which line is which.
6. Leverage consistent color—where two lines are of different colors, label them with words in the same color.

Here is a chart showing marketing expenditure and sales volumes throughout the year. Follow the progression from Excel's base chart as we give the six treatments and add a few more.

[16] International Organization for Standardization (ISO) standard 9241-143 notes that vertical text produces the worst performance of all orientations.

2025 Monthly Spend and Sales		
Month	Marketing Spend ($'000)	Sales Revenue ($'000)
Jan	29	58.74
Feb	34	77.75
Mar	43	88
Apr	43	93.9
May	50	105.2
Jun	55	111.76
Jul	63	121.2
Aug	67	143.13
Sep	72	147.45
Oct	78	156.78
Nov	82	159.24
Dec	94	166.46

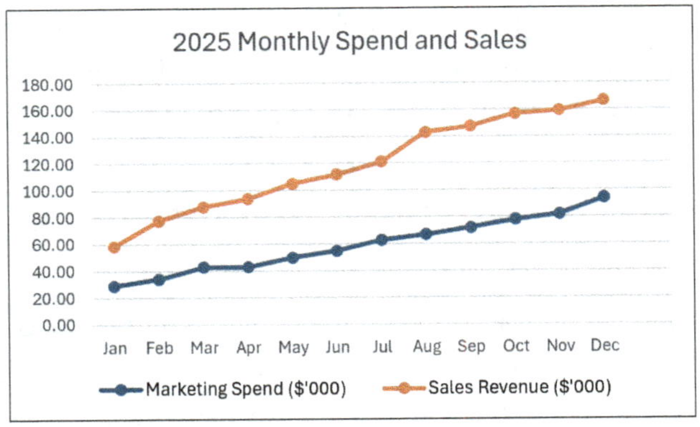

FIGURE 59: Marketing spend and sales revenue

Remove the border:

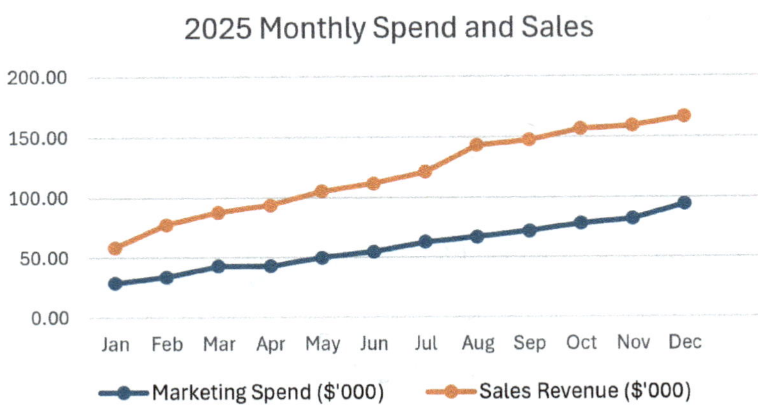

FIGURE 60: Marketing and sales II

Remove the gridlines:

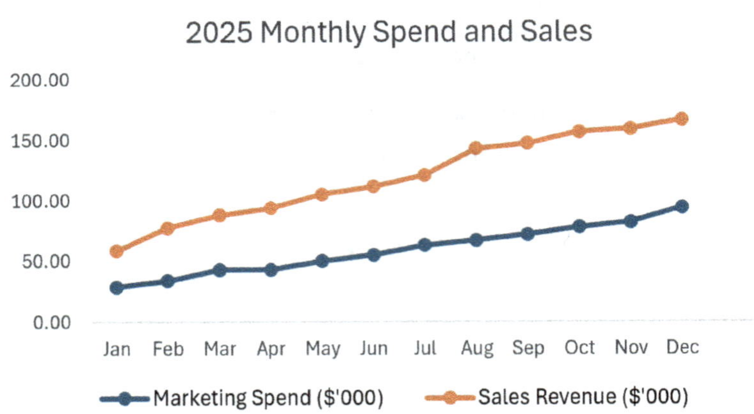

FIGURE 61: Marketing and sales III

Remove the data markers:

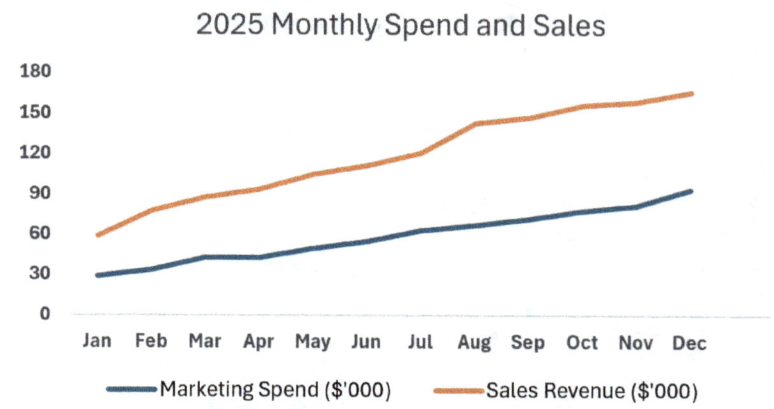

FIGURE 62: Marketing and sales IV

Add necessary axis label(s):

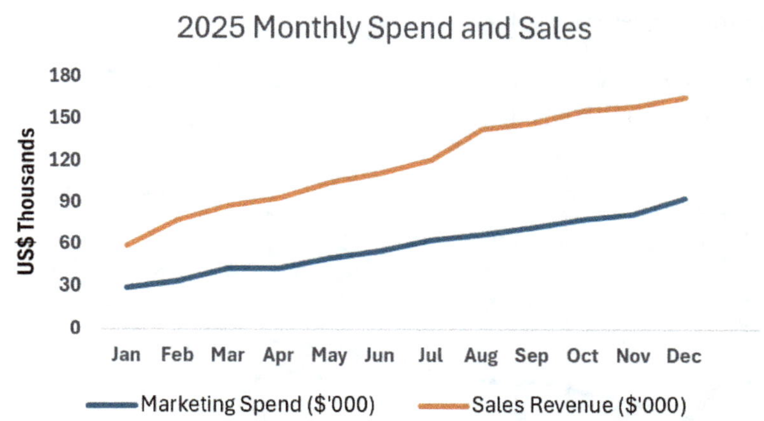

FIGURE 63: Marketing and sales V

Label data directly:

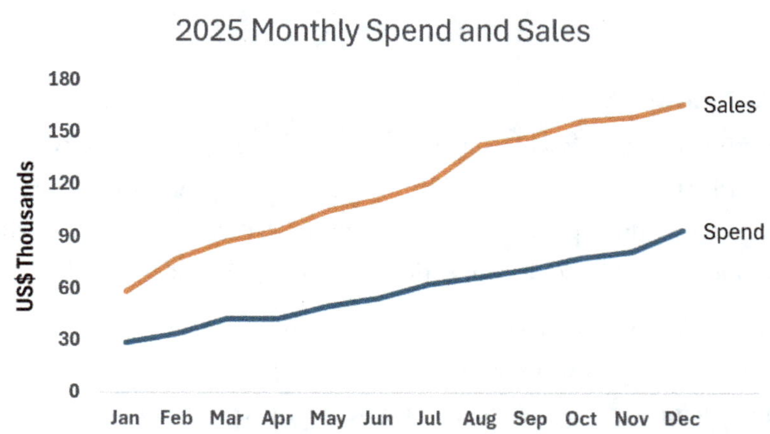

FIGURE 64: Marketing and sales VI

Change colors:

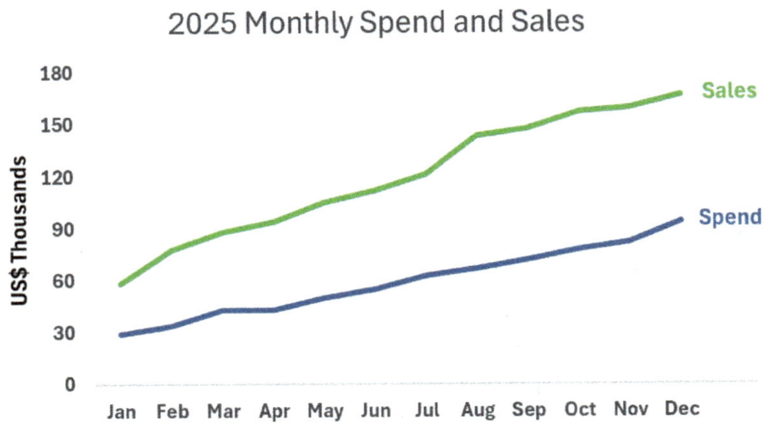

FIGURE 65: Marketing and sales VII

Add title and subtitle at top left, leverage colors:

FIGURE 66: Marketing and sales final

Color and accessibility

Audiences have pre-existing deep beliefs which are not supported by logic but by convention. Maps always have north at the top and south at the bottom, right? Do you have a GPS map in your car? Do you keep north at the top, or do you prefer the cardinal points to move around so that you are always driving up the map? Time almost always runs from left to right. Color conventions are among the most complex that you will encounter.

Color associations are not nearly as universal as you might believe, and there are even differences within culturally similar regions. In a map of world temperatures, most people would be comfortable with a choice of bright red for the highest temperature, and shades of blue for the colder climates. Such an association would not come so easily when mapping crime statistics or accident rates. Red might seem like the obvious color to emphasize a high crime rate in Canada, as it symbolizes danger (red alert); but in India it is symbolic of purity (many wedding dresses are red), while it points to luck and happiness for Chinese audiences. Even in western culture red can also symbolize love (red roses) or festivity (Santa's costume). Romanians don't like red; they associate it with communism and the abuses of the Russian government.

One might be forgiven for thinking that green would always represent nature, the environment, health, as it does in Brazil. It is the national color in Mexico. But in China, wearing a green hat (*戴绿帽子*, dài lǜ màozi) is a symbol of being a cuckold! English people are sometimes "green with envy," but Germans apparently turn yellow!

Surely yellow is OK, though? For most of the world it is viewed as a "warm color" associated with relaxation and happiness. For some Indonesians it is known as the "forbidden color" as it is a symbol of marital infidelity. In France it is associated with betrayal and deceit.

Color theory carefully defines several terms which are commonly used, often mistakenly.

- *Hue* is a pure color without the addition of any white or black. White, black and gray are NOT hues. The primary colors are blue, red and yellow; the secondary colors, which are a mixture of pairs of primary colors, are green, orange and purple. When a human perceives a color, hue is the starting point.
- *Shade* results from the addition of black to a pure color. The more black that is added, the greater the darkness of the starting hue.
- *Tint* is the opposite of shade; it results from the addition of white to a color.
- *Tone* is the only possible remaining combination; it results from the addition of gray to a hue, gray being a mixture of black and white.

This structure creates a powerful toolset for design of visualizations. Not only can one color be used to draw attention, but two can be used to distinguish key concepts, categories or trends. In addition, though, different shades or tints of the same color can be used to create a hierarchy, as we showed earlier in our discussion of choropleths and isopleths.

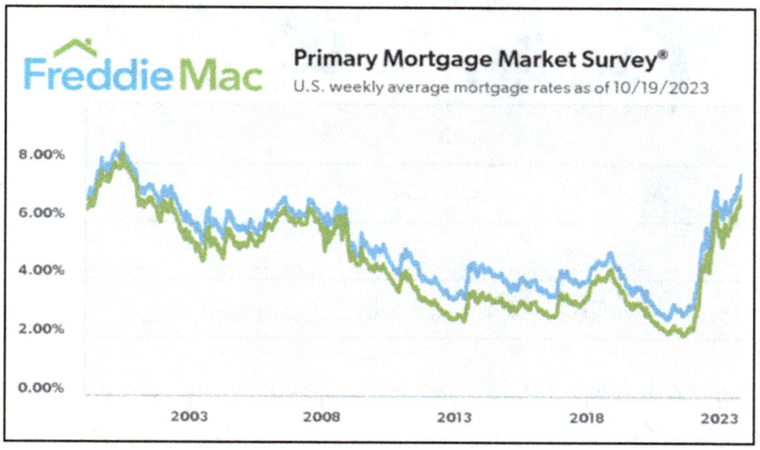

FIGURE 67: Freddie Mac survey

Nice one, Freddie Mac! There are only two time series to be shown, along with their relationship (correlation) which is visually very close. Why did they choose these two colors? These are the colors of the company logo.

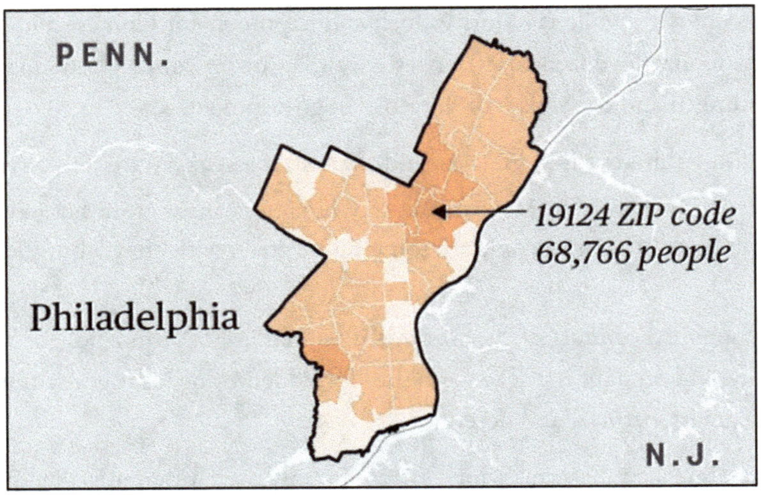

FIGURE 68: Philadelphia population density

This map, published by NBC News with a somewhat unnecessary key, demonstrates the use of tints of a single color (orange) to establish a hierarchy. The meaning of the various tints is intuitive: the lighter the tint, the less dense the population.

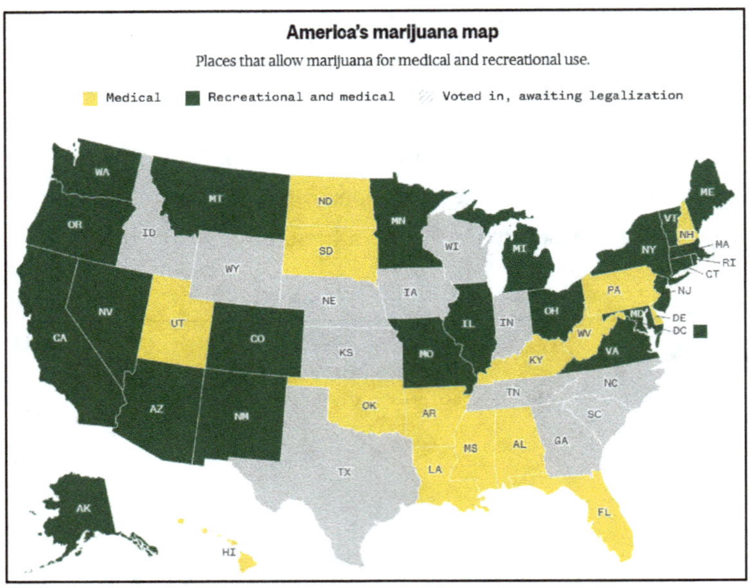

FIGURE 69: American's marijuana map

America's marijuana map (Wu, Silva, & Chiwaya, 2024) asks the viewer to do a little more work. The key is necessary to decode the information, but it's not complex. We intuitively understood the association of green with marijuana, but the orange color for medical use was not quite so intuitive; however, some varieties of marijuana plants have orange flowers. Color was an effective way to distinguish the status of weed among the various states; the viewer can also assess the extent of permission and any geographical clustering.

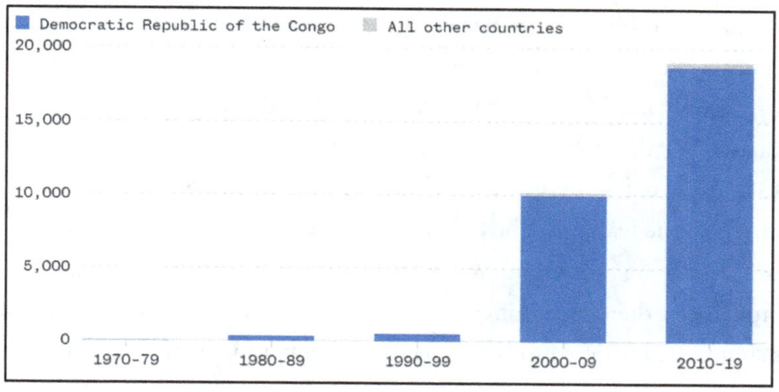

FIGURE 70: Monkeypox in the DRC (Bendix & Carman, 2022)

This chart, from which we've omitted the title and notes, illustrates the point that inappropriate use of color can mask the important information instead of highlighting it. When you look at this histogram, what do you see? Most people will perceive that over the decades there has been an alarming rise in the number of cases of monkeypox in the Democratic Republic of Congo. But that was not the point at all. The article surrounding the graphic is about how almost all cases of monkeypox occur in that one country; look again at the gray element for "All other countries" in the key and try to find it in the chart. It's there, but barely perceptible. We'd say this chart fails to convey the key insight.

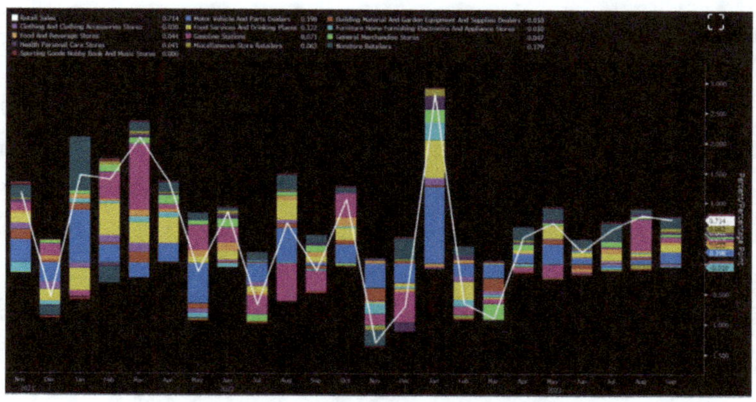

FIGURE 71: Yahoo Finance chart

We certainly don't love this chart, sourced from Yahoo Finance. It demonstrates a disastrous over-use of color, to no effect whatsoever. If you have 10 minutes to waste, spend them looking at this chart and studying the legends; try to determine what information is being conveyed (we failed).

There are other important considerations with color.

- Be attentive to the difficulties of colorblindness. Most often an inherited problem, the commonest form (though not the only one) is an inability to distinguish shades of red from green. About 1 in 200 women suffer from this, but 16x as many men. The gene which commonly causes it is carried on the X chromosome;

women who are not color blind can however carry the gene and pass it on to their children. Wait! You may be thinking. Can people drive if they are color blind? The answer for the UK, Canada and the USA is yes. Color blind drivers only need to know the *position* of the red and green lights; so long as they can see which one is illuminated, they don't need to see the different colors.[17] This is an important lesson for the visual designer; it's OK to use red and green if you have to, but there must be some other attribute which enables viewers to distinguish the features. The better practice is to avoid using red and green for contrasts.

- Color choices can be inappropriate for a profession or business. Some environments demand an unemotional approach; there is significant scholarship around the idea that foreign exchange and stock trading charts should be restricted to black, white and gray to increase trader focus.

Typography and labeling

The words used on a chart are a key part of the message. Effective typography enhances communication, draws out insights, and makes charts more readable. Bad choices can obscure the message and add confusion.

It's important that text is easy to read (you've seen quite a few examples above where it's clearly not). Sans serif fonts like Arial and Helvetica are good choices. Serifs are tiny lines attached to the ends of letters—sans serif means that they are absent ("sans" is French for "without").

T	T
Garamond, a serif font	Montserrat, a sans serif font

Consistent use of fonts keeps a professional appearance; don't be tempted to mix up fonts for artistic effect. If you are using several charts in a presentation, keep your fonts and positioning of written elements consistent. A text hierarchy helps readers work through the information—large, bold titles contain the main message, a subtitle can provide additional context, then axis labels and legends make clear what's being shown. Add data labels, *if necessary*, but don't overwhelm the chart with too many. Sparing use of color, especially if it is consistently used in some text and in other chart elements, can really help to focus attention on the most important message.

---

[17] Waxing anecdotal for a moment; many years ago, the second author was training a new pilot on visual approaches to the main runway at Dublin airport. Most major airports have a system of lights called a "visual approach slope indicator." There are variations on it, but the essence is that there are four lights. When the airplane is positioned at the correct altitude for the distance from the runway, two are green and two are red. Three reds, you are too low—three greens, you are too high. The main danger with four greens is that you won't get to the ground in time to land, but with four reds you might hit the ground before the runway. The student was told to "read the lights" to assess his approach—then confessed that they all appeared to be the same color. Those old jokes about blind pilots are not completely fantastical!

Sometimes it's necessary to add explanatory text or callouts. Keep in mind that these require the viewer to do extra work and strive to keep them simple. Too much text and you have lost the point of visualization.

Accessibility, just as in color choices, is important. Keep in mind that visually impaired viewers may be viewing your chart—use fonts and text sizes that will not deny them the message you are conveying. Canadian law has rapidly developing requirements for digital content (web and mobile applications) to be accessible according to various published standards which are beyond our scope, but we'd encourage you, if you are producing digital content, to become familiar with the requirements in your jurisdiction and particularly to learn about providing "Alt Text" for all visualizations which you produce. Most graphics software makes this a simple process.

A Checklist for Common Errors

Here is a checklist which you can use to review your work as you create visualizations for your data. The answer which you want to achieve (Y or N) is given after each question. If you answer the opposite, your visualization needs more work.

1. Do I have a clear title which captures my main point? Y
2. Does my subtitle convey additional information or context?
3. Are my text sizes hierarchical? Y
4. Have I overloaded the chart with too much information? N
5. Have I truncated any axes, or used any inconsistent intervals? N
6. Have I used appropriate baselines for numerical axes? Y
7. Have I used an appropriate chart type for my data? Y
8. Have I displayed data in an appropriate order?
9. Have I used 3D effects unnecessarily? N
10. Is all my text legible? Y
11. Have I used sans-serif fonts? Y
12. Have I used the same font for all my text? Y
13. Have I considered color-blindness? Y
14. Have I provided alternative text for digital content? Y
15. Have I used too many colors? N
16. Have I used color effectively to highlight the main takeaway(s)? Y
17. Is there any clutter in my chart? N
18. If I have used gridlines, are they necessary and muted? Y
19. Have I removed any unnecessary tick marks?
20. Have I omitted any necessary context such as axis labels or units? N
21. Have I gone for style at the expense of substance? N
22. Does my chart faithfully represent the complete dataset (no cherry-picking)? Y
23. Have I carefully reviewed my chart for all the above? Y
24. Does my chart clearly underline my key message? Y

Practical Application: The Evergreen Checklist

You may be interested to learn how data visualization exercises are graded in academic courses. Broadly, marking typically follows a version of the above list, but we draw our attention to one very popular resource, the Data Visualization Checklist, published by Stephanie Evergreen and Ann K Emery. We would breach copyright rules by reproducing it here, but we encourage you to visit Dr Stephanie's website https://stephanieevergreen.com/data-visualization-checklist/ and register, which will result in her sending you a pdf copy. The site also includes an automated tool for rating your own visualizations using her criteria.

Conclusion

Good visualization design goes far beyond turning numbers into pictures. Deliberate choices following the principles we have outlined in this chapter will help you produce effective charts which assist your viewer in grasping your message with minimal work.

However, we're not finished. Well-designed visualizations support the construction of a storyline to engage and fascinate the audience. In the next chapter, we'll move into the world of data storytelling—starting with data, revealing insights, persuading them of your credibility and moving them to act.

Multiple Choice Questions for Chapter 3

1. The von Restorff effect, which causes people to remember words or imagery that stands out in a picture better than they remember background information, is an example of:
    a. data manipulation.
    b. attention manipulation.
    c. image manipulation
2. The gestalt principles of closure and enclosure are two words for the same concept.
    a. True.
    b. False.
3. The gestalt law of *pragnanz* suggests that:
    a. any object which stands out visually will have first claim on the viewer's attention.
    b. when confronted with a set of complex objects, the brain will simplify them.
    c. humans instinctively perceive objects as either in background or foreground.
    d. Humans instinctively close gaps to convert incomplete figures into complete.

IBM

4. The IBM logo exploits the gestalt principle of
    a. enclosure.
    b. proximity.
    c. closure.
5. Three-dimensional pie charts are deceptive because
    a. the addition of the third dimension further complicates the difficulty of perceiving relative sizes of the slices.
    b. humans perceive objects in the background as larger than they actually are.
    c. moving one slice outwards to emphasize its importance restricts the viewer's ability to understand the whole environment.
    d. comparisons of most populations with a food item are inappropriate.
6. 3D charts
    a. Can make it difficult to see relative sizes.
    b. Don't display trends.
    c. Are not as attractive as 2D charts.
    d. Need gridlines to ensure that viewers correctly read values.
7. ___ is a pure color without the addition of black, white or gray.
    a. Shade
    b. Tint
    c. Tone
    d. Hue

8. To create 50 shades of gray, the mixer must add differing amounts of ____ to the original gray:
   a. gray
   b. white
   c. black
   d. another color
9. The commonest form of colorblindness is
   a. the inability to distinguish red from blue.
   b. the inability to distinguish green from blue.
   c. the inability to distinguish red from green.
10. On a population density map, a lighter tint of color would intuitively indicate
    a. lower density
    b. higher density
    c. neutral density
11. The audience must be carefully considered when selecting colors for a visualization because
    a. different colors have different cultural significance to some nationalities or religions.
    b. different colors indicate different mathematical treatments of the same data.
    c. different colors mean different things to 8% of men and 0.5% of women.
    d. different colors have different effects on long-term memory

4. STORYTELLING

Introduction to Storytelling

Data by themselves, unless they are extremely simple, can be overwhelming, difficult to understand, and harder to interpret. Data don't persuade people to do things—stories built around them do. Whether in business, education or even at home, you can use *data storytelling* to convert raw numbers into a reason to act.

The concept of *data storytelling* is often expressed as *Storytelling with Data*, but we have avoided that phrase as it is the title of the best book ever written on the subject, by Cole Knaflic; it is also the name of her organization's website. Cole is a former Googler (Google employee) who now specializes in training businesspeople in the data visual arts. Her book is beyond excellent—one of the clearest, best expositions we have ever seen on any subject, and we highly recommend it to anyone with an interest in this subject. We will only scratch the surface of what she describes and explains in her work.

Storytelling involves the use of communication to engage human cognition. As we mentioned in the preface to this book, storytelling is deeply rooted in human cultures as a way of conveying knowledge, teaching values, shaping perspectives and proposing or guiding actions.

There is no better example of the importance of understanding the audience and environment than in the timeless history of Indigenous storytelling in Canada. Perhaps because of its importance to preserving cultural values, it has always sought to blend history, local points of view, and the insights of the gathered community. Quite intentionally, Indigenous storytellers strive to direct the attention of the audience to the most important themes and lessons being conveyed (CIKS Anaadi, 2024). Selective emphasis, paying attention to the needs and preferences of the listener, is precisely the best methodology to use in complex business communication.

In business contexts, numbers alone are often insufficient to convey the intended message. The audience must be engaged. Effective storytelling structures numerical information in a way that provides insights, reduces ambiguity and helps decision-makers. A good storyteller organizes data and presents it in a way that it becomes actionable knowledge.

Earlier, we wrote of cognitive load—the amount of work a human mind is required to do, to absorb the important points from information provided. Visual storytelling, the creation of visualizations to draw out the key points, lessens cognitive load and improves the viewer's uptake of the essential information. It enables you, the author, to determine what message the viewer receives. In the simplest cases a table of data will achieve this end. Here is an example.

TABLE 11: World Cup top scorers

#	Name	Country	Goals
1	Klose	Germany	16
2	Ronaldo	Brazil	15
3	Müller	Germany	14
4	Fontaine	France	13
	Messi	Argentina	13
6	Pelé	Brazil	12
	Mbappé	France	12

Which player has scored the most goals, ever, in the FIFA World Cup? It is difficult to think of a visualization that would answer this question more clearly than the table.

The answer is Klose, of Germany. Not the first name that comes to mind, but with 16 lifetime goals he is clearly at the top of the list. Most of the other all time great players who might have come to mind are shown on the list, dispelling the notion that Ronaldo, Messi or Pele might occupy the top spot.

Sometimes, you just don't need a picture.

However, whenever you want your audience to understand and remember insights from data, they need to connect with it at a deeper level. When the brain sees data, it needs to work to process it; when it has to deal with a story, cognitive and emotional pathways are fired up, making the message easier to remember and the associated argument more persuasive. Emotional connection makes the audience more likely to act on the information they receive, while a well-crafted visualization of data can produce a single, compelling insight from hundreds or thousands of data points.

Foundations of Data Storytelling

Before you start to build your story, it's useful to run through a structured list of considerations. You will consider:

- Who is the audience and what do they need?
- What is the environment?
- What medium will you use?
- What cultural factors may affect the audience's perception and interpretation of the story?
- Why are you telling the story?
- The elements of storytelling—context, characters, conflict and resolution.
- How will the story progress (we'll explain how to use The Hero's Journey for this, below)
- How will you simplify the data without losing insight?

We will work through each of these in turn.

Who is the audience and what do they need?

This is the single most important preparatory question.

As you plan visualizations to present data, it is very tempting to focus first on what you know, then secondly on how you present it. Neither of these is the right place to start! Before doing anything else, devote serious thought to the intended audience.

Imagine that you are called into your boss's office to explain poor quarterly sales by your team. You arrive with half a dozen pages of complex spreadsheets showing individual performances, market trends, costs, products and sales by department. Your boss looks at them uncomprehendingly and asks you to explain.

Now imagine, instead, that you prepare an analysis of the key trends in the data and prepare just a couple of charts that pinpoint where the problem is, then a third page or slide which suggests a solution. Which of these approaches do you think has provided your boss with what they need? And which do you think will generate the decision that you would like to see made?

Understanding the audience's expertise, role, and needs allows you to create an *audience-centric* presentation which will fulfill their requirements. Are they financial executives, who can quickly absorb data from a few key ratios, or are they volunteers at a charity, with little financial background? Are they students, who want to learn from your work, or teachers who are evaluating your presentation ability?

Having defined your audience, consider what they need and what use they are going to make of your presentation. They may simply want education or knowledge, but in a business setting there is typically a decision to be made. Put yourself in their place, and ask yourself what they would want to know, and what would persuade them to the result that you want.

What you produce will differ greatly, depending on the answers to these questions.

What is the environment?

Environment refers to the setting, context, and constraints in which your presentation will be delivered. Will you do it in person, or by emailing a report or dashboard? Will you be taking questions from the audience at a large conference, or pitching to half a dozen executives in a boardroom? Or demonstrating your abilities to a class of fellow students?

Timing needs very careful consideration. An *elevator pitch* is a short, sharp, getting-right-to-the-point explanation (the phrase is based on the idea that you meet the decision-maker in an elevator, and have only the travel time to their floor to get your point across). A financial pitch to a funder or investor might take 20 minutes, while a lengthier explanation to a class could be one or two hours. Remember that audience attention spans are very limited; if you are going to be presenting for an hour or two, you will need to use techniques such as questions, exercises or case studies, to regain their attention regularly.

What medium will you use?

The way your presentation and visualizations should be structured will depend on the format. A large conference screen will allow for incorporating video content, bulleted lists (within reason), and pictures; a dashboard for a smartphone can have only one page and too much content will make it too small. A printed report can be several pages long, with multiple visualizations and explanatory text.

Most importantly, business reports should be succinct but capable of deeper exploration; they can be more than one page. Educational presentations (typically PowerPoint presentations) may be many pages long.

What cultural factors may affect the audience's perception and interpretation of the story?

Our combined experience of over 40 years of practicing law and two decades of teaching confirms the essential three-part interpretation of every communication:

- what is intended to be conveyed by the communicator,
- the content of the communication, and
- what is "heard" or understood by the receiver. Paying attention to the fact that these are three different messages pays huge dividends when it comes to communication media.

The cultural differences in how messages are received is a vast subject and indeed the subject of whole books (For example Dignen, 2011). Three principal distinctions are made in scholarly literature.

Some cultures are regarded as *high-context,* such as Japan, China, and the Middle East. *Low-context* refers to places like Canada and the U.S.A. High-context refers to the conveying of meaning through cues and relationships, while low-context indicates that more straightforward, explicit and structured communication is expected.

Hierarchical communication is valued in some cultures, where data stories are presented in the context of there being senior folks who make the decisions. Flat communication is more appropriate in other places, where data are presented then groups discuss and decide.

The third distinction is between relationship-based and science-based credibility. In a relationship-based culture, such as in the Middle East, a great deal of reliance may be placed on the individual delivering the message, meaning that personal stories and opinions are more important. Science-based credibility flows from audiences placing more trust in the data themselves and qualified analysis of it, which is typical of audiences in North America and most of Europe.

Consideration of cultural contexts also requires careful attention to symbolic meanings of visual elements and common phrases. We discussed color earlier; icons and emojis are increasingly used in presentations; beware of different meanings in different communities. Do you like the thumbs up symbol, so commonly used to express strong agreement in Canada? In Iran, Afghanistan and some parts of Africa it is the equivalent of the middle finger gesture in North America. What about the OK symbol made with the thumb and index finger in Canada? In Brazil it is an obscene gesture, while in France it can be interpreted as "zero," or an indication that a person is worthless.

The use of metaphors, particularly from sports, is best avoided with international audiences. Baseball metaphors are widely used in North America—getting to home base, scoring a home run, touching base. Except for Japan and some Caribbean nations, most of the rest of the world does not follow baseball. Full court press from basketball, and Hail Mary pass from American football are also meaningless in many other nations. If you are Canadian or American, do you know what a "sticky wicket" is? (It comes from cricket and refers to ground which is difficult to play on).

Humans in the Western hemisphere generally read printed pages left to right, and top to bottom, in a "Z pattern" This narrative will need to change if the intended audience uses a different script such as Arabic or Farsi, which are read from right to left). This is not the case for visualizations, however. Remember what we learned earlier about pre-attentive attributes; on first seeing a chart, the human viewer will be attracted to its most prominent features, then search the rest for information to further interpret the initial impression. If there is key information which is supported by the detail, place it in the top left corner, or at least in the center of the top row. Larger font sizes and lack of complexity help to draw attention to the most important information. In Power BI "cards" are extremely useful for presenting single key data; bar and column charts are easier to read than pie and donut charts, and 3D visualizations are often disastrous.

Defining your "why"

All the above considerations lead toward this exercise—before creating a presentation, you need to know what you want the audience to take away or do and what need you are addressing. For example, if you are asking a Board of Directors to approve a large investment in a new product, you must ensure that they have enough data to evaluate the proposal, be confident that they are fully informed, and are motivated to approve the project. You need to inform them about the consequences of acting or not acting. Having a clear understanding of "why" will help to sharpen the narrative—anything that doesn't help the story can be discarded, every visualization should add to the principal message, and the takeaway at the end should be clear and explicit.

Principal elements of storytelling

In this section, we'll outline the four principal elements of every story. Then, we will explain in more detail how to structure a story.

- The *context* comes first—it conveys the background information which is needed to understand the data that are to follow.
- The *characters* in the story can be people, data or objects—they players, things or concepts that feature in the story.
- The *conflict* is the issue that the story is about to address. Conflict is a slightly misleading title, because the conflict may be a problem, but it may also be an opportunity. Declining sales, rising fraud, high staff turnover, global warming—these are all negative conflicts. Equally, though, the conflict could be the increase in population of digital currency, growing demand for alternatives to milk, or the closing down of a competitor.
- The *resolution* is what you want your audience to take away from your presentation. It encompasses the solution, changes, or actions you want. It might be increased budget for your department, a signature on a contract, purchasing a new machine, changing marketing strategy, or reducing carbon footprint. The possibilities are endless.

How will the story progress?

In 1949, Joseph Campbell's seminal book *The Hero with a Thousand Faces* was published by the New World Library. It has proved almost timeless and gone through several editions, the latest in 2018. It is widely used in analysis of literature, film, theatre and other arts, and is regarded as the foundational structure for storytelling in business. The Hero's journey, referred to by Campbell as a *monomyth*, is a common patter in stories where a hero leaves the ordinary world for an adventure, faces trials, gains knowledge, and returns to the original world with new wisdom and power. You will quickly recognize the close alignment with the elements of storytelling that we outlined in the previous section.

In the following table we identify the stages of the hero's journey, give their equivalent in data storytelling, and take you through a theoretical presentation to the Board of a video rentals company a few years ago.

TABLE 12: The Hero's Journey

Hero's Journey	Data Storytelling	Presentation
Ordinary World	Things as they are today	We have a recognized national business with over 400 stores renting DVDs to retail customers.
Call to Adventure	The problem, insight or opportunity	Improvements in internet technology have made it possible for people to stream movies to their home computers without visiting a store. Netflix subscriptions grew by over 1200% in the last year.
Crossing the Threshold	Drawing new insights from the data	75% of homes in Canada have at least one computer with internet access. Streaming sign-ups across all providers tripled in just one year, growing from 10% of households to 35% of households in the last year.
Trials & Tribulations	Identifying trends, patterns or roadblocks	Over the last year, our sales have declined 30%. In the next year we may lose a further 50% of sales volume.
Transformation	Summarizing the most significant points	If our sales continue to decline at this rate, we will have net losses of $2.5 billion in the current financial year and severe cash flow problems within two years. Incorporating streaming into our business model is our best way forward.
Return with the Boon	Stressing the decision or action which must be taken based on the data	We must leverage our brand and develop an online platform to rent movies via streaming within the next six months. We must stop renewing leases and commence a rapid shutdown of all our physical stores.

Whatever the type of presentation, it should have a logical start, middle and end—and they should be clear. Then, the various slides, pages or elements should start with the basic information that the audience needs and progress through logic or layers to a conclusion—which should be fully supported by the journey they have just undertaken with you as their guide. If you want an action to be taken based on your analysis, state clear what that action is. If your goal was to convince the audience of something, make sure they understand what you want them to believe.

How will you simplify the story without losing insight?

Your goal in making a presentation is to simplify complex data, without oversimplifying to the extent that insights are lost. Here are the basic rules that will help you.

- Try to define the ONE key thing that you want the audience to remember. "We will go bankrupt if we don't pivot to streaming immediately."
- Less is more—don't try to include everything you know. Stick to the data that support your key message.
- Now try to summarize your message in one sentence with two commas. Using the above story, it might be "Streaming is growing, DVD rentals are going the way of the dinosaurs, we must pivot to streaming immediately."
- Revisit the audience needs and ensure your presentation addresses them. The CEO needs to know that we are about to go out of business if we don't pivot. The finance team needs to know how much investment is required to pivot. The bank needs to know how much we want to borrow, and how we will repay it.
- Don't use jargon or technical terms, unless they are necessary. Not "We can hit a home run by pivoting to streaming," but "An immediate pivot to streaming will keep us in business."
- Consider your audience's need for deeper data. Technical or finance teams, for example, may appreciate the inclusion of appendices with comprehensive data, which will not be shown in a verbal presentation but may be reviewed later.

After creating the first draft of your presentation, it's time to edit it. Ensure that each visualization serves a purpose.

Each visualization will ideally make one point, and only one point.

- For each visualization, slide, or page, determine what point you want to make. Does the visualization seek to document something that is already known, or demonstrate a discovery that was unknown without it? Does the visualization make that point?
- Next, is it correctly positioned in the presentation? This may refer to position on page in a dashboard, but page position in a PowerPoint presentation, for example.
- Is there anything missing from the visualization? If there is a scale, is it clear what the units are? If there are lines, is it clear what each line represents? If color is strategically used, is it clear what the colors signify? Use all the knowledge you gained in the earlier chapters to use Gestalt principles, avoid clutter and distractions, and if you have used a chart, make sure it is the right type.

- "Less is more" also applies to the scope of visualizations. At all costs try to avoid scroll bars and hidden data, and wherever possible get all the essential information for each point into a single visualization.

Conclusion: Data Storytelling, Art and Science

In this chapter, we've seen that data storytelling is both an art and a science. You need scientific analysis of your data to draw the insights, but an eye for visual appeal to make your slides, pages or dashboards visually compelling. Your job is to make sure that your storytelling skills close the gap between raw data and informed decision-making.

Through your whole career, indeed your whole life, you will continually be presenting data, arguments, and requests for decisions to the people around you. Presenting is not just something you do in class or the boardroom—you do it every day with your friends and family. Refining your storytelling skills and ability to persuade using data can have an extraordinary impact not just on your professional career but also on your whole life.

You have an opportunity to guide your audience to a result every time you present data with a view to an action. You must avoid overwhelming them with too many numbers. You can make data storytelling part of your personal competitive advantage. Will you guide your audience towards the result you want, or baffle them with too much data?

Multiple Choice Questions for Chapter 4

1. Cognitive load is:
    a. the amount of work a human mind is required to do.
    b. the amount of information a human can store in iconic memory.
    c. The amount of information a human can store in short-term memory.
2. The all-time leading goal scorer in the FIFA World Cup is:
    a. Ronaldo
    b. Messi
    c. Pele
    d. Klose
3. Which of the following has only one page?
    a. PowerPoint presentation.
    b. Power BI Report.
    c. Dashboard.
4. Western audiences tend to read a page in a pattern signified by which letter?
    a. X.
    b. Y.
    c. Z.
    d. L.
5. What is the primary goal of data storytelling?
    a. To display all available data to the audience
    b. To entertain an audience with creative visuals
    c. To present data in a narrative format that informs or persuades
    d. To make data analysis more difficult to replicate
6. What is the first thing to consider when planning a data story?
    a. The type of software to be used
    b. The dataset's size
    c. The needs of the audience
    d. The design of the charts
7. What does the 'conflict' element in a data story refer to?
    a. A disagreement between team members
    b. A plot twist that entertains the audience
    c. A problem or opportunity that the story addresses
    d. The gap between visual and textual content
8. Which visualization method is often clearer than pictures for showing exact values, according to the chapter?
    a. Pie chart
    b. Bar graph
    c. Table
    d. Donut chart

9. Why is emotional connection important in data storytelling?
    a. It makes the data more humorous
    b. It reduces the need for visuals
    c. It helps the audience remember and act on the information
    d. It adds complexity to the presentation
10. What is a key danger of oversimplifying data in storytelling?
    a. The charts become too colorful
    b. The data might be misrepresented
    c. The audience gets bored
    d. The resolution becomes unclear
11. According to the Hero's Journey model, what stage involves identifying trends and roadblocks?
    a. Ordinary World
    b. Call to Adventure
    c. Trials and Tribulations
    d. Return with the Boon
12. What type of culture places more emphasis on the relationship with the communicator than on the data itself?
    a. Low-context, science-based
    b. High-context, science-based
    c. Relationship-based
    d. Flat communication cultures
13. What is a best practice for individual data visualizations?
    a. Each should include multiple unrelated insights
    b. Each should contain as many colors as possible
    c. Each should aim to make one clear point
    d. Each should avoid using any titles

5. MAKING EFFECTIVE PRESENTATIONS

Planning Your Presentation

During or at the conclusion of your course, you might be required to participate in one or more team presentations. This chapter is not an exhaustive review of presentation technique, but a presentation of some of the guidance we have found most helpful for students in preparing.

Almost all the Work is in the Preparation

Most of the work happens, like in negotiation, before anything is said publicly. With the right materials prepared, the key to success is practice, practice and more practice—accompanied by seeking feedback from anyone and everyone prepared to listen to you.

What does Your Audience need from You?

Before even starting to create slides, a PowerPoint presentation or a practice script, think carefully about the audience. You are going to build a relationship with them, and it must be one in which they are the beneficiaries of your work. Make sure that you address the needs of the audience and follow any specific instructions about length or content.

This consideration can be further broken down into a series of important questions:

- Who is the audience?
- What do they think they want?
- What do they really need?
- What do I want to tell them?

The last three questions are not entirely divorced from each other; they require careful interweaving. If the audience has a strong opinion as to what they want, there is a need for their expectations to be met, or they will not listen to any amount of reasoning. If you determine that they really need something different, the two need to be dovetailed. Then, if you still want to tell them something which is not in their requirements, you need to figure out how to weave that into the presentation without compromising your achievements on the first two.

As a practical example, consider a doctor who has diagnosed a terminal illness in a patient. The patient arrives for their consultation and asks the question "What is wrong with me?" That is the requirement. But the doctor knows the patient needs to understand that they are going to die within a few months. That is what the doctor knows they truly need. The doctor also wants to tell the patient, however, that they will not be particularly sick during the next few months and full advantage should be taken of that time. While this is a dramatic example, it encapsulates the three questions and can be applied to many business situations.

How will you Engage the Audience?

Writing in the Harvard Business Review in 2014, American communications expert Nick Morgan stunningly highlighted a concept which is given scant notice by many writers on data and decisions. Decisions, he pointed out, aren't made based on data, but on emotion. In the unconscious mind, where most desires are manifested and most decisions are made, emotions rule. No amount of conscious reasoning, especially based on data or statistics, will overcome an emotional bias. Therefore, the skilled speaker will evoke the emotional content then address the need for change based on statistics. Here's a dramatic demonstration.

In British Columbia, motorcycles make up about 3% of insured vehicles (and they are largely absent from the roads in the winter months. Yet, motorcycles are involved in approximately 10% of road deaths (British Columbia Government, 2022). That's a relatively mild part of the statistics. In 2019, 73 people died on our roads; 31 of them, or over 42%, were motorcyclists (RoadSafetyBC, 2020).

My (Paul) 17-year-old son is a petrol head. On turning 16, he wanted nothing more than to buy a motorcycle. I didn't want him to have the motorcycle and refused to buy it for him. He took a part-time job to save up for it. As a family, we argued and argued. I presented the above statistics many times. My son believed he would be the exception to the statistics, an invulnerable survivor. Nothing worked. I even bought him his own car so that he could look forward to being independent on the roads at 17. Nothing changed.

Halfway through his 16th year, I read Nick Morgan's article and adopted a different approach. Starting our umpteenth family discussion of "the bike," I started off by evoking a picture of my son going to my funeral. Sad, we agreed, but part of life's normal course. Then I painted a verbal picture of his parents attending his funeral and asked him how he thought we would feel. Then I called up the statistics again. That day, he agreed never to ride a motorcycle on our roads. You might shake your head and wonder if it could really be so simple. But it was. Our son is still alive and healthy, and there is no motorbike.

Consider your Title Carefully

It is likely that your title page will spend more time on the screen than any other slide. The title should be impactful, invoke curiosity in the audience and be the first step in communication of your professionalism. When we prepared a presentation on this topic, we postulated four possible titles:

Getting Top Marks for Your Presentation

Presentations—Some Guidelines

How to Speak to the Class

Presentations—Written and Verbal

We trust you have quickly concluded that while all four titles are truthful and to the point, only the first one passes the acid test of invoking increased interest from the audience.

What Does the Audience See and Hear?

TABLE 13: Elements of audience communication

Rank	Element	Aspects	Detail
1	Audio	Delivery & engagement	Anthropologist Ray Birdwhistell, who invented the concept of *kinesics*," demonstrated that no more than 30-35% of communication is achieved through the words used (McDermott, 1980).
2	Non-verbal	Body language & appearance	Sascha Schneider and colleagues (2022) demonstrated the significant increase in learning outcomes in educational settings when presenters use appropriate gestures and facial expressions.
3	Visual content	Text. Pictures, & charts	Pictures are important. Visual information is processed more efficiently than text – some estimates are up to 60,000 times faster. This is known as the *picture superiority effect*. But it is the combination of pictures with presentation that is truly effective. If they are poorly integrated, the *split attention effect* can overwhelm the viewer.
4	Other	Environment, prior knowledge, & emotions	Prior knowledge reduces cognitive load, while the environment affects motivation and openness to new information. Positive emotions influence perception, attention, and memory. However, these three aspects largely operate in background as amplifiers or reducers of the primary channels.

You may have heard of the 7-38-55 rule. It's based on the work of American psychologist Albert Mehrabian, who summarized his findings in his 1971 book *Silent Messages*. Mehrabian's work focused only on feelings and attitudes, not business or classroom communication, However, it is frequently cited as proof that words spoken are only used as 7% of the interpretation of messages, while 38% depends on vocal elements and 55% on non-verbal cues. This is not helpful in considering how to deliver a slideshow to a boardroom or classroom. The table above summarizes the extensive field of academic study of presentation delivery and audience attention/retention.

There are two important techniques which will substantially affect the audience's engagement.

- If you have a great visualization which makes a good point, place the slide on the screen and stay quiet. Resist the temptation to say anything at all. For several seconds, let the audience absorb the visualization—maybe someone will say something, maybe not. Everyone will feel uncomfortable, but almost everyone will get the message.
- Once you have given the audience time to absorb the message, and especially if the slide has a lot of data or complexity, turn off the projector and just speak to the point. If the audience can give you all its attention,

instead of trying to absorb a visualization at the same time, you will be more effective in delivering your verbal message.

Even more important—the impressions that are gained of you as a professional are formed *in less than ten seconds*. From the moment you appear at the front of your room, your demeanor, dress, grooming and stage presence are being keenly studied by the audience.

You Never get a Second Chance to make a First Impression

FIGURE 72: Dress for the context

That's not to say that there is one way, or only one way, to dress or groom for any given situation. The young professional to the left has made choices about her appearance geared to the occasion. On the left, she was to address a room full of programming staff at Google. On the right, the audience was a group of trial lawyers.

What is universal, however, is that audiences will pay very limited attention to a speaker whose presentation is marred by an appearance inappropriate to the context, severely distracting personal habits, or other distractions. Common "appearance" mistakes vary with the context:

- In live demonstrations (particularly with a view to employment), it is a mistake to dress for your current "level." Dress for the level you are seeking to achieve. If you are a student, but want to join an accounting firm, dress professionally so that the interviewer can picture you in the role.
- In virtual appearances, presenters often fail to fit the content to the frame.
- In Zoom and Microsoft Teams calls, presenters often fail to consider the background. If you work in a messy office, or present from your basement, Zoom is full of tools to modify the background so that the audience doesn't have to see your environment!

First impressions, once formed, are very hard to change. But how long do they take to form? You have less than 30 seconds before your audience crystallizes their beliefs about you:

- *Less than one second* for an initial impression of trustworthiness and attractiveness (Willis & Todorov, 2006);
- *Less than 15 seconds* to form an assessment of competence and confidence (Ambady & Rosenthal, 1993);
- *A minute or less* before they've reached a conclusion on expertise and credibility (Schmälzle et al., 2025).

Before you speak, if possible, try to find quiet time for a "re-set." Treat yourself to a minute or two of deep breathing, relaxing, and reassuring yourself.

When you start to speak, be professional and appropriate from the first moment. Don't start with "Aaah," or "So." Smile, look the audience in the eye, and greet them. You are under no obligation to make a sound in the first few seconds. You can build anticipation by smiling, looking around the room, and making eye contact with a few people.

If you have dignitaries in the audience, they should be acknowledged early. If it's a team presentation, introduce the team.

Then do this. Always.

- Say what you are going to talk about.
- Talk about it.
- Wrap up by summarizing what you have said.[18]

First impressions also apply to each individual slide in a PowerPoint presentation. We have spent considerable time in earlier chapters discussing visualizations—there is one more issue. The *title space* on each slide is valuable, and almost always the first thing that people see or read. Don't squander it! A heading is good, but an actionable heading is better. Compare these two headings in a presentation to the Sales Manager who may decide on your promotion soon:

ANNUAL SALES

Or

ANNUAL SALES ARE UP 50%

75% of People Suffer from Glossophobia

That is, the fear of public speaking. The good news is that 92% of those people report that their fears are reduced by having a well-developed presentation.

Record Yourself, and Listen

Practice your presentation, then listen to yourself. Try to pick out any distracting habits or other problems before someone else does. The commonest mistakes are:

- An affectation, or bad habit, of punctuating speech with "aaah," "aaam," or catch-phrases like "you know," "you know what I mean," "and stuff," etc. You can teach yourself not to make any of these mistakes.
- Speaking too quickly. Less is more. Make what you say important. Deliver it slowly so that people have time to absorb what you are saying.

---

[18] The sentiment is attributed to Dale Carnegie who expressed it thus: "Tell the audience what you're going to say, say it; then tell them what you've said."

- Reading Out a PowerPoint presentation. People read more quickly than you can speak. If you put up a wordy PowerPoint, most of the audience will either read it and disregard what you are saying (or reading) or continue to listen to you and ignore the slide. Let your slides contain key points, not explanations or scripts. A good rule of thumb is that one slide should not contain more than 25 words; but less than that is even more powerful.
- Thinking that you need to be speaking all the time. After making a key point, or going to a new slide with a powerful, clear message, pause. Count silently in your head for at least three seconds. Allow the point to sink in.

Body Language Speaks Louder than Words

You can have great content but still disenchant your audience by exhibiting poor body language. There are whole books on this subject, but the big five no-nos are:

- Slouching
- Failing to make eye contact with members of the audience
- Exaggerated gesturing
- Using the podium as a crutch (life preserver)
- Covering the mouth with a hand

On the other hand, open body language buys audience engagement. Practice

- Open hands
- Open face
- Relaxed shoulders
- Natural movement

Practice in front of a mirror, then record yourself using your phone or computer. When you think you have it, practice in front of family or friends. Ask them to be brutally honest and tell them what to look for.

Visual Aids—Less is More

We've already pointed out that audiences don't take much in from the visual presentation. This becomes even more of a problem when

- there is too much text on the screen.
- the slides are changed too quickly.
- there are "clever" visual effects which distract from the data.

Content is Still Important

All the preparation you can do, all the skills you can muster, will still not save you if the content of your presentation is poor, as determined by the audience. Imagine that you attend a presentation where a highly skilled performer argues that the earth is flat. Would you come away convinced, or would you only have experienced an interesting demonstration of nonsense?

Stories, especially personal experiences, are a great way to hold or re-kindle audience attention. Make sure they are relevant, interesting, and above all short. Make sure you can tell them in two minutes or less.

Presenting as a Team

When you present as part of a team, there are some rules which will greatly enhance your performance.

- Determine who are your strongest two speakers and place them in the first and last speaking positions.
- Allow less confident speakers room to grow, don't cut their time too short.
- Make sure every team member has a clearly defined role.
- Practice individually, and together.
- Have the first speaker introduce the team; then, have each speaker hand off to the next by name.
- Determine in advance who will respond to questions, or how you will decide that in the moment (perhaps depending on content)
- When one presenter has answered a question, never allow another presenter to disagree or undermine them. Gentle supplementary comments may be helpful, but it's important they don't make the first responder look inadequate.
- At all times, display respect and good manners towards both the audience and fellow presenters.

One Last Statistic

In a typical presentation, 90% of the audience have checked out after 10 minutes (Gallo, 2024). It's not hard to observe this, from the hand movements usually involved in looking at the mobile phone. If your presentation is longer than this, develop some audience engagement techniques to bring them back—"show of hands" type questions, audience exercises, asking the audience questions—there is a long list, and the limits are of the imagination of the presenter. Questions do not have to be related to the subject of your presentation (What is the second largest city in Manitoba?[19]).

Conclusion

The dashboard, which we've already mentioned several times, is the ultimate test of your ability to convey a well-supported message succinctly and clearly. In the next chapter, we'll look at how to do just that.

---

[19] Brandon, known as the "Wheat City." At the end of 2024 it had a population of approximately 50,000.

Multiple Choice Questions for Chapter 5

1. What percentage of audience attention is given to visual content such as text, pictures and charts?
    a. Approximately 35%
    b. Approximately 7%
    c. Approximately 55%
2. An audience's first impression of a speaker is formed in the first:
    a. 5 minutes.
    b. minute.
    c. 10 seconds.
3. How often do you get a second chance to make a first impression?
    a. Often.
    b. Rarely.
    c. Never.
4. 90% of the audience in a typical presentation lose attention after how long, if it is not re-kindled?
    a. half an hour.
    b. 20 minutes.
    c. 10 minutes.
5. What is the purpose of the question about the second largest city in Manitoba used as an example in this chapter?
    a. To engage the audience's love of trivia.
    b. To add Canadian content to a presentation.
    c. To re-engage the audience as their attention drifts away from the presenter.
6. Which of the following is an important habit to develop when learning presentation skills?
    a. Using gestures to provide natural emphasis on key points.
    b. Keeping still, to remain authoritative.
    c. Speaking in a monotonous voice, to avoid creating distractions.
    d. Avoiding eye contact with the audience, so that you don't get nervous.
7. The most useful visualizations to accompany verbal presentation are
    a. Data-rich.
    b. Complex and technical.
    c. Filled with additional information not presented by the speaker.
    d. Minimal and impactful.

6. DASHBOARDS

Dashboard Theory and Technique

> A dashboard is a visual display of the most important information needed to achieve one or more objectives, consolidated and arranged on a single screen, so the information can be monitored at a glance (Treacy, n.d.).

Mynda Treacy's words encapsulate the critical difference between a dashboard any other form of report using visualizations—it is all on one page, and the "pictures" must address the main points to be conveyed.

> A large share of ink on a graphic should present data-information, the ink changing as the data change. Data-ink is the non-erasable core of a graphic, the non-redundant ink arranged in response to variation in the numbers represented (Tufte, 1983).

You may be amused to know that Edward R Tufte, the data visualization expert who wrote these words, was affectionately nicknamed "ET." Although he wrote these words 40 years ago, they are as valid today as they were then. Tufte was sometimes referred to as a minimalist. He stressed that visualizations should be simple; they cannot be overloaded with too much information. If visualizations are too small, too crowded, or contain too many elements or colors, the story is lost. Even having the colors too bright or garish can reduce visual effectiveness.

Here are some basic planning elements which will assist in creating an effective dashboard.

Think about the audience

Who will see the dashboard? How familiar are they with the subject, or the data being addressed? What questions are they likely to have? Will their questions be answered on the dashboard, or will they have a need to drill down? The exact same data may need to be presented very differently to different viewers; imagine for example showing performance statistics for a car engine to (a) a high school class in its first engineering course, and (b) the design engineers of a Formula 1 team.

Think about the medium

Will your dashboard be delivered by email to an Excel user? On paper in a briefing package? On a big screen at a conference? If it's to be a .pdf print-out, users won't be able to drill down or use slicers. If they will download it and use it in Excel, they will have much more flexibility (and so will you).

Think about the result

Don't be afraid to use pencil and paper (and an eraser!) or your favorite graphic design program (like Paint or even AutoCAD). When you know what you want to convey, think about the visualizations that will do the job, how big they will need to be (including in relation to each other), and what headings and labels they might need. None of this is written in stone, it will evolve as you progress—but it's important to have an idea where you're going, before you set off.

Make the dashboard tell the story

Recall what we learned earlier about the Z pattern of reading (for Western audiences). Group visualizations that belong together must be in the same area—don't force the reader to jump around the page. Two visualizations which demonstrate "before and after" effects are best placed in the same row, with before to the left of after. Visualizations which compare two of something should be side-by-side, with the same scales so that the first glance gives the correct impression.

Choose your visualizations wisely

Although there is a bewildering variety of possible chart types (and new ones are being introduced continually), there are right and wrong selections for different demonstrations. Most often the old standard displays are the most effective.

- Bar charts are usually the most effective for comparing values across categories.
- Line charts are usually the most effective for a time series, though bar charts can also work.
- Map visualizations are increasingly more sophisticated and can be very effective for showing regional disparities.
- Pie charts are almost always a bad choice.

Building a Dashboard in Excel

Excel, in this as in other areas, has a vast and rich array of tools and functions for creating great visualizations. It would be too much, here, to catalog them all; certainly, though, we wouldn't discourage experimentation and exploration. Here, we will work through the building of one dashboard and demonstrate most of the key techniques necessary to get started.

There is no one correct way, eschewing all others, to do anything in Excel. This applies as much to dashboards as to any other procedure.

Some basic decisions

It will speed progress and secure success if the base data and Excel tools chosen as the source for any dashboard are optimized.

- The data should be formatted into a table or tables, with appropriate headers.
- There will be a separate worksheet for the dashboard itself, then one sheet for each pivot table, from which the dashboard charts will be generated.
- The more complex the dashboard, the more important it is to make use of naming—for Tables, Ranges, Worksheets, Pivot Tables and so on. This makes it much easier to resume work after a pause, and easier to identify sources when modifications are needed.
- We can build a dashboard without any coding. Excel has sufficient tools and functions to make this possible.

The exercise: Precipitation in Vancouver

It's early 2024. We have just been elected to the rotating presidency of an English vacation club; the 2024 destination is Vancouver. Our members are sunseekers (they are tired of the English rain) and want to plan the outing with the minimum chance of rain and the maximum chance of staying dry. When should they travel?

To display our research, we are going to build an Excel dashboard to analyze the "truth" about how much it rains (and snows) in Vancouver. We have raw data for 2020–22, and some new data for 2023 which we will add later. Please download the file Precipitation Shell.xlsx. You will see it has three sheets already populated and named: Dashboard, Precip, and 2023. The first of these has only the heading, this is where we will build an interactive dashboard.

Click on the tab "Precip" to see the raw data. This is a list of months (since January 2020) and the total precipitation for each, in millimeters.

1. Convert the data to a table. Click anywhere in it, then Ctrl+T, Excel will confirm the range ($A$1:$B$37) and be sure to check-mark the box for *My table has headers.* Click OK. Using the box near the top left of the sheet, underneath File, name the Table "Precipitation."
2. Click anywhere on the table. Still on the Table Design ribbon, click on *Summarize with PivotTable.* The table Precipitation is to be used, if necessary, select *New Worksheet* for the location. Click OK. A new sheet will appear, right-click on the tab to rename it "AllDataPivot." Click and drag the worksheet (on its tab) to the right-hand side of the existing tabs.

It's tempting to use Excel charts directly to build a dashboard. However, using intermediary pivot tables gives us a lot more interactivity. Here is a key difference. Excel charts update automatically when the underlying data are changed or updated. Pivot tables and pivot charts do not. They need to be refreshed.

---

3. Click in the "to build a report" area to the left to bring up the PivotTable Fields. Select Month; Excel will automatically summarize by year. Press Ctrl+Z to remove the summarization. Now select Total, which will place "Sum of Total" in the Values area.
4. Click on the *PivotTableAnalyze* tab and select *PivotChart.* Select the Clustered Column Chart and OK; the chart will look like this:

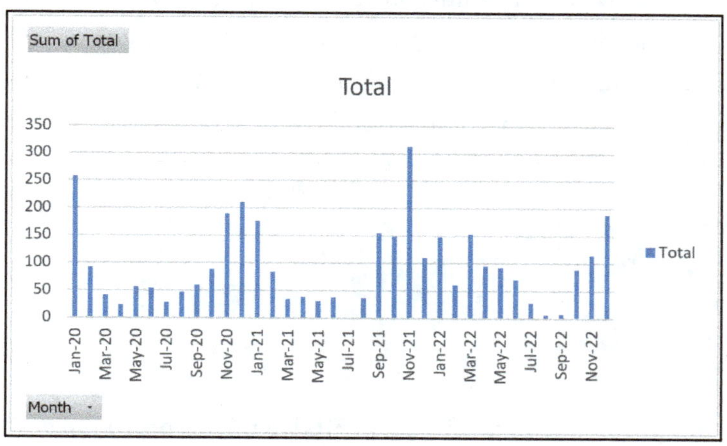

FIGURE 73: Precipitation pivot chart

Right-click on the "Sum of Total" button in the top right, then select *Hide all Field Buttons on Chart.* Next right-click on the "Total" legend on the right, and press *Delete* to remove it. Double-click on the header ("Total") and change it to "Monthly Precipitation." Click outside the chart, then right-click on the new title, select *Font*, and edit the size to 12 and the style to bold. Click OK, then click and drag the title to the top left of the chart. Click anywhere in the chart to bring up the editing buttons; select the + button and use the "Chart Elements" menu: uncheck gridlines. Go back to the + sign and hover on "Axis Titles." Click the right-arrow and use the fill boxes to select only a vertical axis title. Go back to the chart, double-click on "Axis Title" and change it to "mm." Click out of the chart, then right-click on the "mm" and change the font size to 9. Make it bold. The bars are too thin. Right-click on any bar, choose *Format Data Point* and re-set the gap to 90%. The bars will fatten accordingly.

You will note that Excel doesn't display the name of every month. It doesn't have room to do this, but when we transfer it to the dashboard, we will re-size it and there will be enough space for all months to be labelled.

5. We can either Cut and Paste (Ctrl+X, Ctrl+V) or Copy and Paste (Ctrl+C, Ctrl+V) to create a duplicate on the Dashboard. Do either of these, and paste the chart with the top left corner at the top of cell A23. Hold down the Alt key, then click in the chart and click and drag to re-size it until it covers columns A-K and is 10 rows high. Holding the Alt key causes the boundaries to lock, or snap, onto the gridlines of the cells.

Excel is always guessing what you might want or intend, and it isn't always right. Possibly, when you re-size the chart on the dashboard, it will insert "Quarter" analysis. To remove this, click in the chart and uncheck "Quarter" in the fields list.

We are going to need four pivot tables in total. The next instruction is a time-saver to create new pivot worksheets quickly.

6. Go back to the AllDataPivot worksheet, hold down Ctrl, click on the tab and drag it to the right. A second sheet will appear—rename it "WettestPivot." Later, we will do this again to create additional pivot sheets. In this sheet, click on the Monthly Precipitation chart and press *Delete* to remove it. Uncheck Month and Table in the PivotTable Fields area, check them again, and uncheck Quarters and Years. You will now have a total of sums by month.

TABLE 14: Precipitation

Row Labels	Sum of Total
⊞Nov	615.5
⊞Jan	579.6
⊞Dec	507.3
⊞Oct	324.6
⊞Feb	234.6
⊞Mar	227.8
⊞Sep	221.2
⊞May	178.3
⊞Jun	160.1
⊞Apr	155.4
⊞Aug	89.6
⊞Jul	55.1
Grand Total	3349.1

We want the months ordered from largest to smallest; right-click on any value in the Sum of Total column, select *Sort*, and *Largest to Smallest.* Click on the down arrow in the Row Labels header, select *Value Filters*, and *Top Ten…* In the dialog box change the 10 to a 6 and *OK.*

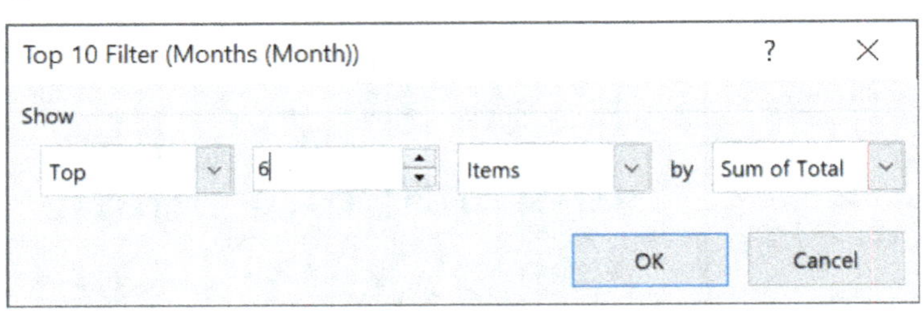

FIGURE 74: Top 10 filter

Click on the *PivotTableAnalyze* tab, select PivotChart, and choose the Clustered Column Chart again. Use the techniques learned above to make formatting changes to the chart, with the title "Average Wettest Six Months." Click on any column to select them all, then use the color palette on the Home Tab, Font group, to change the colors to gray.

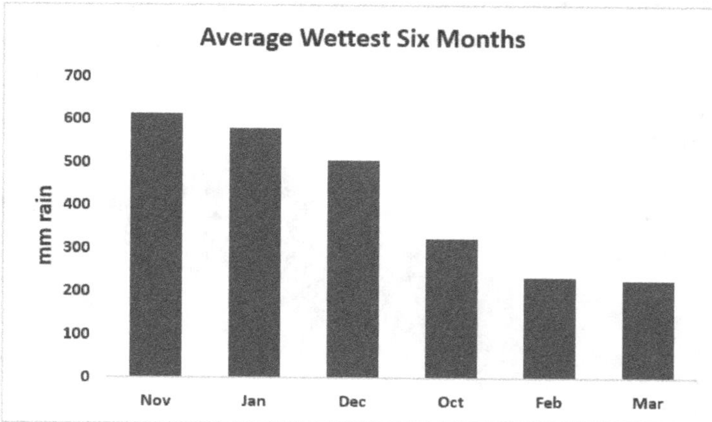

FIGURE 75: Average wettest six months

Copy or move this chart, as above, to cell D3 on the dashboard, and re-size it until it is four columns wide and 10 high.

On copying, some formatting changes may occur. For example, the title may wrap onto two lines, or the vertical scale may change. Use options on the Home tab to change font sizes, and Format Axis to re-establish the scale as 0-700, with increments of 100.

7. Go back to the WettestPivot worksheet. Use all the techniques above to create a similar chart for the Average Driest Six Months. Color all the bars in the same grey, but then click twice on the driest two months and change their color to green. This will draw attention to them as the best months to visit. Copy this graph to the dashboard, positioning it immediately to the right of the Wettest chart. You will have to make some logical changes such as ordering lowest to highest and selecting the Bottom 6 months.

We have a perception problem now. It looks as though September (in the dry frame) has more rain than November (the wettest month, on average). There are two different ranges in the vertical scales. We need to convert the scale in the driest box.

8. Right-click among the numbers on the vertical axis, select *Format Axis,* then reset the bounds to 0 and 700, to match the wettest chart. Fix any other formatting problems that arise after copying. Use standard editing features like font size and bolding to ensure consistency among your tiles.

All being well, your dashboard will now look like this:

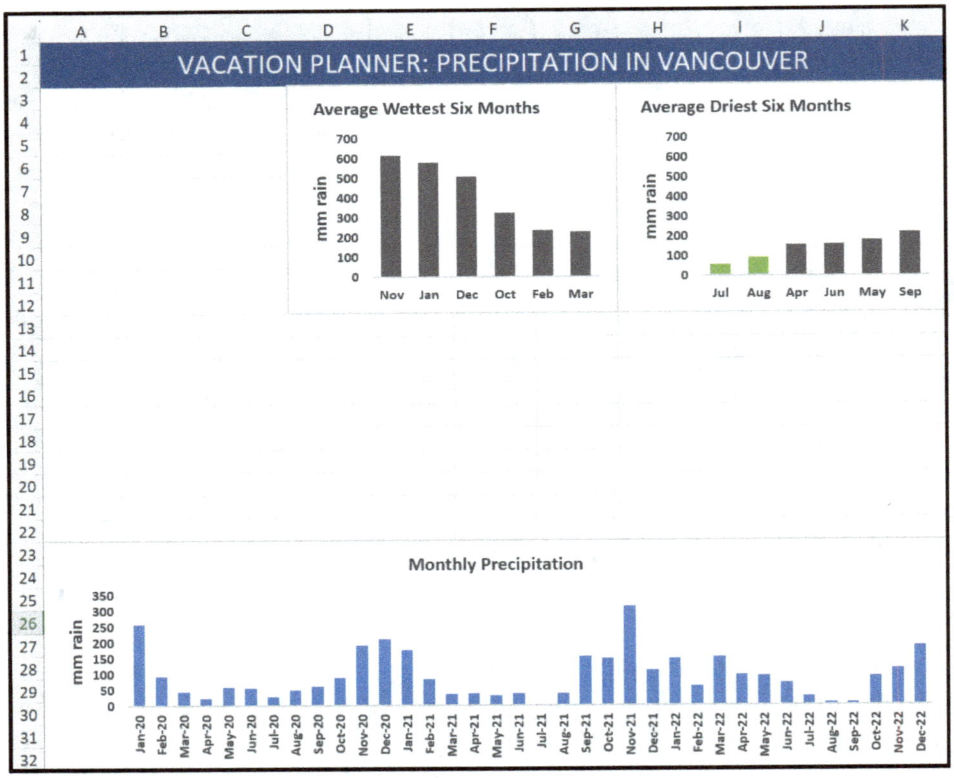

FIGURE 76: Precipitation tiles

We think that our members might be interested in the longer-term trend; they might be wondering whether Vancouver should be postponed to a later year. We'll create a line chart to determine the overall trend.

Use the AllDataPivot to create a copy and name it LongTermPivot. Select and *Delete* the chart, unselect all the fields then re-select Total and Years. From the *PivotTableAnalyze* tab create a line chart and clean it up using the techniques learned above. Copy it to the Dashboard, position it at cell D12 and re-size it so that it fills the gap down to the "Precipitation by Month" chart. Oh no! We forgot to put a trendline on the original chart. No worries, we can add it on the dashboard in the same way as we would on the original chart.

This brings up an important consideration. The charts placed on the dashboard can be edited and formatted using the same tools as on their original versions. Editing the copies on the dashboard does not change the originals; and if the originals are deleted, those on the dashboard will remain. They address the source data, not the source designs.

Now we are going to make the dashboard interactive by adding a Timeline and a Slicer.

9. On the dashboard, click in any one of the charts, select the *PivotChart Analyze* tab, then from the *Filter* group select *Insert Timeline.* Check the *Month* box. Position and resize the timeline to the left of the Wettest Months chart.

10. Click in any chart, again, and from the PivotChart Analyze tab select *Insert Slicer.* Select "Years" as the type, move the slicer to fill the remaining space at the left of the chart, and right-click on the symbol, select *Slicer Settings* and remove the header. Check the box for *Hide items with no data.* Re-size and re-position the slicer in the last empty space, at cell A13.

If you select a year or years in the slicer, you will see that it presently affects only one chart.

11. To connect it to all the charts, right-click on any year in the slicer, select *Report Connections* and fill in the boxes for each Pivot Chart. Do the same for the timeline. Selections in the timeline and slicer will now affect all the pivot charts.

In the slicer, if any years are unselected and you wish to select all, click in the top year and drag down through the others.

The dashboard should now look like this:

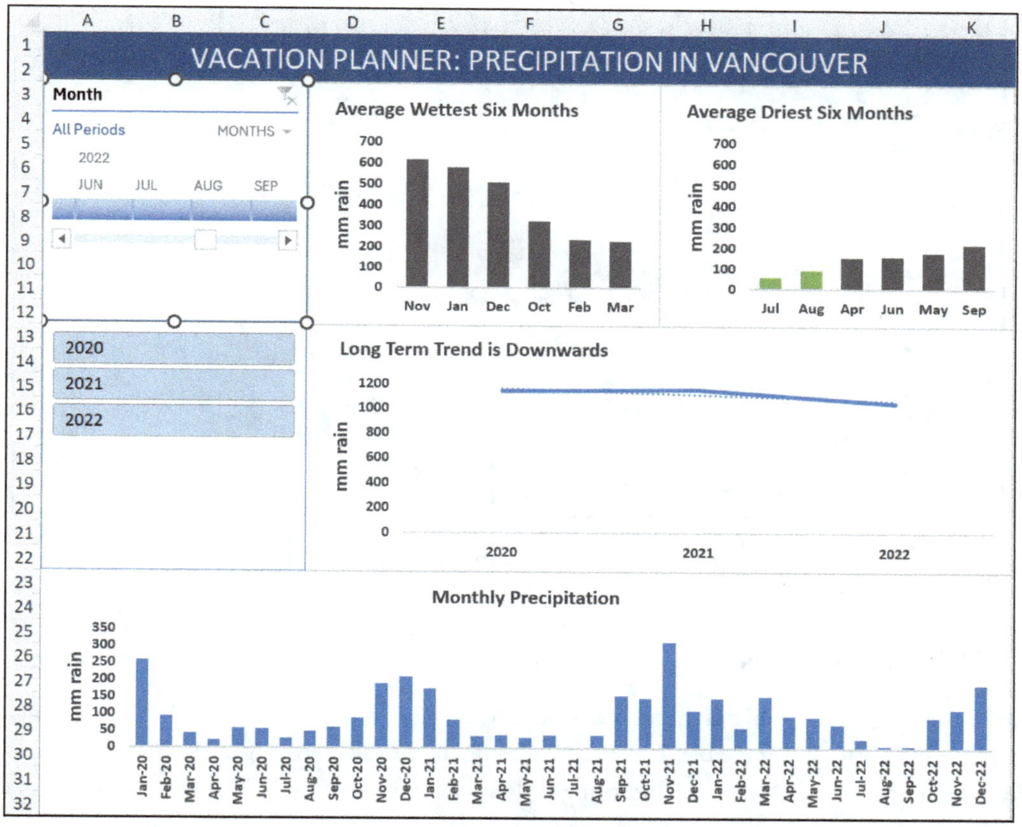

FIGURE 77: Dashboard with timeline and slicer

Another annoying feature is that the borders on the slicer and timeline are different. To rectify this, we'll "frame" them.

12. Move them off the dashboard into the space to the right. Right-click on each in turn, select *Size and Properties,* and make the height and width 1.87."

13. Highlight cells A3 to C22. Fill them with gray shade, then drag the timeline and slicer onto the gray area. Use the directional arrow keys on the keyboard to position them very neatly above each other.

Our dashboard is "complete," and it looks pretty good ... but we now have new data for 2023, and it isn't included yet.

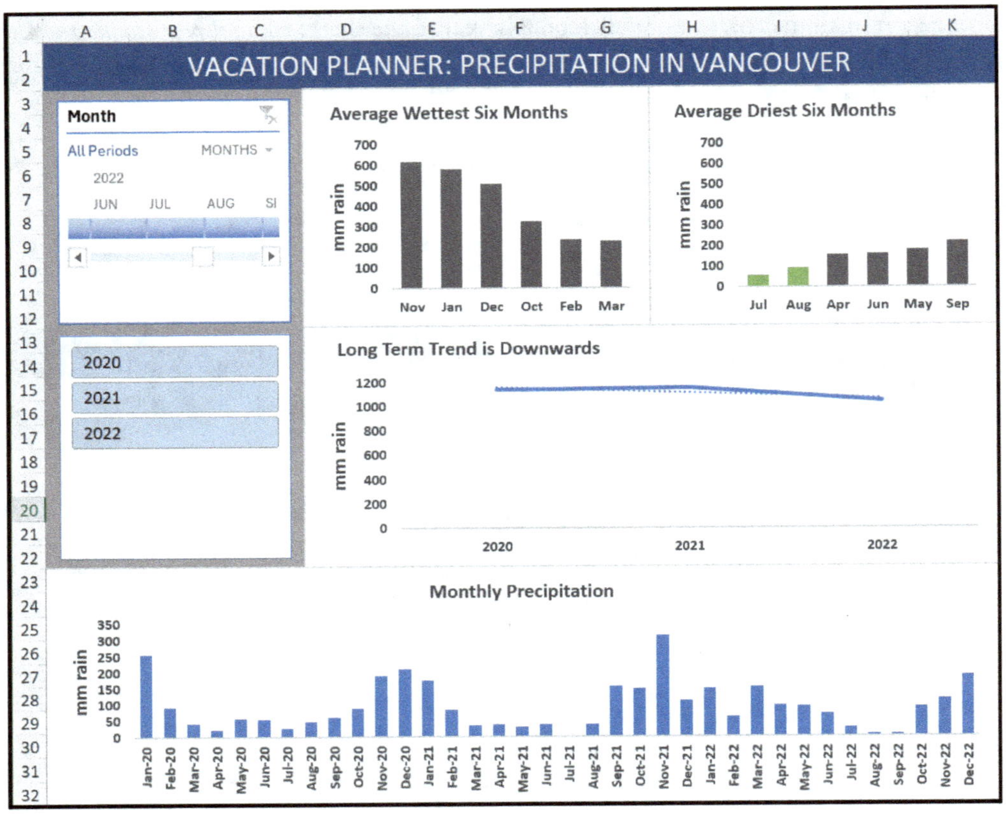

FIGURE 78: Final three-year dashboard

IMPORTANT NOTE: Remember that when you update data, pivot tables are not automatically refreshed.

14. Go to the 2023 tab and highlight all the data in it, then press Ctrl+C to copy it. Go to the Precip tab and add it to the bottom of the table. Excel does not update the table array to include the new data—click and drag the fill handle from Dec-22 and bring it down to include Oct-23. The table now covers all the data. *Notice that on the dashboard, the charts are not yet updated.*
15. Click in any pivot table, click on *PivotChart Analyze,* from the Data group select *Refresh*, and *Refresh All.* All the pivot tables on the dashboard and through the workbook will automatically update.
16. On the bottom chart, Monthly Precipitation, when 2023 data were added, Excel may have dropped some of the month labels. We want them all to show. Right-click anywhere in the month-name axis labels, select *Format Axis,* then on the right-arrow next to *Labels.* Under *Interval between labels* select *Specify Interval Unit* and make sure it is "1." All the month abbreviations will now be shown.

If you were planning to send this dashboard to someone, or show it in a presentation, you might not want all the working sheets showing as tabs. Select them, right-click and choose Hide. (To restore them, right-click on the Dashboard tab and select Unhide).

There are a few final touches we can apply to enhance the dashboard even further.

17. Move the "mm" titles on the vertical axes up closer to the titles. This brings them into closer contact with the "Z" reading pattern favored by viewers.
18. Change the two "Average" titles to reflect the conclusions to be drawn, making them more of a call to action.
19. Right-click on the X axis labels in the Monthly Precipitation chart, select *Format Axis*, then use the *Labels* and *Number* menus on the AxisOptions tab at right to set the interval between labels to 1, activate Multilevel Category Labels, set the Number category and Format code to General, and link the numbers to the source.

The finished dashboard should look like this:

FIGURE 79: Complete dashboard

Now please consider and use it to answer the following questions:

1. The three driest months for all the data are July, August and June, in that order. Does the order change for any individual year, or any series of years, from 2020 to 2022?
2. In the entire period under review, was there any month with no precipitation at all?
3. If we look only at the period 2020–21, is the annual trend upwards or downwards?
4. If we consider the period 2020–22, what are the wettest three months?
5. Can you add a trendline to the Precipitation by Month chart that was generated by Excel, on the dashboard page? Is there more than one option? Is it useful?
6. In the entire period under review, which month had more rain than any other?
7. If you hate the rain, which month next year should you plan your Vancouver vacation?
8. If you had precipitation data for Calgary or Seattle for the same years, how much work would you have to do to re-use your dashboard? How many steps would it take?

Using the dashboard

Throughout the work above, we've talked about the reason for building the dashboard and how it should tell a story. This is not always a stand-alone requirement—the end use will determine what exactly must be explained on the dashboard and what it contains.

We might, for example, be planning to put the Excel dashboard itself onto the screen during a presentation and use some of the interactivity. It might be emailed to people who would play with it themselves, perhaps using the slicers to answer their own questions. Or we might take some or all the visualizations and add them to PowerPoint slides, to accompany a verbal or on-line presentation.

Thinking critically about this dashboard, we might ask "If we are interested in the driest months, why do we have a visualization for the wettest months?" The answer might be that we want to show those most to be avoided. Why do we have all twelve months in the two six-month analyses? Possibly we just want to show that we haven't missed anything!

If we are searching for the driest months, which are clearly July and August, what is the use of also showing the next four driest months? Maybe some of our group can't travel during the school holidays; the Average Driest Six Months demonstrates the next best alternatives, June and May; there is not much difference between them. What is the purpose of the long-term trend? It might help us to think about whether now is the best time to plan for Vancouver, or whether we might get a better chance of remaining dry if we wait a couple of years.

The way we have built this dashboard would also enable us to deploy it for totally different questions and different destinations. Suppose that our group includes several skiers and snowboarders. We could take the snowfall statistics from Taos, New Mexico, or Denver, Colorado, and substitute them onto the Precip sheet. With one refresh we would have a similar analysis, but now we'd be looking for the most precipitation (and thus justifying the inclusion of the "wettest" analysis).

Multiple Choice Questions for Chapter 6

1. Which of the following is most effective for portraying a time series?
    a. Line chart.
    b. Map visualization.
    c. Pie chart.
2. Data for an Excel dashboard are best organized into:
    a. worksheets.
    b. named ranges.
    c. tables.
3. Fattening bars on a clustered bar chart is achieved in which Excel area?
    a. Format Data Point.
    b. Hide all Buttons on Chart.
    c. Format Major Gridlines.
4. If you copy a Pivot Chart from an Excel sheet to a dashboard, changes to the original are automatically made to the dashboard.
    a. True.
    b. False.
5. A dashboard slicer is automatically connected to all charts on the same Excel worksheet.
    a. True.
    b. False.
6. It has rained every month in Vancouver for the last four years.
    a. True.
    b. False.
7. The main advantage of slicers in dashboards is
    a. Users can filter data interactively and see the results visually.
    b. They increase the amount of data that can be stored on screen
    c. They automatically index and summarize data.
    d. They are a gateway to creating good pivot tables.
8. What is the primary governor of dashboard content?
    a. A need to fit all screen sizes.
    b. The audience's specific needs.
    c. The variety of fonds and colors needed for clarity.
    d. The need to maximize number of visualizations for efficiency.
9. Why do we limit use of 3D charts in dashboards?
    a. Because they are not supported by dashboard tools.
    b. Because they are incompatible with slicers and timelines.
    c. Because they create visual distortions.
    d. Because they take up too much memory.

10. The standard font and formatting commands from the Excel Home ribbon can be used to change the appearance of titles and legends in visualizations and pivot tables?
    a. True.
    b. False.
    c. True for visualizations, but not for pivot tables.
    d. True for pivot tables, but not for visualizations.

7. POWER BI

Introduction

Power BI is part of the Microsoft Power Platform. BI stands for "business intelligence" and refers to its intention of providing a visualization tool for business data. The ever-expanding Microsoft suite currently includes 12 different components of Power BI, many of which are variations created to cope with differences in licensing and security. While it is not the only analysis tool for business data, it is one of the most popular.

This book is all about interpreting, analyzing and presenting business data in a format which is user friendly. Familiarity with Power BI is an essential tool for these purposes and a key feature of many professional examinations. Please take the time to download and install Power BI Desktop, become familiar with its use and develop an innate ability to create and manipulate dashboards within the app from raw data. The investment of time will pay off as you progress through your university career and professional life.

Power BI Components

Power BI Desktop is downloaded (free of charge) onto a standalone laptop or desktop computer and can be used to load, analyze and visually present summaries of vast amounts of interconnected data.

The other two components you are most likely to encounter early in your accounting career are Power BI Service, and Power BI Mobile Apps. Once you have created a dashboard presentation in Power BI, you can *publish* it—*i.e.* upload it to the software-as-a-service site, where it will be stored and made available from the cloud. Others in your organization can then use the Power BI Mobile Apps to view your work on iOS and Android devices, Windows phones and tablets.

While there is no additional charge for the Power BI Service or Mobile Apps, using them requires a login from an email address associated with an organization with a paid Microsoft subscription. If you have a work email address that qualifies, you will be able to experiment with these elements.

Installing Power BI Desktop

Power BI on Windows PCs

You will need to download and install Power BI on your laptop or desktop computer. There are several ways to download Power BI on a laptop or desktop computer.

Power BI is currently available in over 40 languages. It requires Windows 8.1 or later, and Internet Explorer is not supported (you need Microsoft Edge or another compatible browser). If you have for any reason made changes to display text sizes or apps at more than 100%, some parts of Power BI will not work; the fix is to go to *Settings* > *System* > *Display* where you can move the slider to return to 100%.

Power BI is available free from the Microsoft Store. Go to https://www.microsoft.com/en-ca/store/ then use the search function by clicking on the magnifying glass icon and typing in Power BI. Select Power BI Desktop, click the blue button "Get in Store app," and then "Open Microsoft Store," and "Install." The download and installation procedures run automatically, and when finished an "Open" button appears—click on it and the program will run.

A similar procedure can be followed on the powerbi.com website. Go to https://powerbi.microsoft.com/en-ca/desktop/ then click on *Download free* >, which will take you to the *Install* button, after which the procedure is identical to the above.

There are also many third-party sites which can be used to install Power BI.

Power BI is updated monthly. Often the changes are insignificant and even transparent to the non-technical user. We *highly recommend* that you obtain the current version directly from the Microsoft Store, as it comes with the following advantages:

- *Automatic updating*—you will never need to use manual procedures to obtain the latest updates, as Windows will download updates without prompting as soon as they are available; this has the consequence that the screenshots shown here will almost always be slightly out-of-date, as new icons and features are constantly added Sometimes important features move to a completely new place; this can be frustrating.
- *No Admin Privilege*—if you obtain an executable file then install from it, you must have administrator privileges on your desktop or laptop. This is not necessary for the store download.
- *Automatic language preferences*—Each time you run Power BI, it checks the language currently in use on your computer and presents that version. However, models created previously in other languages are maintained in their original language.
- *Partial updating*—the update procedure (which runs in background) downloads only changed components. Other types of installation can result in full downloading and re-installation of Power BI.

IMPORTANT NOTE

Due to the automatic updating of Power BI every 30 days, it is highly unlikely that the on-screen presentation of every element which you see on your PC or laptop will exactly match what you see here in this book. Microsoft quite regularly moves tools, re-formats menus, and adds or removes icons. As you gain familiarity with Power BI, however, you should gain enough familiarity to find the things you need, even if they are no longer where they were when we last updated this chapter.

Power BI on Mac devices

In the early editions of *Information Systems for accountants* we wrote the following:

> There are versions of Excel which run on a PC, and versions which run on Mac computers. Using the advanced features of Excel on a Mac requires the implementation of workarounds, acceptance that some things just can't be done, and a full understanding of why certain things don't work or work incorrectly. Let us say this in the most straightforward manner possible: *put the Mac away and get used to using Excel on a PC.* This will earn a big reward in terms of marks, efficiency and overall satisfaction. It's possible to make

> it through a Power BI course on a Mac with workarounds, but in more advanced data visualization there are whole routines which are not available on the Mac. Wean yourself off now—to get the most out of [Power BI], please learn to use a PC *now*.

Here we are. We hope that you followed this recommendation. If you did not, then the transition has become even more urgent. There are three ways to run Power BI on a Mac, none of them convenient or sensible. They are:

- Install Power BI on a virtual machine, then run that machine remotely from a Mac.
- Install Power BI on a PC, then use a remote viewer to see that machine from a Mac.
- Install Windows on an Intel-based Mac, using Boot Camp.

Technical writers on business intelligence usually offer a fourth alternative for Mac users—don't use Power BI, find an alternative!

We hope you will understand that none of these make sense. As to using an alternative program, then you won't be learning to deploy Power BI. Of the three technical solutions, two of them involve linking Power BI to a PC environment anyway, and the third involves an extensive work-around (Boot Camp) which does not always function in a satisfactory manner. *Use a PC and install Power BI on it. Every other solution is just inviting problems into your studies; you will definitely incur time losses, and you are likely to lose some facilities.*

Microsoft has no current intention to develop Power BI versions for Mac computers and does not support Mac use of the program.

Loading Data

Power BI has vast capabilities in the range of data types which it can import, including the ability to hold, analyze and integrate data from different source types. The commoner sources are Excel, SQL databases, text documents (including .txt and .csv files), .pdf files and web sources, but there are many addressable resources including sample data from the Power BI Service and data already stored in Microsoft's Dataverse. All work in quite a similar fashion, and here we are going to use exclusively Excel files as the data source.

After installing Power BI and on first opening the program, a screen like the following will display:

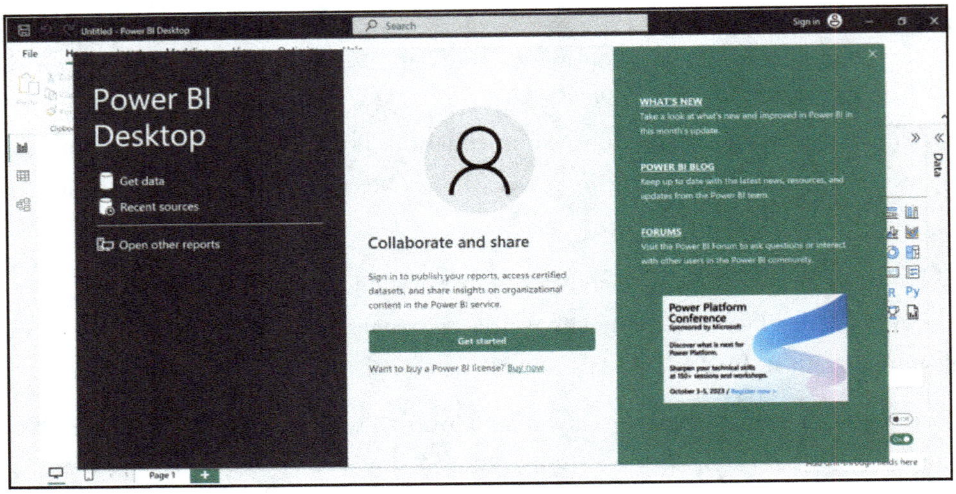

FIGURE 80: Power BI Desktop

For a moment, ignore the main Power BI presentation which lies in background. There are a few things to note about this view. On the left (black) panel, there is an option to jump immediately to getting data, which can be a useful shortcut. Below the white line, if you have previously created Power BI presentations, the most recent will be listed. You can right-click on any of them to see a list of options such as removing them from the list or double-click on one to load the last version you saved. The center panel is used to access the software-as-a-service element to publish and share presentations. The right (green) panel gives the opportunity to see the latest monthly updates, visit discussion platforms and read advertising from Microsoft. The left and right panels will update frequently. The entire pop-up can be removed by clicking on the white X in the top right corner. If you do that, you will see this something like this working canvas.

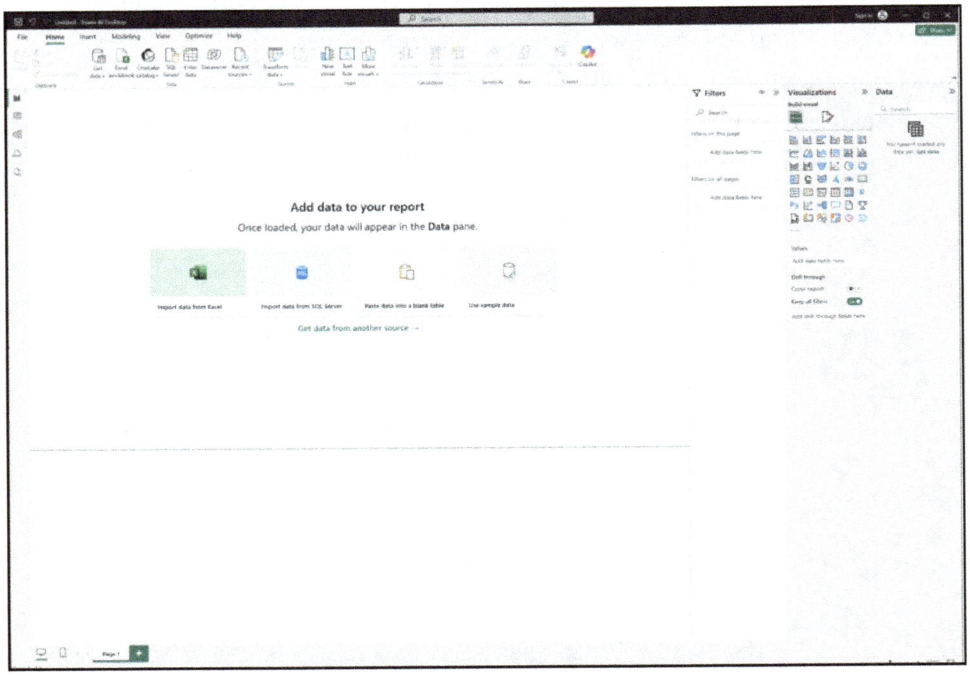

FIGURE 81: Power BI working canvas

The Filters, Visualizations, and Data panes to the right can be displayed or hidden using the double arrows at their tops.

There is a lot to be unpacked here—but virtually everything we want to discuss will be better exemplified when there are data to work with. Please go to the website https://powerbidocs.com/2019/11/28/power-bi-sample-data-set-for-practice/ and download the third dataset, "Global Super Store Dataset 2016." The site may require you to download a Chrome Extension before you can access the dataset; you can do this, then immediately remove it and you will still have access to the dataset. Save it in a place which is convenient for you, then in this screen click on "Import data from Excel," navigate to the file and double-click on it. Power BI will take you to a Navigator screen like this:

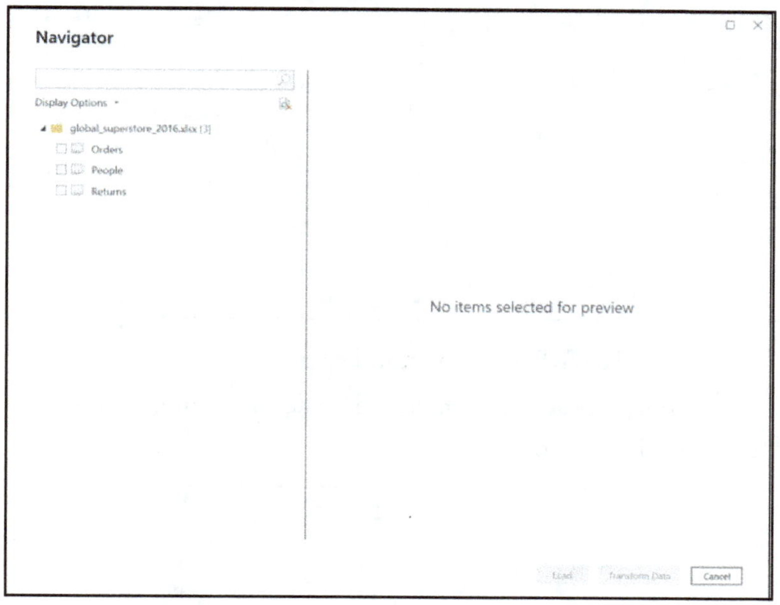

FIGURE 82: Power BI Navigator menu

The file is now presented as if it were a folder, and that the three sheets in the file are shown (correctly) as sheets. This is a first hint that the data with which we are going to work is not in an ideal format—but let's progress for now. Shortly, we'll undo the work so far and start from a better place.

While the navigator drop-down menu is live, we have the option to view a selection of the data. Clicking on one of the sheets will cause a partial table to display as follows:

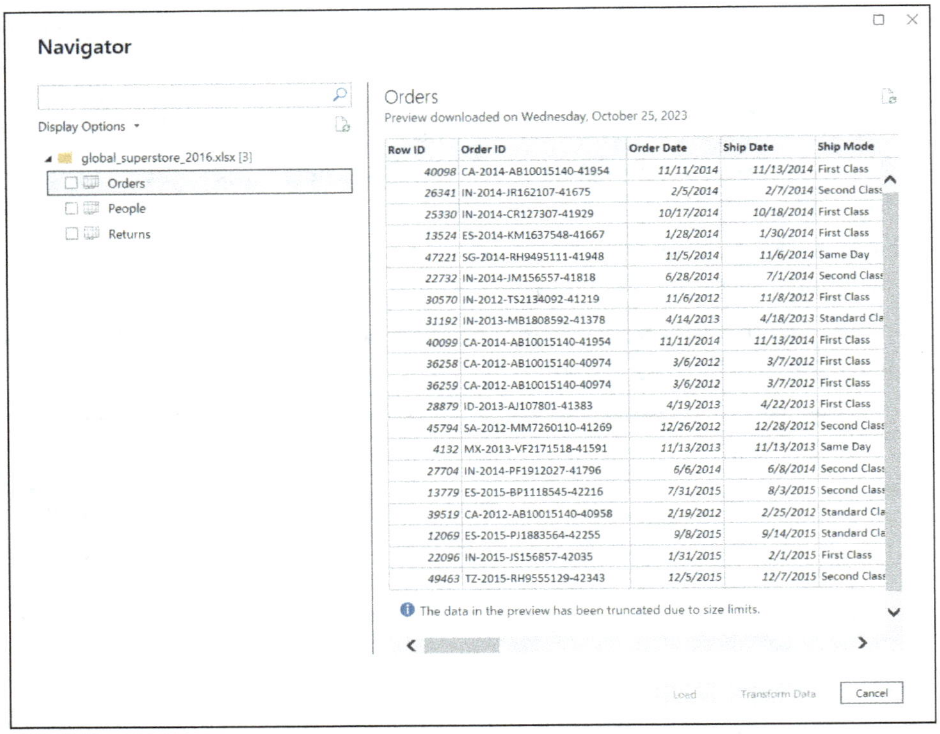

FIGURE 83: Power BI data preview - orders

Note that in this sheet, the top row (headers) contains the header titles for the data. However, if you now click on the "People" sheet the result is different:

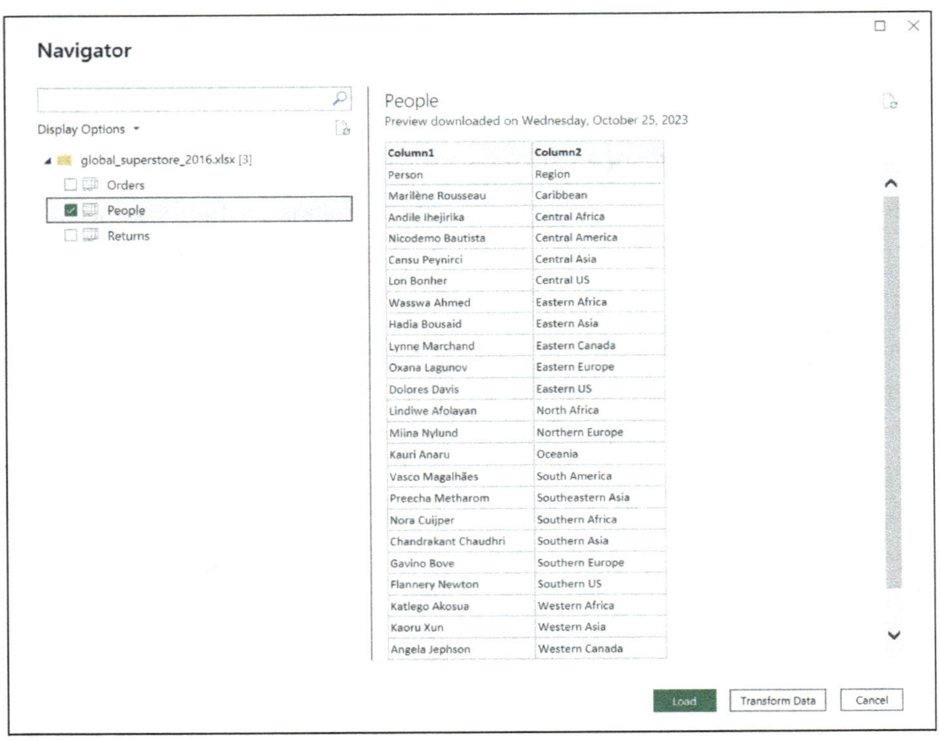

FIGURE 84: Power BI data preview - no column headers

The column headers are now "Column1" and "Column2." This is going to cause some extra work which can be avoided. We'll keep going to demonstrate this and some possible fixes.

Click to fill all three boxes next to the sheets, then examine the options at the bottom right of the screen. We can elect to "Load," or "Transform Data." For now, let's load—but let's also pause to absorb some *very good news*—if we select "Transform Data," the *Power Query* editor will load, and sheet by sheet we will have the opportunity to work on the data to generate a better result. It will load up with a list of all the sheets on the left side, and we can select them one by one to apply changes to the data.

Why is this such great news? If you are familiar with Power Query Editor's capabilities, you already have a solid foundation for cleaning data to use in Power BI and your dashboards.

There's more good news. If you "Load" at this point, but then spot some changes you wish you'd made, you can still select "Transform Data" from the ribbon and go back to work on the original data as if you had selected "Transform Data" at the loading stage.

There's another useful feature here. If you have been working on your source data, but did not save your changes, Power BI will recognize this and ask whether you want to incorporate the saved changes or disregard them for this load. This is great stuff—most programs, for instance most email applications, fail to notice unsaved changes and work only with the previously saved version of your basic data.

Here is what you will see after loading the three sheets of sample data:

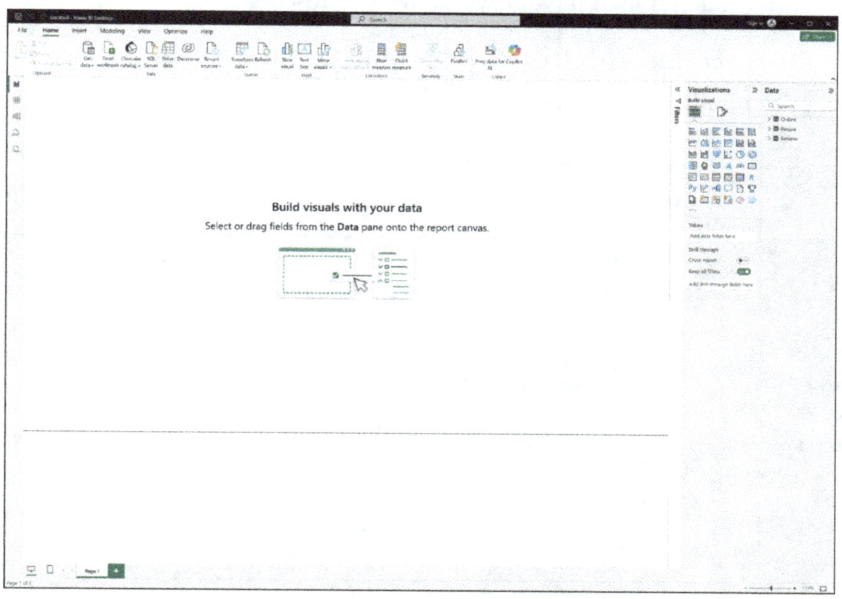

FIGURE 85: Power BI data panel extension

On the right of the screen, the panel "Data" has now expanded to show a list of the available data. Just above the Data heading is an up arrow, which allows hiding of the ribbon if you want more screen on which to work. The three sheets are listed, and alongside each is a right arrow—clicking on it will display a list of the columns in that sheet. You may sometimes see the list of columns referred to as "fields" which is also technically correct, but here we'll stay with "columns" for consistency.

We hinted above that what we have done so far is not ideal. We will show why, and the fix, as we next examine the three views available in the Power BI main screen. Please read, learn and get ready to apply this statement:

It is best practice in Power BI to work with TABLES. Power BI will often present a list of tables and the worksheets on which they live; but only the tables update automatically when new rows are added.

The Four Views

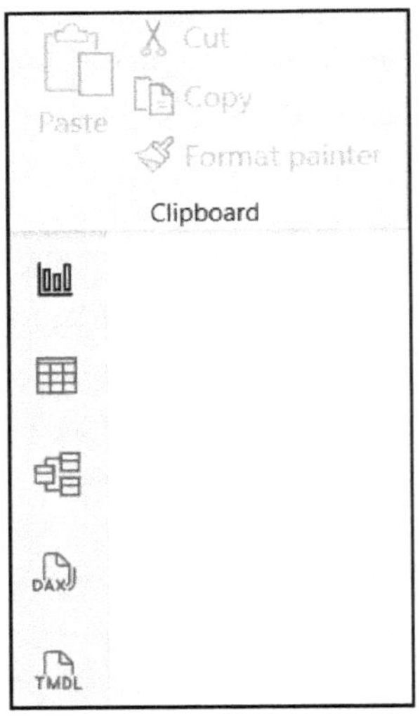

FIGURE 86: View icons

At the top left of the screen, below the File tab and clipboard icon, there are four symbols. The first, which looks like a bar chart, selects the "Report View"—a presentation of the data visualization which is being created.

The second symbol, which looks like an Excel table, selects "Table View" and allows you to view the source data in tabular form.

The third symbol selects "Model View" which maps the relationships between various datasets—in this case, between the three sheets we have loaded.

The fourth symbol opens a DAX Query View which allows evaluation of DAX queries used in your work. We will discuss this later.

To the left of one of the symbols there will always be a colored vertical bar, indicating which is selected.

Selecting "Model View" for the current data produces this schema (you may need to collapse panes at the right using the >> button to see the full set of sheets):

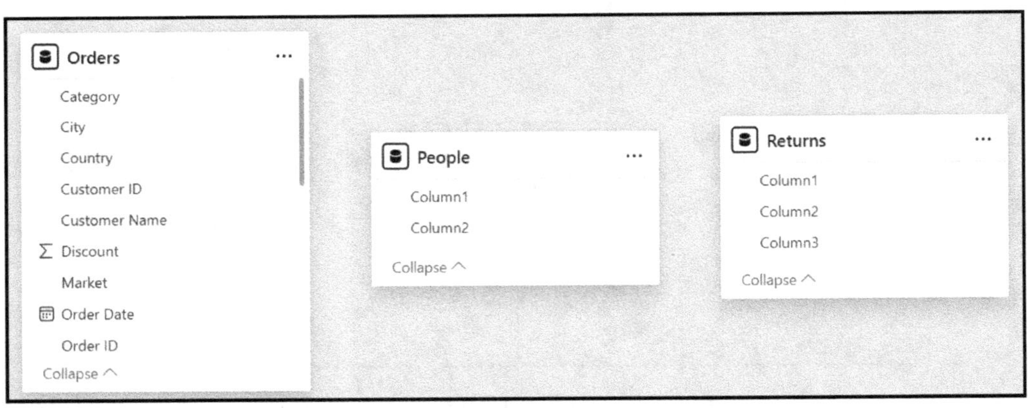

FIGURE 87: Model view

Instantly we see a budding problem—there are no relationships. This is slightly surprising because Power BI is very good at detecting relationships, even when there is no common naming of columns. But in this case, it has failed to spot any relationships—and has wisely avoided concluding that because there is a Column1 in both the People and Returns sheets, they signify a relationship.

We have caused this problem by uploading data which wasn't in an ideal format and failing to transform it when we had the chance. In the next section we will explore various ways of creating connections.

Connecting Data

There are three ways we could deal with the absence of relationships:

- We can manually create the relationships we want, by clicking and dragging common fields between sheets (for example, Order ID in the Orders sheet can match up with Column2 in the Returns sheet). After creating this relationship, the schema now appears like this:

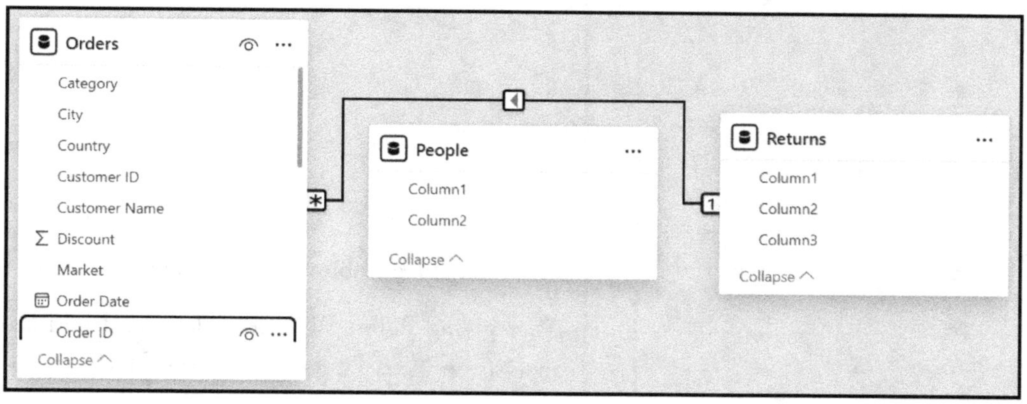

FIGURE 88: Relationships

- We can select "Transform Data" from the ribbon, go to each sheet and promote the first rows to headers in the People and Returns sheets. When this is done, Power BI will re-evaluate possible relationships, but it is not a given that it will get it right—with these data, the result is a connection between Region in the two altered sheets, but no determination that Order ID is a linking element between Orders and Returns:

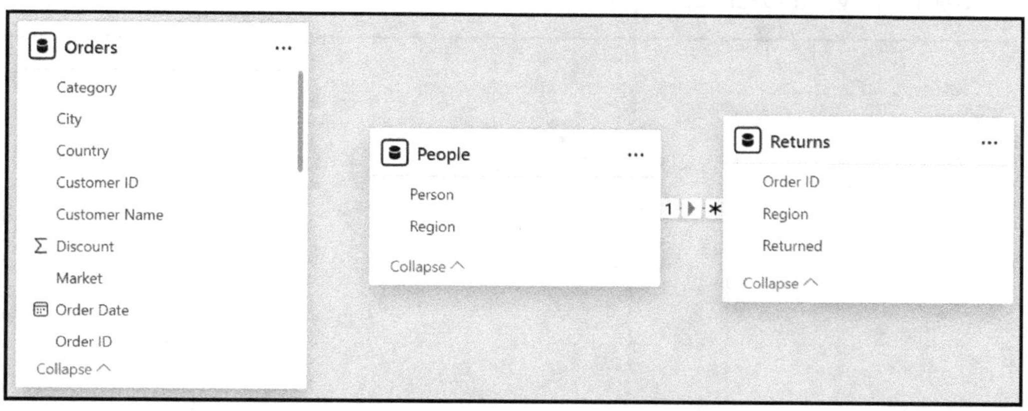

FIGURE 89: Missing relationship (Power BI has not connected Order ID in the first and third tables

To examine the relationship between sheets, move the cursor over the link and the connected columns will be highlighted. To remove a connection, right-click on the connection and select "Delete."

This solution, fixing on the fly, is useful if a lot of prior work is likely to be wasted, but is not ideal. Earlier we said that best practice is to work from Tables: so please click the top right X to exit from Power BI, click on "Don't Save" and re-open the original data in Excel.

Now go to each sheet and convert the data into a table (click on any cell, Ctrl+T, select "My data has headers" and OK). Save the workbook and re-open Power BI; then follow the procedure to load data from Excel and select the revised workbook. This time the Navigator looks different:

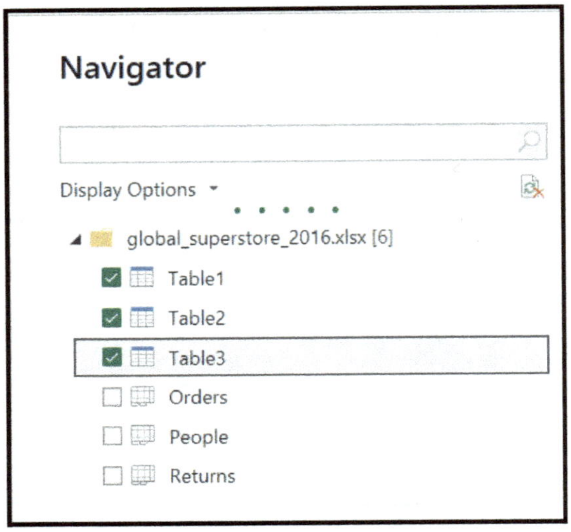

FIGURE 90: Selection of tables

Select the three Tables (as shown), and Load.

After giving Power BI time to load and perform its initial analysis on the data, go again to the Model View.

If the tables are not shown in the positions you would like them, move them around by clicking and dragging the title bar in each one. In this case it may be necessary to again manually create the Order ID relationships; eventually the Model View can be made to look like this:

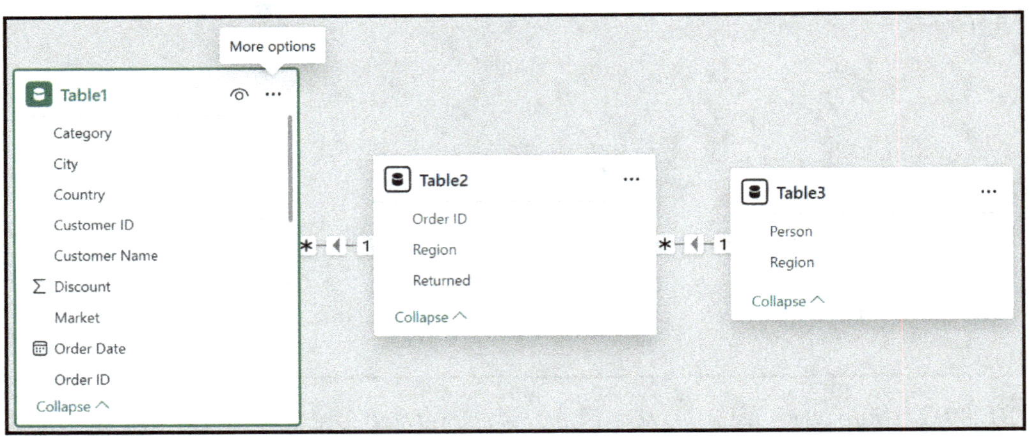

FIGURE 91: More options

In this snapshot we have left visible the "More options" icon at the top right of Table 1—clicking on this opens a lengthy dropdown menu of possible actions for the model. Spend some time to review and experiment with them. You will discover that very like in Excel, there are many ways to perform various tasks and multiple places to start them.

Terminology and Data Currency

Words

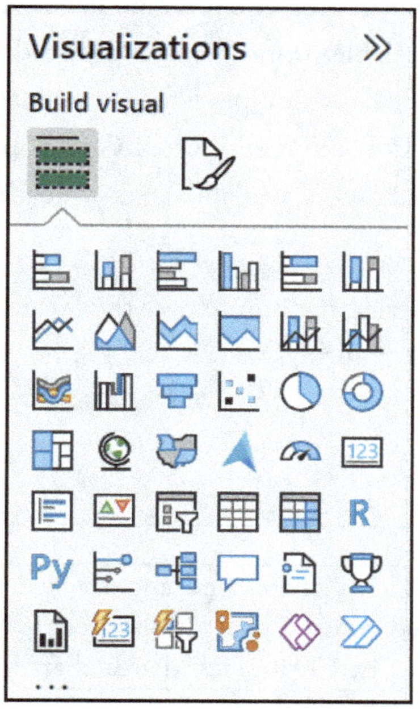

FIGURE 92: Visualization icons

The Power in Power BI flows from its ability to analyze and present summaries of vast amounts of data in pictorial form, making it easy to understand and contextualize.

Every exercise in Power BI is built on a *dataset*—the collection of data on which the summarization and analysis is based. When you load Power BI ready for action you see a *report canvas*—a single page ready for a collection of visualizations, also known as visuals.

A *report* can have many pages, always based on a dataset. In the Power BI online service, you can also create a *dashboard*, a single page constructed from *tiles* from one or several report visuals. To be clear: dashboards are made of tiles, while reports are made of visuals. Confused? It's easy to be, not least because Microsoft interchangeably uses "visualization" and "visual." It's perhaps easiest to understand the elements of a report as a process flow.

After loading a dataset, you build visuals on a report canvas. If you're in Power BI service, you can pin selected visuals to a dashboard as tiles. Dashboards give a summary overview; reports provide deeper exploration of the data.

Data currency

FIGURE 93: Refresh Button

While historical data may be static, in a going concern new data are always coming along. It would be a shame if all the work of creating a report had to be re-done when new data are updated.

Do you remember from your study of pivot tables that after creating them, they wouldn't update unless Excel was specifically instructed to refresh? This also applies to Power BI. After you have created your report, if the data are updated there is no need to re-do the creative work—but you must remember to refresh the report. There is a Refresh icon on the ribbon; a click on it will update everything to conform to the latest data.

Visualization Types

On the next page is a chart of the standard visualization types that were available directly on the current version of Power BI in August 2025. Microsoft adds and changes these on a regular basis, so it should not be a surprise if something you see on your latest version is different to the ones shown here. We have grouped them for convenience roughly in line with how they are best used.

If you have put data into a visualization but then decide you want to use a different one, all that is required is to click on the visualization to be changed, then click on a different icon. The tile will automatically update to the new format and display the same data.

These are not the only visualizations available. From within the visualizations pane, there is a function denoted by three dots that will take the user to a new page where many more are available, from inside and outside Microsoft. There are literally hundreds of others to choose from, including some familiar types like histograms, Gantt and bubble charts, and some highly specialized applications like Microsoft's Force-Directed Graph. If you can think of a visualization you want, it has almost certainly been created and is available to download, usually free.

All the icons on the Visualization panel have a name, which is revealed by hovering the mouse over the image. The following table groups the visualizations available in mid-2025 by use case groups.

TABLE 15: Power BI visualization groups

Use Cases	Visualization Types
Time Series, progress	Line chart, area chart, stacked area chart, line and stacked column chart, line and clustered column chart, ribbon chart, waterfall chart, funnel, gauge, goals, 100% stacked area chart.
Comparison, ranking, part-to-whole	Stacked bar chart, stacked column chart, clustered ar chart, clustered column chart, 100% stacked bar chart, 100% stacked column chart, table.
Data analysis, examination, relationships	KPI, decomposition tree, matrix, key influencers, scatter chart.
Advanced analytics and programming	R script visual, Python visual, Power apps, Power Automate, Paginated report.
Spatial, geographical	Map, Filled map, Azure map, Arc GIS map.
Part-to-whole	Pie chart, donut chart, Treemap.
Reporting	Q&A, narrative, slicer, card, card (new), multi-row card, button slicer.

Visualizations and Tiles

Let's commencing building a Power BI report. It's time to create a tile. Creating a good tile involves assessing the synergy between the data to be presented and the visualization type. There are several ways to place a new tile on the dashboard; we will use just two.

Start with a visualization type

Click on a visualization type in the Visualizations panel; in this example, we have selected the top left type, stacked bar chart. Power BI has created a tile on the dashboard ready to display data.

FIGURE 94: Selecting visualization type

In this tile we want to show sales by country. It's now necessary to select the fields from the data tables; in the Data panel to the right of the screen, click on the right arrow next to Table 1 to display the list of fields, then click to select "Country" and "Σ Sales."

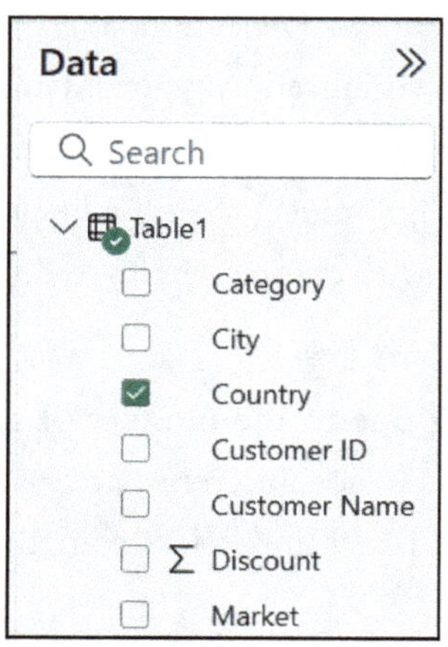

FIGURE 95: Selecting data

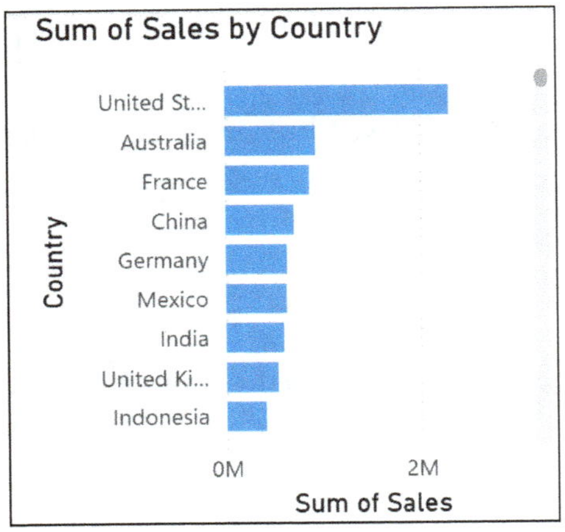

FIGURE 96: Top 9 countries

The result is a meaningful tile, even if it is not yet very elegant. Though there are many countries not visible on this list, we have a list of our top nine and we can easily see that our sales in the United States are more than double the next country on the list, and a multiple of all other national territories. There are many things we could do with this tile. It can be resized using the handles mid-point on the sides and on the corners. It can be moved around the dashboard by dragging and dropping. Its format and content can be edited. We can retain the same data in a completely different visualization format, by keeping it selected and clicking on a different icon in the visualization panel. This is an especially handy tool as we can quickly experiment with different formats and see which best presents the intended message. The tile can also be deleted by selecting it by clicking anywhere within it and pressing the *Delete* key.

As it turns out, the selection of the stacked bar chart was one of the best for this portion of the data. A pie chart, by contrast, would have been one of the worst!

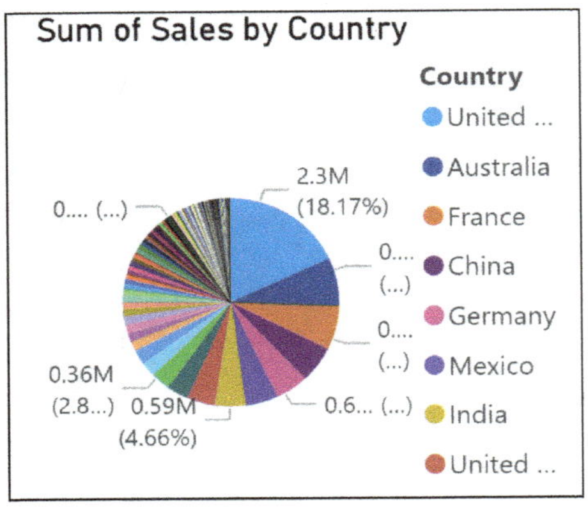

FIGURE 97: Overcrowded pie chart

Or start with the data

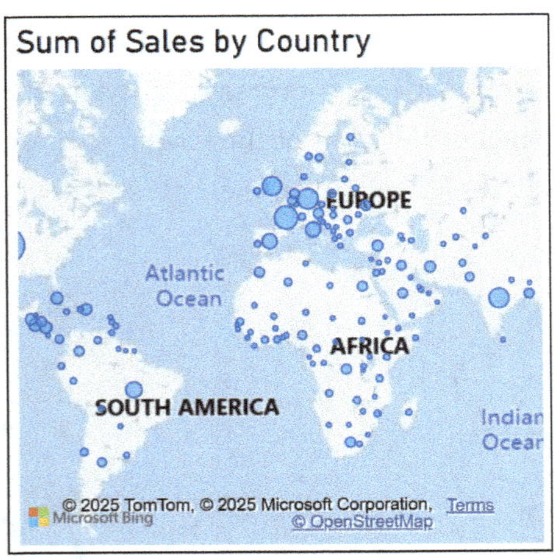

FIGURE 98: Power BI map

Another method of creating a new tile first selects a data category from the Data panel. As soon as you make your first selection, Power BI will guess what might be an appropriate visualization type and create a tile in that format. Using the same fields, a selection of a geographical field like "Country" or "City" plus Σ Sales is likely to create a bubble map, a geographical map with colored circles to depict relative revenue volumes.

This is not a helpful visualization at all due to the number of data points; we would need to add slider bars to see different parts of the world. To fix, go to the Visualizations panel and select something more appropriate.

Which data?

Both above illustrations employed just two columns of data, Country and ∑ Sales. However, there is no limit to the number of columns that can be added to a tile nor to the number of sources. A common procedure would be to add a time element to sales data to complement geographical analysis; data could then be viewed by month or year. Provided the necessary links are in place to allow Power BI to connect associated data, columns from different Excel tables may be drawn into the same visualization.

To keep things simple, at this stage we have ignored orders which were returned, treating all sales as final. Later we will correct this detail using filtering.

Special visualizations

It would be boring and somewhat repetitive for us to go through all the different visualizations here. Many are self-explanatory and probably already familiar from the Excel chart function. There are however a small number that deserve individual treatment.

Before we go on to add a second tile, please be aware that if you select a visualization type while you are still "live" in a tile, that tile will change to the type selected. When you are ready to add the next tile, first click once in the empty space away from existing tiles.

FIGURE 99: Single line card icon

One of the most impactful tiles that can be created is a *card*. Creating a single line card is very straightforward; click on the card icon in the Visualizations panel, then select the desired data in the data panel. In this example, we have moved the "Sales by Country" tile towards the center of the dashboard, then created a card for Total Sales to its left, and one for Total Profit to its right.

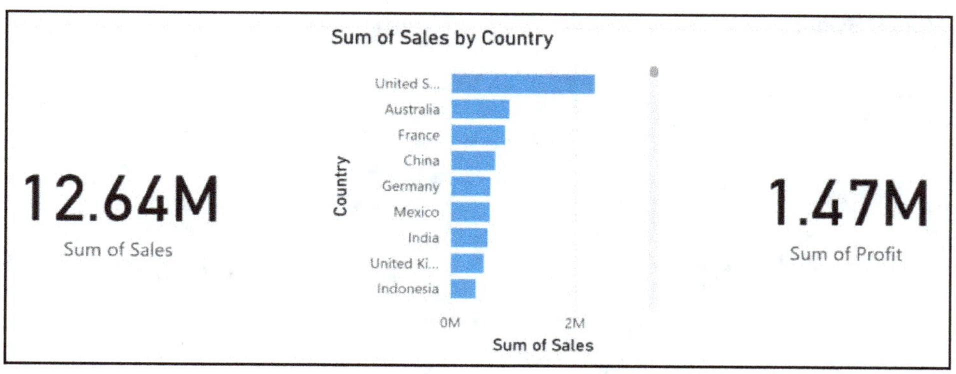

FIGURE 100: Two sard tiles bracket the bar chart

FIGURE 101: Multi-row card

There is also a visualization type known as "multi-row card," which can be used to show a list of key data points analyzed by a second column. This tends to be useful only where there are few data points; its use for sales by country, for example, produces a lengthy list of countries with their individual sales totals, most of which are hidden due to space limitations.

Time columns

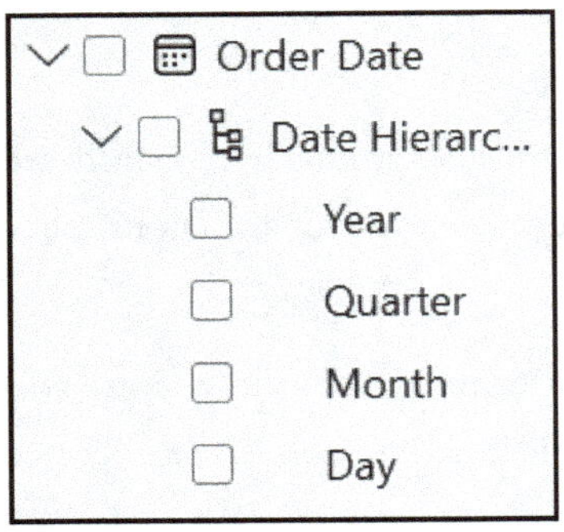

FIGURE 102: Time columns

Columns which refer to dates and/or times introduce new facilities which are important in trend and performance analyses. Such columns are identified in the field list in the Data panel by a calendar icon next to the check box, and a right arrow > to the left. Clicking on the right arrow changes it to a down arrow and displays the text "Date Hierarchy" with its own right arrow—click on this and Power BI presents a list of the available divisions of time. Here we are offered Year, Quarter, Month and Day, and these can be selected like other columns to produce more detailed summary data.

TABLE 16: Sales totals

Year	Sum of Sales
2012	2,259,450.90
2013	2,677,438.69
2014	3,405,746.45
2015	4,299,865.87
Total	**12,642,501.91**

Select Year from the Order Date Hierarchy, then Σ Sales. Power BI decides to present this as a table, which is a reasonable choice as it is quite small. Note now that there is interactivity between this table and the other tiles—if for example we click on the year 2012 in the table, the other tiles will immediately change to depict the data for that year only.

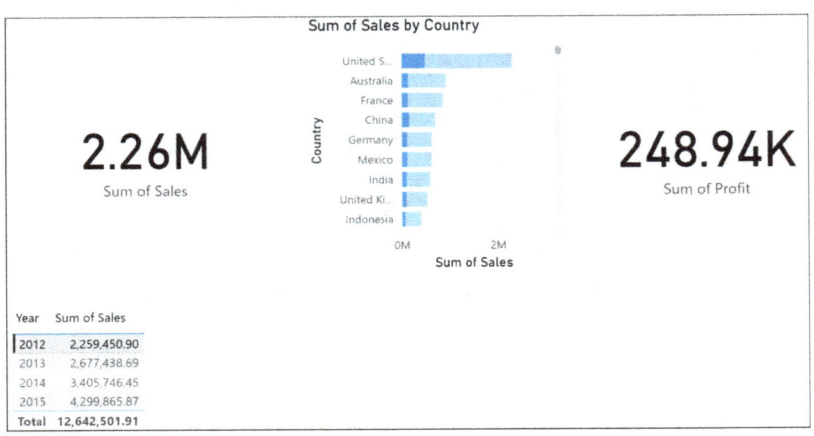

FIGURE 103: Table interactivity

Time progressions in data are often much easier to understand if presented graphically rather than in a table or matrix. This is the case here. Keeping the table as the active tile, click on the Line chart icon in the Visualizations panel, then go over to the Data panel and add the ∑ Profit column. The chart is rather narrow so extend it to the right. Now the picture seems to tell an interesting story—although sales have increased at an accelerating rate, profit looks as though it has failed to keep up with the growth in volume and the gap between the two lines is increasing year by year.

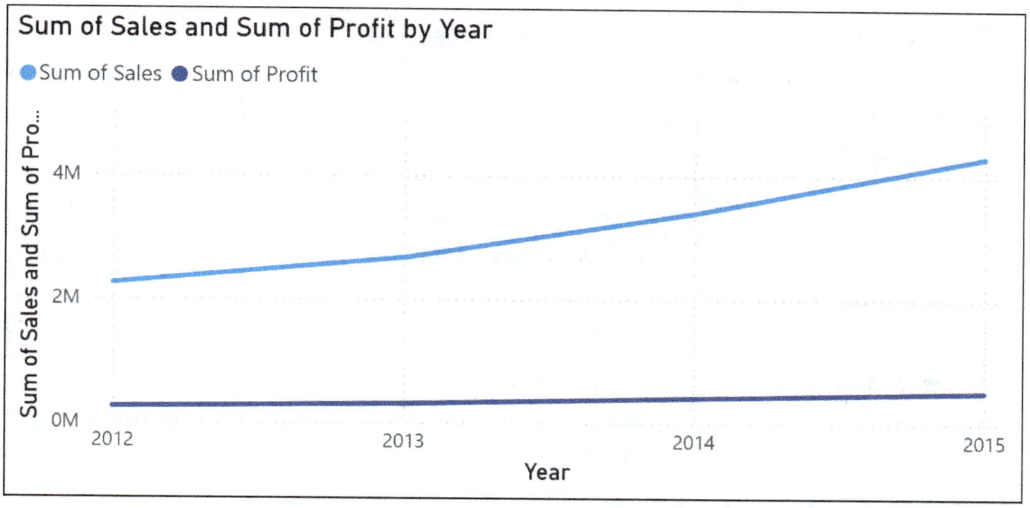

FIGURE 104: Sales and profit line chart

This, however, is a false impression created by using the same scale for two vastly disparate sets of numbers. To correctly compare the two trends, we'll create a second tile just for profit, with its own scales, and compare the slopes.

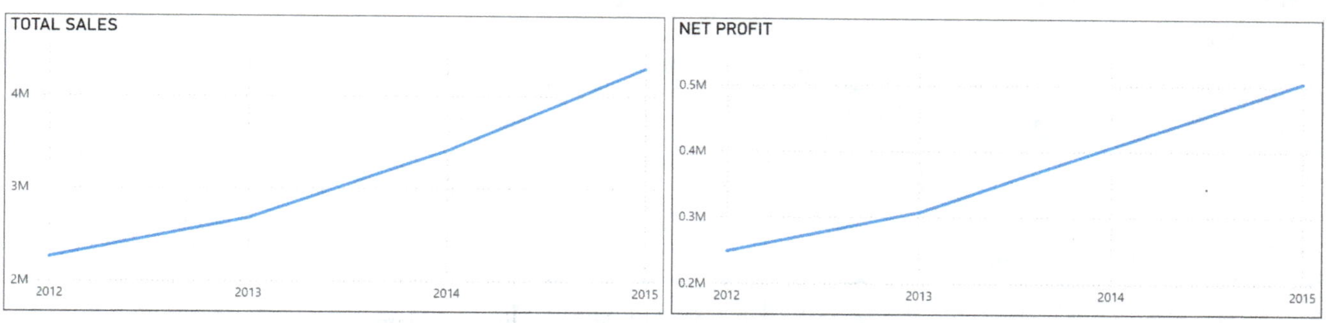

FIGURE 105: Comparison of slopes

When each visualization has its own proportions, the slopes look closely similar. If you want to be sure which impression is correct, analyze the source data to see the profitability ratio in each of the four years. It always falls between 11 and 12.5 percent, meaning that the more we sell, the more we make. On a percentage basis, though, the company is not growing at the same rate over the last three years, despite the steady uphill slope. Sales and profits have grown by roughly the same *amount* each year, but by a diminishing percentage.

Slicers

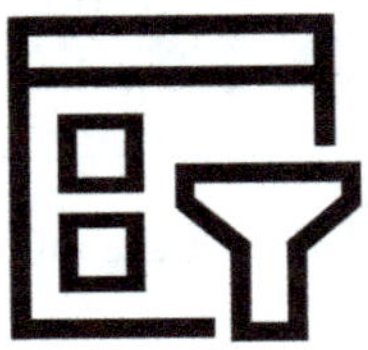

FIGURE 106: Slicer icon

To create a slicer, click in the empty space on the dashboard then on the slicer icon in the Visualizations panel.

There are several different types of slicers available. Power BI will select the appropriate type depending on the columns selected by the user. The three most common types are categorical slicers (which enable selection of data for categorical columns, such as countries, regions, products or people), relative date slicers (which enable the presentation of data for a selected calendar period) and relative time slicers (which enable restriction of data to a specific time, such as the last hour or the last three hours. Here we will use a categorical slicer to examine the relationship between shipping methods and profitability.

Having created a tile for the slicer by clicking on the icon, select "Ship Mode" in the Data panel. No immediate change occurs to the remaining tiles, but the slicer now contains a list of shipping methods with check boxes. Clicking in the check box next to any method will cause the displays in all other tiles to update to select only transactions using that method. With a few clicks we can learn and demonstrate that product shipped by Standard Class has far and away the highest volume and yields the most profit.

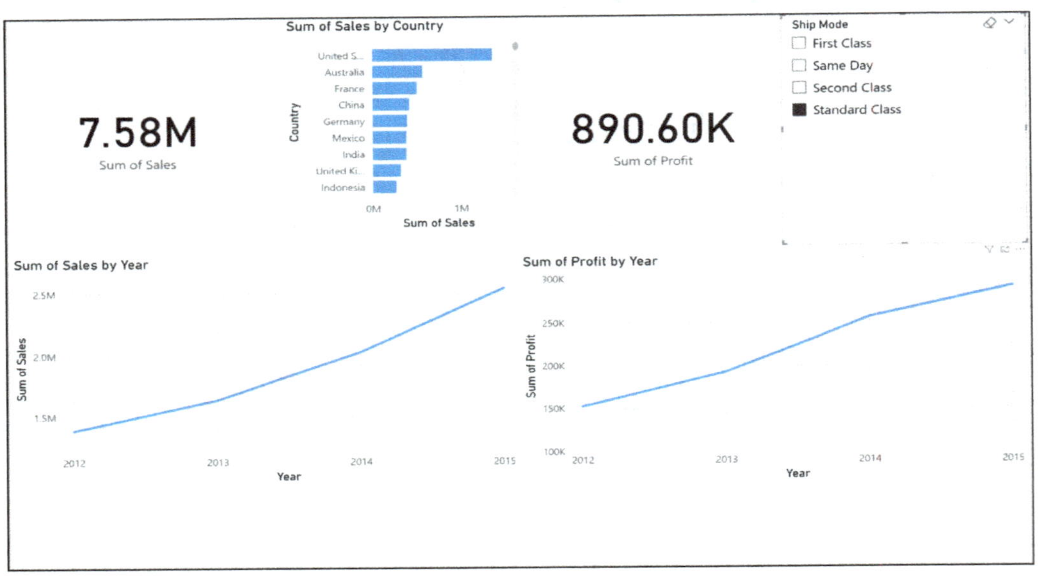

FIGURE 107: Standard class shipping data

We might be interested to see the profitability curve for goods delivered by Same Day service, which falls steadily for the first three years but then ratchets remarkably upwards in the fourth year. To return to the full display after deploying a slicer, click to clear the selected box and all the data will again be analyzed.

You may have noticed that *all* tiles in the report are updating according to the slicer selections. This is the default treatment by Power BI but is customizable—the user can select which individual tiles are affected by the slicer. If you wish to try this, click on the slicer visual, then the Format tab in the top ribbon. Click "Edit interactions" then for each visual on the page, select Filter icon, No icon, or Highlight icon. These slections operate as on/off toggles. When finished, click Edit interactions again to exit the mode.

Individual tile setting only works within the same report page. To work with multiple pages, use Sync slicers, which is in the View tab.

Maps

FIGURE 108: Map icon

The map visualizations in Power BI presently beat most of the others for "wow factor." Power BI has mapped almost the entire world. When countries, states or cities (among others) are available in data, it can make mind-blowing graphics which analyze and depict data geographically. Just how useful those depictions are varies greatly between datasets, but there is no doubt that the ability to place data into terrestrial contexts is impressive. There are four map types available in Power BI, but we are going to focus only on the basic form. Maps are most useful to display insights about numbers that are somehow related to locations or distances between them.

As the dashboard from the earlier exercises is quite full, create a second page (a new canvas) by clicking on the + sign next to "Page 1" at the bottom of the screen. We have a new empty dashboard to work on.

Select the map icon (it depicts a globe, which is a three-dimensional map) in the Visualization panel, then expand it to fill the canvas, which will make it easier to view results. Now experiment putting different columns, or groups of columns, into the tile.[20] Where are we making the most profit? The largest circle is in the U.S.A., no surprise as we saw the sales figures earlier. Are we selling to the whole world? Pretty much, though interestingly we are making no sales in Iceland (one of the world's richest countries) yet shipping goods to Papua New Guinea. We are apparently shipping goods to Cuba—that might be worth some attention if our company is US-based.

It's not difficult to think of useful applications of the map visualization. National Post Offices might use them to emphasize areas of high loss due to theft; weather forecasting services might discern interesting patterns in the distribution of dangerous weather phenomena. Please experiment with this or other data and the map visualization, then return to Page 1 as we have more work to do, and much more to learn.

Measures and DAX

Power BI incorporates a sophisticated tool which allows you to create new value fields from within your data, without going back to modify the data at source or calling up the Power Query editor. A new calculation based on aggregated data is known to Power BI as a "measure."

As with so many Microsoft features, there are several ways to create a measure, not to mention several points of view as to what constitutes best practice. As an example, some authors insist that new measures should be added to the field list for the table they are principally drawn from. Others suggest creation of a brand new table to contain all your measures. Ultimately, if you know where to find your measures, this isn't important.

---

[20] Data can be added to the visualization bar of the map tile—for example, count of x data can be added to the "Bubble size" area of the visualization bar to make the bubbles different sizes for non-numbered data.

We are going to demonstrate use of two measures. While it might be rather obvious that Sales minus Profit equals costs, we'll use a measure to display costs and verify it with reference to the Visualizations already in use. Then, we'll take a broad brush to compare the efficiency of different countries in getting goods out of the door—by comparing the average delays between order and ship dates. We're going to need a new canvas for this presentation; please create one by clicking on the + sign next to the page tabs at the bottom of the screen.

Measures use DAX, a formula expression language or query language, to execute mathematical operations on data. The words "formula" and "expression" must importantly be used together; DAX is not an expression language but limited to formula expression. You may see DAX (which stands for "data analysis expressions") referred to as a "programming language." Don't let the idea of a new language intimidate you—it has much in common with the language you already know so well from Excel, though it has some formats and vocabulary of its own. We'll demonstrate as we go along.

Although this might be the first time you are seeing a discussion of DAX, it is not the first time you have used it. In background, Power BI uses DAX formulas for almost every tile it creates, though you cannot see them running seamlessly in background.

What are our Costs?

FIGURE 109: New measure icon

Click on the Modeling tab then on "New measure." Power BI will create a new field called "Measure" and place it in the field list for Table1. After creating it, you can right-click and select "Rename" to give it a new name, which will move it to the correct alphabetical position in the list. You can also change the name in the "Name" box or edit the first word in the formula bar. In this case, we are going to call it "Costs." But not yet![21] At the top left, Power BI opens a formula bar as follows:

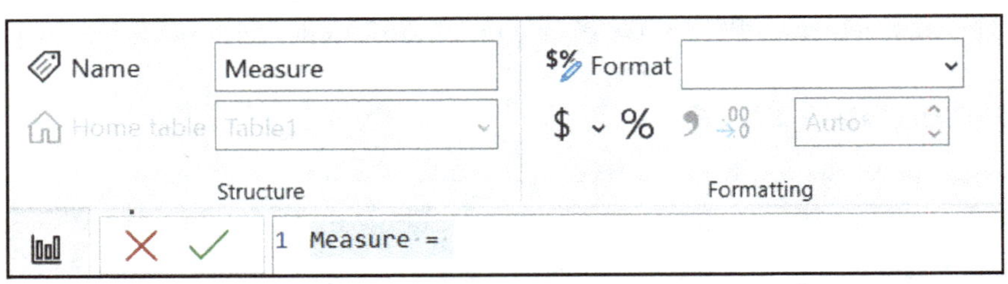

FIGURE 110: DAX formula box

Focus for a moment on the pale blue rectangle—this is where the DAX formula will be composed. The = sign operates to signify the start of a formula just like in Excel—all DAX formulas start with this symbol. Start to

[21] Some users may experience difficulties with re-naming; there is a well-known bug which may cause the measure to disappear, then when re-selected the Measure function causes Power BI to crash completely. It is best left until after the measure has been created and saved.

type the DAX function SUM. As soon as you start to type, you will see suggestions as to functions you might intend (again, just like Excel). You can continue typing or select one with a click.

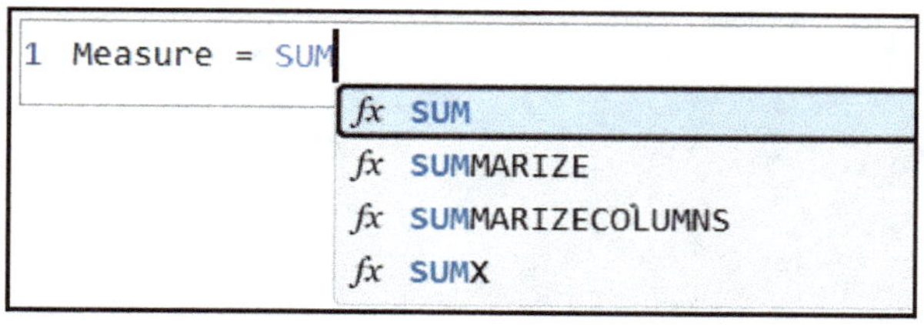

FIGURE 111: SUM measure

With SUM selected, Power BI will add an opening round bracket, then present a list of possible fields from which you can select. Choose Table1[Σ Sales] and close this part of the equation with the closing round bracket).

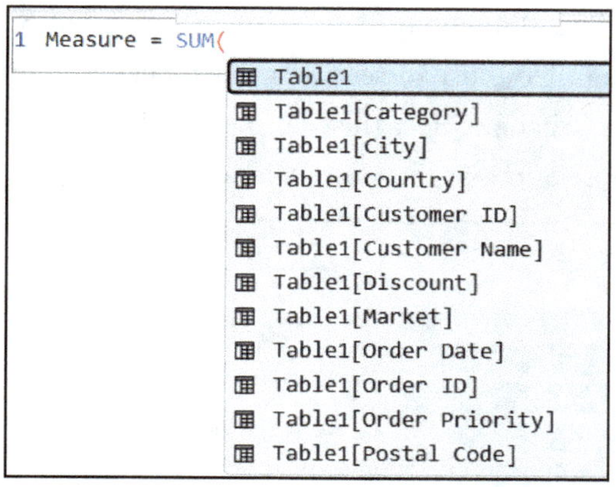

FIGURE 112: Field selection list

Next type in a space, the minus sign, then another space, then SUM again and this time include the field Table1[Σ Profit]. Don't forget to close off with a round bracket.

The syntax is now

Measure = SUM(Table1[Sales])-SUM(Table1[Profit])

And when you press "Enter" to accept the formula, Power BI will complete the measure. You can now click in the name box to rename the measure "Costs" and, should you wish, change its location to another table in the box alongside.

Now we can create a visualization for this new value and see if it agrees with what we expect.

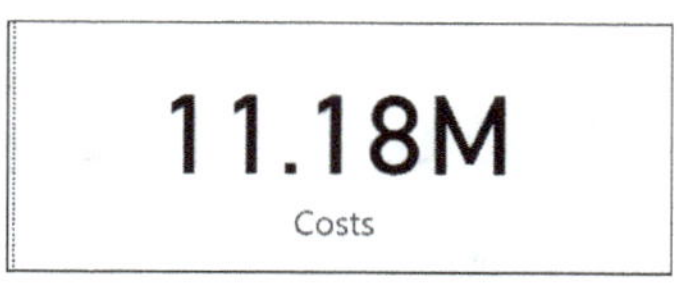

FIGURE 113: Costs card

Place a card on the canvas, then select "Costs" from the field list to insert the calculated value into it. 11.18 million—is that correct? Keeping in mind that these figures are rounded, from the main page the total sales were approximately 12.64 million and profit was 1.47 million. Yes. That works.

Where are we most efficient?

To compare shipping efficiency after receiving an order, we're going to need to use a different DAX function, AVERAGE.[22] Here are the steps to create that analysis:

Modeling Tab: New measure

```
= AVERAGE(Table1[Ship Date]) - AVERAGE(Table1[Order Date])
```

[22] Once again, there are alternative ways to achieve this goal. For example, DAX contains a function "DATEDIFF" which can be used in an expression to calculate the number of days, hours, minutes etc. between two dates.

Rename the measure "Delay"

Enter

Select the Stacked Bar Chart icon

Check the box for "Country"

Check the box for "Delay"

Expand the chart to the right for a better view

Our question was about efficiency. Presently, the countries are sorted from the longest delay to the shortest, so those displayed at the top of the list are the least efficient (Belize, Bhutan and Laos with an average of 6 days from order to shipment). We must go to reverse the ranking of the list to see the most efficient countries (Bahrain, Chad, Kuwait, Luxembourg, Malawi, and Western Sahara). Select the tile, then click on the three dot symbol in the top right corner. From the pop-up list, choose Sort axis then Sort ascending.

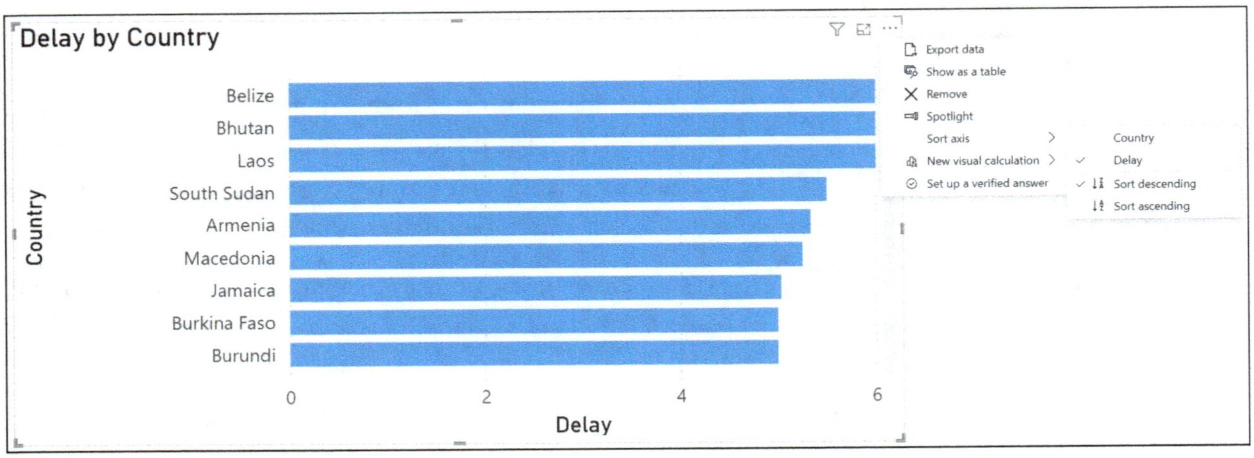

FIGURE 114: Finding the sort functions

Here we have demonstrated just two uses of DAX queries. There is a very long list of functions available in DAX. There is no requirement to learn most of them, and the most popular are for the most part the same as, or very similar to, Excel functions. You will find a DAX chart among the course materials—for the most part, though, you'll be able to rely on the interactive prompts shown on-screen as you work.

Calculated columns and DAX

DAX formulas are also used to create new columns derived from existing data. In our report, we want to create a new column which contains both city and country. This is useful for many purposes, but one very particular use is to correct errors made in map visualizations by the existence of similarly named cities in different countries. London could refer to the capital of England or a small city in Ontario, Canada. There is a Dublin in Ireland and another in California. If Power BI is making mapping mistakes for this reason, one solution is to create a new column which contains both city and country.

Start with the Table name in the right-hand pane, right-click on it and select "New column." A dialog layout will appear, identical to what you have already seen when creating a new measure. In this case, type in the syntax [City]&","&" "&[Country]

This instructs Power BI to place the City name, followed by a comma (special characters are enclosed in double quotation marks), followed by a space, followed by the country. This looks very much like an Excel formula, the only difference being the square brackets to denote columns from within the table.

A new column will appear in the list to the right. Rename the new column CityCountry.

To see if it is correctly calculated, install a new tile in Table format on Page 3 of the report, and bring in the new column. If all is well, the first row will read Aachen, Germany.

If the calculated columns function is used while in Data view, Power BI will display the source data, and you will see the new column at the right of the existing data. There is no change to the methodology.

The difference between measures and calculated columns

At first glance these two procedures look quite similar—they invoke formulaic procedures performed on the source data. However, they work in different ways to produce different types of result.

As we have seen, a calculated column adds a new column of data based on a mathematical operation for each row of data. In the new column, there is a result for every line item. Measures, however, perform operations on the aggregate of the data. No new column is created, and there is no result for each line item—only for the whole of the data (or a filtered subset of it).

Why is this important? An illustration is the calculation of percentage profit for either the whole enterprise, or a region or product. If a calculated column is created, we will see the percentage profit on each order. But there is no way to produce an overall profitability percentage from this column, because an average of averages would not be weighted for the individual values. A measure, however, which does not produce individual results, would start from the aggregated data and calculate a single result for all the orders.

Drilling down

A key feature of Power BI which makes it possible to present simple, summary data but then allow the user to examine more detail is the *drill down* feature. For any data which form a hierarchy, it's possible at the click of the mouse to move up and down the hierarchy and see more or less detailed analyses. A *Data Hierarchy* is "a series of ordered groupings in a system, beginning with the smallest unit to the largest" (Roch et al., 2022). The most common hierarchy is date; sales data, for example, may be presented for an entire period, by year, quarter, month or even day. Fast-paced data such as TV viewing statistics may be captured by the hour, minute or even second.

Create a new page in the report and add a tile with the "Stacked Column Chart" icon. From Table1, select ∑ Sales and Order Date.

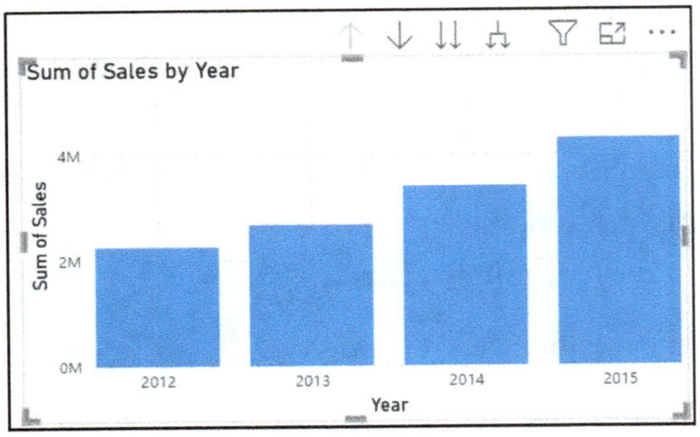

FIGURE 115: Sales totals by year

The tile now displays columns representing total sales by year. At the top right, because there is a hierarchy in the "Order Date" column, there are four different arrow symbols—the first enables drilling up (three clicks) to the year, the others allow drilling down.

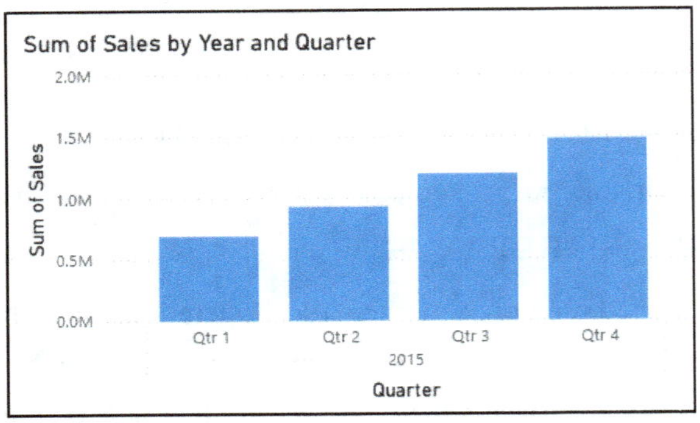

FIGURE 116: Sales totals by quarter, for one year

Click on the down arrow, which enables drilling down, then on one of the columns. The chart will change to display the data for that specific year at the next level, by quarter. Ctrl+Z or the single up arrow will return to the previous level. Clicking again on a column will take the display to the next level, months (not illustrated). Note that clicking on a bar will create a chart which shows months for *that period*, while the branched double down arrow will display all months for all the columns the year.

FIGURE 117: Branched double down arrow

SCATTER CHARTS

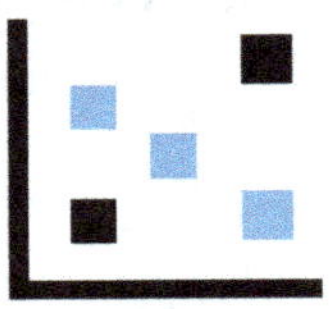

FIGURE 118: Scatter chart icon

The scatter chart visualization is a powerful tool for data analytics, where we want to explore the relationship between two variables. Create a new dashboard and click on the icon, then click and drag Σ Profit from Table 1 to the Y axis on the Visualizations pane, and Σ Sales to the X axis. Click on the down arrow on the editing pane for each axis then select "Don't summarize" from the drop-down menu. Resize the tile, to obtain a visualization like this:

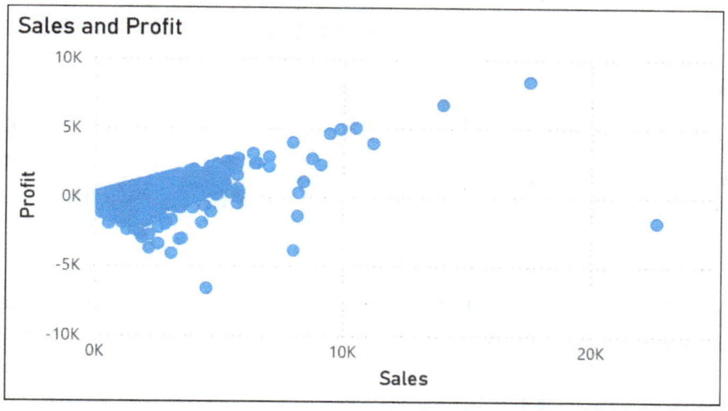

FIGURE 119: Scatter plot

Think like an auditor and note the outliers—how can it be that the largest sale in the period, over $22,000, resulted in a loss; and how did a single sale of around $4,500 result in a $7,000 loss? There could be valid reasons for this, they could be mistakes in the data—or they could be fraud.

Formatting

In the earlier sections, we created a pair of dashboards using default options presented by Power BI. The presentation of Page 1, on which we will focus, is quite basic as is the data analysis, and there's nothing wrong with that. We've presented a four-year window of activity, highlighted sales and profits, shown trends for both, demonstrated where the bulk of our sales occur, and enabled interactive analysis of the relationships between sales, profits and shipping methods. In selecting these themes, we concentrated mainly on finding summaries and analyses that demonstrated key features of Power BI, rather than directing our work to a particular audience or business need.

Our work so far is effective, but it looks neither professional nor elegant. The company is not identified, fonts and labels are quite random, and we've given no thought to axes, frames, colors or layout. Using Power BI's formatting options, we can change all that.

The whole dashboard

FIGURE 120: Format icon

We can't work on the appearance of the whole dashboard while any tile is selected. On Page 1, click in the empty space beneath the tiles and observe that the Visualizations panel now has a formatting icon in the top space, which is unselected. Click on it to produce a short menu of six possible selections, each with its own right arrow > for further choices.

Page Information allows a change to the tab name at the bottom of the page. You can also do this by double-clicking and editing the tab itself, or right-clicking it and selecting "Rename Page." Three different ways to achieve the same object. The other menu items are further format settings:

- *Canvas Settings* allow selection of ratios of width to height, and alignment of the tiles.
- *Canvas background* allows the choice of a background color which may be visible in any unused space, and insertion of a background image. A transparency slider defaults to 100%, where even if selected neither of these will be visible. Moving the slider down progressively increases the intensity of the background color or image.

- *Wallpaper* covers are larger area and overlaps the canvas background. Here however the most intense display is with the transparency slider set to 0%.
- *Filter pane* has no effect on the canvas but sets up fonts, colors and sizes for the interactive Filter pane.

This is fairly technical stuff; most users will probably never change or use these functions.

The individual tiles

Formatting becomes *much* more interesting when we apply it to individual visualizations. The presentation and formatting options change according to the type selected.

FIGURE 122: Add data icon

Starting with the Sum of Sales card at the top left, select it, click on the "Add Data" icon in the Visualizations pane, then look below the individual visualization icons. As this is a single field, there is only one "bucket" and it presently shows as "Sum of Sales." There is however a down arrow next to the field name; clicking on this will present a drop-down menu with a range of possible mathematical functions. The penultimate option is "Show value as" which allows a further choice between "No calculation" (the default) and Percent of Grand Total.

FIGURE 121: Format visual icon

Now click on the "Format Visual" icon in the Visualizations pane. You will immediately see a toggle switch for "Category label," which can be kept in the On position or moved to Off to remove "Sum of Sales" from beneath the displayed figure. There are also options available to change the presentation of that text. Click on the General tab to reveal many more formatting options.

Title, if toggled on, allows the placement and formatting of a title inside the tile. A background color can be selected and the placement of the title within the tile can be manipulated.

Move to the Sum of Sales by Country tile. As this is a two-axis chart, there are two "buckets" below the Visualizations icons. Different columns can be clicked and dragged into the Y-axis and X-axis buckets, each then presented with a down arrow for further options. Categorical data have a limited range, while numerical data are given the full list of mathematical options. Clicking the Format visual icon produces a series of options under the Visual tab. Here you can select the Y and X axes to be on or off, format the text on them, switch to logarithmic scales and much more. Gridlines can be turned on or off. Colors can be selected for the bars, data labels can be switched on or off, and much more. On the General tab the options are the same as they were for the Sum of Sales card, including the option to include, edit and format the header.

On the slicer tile, the Visualizations pane again shows only one bucket, for the field which will define the slicer. The Visual tab gives three options for presentation—a vertical list, tiles within the tile, or a drop-down menu. A range of other formatting options, like those used for the previous tiles, is also presented in several sub-menus within the General menu. Importantly the text size can be adjusted to fill the box so that it doesn't have awkward space below the list.

If you've worked through these menus and tried out various options, formatting the two-line charts will become instinctively easy. It's unnecessary to recite all the options and techniques repetitively; note, however, that here the buckets can have more than one field dragged into them if there is a time element involved; here Order Date and Year are both listed in the X-axis bucket.

MAPS

The map visualizations have impressive formatting features. For the basic map there are five style options—the default is "Road"—then there are three shades, dark, light and grayscale. These are accessed from the Visualizations pane, selecting the format icon, then the down arrow next to Map settings. While the road map is probably the clearest for most applications, the aerial view may well be the most impressive.

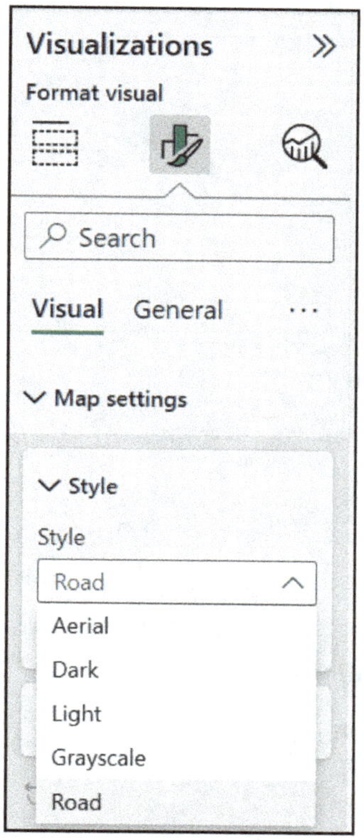

FIGURE 124: Map selections

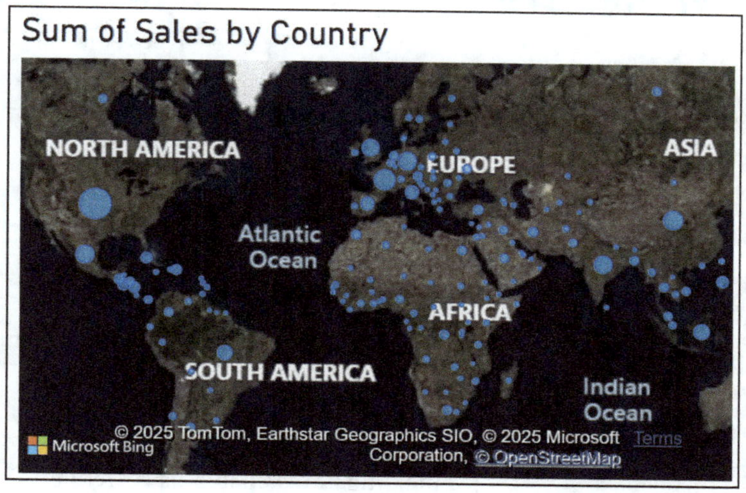

FIGURE 123: Aerial bubble map

Non-tile elements

FIGURE 125: Text box icon

The Dashboard is missing one essential element: a title. This must be created as a separate element. The device is a text box, which may be familiar from other Microsoft suite applications. After creating space for the box, click on the Text Box icon and re-size the box to fit. Type the required text into the box and use the pop-up editing strip to format it. The result looks much better than the bare presentation we started with. To familiarize yourself with the procedures described above, take this screenshot as a model and experiment with formatting features first to copy it, then to improve it.

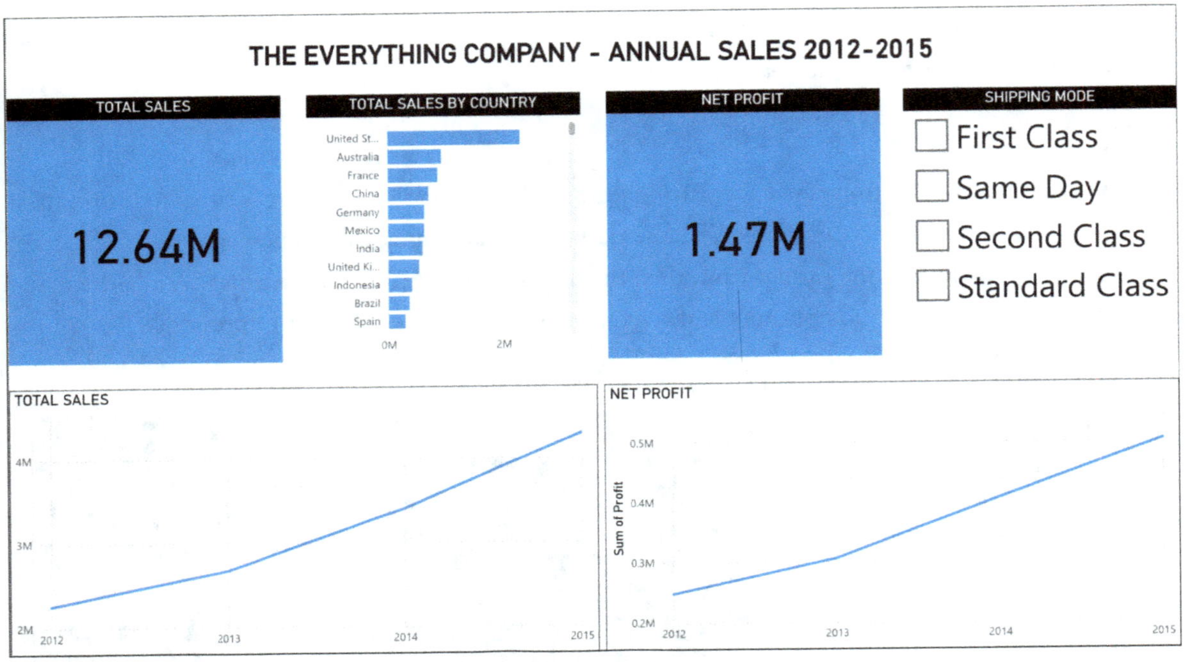

FIGURE 126: Everything Company annual sales

Filters

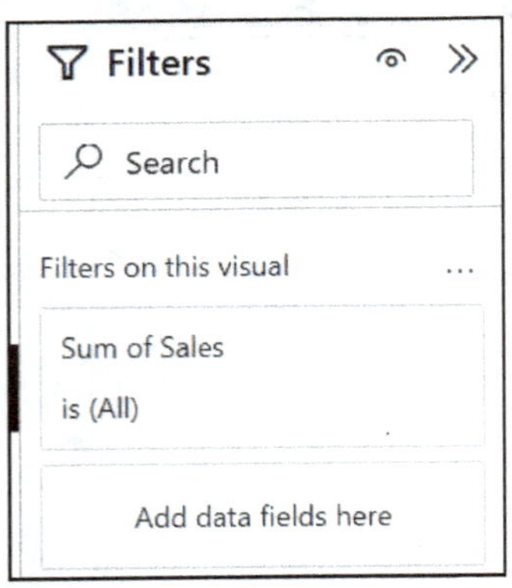

FIGURE 127: Filters

Filter functions enable us to refine the data in a tile according to parameters which we set, or selections that we make. Select the Total Sales by Country tile by clicking in it. Then open the Filters pane, if it is not displayed, by clicking on the double left arrow to the left of the Visualizations title..

The list of filters tells that we have one data column selected—Sum of Sales—and that the data summarized is "All).

There is an empty box beneath the list of filters, into which you can drag *any* column that you want to use as a filter. It is not necessary, though it is possible, that the chosen column be one of those already listed.

To see the same statistics but for specific countries, drag and drop the column Country into the empty box.

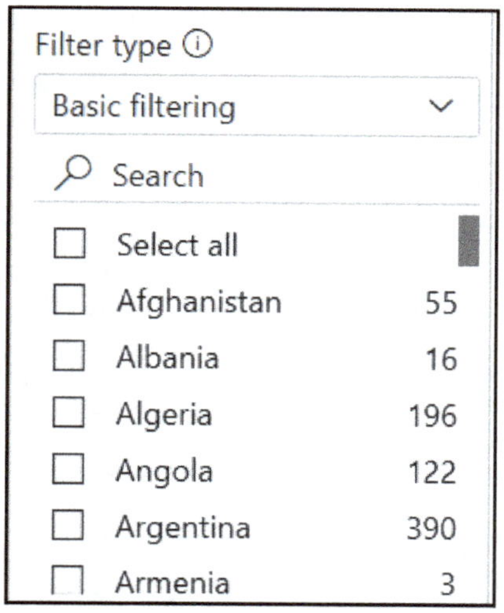

FIGURE 128: Filter Dialog Box

Immediately we are presented with a complete list of the countries in the database, from which we can make manual selections. One is "Select all" (which would be pointless for our purposes[23]); we could search for countries of interest or perform any number of manual combinations (for example, all countries beginning with A). Note the "Require single selection" checkbox below the list—if this is checked, the user will only be able to select one country at a time.

We might well decide, however, that selecting single countries is not very efficient, especially if we are interested in regional performance. Instead of dragging "Country" into the third box, remove it (using the X) and drag "Region" into the box instead. Then select "Caribbean" and check that the tile now displays total sales of 324.28K or 0.32M.

This snapshot draws our attention to the drop-down menu available under "Filter type." The default is "Basic filtering," but two other types are available: Select "Advanced filtering" to reveal this dropdown menu:

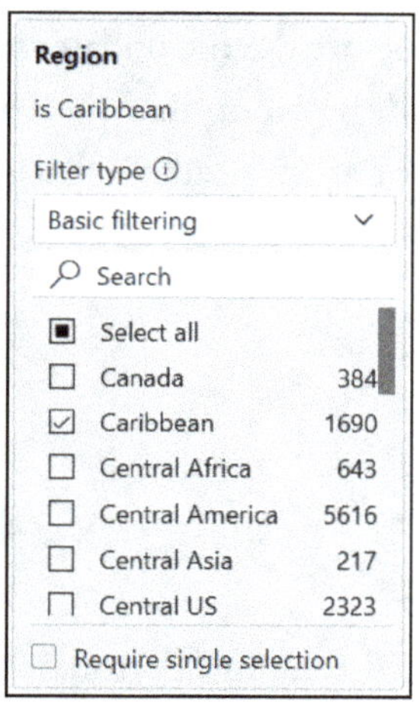

FIGURE 130: Regional selection

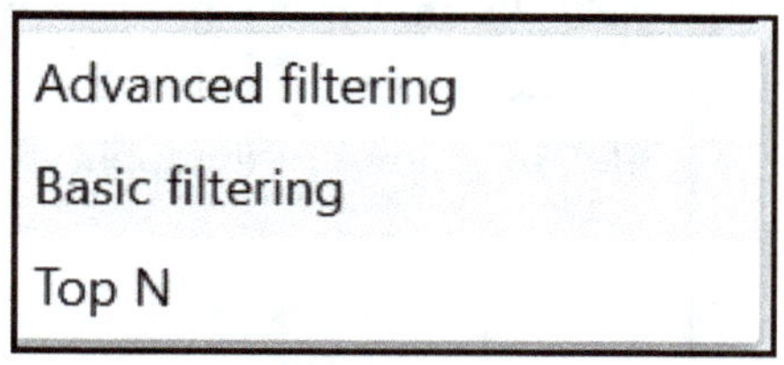

FIGURE 129: Filter types

[23] This option may be helpful when the user wishes to remove a small number of outliers to give viewers a more accurate image of averages (for example, select all the people in a Microsoft meeting then remove Bill Gates to obtain a more representative calculation of average rider salary).

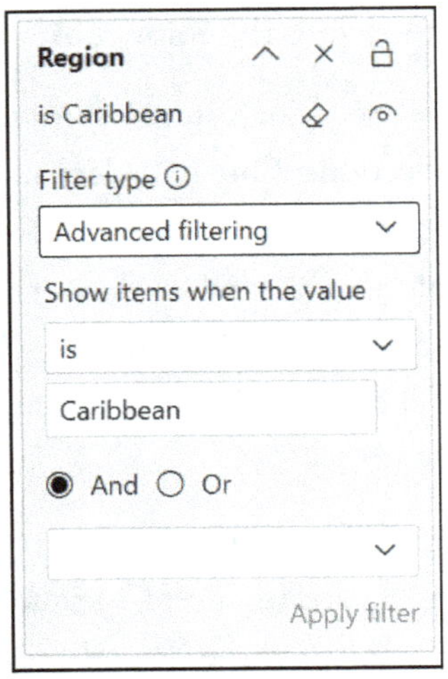

FIGURE 131: Advanced filtering

In most cases it is more suitable for numerical fields but can be used for categorical filtering. For example, the Or box could be used to include empty fields in the Region column.

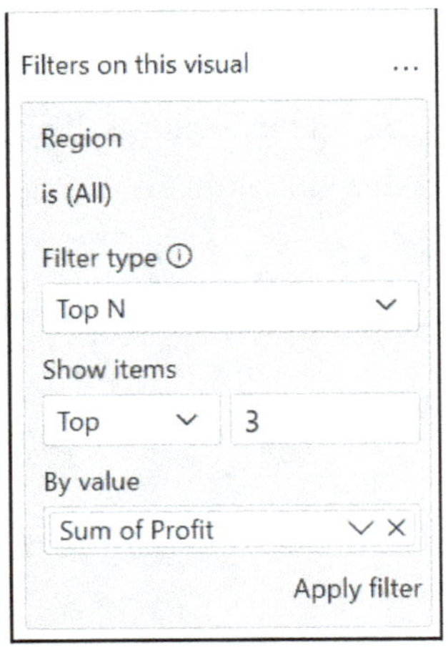

FIGURE 132: Top 3 filtering

"Top N" filtering may also be familiar from other Microsoft programs—in this example, we have configured the dialog to ask the question "What are the total sales from the three regions yielding the most profit?"

There are two important points worth noting here; first, before the tile updates to yield the answer, we must click on "Apply filter"; second, be aware that ONLY the selected tile is updating. Filtering on one tile does not affect results in other tiles, in contrast to the application of a slicer.

A cautionary note—when looking at a dashboard, it is easy to forget that you've applied filtering. Fortunately for each tile type where filters can be applied, Power BI places the filter symbol (a funnel shape) above the tile. Hovering the cursor on this symbol will produce a pop-up box which informs the viewer whether any filters are applied, and if so which ones.

FIGURE 133: Filters and slicers notification

Earlier we mentioned that for simplicity, returned orders would be ignored up until this point. Now we'll use a filter to remove returned orders from our calculations.

In the main page of the report, select the "TOTAL SALES" tile by clicking on it, remove the previous figures by returning to Basic filtering and selecting all, then note the figure, 12.64M. Ensure that the Filters pane is visible. "Country" and "Sum of Sales" are presently set to all.

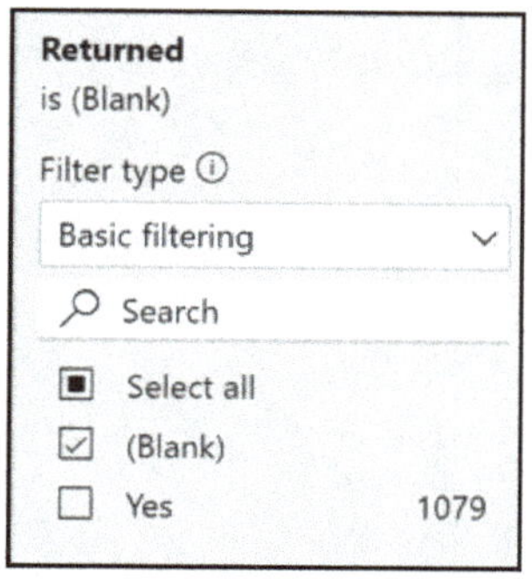

FIGURE 134: Filtering selection

Go to the Data pane and click on the right arrow next to Table 2 to bring up the column list; click and drag the "Returned" column into the first available filter box, then click to select "(Blank)" from the list of options.

You have instructed Power BI to calculate total sales for all orders that were NOT returned (*i.e.*, there is no datum indicating that the order was returned). The total sales will drop to 12.12M but note that the Profit calculation in the third tile has not changed. It will be necessary to repeat this procedure to remove calculated profits on orders that were returned or add a page-level filter. Profit will drop to 1.41M; hovering on the filter symbol will confirm that returned orders are now removed.

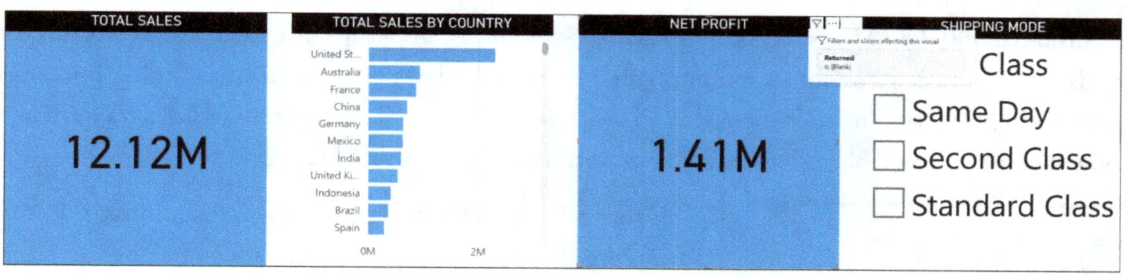

FIGURE 135: Sales and profits filtered for returns

Parameters (What-If Analysis)

Power BI can capture user input and update its calculations to provide dynamic profit calculations, break even points, and more.

Power Boats, Inc. is a small boatbuilder. It specializes in custom twin-engine craft for private use. Please download the Power BI file Power Boats.pbix; it contains the basic fixed and variable costs for the business, with two card visualizations already created for fixed and variable costs. The visualizations show only costs. Management believes it can sell its boats for a price between $200,000 and $300,000 each; it would like to know what price it must charge and how many boats it must sell next year to break even.

Click on the *Modeling tab,* then on *New Parameter*, select *Numeric range* to reveal this dialog box:

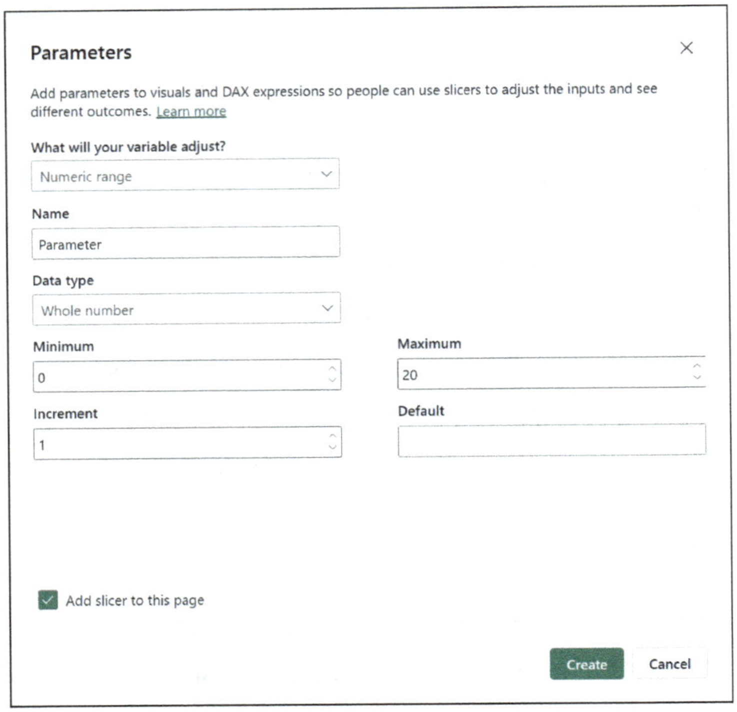

FIGURE 136: Parameter dialog box

For name change “Parameter” to "Selling Price,” make the minimum and numbers 200,000 and 300,000, with increments of 10,000. Leave the slicer box checked. Click *Create*. This results in a visualization box that includes the words Selling Price, a box for user input, and a slicer that allows the user to select selling prices between $200,000 and $300,000. The user input data are captured in a variable called Selling Price Value. The Fields pane now includes a new table called Selling Price with the following variables:

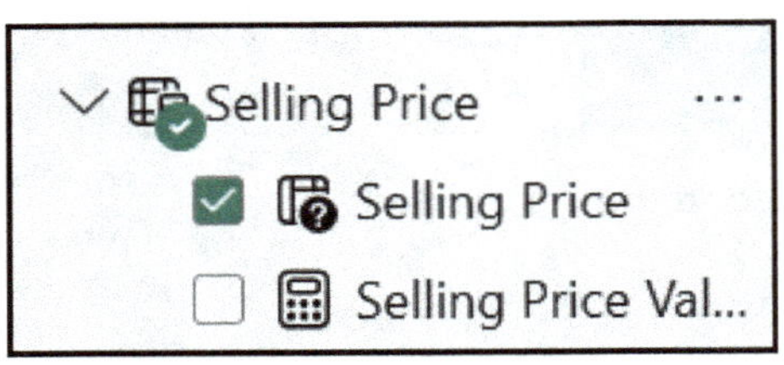

FIGURE 137: Selling price variables

This new table is not part of the original data; instead, it is created to capture the Selling Price Value variable input by the user. Click on the button on the slider which has appeared in its own tile then move it across the bar, experimenting with different prices. The appearance of the slider can be modified as with any other tile.

Next we will calculate the breakeven point. Because the dashboard is dynamic, the breakeven point (the number of boats) should change each time a different selling price is entered. We must create a formula which uses the known variables. In the Data pane, hover over the Selling Price title and click on the three dots which appear to the right. Select *New Measure*. Delete the suggested formula and put instead:

```
BE = SUM(Table2[Cost]) / ('Selling Price'[Selling Price Value] - SUM(Table3[Vvalue]))
```

A new field will appear under Selling Price, called BE. Click outside the existing visualizations then click on the card visualization icon. Select the BE from the Data pane and click on the Selling Price slider to establish a selling price of $200,000. The breakeven requirement, 48.97 boats, will appear in the breakeven tile.

Experiment with moving the slider, as the price increases the breakeven number of boats will become smaller. At a selling price of $300,000, the company need only sell 6.75 boats in the year.[24]

Following are the cards and slicer which will be on your screen. They can be reformatted just as we did earlier, but here we won't do that as we have achieved our main object.

FIGURE 138: Dynamic break even calculation for Power Boats

Publishing and Embedding

It is stunningly easy to share your Power BI work with a team, embed it into a PowerPoint presentation and have it update continuously as you refresh data. Demonstrating these features to new users will certainly deliver a "wow factor" to your audience.

FIGURE 139: Publish button

Here, "Publish" has a particular meaning—to upload a Power BI report to Microsoft's software-as-a-service product, Power BI service. This is the steppingstone to sharing a presentation on Power BI mobile and other add-on products, and embedding Power BI work into a PowerPoint presentation.

You must have a work or organization email account which is tied to a Microsoft subscription. Once you are logged in, publishing Power BI work is extremely straightforward. If you're not logged in when you try, Microsoft will walk you through the steps to register and enroll you in Microsoft Fabric, a free product which opens the Power BI doors on the cloud.

---

[24] You might question whether whole numbers should be specified. For larger capital items like boats, planes and houses, from a manufacturer's point of view it is quite reasonable to reckon work-in-progress on the last item of the year as a fractional sale.

With your Power BI work open, click on the File tab then on the vertical ribbon, select Publish. If you have unsaved changes, Power BI will prompt you to save them, then show this dialog box:

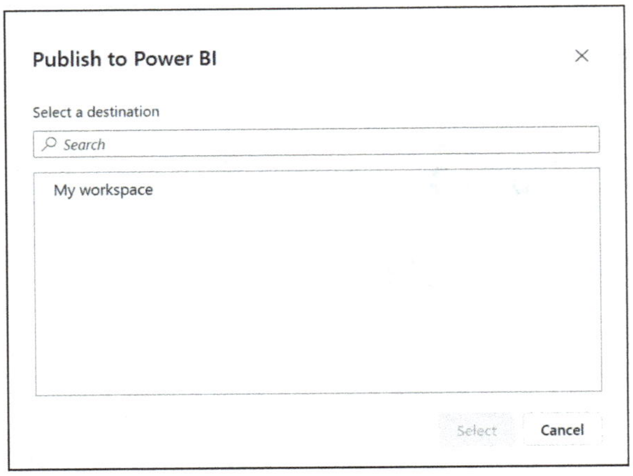

FIGURE 140: Publish dialog box

Double-click to select "My workspace" then click the Select button. After a brief pause for uploading, success will be confirmed on this screen:

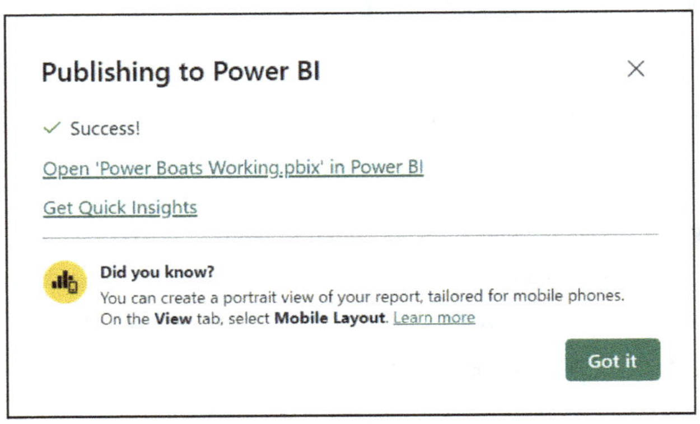

FIGURE 141: Published success notification

If you now click on the link immediately below "Success!" your presentation will open on the cloud, and importantly the browser will now display the URL for your work. You will need this if you wish to embed the report in a PowerPoint presentation.

Embedding requires use of the Power BI Service, the Microsoft SaaS element that allows you to store your Power BI work on the cloud. Once you have done so, you will have access to a URL which identifies your stored work.

In PowerPoint, open a new or existing slide and click on the Insert tab.

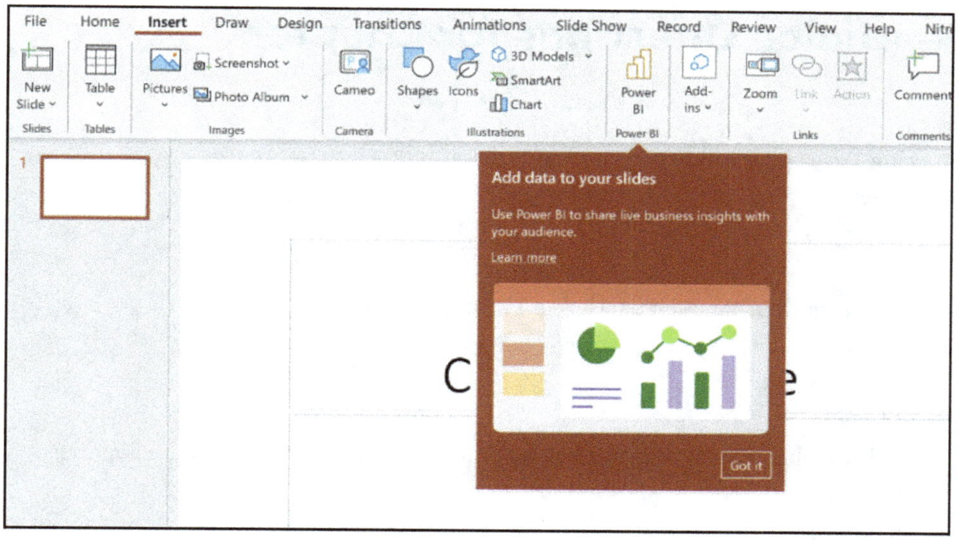

FIGURE 142: Embedding Power BI

Just to the right of the Slide Show tab, there is a Power BI button. If the pop-up graphic shows, click "Got it" to clear it, or "Learn more" if you would like to. Click on the Power BI button, and Microsoft will ask you to identify your user account by email address. Once you've done that, insert the URL for your Power BI report and PowerPoint will do the rest.

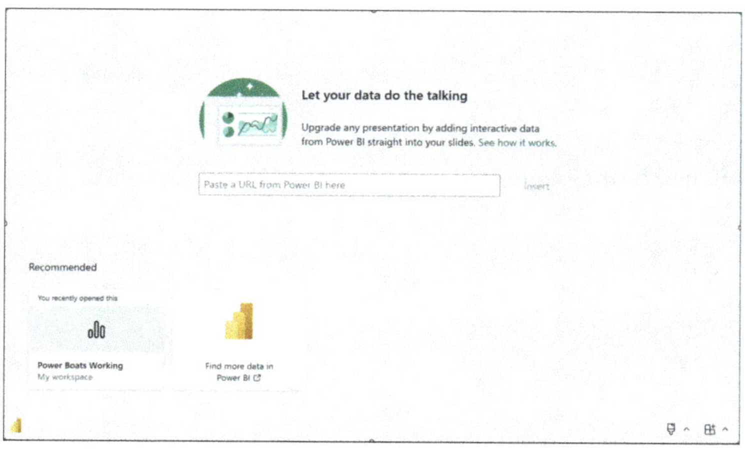

FIGURE 143: Let your data do the talking

As you update your Power BI presentation and publish it, it will be automatically updated each time you open your presentation.

As PowerPoint says, you really can then "Let your data do the talking."

Multiple Choice Questions for Chapter 7

1. When using Power BI to address data from Excel, it is best practice to work with
   a. sheets
   b. tables
   c. ranges
2. To see the relationships between datasets in Power BI, which view is used?
   a. Report
   b. Table
   c. Model
3. In Power BI, which of these is constructed by pinning visuals from one or more reports?
   a. dashboard.
   b. report.
   c. canvas.
4. When original data are updated, visualizations in Power BI automatically reflect the new data.
   a. True
   b. False
5. A new calculation in Power BI based on existing aggregated data is known as
   a. a tile.
   b. a measure.
   c. a calculated column.
6. DAX is
   a. a programming language.
   b. a formula expression language.
   c. neither a query nor programming language.
7. An individual visualization in a Power BI dashboard is known as a(n):
   a. tile.
   b. element.
   c. mosaic.
8. Time columns imported to PowerBI are identified by
   a. a calendar icon.
   b. a clock icon.
   c. an empty hierarchy icon.
9. Power Query Editor is an important tool which can be used in the process of importing data to Power BI.
   a. True
   b. False
10. Power BI runs flawlessly on Mac computers.
    a. True
    b. False

PART II. ANALYZING BUSINESS DATA

8. TOOLS FOR BUSINESS ANALYTICS

This chapter introduces several techniques which use existing or hypothetical data as support for decisions or predictions. Not all will be used in any one business model.

Sales Prediction with Varying Price

In this exercise we will demonstrate the use of Excel's trendline feature to predict outcomes in one variable from changes in another. The trendline which gives the best results will vary with the type of data. Excel gives six choices; we will execute three and show the tools for comparing them. First a few words about the types we will *not* demonstrate.

Logarithmic trendlines are most suited to situations where something increases or decreases at first but then flattens off. An example might be the relationship between advertising and sales. As a new product is launched, the advertising spend will determine the reach—but at a certain point the market starts to become saturated and even if more advertising is bought, the return on it becomes less and less.

Polynomial trendlines are used for relationships that change direction—that is, they first increase then decrease, or first decrease then increase. Polynomial equations are largely used in technical fields such as aviation, engineering and pharmaceuticals. Consider an object which is thrown up in the air—its distance from the ground will increase at a diminishing rate, then decrease at an accelerating rate, until it hits the ground. In jet aircraft, normally adding power will increase the speed, but there are situations in slow flight where adding power decreases the speed.

Moving average trendlines are used to flatten the curve in a relationship that is difficult to see from the data because there are so many ups and downs. An example might be inflation rates calculated monthly, or corporate bond rates over a lengthy period.

At a hypothetical university (UZO—the University of Zoology), Animal Medication 1.01 is a compulsory course. It is offered four times per year, with a maximum enrolment of 100. The teachers of the course have authored and published a textbook, *Animal Medication*.

Students *need* access to the book. They can purchase a softcover copy from the university bookstore; they can purchase an eBook online for $60, and if they want to print and bind a copy of the eBook, the total cost is $90 more. The book is very technical; students often need a copy of the book open beside them as they work on problems and assignments. It is not convenient for all students to work from the online copy alone. Students wishing to save money also have the option of buying used copies from students who have finished the course. Because of the range of options, sales of new copies are highly sensitive to price.

Table 17: Book sales

Animal Medication 1.01
Text Book Sales 2022-2023

Term	Price	Sales
1	100	2
2	40	72
3	60	53
4	80	9
5	70	50
6	50	70
7	30	90
8	90	3

Each copy of the book costs $25 to produce, regardless of quantity. Over the last eight semesters (two years), the price charged for a new book has varied between $30 and $100; the bookstore has kept records of the number sold. After eight semesters there are now enough data to measure the impact of price on demand (sales).

The file Animal Medication.xlsx is downloadable, or you can copy the data into a new spreadsheet. Our objective is to determine the price at which the book will be most profitable for the bookstore.

The first step is to produce a scatterplot (Select the Price and Sales data B4:C12, Insert tab, Scatter) showing the relationship between the two datasets. Predictably, it's a downward trend; at a price of $30, 90 students in the course buy a copy as the price is lower than the eBook and even second-hand copies are unlikely to be available. As the price increases, however, demand drops off and at $100, only two students buy an original copy—even printing out the eBook is now cheaper.

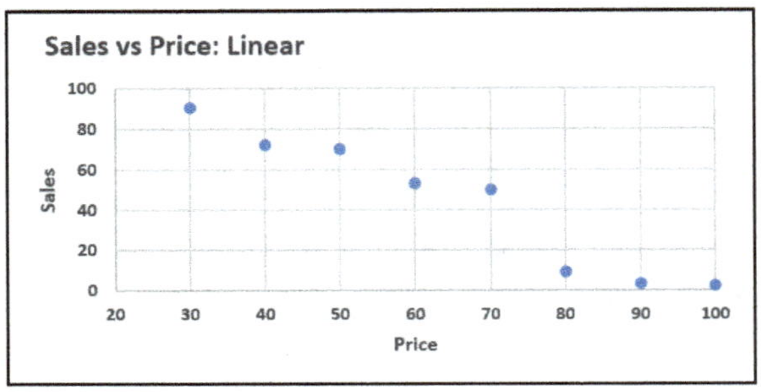

FIGURE 144: Sales vs Price scatterplot

We can now use Excel's powerful charting features to depict and calculate some formulas which show the relationship between sales and price. There are various types of relationship curves; we will explore and evaluate three of them.

Linear curve

Clicking inside the chart produces editing symbols to the right—select the + icon which presents a selection of chart elements; from the list select *Trendline*, click on the arrow to the right and select *More Options*. This will produce the Format Trendline Menu with three tabs – select the one that looks like a column chart, select Linear, and check the box for Display Equation on chart. Click and drag the equation into the empty space above the line and enlarge the font size so that it's easier to read.

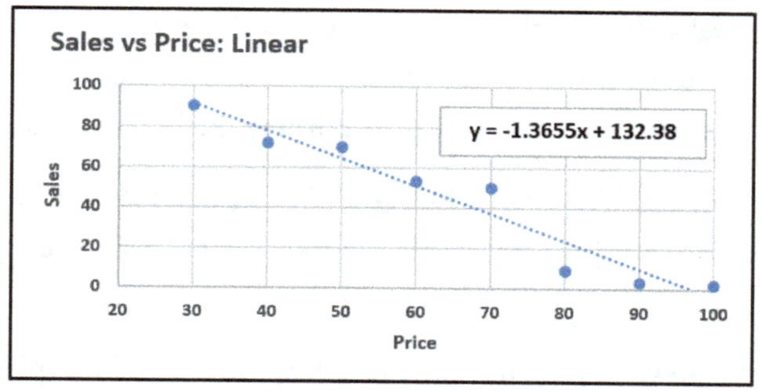

FIGURE 145: Linear trendline

The linear trendline is a straight line, quantifying what we intuitively expected—the higher the price, the less the sales. Linear trendlines are most suitable in this kind of situation, where there is a relationship between two axes that approximates a straight line. Excel has also created an equation for this relationship—the sales at any price in our range will be -1.3655 times the price, plus 132.38. From this you could predict for example that at a price of $55, 57 books would be sold. The intercept—the point on the Y axis at which the line crosses, is 132.38, and -1.3655 is the slope of the line.

The linear equation always results in a straight line—for each dollar increase in price, sales will decrease by a fixed amount. Linear equations are the easiest to understand, and the easiest to apply. However, they may not always be the most accurate. A defining feature of linear equations is that all exponents are 1 – this keeps them relatively simple but does not always reflect reality.

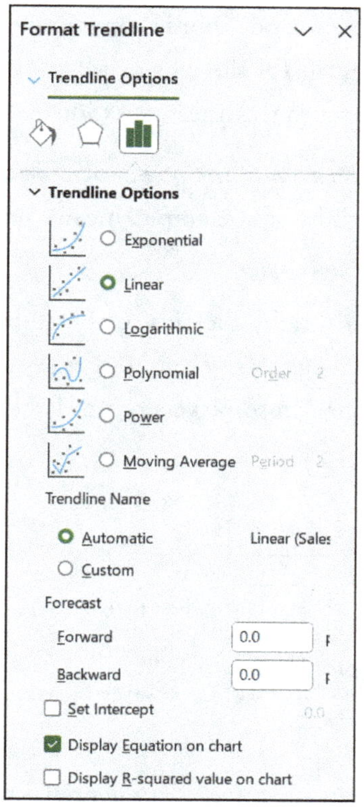

FIGURE 146: Trendline options menu

Power curve

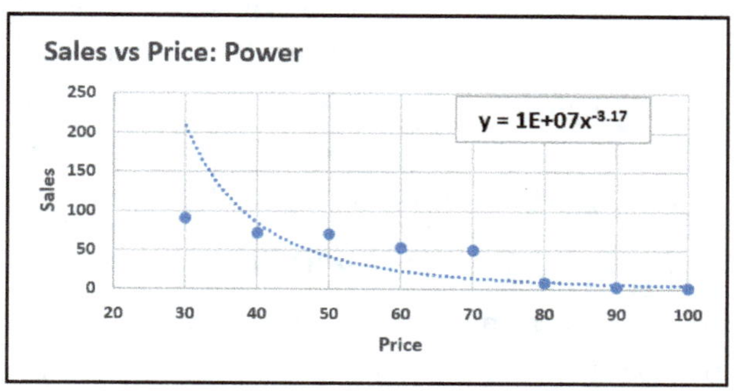

FIGURE 147: Power trendline

The second curve to be created is the Power Curve. We might predict, before creating it, that it is not going to be well suited to the data. By its very name, the power curve indicates that is most appropriate for data which measure the results of increasing inputs on performance—it is highly appropriate for measuring car or aircraft engine performance, or efforts of athletes. However, we'll try it since it will give us a comparable to help in evaluating other curve types.

Our fears are realized: to fit the power curve, Excel has used a scale which is outside the possibilities (maximum sales in any one term are 100) and the curve does not visually seem to reflect best fit for the data as we know them. We do however have a formula, and it now includes an exponent (in contrast to the linear equation).

The formula contains a letter E. This stands for exponent and is shorthand for "times ten to the power of". This type of expression, known as scientific notation, avoids using very long numbers. 5E5, for example, means 5 x 10^5, or 500,000.

To convert the power equation into a number which can be copied into equations, right-click on the formula and select Format Trendline Label. In the panel that appears to the right, change the category to Number. You can also change the number of decimal places displayed (here, we have chosen four). In some versions of Excel you will need to uncheck and recheck the Display Equation box to effect the change.

$$y = 10{,}035{,}453.94x^{-3.1700}$$

FIGURE 148: Power equation

The formula tells us that for every 1% increase in price, sales will decrease by approximately 3.17%.

Exponential curve

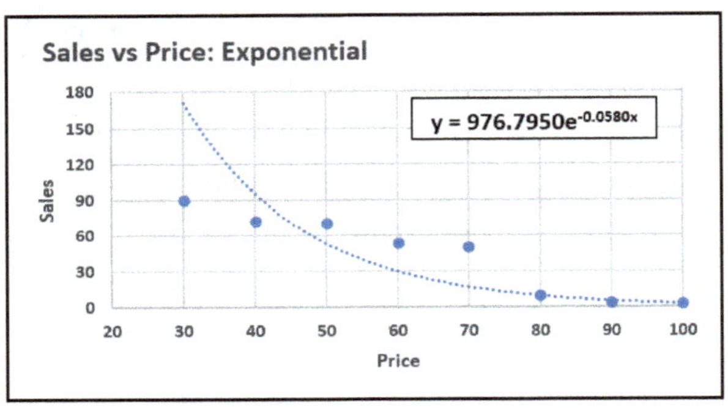

FIGURE 149: Exponential Curve

Now let's try the exponential curve. Exponential fit, like power, expresses what happens if there is a 1% increase in price.

Exponential curves work best with data which increase or decrease at, respectively, an increasing or decreasing rate in relation to the other variable. World population is a great example; the rate of growth increases constantly over time. By contrast, animal species nearing extinction tend to die off at an increasing rate. Carbon dating is another example: exponential models are used to calculate the age of plants and bones based on knowledge of the exponential rate of decay.

Here, the constant is 976.8e, while the exponent is -0.058. The lower case e signifies Euler's number, in contrast to the upper case E discussed above. Euler's number is approximately 2.71828, and represents in this case an exponential decay function, because the exponent is negative. Unlike the previous case, we cannot force Excel to converting to pure numbers though we can select the number of decimal places. If you type e in an formula which you create, Excel will return an error code. Instead, use the EXP function: to convert this equation, for example, for a sale price of $60, for example, you would type

```
=976.7950 * EXP(-0.0580 * 60)
```

Evaluating the methods

We want to know which of these three curves is the best predictor of sales at any given price. We'll employ Excel to do most of the work. In each case we calculate the difference between what each curve would have predicted for sales, and the actual sales that we already know for our price points.

Mean absolute percentage error

For each curve, we can calculate the absolute percentage error for each prediction versus actual sales, then take an average of those errors. This will calculate the average percentage by which the curve missed the mark. First, we'll set up a framework for calculating MAPEs for each curve.

TABLE 18: Curve statistics

Curve Statistics	
Linear	
Slope	-1.3655
Intercept	132.38
Power	
Constant	10035453.94
Exponent	-3.17
Exponential	
Constant	976.8
Exponent	-0.058

The numbers placed under "Curve Statistics" are the exact numbers from the formulas exhibited by Excel for each curve. Using these, we can calculate the predicted sales for each term.

TABLE 19: Predicted sales

Predicted Sales		
Linear	Power	Exponent
-4	5	3
78	84	96
50	23	30
23	9	9
37	14	17
64	41	54
91	208	171
9	6	5

In the linear column, the formula will refer to the prices set in Column B:

```
=B5*$B$26+$B$27
```

The locking $ signs are to keep the calculation focused on the intercept and slope. The formula can be dragged down for all eight terms. The power curve calculation will be

```
=$B$29*B5^$B$30
```

And the exponential:

```
=$B$32*EXP($B$33*B5)
```

We now have a set of predicted sales using each curve. We've reduced the display to remove decimal places for each, though Excel still knows the complete figures. Of course we can't sell 4.587 books, let alone -4.17; if the exercise was to stop here, we would round the figures and use them to guide production ahead of term. However, our objective is to evaluate the production methods and decide which curve works best given what we know from actual sales in previous terms.

TABLE 20: MAPE calculation

Linear	Power	Exponent
308%	129%	48%
8%	16%	33%
5%	56%	43%
157%	3%	5%
26%	72%	66%
8%	41%	23%
2%	132%	90%
216%	114%	76%
Mean Average Percentage Error		
91%	70%	48%

We calculate MAPE using the formula:

```
=ABS(D26-C5)/$C5
```

That is, the absolute value of the predicted sales—actual sales, divided by actual sales to give percentage error for each term. Because we provided an absolute reference to the correct letters and numbers in the first formula in row 36, we can drag across and down to fill all the squares in this table.

After taking the average (mean) of the percentage errors, we have an indication that the exponential relationship is the best predictor (though it's not particularly accurate).

This is not the only way to test the predictions.

Root mean squared error

TABLE 21: RMSE

Linear	Power	Exponent
38.07	6.69	0.92
33.18	138.16	575.69
6.50	890.24	524.75
199.94	0.09	0.19
174.37	1280.97	1099.00
34.75	824.50	264.17
2.00	14037.31	6633.83
42.06	11.60	5.21
Root Mean Squared Error		
23.04	131.11	95.41

The root mean squared error "does what it says on the can." It is the square root of the total of the squares of the individual errors. As both negative and positive numbers, squared, are positive, we have no need of the ABS function this time.

The formula for the linear squared mean error will be:

```
=($C5-D26)^2
```

Again, the formula can be copied down and across to fill a new frame. This time, however, to reach the root mean squared error, the bottom line will be

```
=SQRT(SUM(D36:D43))
```

It too can be copied across the three cells, and this time the linear equation looks like the best predictor, having the lowest value.

Mean absolute error

TABLE 22: MAE

Linear	Power	Exponent
6.17	2.59	0.96
5.76	11.75	23.99
2.55	29.84	22.91
14.14	0.31	0.43
13.21	35.79	33.15
5.90	28.71	16.25
1.41	118.48	81.45
6.49	3.41	2.28
Mean Absolute Error		
6.95	28.86	22.68

Mean absolute error is a variation on root mean squared error, and in all most all cases will give the same indication as to the more reliable test. The formula for the first cell will be:

```
=ABS($C5-D26)
```

This again can be dragged down and across to fill all the cells.

As anticipated, the linear prediction proves to be the one which comes nearest to observed values. That is what we will now use to estimate the price which will produce the most profit.

Profit Maximization: Advanced Data Tables

Profitability versus price

Building on the data we have already generated we can estimate the price which will generate the most profit from sales of the book.

Excel needs some additional inputs. It already has the intercept and slope for the linear equation, but we have not incorporated our cost. That is $25 per book, and for now will not vary with quantity. Then, we will need to choose one potential price to serve as an anchor for a tiny Income Statement. These are added to the spreadsheet commencing at Row 47. We can reduce the risk of error by naming some of these cells: Slope and Intercept for example will work very well.

Having entered the cost as a fixed input and placed $60 in the green cell for decision variable, we can then construct an initial Income Statement. Predicted sales come from the application of the linear equation to the test value: Excel's ROUNDDOWN function is deployed because we can't sell a fraction of a book.

```
=ROUNDDOWN((C48*Slope)+Intercept,2)
```

Revenue is then Predicted sales*Test Value, Net cost is Cost per book*Predicted sales, and Gross Profit is the difference. In this model there will always be a gross profit because the only cost calculated is the fixed price per book, and the selling price is always more than cost. For this small revenue calculation we would recommend asking Excel not to display decimal places but just whole numbers; the model will feel more realistic if there are no parts of books, and the cents are immaterial.

You may have observed that in some of the predictions, losses were incurred. This reflects the inaccuracy of the predictions, because in our simplistic model a loss cannot happen—the lowest selling price is $30, while each book costs $25.

TABLE 23: Rounding to Whole Numbers

		Income Statement	
Cost per book	$ 25	Revenue (Sales * Price)	$ 3,061
Test value	$ 59	Net Cost (Cost * Sales)	$ 1,300
Predicted sales	52	Gross Profit	$ 1,761

TABLE 25: One-Way data table

Prices and Profits	
Price	Profit
	$ 1,761
$ 30	$ 455
$ 40	$ 1,155
$ 50	$ 1,600
$ 60	$ 1,750
$ 70	$ 1,620
$ 80	$ 1,265
$ 90	$ 585
$ 100	$ (300)

Now we can build a one-way data table to figure out the maximum profit. First populate the left column with the potential prices from $30 to $100, then create a second column for profits, placing the profit calculated in the Income Statement by cross-reference into the top right data cell. Selecting the whole table area, we go to Data tab, What-if Analysis Group, Data Table, and select the Test Value (C48 in this model) as the column variable.

TABLE 24: Prices and profits

Prices and Profits	
Price	Profit
	$ 1,761
$ 53	$ 1,680
$ 55	$ 1,710
$ 57	$ 1,728
$ 59	$ 1,734
$ 61	$ 1,764
$ 63	$ 1,748
$ 65	$ 1,720
$ 67	$ 1,680
$ 69	$ 1,672

Coincidentally, it seems that we selected the best price as our test value, as $60 is the price at which we will secure the most profit. It's also worth noting that we are not limited to the price increments in our original observed data; the use of the predictive formula would also allow us to evaluate price points between $50 and $70 at smaller intervals, as shown.

There is scope to enhance the value of these tables using two familiar techniques. Conditional formatting is used to highlight the highest profit, and INDEX and MATCH can be used together to pull out and re-display the highest price in a separate area. We have done this in the sample workbook, but we will not belabor the method here. We have more exciting stuff ahead of us!

Profitability with variable cost

If the opportunity arises to vary the cost of the book, perhaps by choosing different qualities of paper, ink or cover, will the most profitable price point remain the same? To determine this, we will need a two-way data table.

The set-up involves selecting a cell to hold a calculation of gross profit, then setting out potential costs across the top of the table and selling prices down the left column. The gross profit calculation is shown in the text income statement, above.

When the two-way data table is created, we see that indeed, in this instance at any level of cost, the most profitable selling price (out of the selection offered) is $60.

TABLE 26: Two-Way data table

Prices, Profits and Costs						
$1,761	$15	$17	$19	$21	$23	$25
$30	1365	1183	1001	819	637	455
$40	1925	1771	1617	1463	1309	1155
$50	2240	2112	1984	1856	1728	1600
$60	2250	2150	2050	1950	1850	1750
$70	1980	1908	1836	1764	1692	1620
$80	1495	1449	1403	1357	1311	1265
$90	675	657	639	621	603	585
$100	-340	-332	-324	-316	-308	-300

Profitability versus cost and price

Up to this point we have assumed a single fixed cost per book. Mostly, in real life, larger quantities ordered result in lower prices. We can continue to use our predictive formula to maximize predicted profit when costs change with volume. We'll start by creating a lookup table for costs. We will also need to create a new Income Statement, with the same calculations as previously except in the Net cost line—we'll use VLOOKUP to create a cost with reference to the quantity predicted to be sold.

TABLE 27: Variable Ccosts

Variable Costs Table	
Order	Cost
1	$25
20	$ 23
40	$ 21
60	$ 19
80	$ 17
100	$ 15

Income Statement	
Revenue (Sales * Price)	$ 3,061
Net cost (cost * sales)	$ 1,092
Gross Profit (Revenue - Cost)	$ 1,969

Observe that the profitability of selling 50 books has now risen, because the cost is lower. Has this moved the "sweet spot" from the $61 optimum price that we determined earlier?

If you are already familiar with Excel's Solver add-on, you might well conclude that it is the best tool to handle this question. Unfortunately, because we are using a predictive formula and VLOOKUP, we encounter one of its most significant limitations—it doesn't handle these, or nested IF statements, very well at all. We have added a demonstration of this "broken Solver" problem in an Appendix.

In this predictive environment, we will have to do some extra work to establish the most profitable price. We already have a lookup table for cost; now, we will need to create a lookup table for sales, using the formula created above.

TABLE 28: Variable costs and sales

Variable Sales Table

Price	Sales	Cost	Profit	Price	Sales	Cost	Profit
25	98	17	784	61	49	21	1960
26	96	17	864	62	47	21	1927
27	95	17	950	63	46	21	1932
28	94	17	1034	64	44	21	1892
29	92	17	1104	65	43	21	1892
30	91	17	1183	66	42	21	1890
31	90	17	1260	67	40	21	1840
32	88	17	1320	68	39	23	1755
33	87	17	1392	69	38	23	1748
34	85	17	1445	70	36	23	1692
35	84	17	1512	71	35	23	1680
36	83	17	1577	72	34	23	1666
37	81	17	1620	73	32	23	1600
38	80	17	1680	74	31	23	1581
39	79	19	1580	75	29	23	1508
40	77	19	1617	76	28	23	1484
41	76	19	1672	77	27	23	1458
42	75	19	1725	78	25	23	1375
43	73	19	1752	79	24	23	1344
44	72	19	1800	80	23	23	1311
45	70	19	1820	81	21	23	1218
46	69	19	1863	82	20	23	1180
47	68	19	1904	83	19	25	1102
48	66	19	1914	84	17	25	1003
49	65	19	1950	85	16	25	960
50	64	19	1984	86	14	25	854
51	62	19	1984	87	13	25	806
52	61	19	2013	88	12	25	756
53	60	19	2040	89	10	25	640
54	58	21	1914	90	9	25	585
55	57	21	1938	91	8	25	528
56	55	21	1925	92	6	25	402
57	54	21	1944	93	5	25	340
58	53	21	1961	94	4	25	276
59	51	21	1938	95	2	25	140
60	50	21	1950	96	1	25	71

Create a Variable Sales Tablewith the range of price from 25 to 100 in the first column. On your Excel worksheet this will be just four columns, but we've broken it into two halves here to keep it readable. In the second column, we want to predict the number of books to be sold at the price, using the ROUNDDOWN function of Excel—we can't sell part of a book!

```
=ROUNDDOWN((A88*Slope)+Intercept,0)
```

This formula can be copied all the way down the table (use double-click on the fill handle) because Slope and Intercept, being named, are automatically locked cell addresses.

Go to the Variable Costs Table, highlight all the data, and name it Variable_Costs_Table.

For cost, use the familiar VLOOKUP function to refer to the Variable Costs Table.

```
=VLOOKUP(B88,Variable_Costs_Table,2)
```

Again, fill down using the fill handle.

Finally, calculate the Profit for each combination using Sales (B88) x Price - Cost (A88–C88). Fill down again.

Use the MAX function or conditional formatting to find the highest profit. You'll see it's achieved with sales of 60 books at a price of $53.

Breakeven Analysis

Breakeven analysis is an essential component of business planning. In the previous sections, we have already touched on all the tools necessary to understand and complete such an analysis. It remains for us to make sure we understand a few definitions and how to use the tools to find the key numbers.

The *breakeven point* is the point at which a business's revenue is equal to total costs (fixed and variable). This same concept can be expressed in different ways; for example, breakeven also occurs when contribution margin is equal to fixed costs. As a formula it is usually expressed as

```
BEP = Fixed Costs/(Average Price - Variable Costs)
```

All these definitions lead to the same point—when you are neither making nor losing money. Depending on what you know, breakeven analysis will tell you a number. If you know the price at which you sell your product, BEP will tell you how many you need to sell to break even. If you know how many you can sell, BEP will tell you what price you need to achieve to break even.

Breakeven analysis is subject to some limitations. Importantly, it is not a predictor of sales, it determines what level of sales are needed to cover all costs. A typical breakeven analysis refers only to one product, though tools like Solver do make it possible to calculate breakeven points with multiple products in play. The most significant weakness however is that breakeven analyses find it difficult to account for changes over time, or for the actions of competitors. They tend to be static and limited in scope.

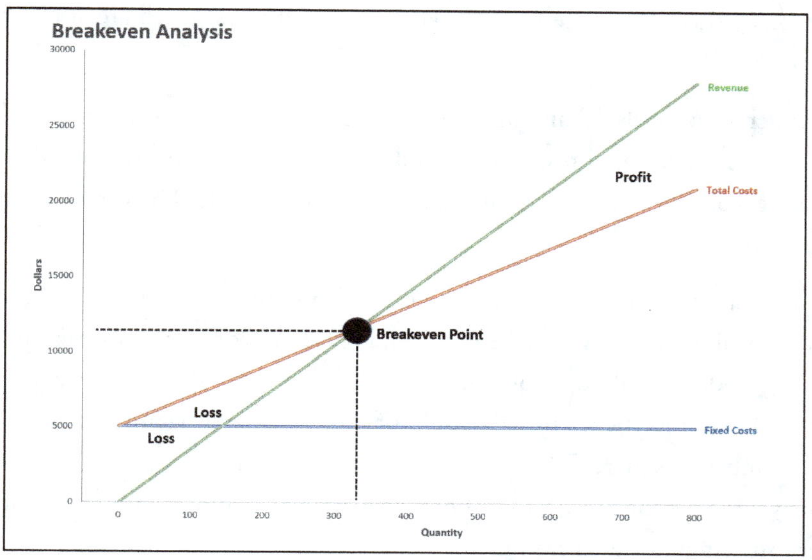

FIGURE 150: Breakeven chart

Visualization of breakeven is usually best accomplished by a special application of the line chart, known as a *breakeven chart.* An example is illustrated at left.

Solver

Solver should appear as an option in the Analyze area of the Data ribbon. If it does not, you need to add it to your Excel – *File* tab, selection *Options,* then *Add-ins,* then *Go* next to Manage: Excel Add-ins, click the box next to Solver and *OK.* Solver is not actually a Microsoft product but was developed by a separate company, Frontline Systems. Introduced in 2008, its original name was What-if Solver.

In earlier sections we have examined Excel functions which assist in making management decisions. Goal Seek allows pursuit of a desired outcome while changing one input variable; data tables allow review of a range of outcomes depending on one or two inputs. Solver may be regarded as the combination of these two tools with the possibility of many further parameters.

Accounting students most often encounter Solver in the context of Cost Accounting. It is a strong tool for finding the best outcome from a range of possibilities. However, Solver's algorithms can also support other business functions, such as promotional spending, staff rostering, inventory management, and bond trading.

Before plunging into a live example and demonstration, please take a little time to read and understand the following paragraphs which explain and rationalize the key concepts that govern the use of Solver.

The *objective cell* is critical to the use of Solver. There can only be one; it reflects the result of all calculations in the model; it is the first item requested in the Solver dialog box. There are three options: Max, Min and Value of. In a profitability model, we would normally want to maximize profit; in cost comparisons, minimize; and in other scenarios like break-even analysis; a set figure might be sought (in the case of break-even, 0).

Interconnectivity. Solver performs the equivalent of an iterative process, testing all the combinations of numbers that could be in your decision variables to find the best solution. It follows from this that all cells which you want it to take into account must be somehow connected, even if at a distance, to the objective cell. It is not possible to limit fields in the sheet by constraints, if they are not calculated from numbers which are also part of the calculation of the objective.

Variable cells (please note the plural) which Excel calls "changing cells." These cells contain the values which can be changed by Solver in order to achieve the optimal result. In a product mix exercise, for example, these decision variables will be the actual numbers of products best produced for the desired result. The variable cells can only contain numbers; they cannot contain formulas.

Constraints allow the user to specify limits upon what resources can be called upon or outcomes achieved. A wide range of constraints may exist in the real world; they may be physical, logical or economic. For example, a company may be capable of producing 100,000 lollipops, but that would be pointless if there was only a market for 20,000 (physical constraint). There may be a limited supply of a raw material, labor or machine hours; there may be a set limit on the number of square feet that can be occupied (also physical constraints). There may be a limited amount of money available for a project (economic constraint). All these numerical data can be put into the model, then Solver instructed not to exceed them.

One useful device is the *integer constraint;* there may be situations in which parts of a whole cannot be meaningfully produced or used. Rounding in Excel is not the ideal solution; Solver however can be instructed to find the best solution with whole numbers. Integer constraints are very particular to the product and process; a bakery which produces in the morning and sells till evening cannot produce half a pie; but an aircraft manufacturer may very well meaningfully perform half of the production of an aircraft in December, carry it through year end, and finish the other half in January. As a broad generalization, the more expensive a product, the more likely that integer constraints will not be useful.

Solver having run will characterize constraints as either binding or non-binding. Binding constraints are those which are at their limit when the objective cell is optimized; any change in them would result in a different solution. Non-binding constraints are those which, while they exist, would not affect the result if they are altered. That is because they have *slack*, a term indicating that there is unused capacity. This is important to sensitivity analysis, which will be explored below.

Non-Negative unconstrained variables sound intimidating! Solver contains a check box to require this outcome; in a production environment it makes perfect sense—you can't make -10 cameras or bake -20 pies; you can't eat negative calories, and you can't run negative miles.

Solving methods is an area upon which volumes could be written. Solver has three, but in the vast majority of cases encountered at this level the first, Simplex LP, will be sufficient. Solver's algorithms are geared to create for smooth, linear relationships (Simplex LP). The second algorithm, GRG Nonlinear, is more appropriate for relationships that are smooth (*i.e.* there are no "jumps" in them) but more curved. It is not uncommon to encounter a problem which appears to be solvable using Simplex LP, but have Solver struggle a little and return a better solution with GRG Nonlinear. In most cases both will return very similar results. The *evolutionary* method is really beyond our scope—but we know you're curious. It finds its home in complex scientific calculations; the distinguishing feature is that it doesn't know when to stop. Even when it thinks it has found a solution, it will often keep running to see if it can find a better one. Users report that sometimes the evolutionary method is run two or three times on the same data and produces a better result each time!

Solver reports are available on demand after running Solver. There are three types: Answer Report, Sensitivity Report and Limits Report. We'll produce them in our exercise below and study their contents individually. While different solving algorithms might produce the same basic results, they often produce different reports.

Named Cells and Ranges work beautifully within Solver. Indeed, in complex models they make life much easier; pure reference to cell addresses can become cumbersome, while named items are intuitive.

The view should be clarified as we work through a live example. In the next section is a problem typical of the type you might encounter at a high level in a manufacturing company. It considers three products competing for resources; however, please be aware that Solver can deal with much larger numbers of decision variables.

There are two main stages or steps to be performed. First is the model development step, where the spreadsheet is built to contain all the necessary data. In this step, we will follow the rules we have learned for model building. This step contains most of the work; the equivalent in the pre-Excel world was the development of algebraic equations. The second step is optimization; here, the values of the decision variables are chosen to achieve the objective. Any solution which satisfies all the constraints is known as a *feasible solution;* a collection of all the feasible solutions is called the *feasible region.* The best feasible solution is the *optimal solution.*

Any solution which violates a constraint is labelled an *infeasible solution.* Infeasible solutions are not allowed by Solver.

A Solver Demonstration

The question

The Boeing Company is one of the world's most recognizable businesses. On the global stage it competes head-to-head with Airbus for a large percentage of the commercial airliner market. The following numbers and facts are imaginary, and only coincidentally resemble any part of Boeing's actual business.

The following is a typical textbook or exam question. The values and constraints are given. In the real world, the most difficult part of the project might be acquiring usable data. Having obtained them, critical thinking must continue to be deployed as we create and examine results.

For this exercise, imagine that Boeing makes three principal aircraft types. The "narrow body" 737 is the workhorse of short-to-medium haul commercial aviation, and one of the most-sold airliners in the world. It sells for 124.8 million US dollars; it takes 9 days to build one. 125 workers are employed for those 9 days on each aircraft.

The classic "wide body" double-decker 747 costs over three times as much, 418.4 million USD.[25] It takes 120 days to assemble this model, with 180 workers devoted to each one.

The new generation of Boeing aircraft is exemplified by the 787 series, which are quieter, more fuel-efficient and more comfortable than the 747. It takes 160 workers 30 days to assemble each one. It sells for $248.3 million.

The 737 is the most sold commercial aircraft in the world, and Boeing estimates the market at 600 per year. 787s are growing in popularity and next year there will be demand for 350. 747s are going out of style, and Boeing estimates it can only sell 30 next year.

Assembly workers on all three models are paid at a flat rate of $200 per day. Skilled assemblers are in short supply, and the most Boeing can expect to have on payroll on any one day (the production lines run all year without stopping) is 10,000. The components (direct materials) required to produce one aircraft cost respectively $50 million for a 737, $200 million for a 747 and $75 million for a 787.

There is one more significant limitation on production. The galleys (kitchens) on these aircraft are produced by an outside supplier which monopolizes the market. They are the same for all three aircraft, but the 737 has two, the 747 has four and the 787 has three. Despite pressure from Boeing to increase its production, the galley supplier is unable to produce more than 2,200 galleys in a year.

How many of each type of plane should Boeing produce next year, to maximize revenue?

Setting up for Solver

Please download and open the completed workbook Boeing.xlsx.

Different authors and books have different conventions for optimization models. The one we use here is not the only possible format. Four elements are common to all: inputs, changing cells, one objective cell and constraints.

The first half of the worksheet is a standard, straightforward, contribution margin statement with the three products identified individually. Totals are on the right. The sheet starts with the selling price of each product, multiplied by the number produced, to arrive at total sales revenue. The "number produced" cells will be output cells for solver; at this stage, anything can be typed into them—0, random guesses, or just a single random number which we have used here—20 of each aircraft. The changing cells are given a pink background. Input cells have black text on a pale blue background.

---

[25] Boeing discontinued making 747s in January 2023, delivering the last of 1,574 aircraft to Atlas Air.

Below that, we input the variable costs of production—in this case, direct materials (which were given), and labor costs—days x number of workers x pay rate for each type. *Note that there are no magic numbers in the formulas*—everything is on the face of the calculation. By summing the variable costs and deducting them from the Sales Revenue, we arrive at the contribution margin for each type and can derive a total contribution margin at the right.

We have no interest in fixed costs. They are the same whatever Boeing produces; if they are more than the total contribution margin the company will make a loss; if they are less, then there will be a profit. Finding the optimum result from production plans focuses only on the contribution margin. The total contribution margin, thus, will be the objective cell; this is typically colored with a gray background. In this example, we've also placed a box around it.

TABLE 29: Boeing Company pre-optimization

	A	B	C	D	E	F	G	H
1	The Boeing Company							
2	Optimization Model - 2024 Production							
3								
4			Boeing 737		Boeing 747		Boeing 787	TOTAL
5	Selling Price		124,800,000		418,400,000		248,300,000	791,500,000
6	Number Produced		20		20		20	
7	Sales Revenue		2,496,000,000		8,368,000,000		4,966,000,000	15,830,000,000
8								
9	Direct Materials	50,000,000	1,000,000,000	200,000,000	4,000,000,000	75,000,000	1,500,000,000	6,500,000,000
10	Direct Labor: Days	9		120		30		
11	Workers	125		180		160		-
12	Rate	200		200		200		
13			4,500,000		86,400,000		19,200,000	110,100,000
14	Variable Costs		1,004,500,000		4,086,400,000		1,519,200,000	6,610,100,000
15								
16	Contribution Margin		1,491,500,000		4,281,600,000		3,446,800,000	9,219,900,000
17								
18	CONSTRAINTS							
19	Market Sales		600		30		350	
20	Galleys per aircraft	2	40	4	80	3	60	180
21	Maximum Galleys	2,200						-
22	Workers	10,000						
23	Working Days/Year	240						
24	Rate	200						
25	Total Available	480,000,000						

Name	Value	Refers To
Limit_Galleys	2,200	=Sheet1!$B$21
Limit_Pay	480,000,000	=Sheet1!$B$25
Market_737	600	=Sheet1!$C$19
Market_747	30	=Sheet1!$E$19
Market_787	350	=Sheet1!$G$19
Produce_737	567	=Sheet1!$C$6
Produce_747	4	=Sheet1!$E$6
Produce_787	350	=Sheet1!$G$6
Total_CM	103,445,000,000	=Sheet1!$H$16
Total_Galleys	2,200	=Sheet1!$H$20
Total_Pay	480,000,000	=Sheet1!$H$13

FIGURE 151: Named Cells

We have named a small number of cells in the worksheet; the names are shown in the list on the left. These are the cells that will be implicated in the constraints when Solver is applied to the model.

Returning to the full sheet, the constraints are set up in a separate section, to avoid complicating the contribution margin statement. Where they apply to specific aircraft, however, they follow the columns from the first section. The limits of sales for each model are positioned on the first line; the number of galleys required for each type, with a calculation of total galleys, are next, with the supplier's limit shown in a separate cell; finally, the available workers are multiplied by the days each will work in a year (240) and the rate, to conveniently calculate a total spend on labor which can be used as a constraint. It's time to set up Solver and try for a result.

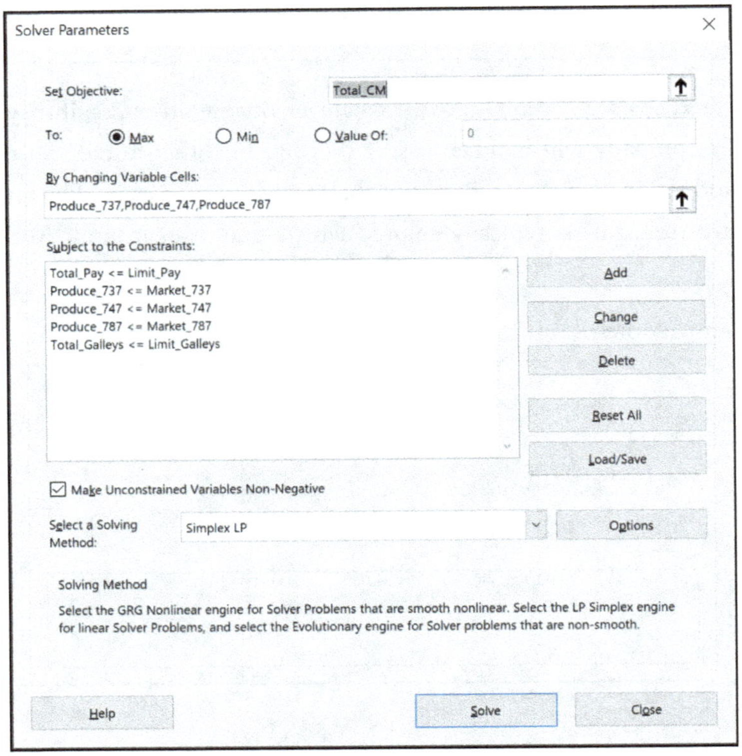

FIGURE 152: Solver parameters

The Solver set-up is shown above. Maximization of the contribution margin is the goal; the variable cells are model production quantities; constraints are listed in the box. To add each one, click on the Add button, then either clicking on the appropriate cell or key in its location or name. Here it is easy to see the value of naming cells, as the constraints are easy to understand, and mistakes will quickly be apparent. We can't produce a negative number of aircraft, so unconstrained variables are made non-negative, and Simplex LP should be sufficient for a calculation of this limited complexity.

Boom! In an instant, Solver has looked at all the possible combinations of production and found the one which gives the greatest contribution margin. The results box narrates that all constraints and optimality conditions are satisfied. At this point there are some options; three possible reports, and to keep the Solver solution or return to the previous figures. For most purposes, the Sensitivity Report is likely to be critical, but the Answer Report provides valuable binding/non-binding and slack information. We've selected all three and agreed to keep the Solver Solution.

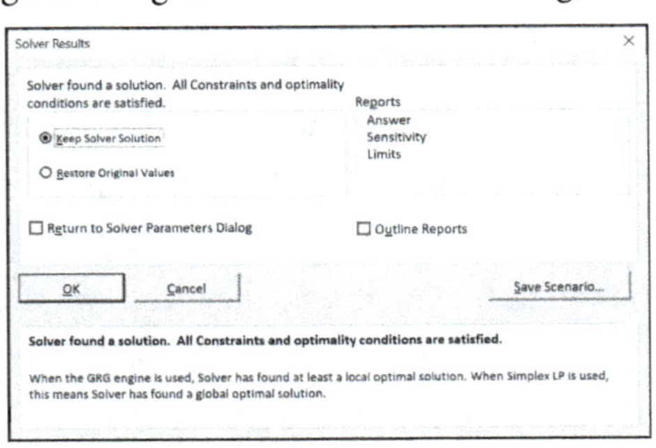

FIGURE 153: Solver found a solution

The necessary production figures and all the flow-through calculations are updated in the original sheet.

TABLE 30: Solver solution inserted

	A	B	C	D	E	F	G	H
1	The Boeing Company							
2	Optimization Model - 2024 Production							
3								
4			Boeing 737		Boeing 747		Boeing 787	TOTAL
5	Selling Price		124,800,000		418,400,000		248,300,000	791,500,000
6	Number Produced		567		4		350	
7	Sales Revenue		70,816,744,186		1,581,162,791		86,905,000,000	159,302,906,977
8								
9	Direct Materials	50,000,000	28,372,093,023	200,000,000	755,813,953	75,000,000	26,250,000,000	55,377,906,977
10	Direct Labor: Days	9		120		30		
11	Workers	125		180		160		
12	Rate	200		200		200		-
13			127,674,419		16,325,581		336,000,000	480,000,000
14	Variable Costs		28,499,767,442		772,139,535		26,586,000,000	55,857,906,977
15								
16	Contribution Margin		42,316,976,744		809,023,256		60,319,000,000	103,445,000,000
17								
18	CONSTRAINTS							
19	Market Sales		600		30		350	
20	Galleys per aircraft	2	1,135	4	15	3	1,050	2,200
21	Maximum Galleys	2,200						-
22	Workers	10,000						
23	Working Days/Year	240						
24	Rate	200						
25	Total Available	480,000,000						

The optimal numbers of aircraft to produce have been inserted into the production cells, all the resulting calculations are updated, and contribution is optimized at just over $103 billion. Solver has managed to use all the available working hours and all the available galleys.

Microsoft Excel 16.0 Sensitivity Report
Worksheet: [Book1]Sheet1
Report Created: 10/4/2023 12:24:27 PM

Variable Cells

Cell	Name	Final Value	Reduced Cost	Objective Coefficient	Allowable Increase	Allowable Decrease
$C$6	Produce_737	567.4418605	0	74575000	32465000	63425000
$E$6	Produce_747	3.779069767	0	214080000	311050602.4	64930000
$G$6	Produce_787	350	50033333	172340000	1.00E+30	50033333

Constraints

Cell	Name	Final Value	Shadow Price	Constraint R.H. Side	Allowable Increase	Allowable Decrease
$H$13	Total_Pay	480000000	16.777778	480000000	101475000	14625000
$H$20	Total_Galleys	2200	35400000	2200	58.33333333	902

FIGURE 154: Solver Sensitivity Report

The three reports have been loaded into separate worksheets. First, the Sensitivity Report. A few terms merit further explanation.

A coefficient is a number or value placed before a constant in an equation. In 2x + 4y, for example, the 2 and 4 are coefficients while the letters are constants. When we asked Solver to maximize contribution margin, it created an algebraic formula to calculate it—the number of 737s multiplied by the profit on each one, the number of 747s multiplied by the profit on each one, and the number of 787s multiplied by the profit on each one. The profit per unit on each model is not visible on the spreadsheet, but it is calculated on the sensitivity report. Under this model, Boeing earns a contribution margin of 74,575,000 on each 737, 214.080,000 on each 747 and 172,340,000 on each 787. That sounds like a lot, until you consider the likely fixed costs of the company. If the 737 is x, 747 is y and 787 is z, Total Contribution Margin = 74575000x + 214080000y + 172340000z. That is the information in the first part of the report, under "Objective Coefficient." Nothing more complicated than that.

For each coefficient there is an Allowable Increase and Allowable Decrease. These are the amounts by which the margin on each individual plane could increase or decrease before the optimal mix of products *might* (not *will)* change. Taking the 787 line for example, the profit on each individual one could increase by a vast amount—1,000,000,000,000,000,000,000,000,000,000 (effectively, infinity)—and the optimal mix would not change. That's logical because the solution already recommends producing the maximum number that can be sold. The margin on a 787 could also increase by a lot—just over $50 million—without Solver suggesting that the production be reduced in favor of another model.

A reduced cost only shows up if the constraint is at its upper or lower boundary. If the recommended production level is 0 (in the Final Value column), then the reduced cost will show how much better the objective coefficient will have to be before a positive value is indicated for production. If, however, the final value is equivalent to the constraint, then the reduced cost shows how much the margin would have to deteriorate before the final value falls below the constraint. Those are logically the same numbers as the allowable decrease, as demonstrated by the 787 line.

The second half of this report deals with the constraints. They are identified, and the Final Value column shows how much of them has been used (in this case, all). The next column shows the *Shadow Price*, in many ways the most useful figure on the report. The Shadow Price shows how much extra contribution margin we would make with an increase of one in the constraint; it works for a reduction of one in the constraint. Shadow price is equal to the reduction in contribution margin that would be caused by a decrease of one in the constraint.

If the total pay available is increased by just $1, there will be $16.77 of extra contribution margin. The Allowable Increase column tells us that this is true, all the way up to an increase of $101,475,000. Boeing should clearly be thinking about finding a way to increase the workforce. The galley limit is even more restrictive. If Boeing can source just one extra galley, its contribution margin will increase by over $35 million. That holds true all the way up to an extra 58 galleys. On the generous assumption that each galley might cost $1 million, there is a powerful incentive for Boeing to find a way to procure extra galleys—even purchasing just 58 more will generate extra margin of 58 x $35.4 million (over $2 billion).

The Constraint R.H. Side column repeats the constraints, with the extra information that they are RH Side—that is, upper limits. Finally, the Allowable Decrease column shows the amount by which the constraints could be reduced with the shadow price calculation holding true.

Next the *Answer Report*

Microsoft Excel 16.0 Answer Report
Worksheet: [Book1]Sheet1
Report Created: 10/4/2023 12:24:27 PM
Result: Solver found a solution. All Constraints and optimality conditions are satisfied.
Solver Engine
Solver Options

Objective Cell (Max)

Cell	Name	Original Value	Final Value
$H$16	Total_CM	9,219,900,000	103,445,000,000

Variable Cells

Cell	Name	Original Value	Final Value	Integer
$C$6	Produce_737	20	567	Contin
$E$6	Produce_747	20	4	Contin
$G$6	Produce_787	20	350	Contin

Constraints

Cell	Name	Cell Value	Formula	Status	Slack
$H$13	Total_Pay	480,000,000	$H$13<=$B$25	Binding	0
$H$20	Total_Galleys	2,200	$H$20<=$A$21	Binding	0
$C$6	Produce_737	567	$C$6<=$C$19	Not Binding	32.55813953
$E$6	Produce_747	4	$E$6<=$E$19	Not Binding	26.22093023
$G$6	Produce_787	350	$G$6<=$G$19	Binding	0

FIGURE 155: Solver Answer Report

The Answer Report mainly informs about how the model was constructed and changed, rather than showing actionable data. It considers the Objective Cell, reminds us that it is maximized, gives its name and the original and final values. The original value in this instance is irrelevant, it was calculated from random numbers that were placed in the variable cells.

The same applies to the table of variable cells. The report reminds us which they are, what numbers we originally inserted, and the final values calculated by Solver. The one useful element here is the Integer column, which tells us that we did not impose an integer constraint. The numbers are however rounded to whole numbers because that's how we chose to display them on the original worksheet.

The third section deals with the constraints; here there is useful information. It repeats the constraints that were imposed on the model and tells us whether their limits were reached. In this model, both Total Pay and Total Galleys were achieved; however, the possible sales limits of 737s and 747s were not—"Not Binding." The *Slack* column calculates how much room was left in those constraints (*i.e.* how many more could be made before the limit is reached).

The *Limits Report* deals purely with the calculation of the objective cell with relation to the variables and constraints.

Microsoft Excel 16.0 Limits Report
Worksheet: [Book1]Sheet1
Report Created: 10/4/2023 12:24:27 PM

Cell	Objective Name	Value
$H$16	Total_CM	103,445,000,000

Cell	Variable Name	Value	Lower Limit	Objective Result	Upper Limit	Objective Result
$C$6	Produce_737	567	-	61,128,023,256	567	103,445,000,000
$E$6	Produce_747	4	-	102,635,976,744	4	103,445,000,000
$G$6	Produce_787	350	-	43,126,000,000	350	103,445,000,000

FIGURE 156: Solver Limits Report

The result in the objective cell is reported, along with the numbers placed by Solver into the variable cells. In the remaining areas, the lower limits (if there were any) are reported, along with the contribution margin for each product type, the upper limits, and the objective result (which is the same as in the first section). We would take some persuading that this report is of any practical use, given that all the information in it is readily available elsewhere in the spreadsheet and the other two reports.

Solver errors

Two types of error are commonly encountered when using Solver.

Infeasibility is reported when there is no feasible solution to the model. Most often one or both of two errors will have occurred:

- There is a mistake in the inputs to the model, such as a wrong arithmetical function in a constraint; or
- The constraints specified do not permit even one solution to be obtained.

It is quite possible that a model is correctly built and there are no feasible solutions; in this case, the only solution is change or elimination of at least one constraint.

Unboundedness is reported when there are not enough constraints; Excel is saying that it can find any number of feasible solutions, without limit. A reasonable model cannot be unbounded; therefore, there must be a mistake such as omission of a constraint, a wrong input or a logical error.

In the first half of this chapter, we looked at techniques which are used mainly to help make internal decisions about production, sales and marketing. In the second half, we will look into the valuation of businesses and investments. We will then perform a full valuation of an existing business.

CAPM

Calculating the cost of capital is one of the first steps in valuing a business. One component of that, and the most difficult to determine, is the cost of equity capital (ordinary stocks or shares). CAPM is one of two common methods for calculating the cost of capital. You may also see it referred to as "RRR"—the *required rate of return*, or the *hurdle rate*. It is a measure of the rate of return required by an investor as a minimum to put their money into the stock. It's an essential component in calculating the overall cost of a company's capital.

CAPM stands for "Capital Asset Pricing Model" and is based on the application of a formula:

$$Ke = Rf + \beta(Rm - Rf)$$

In some cases there are additional elements and the formula becomes

$$Ke = Rf + \beta(Rm - Rf) + CSRP + CRP$$

Ke is the standard abbreviation for the cost of capital itself. Rf is the risk-free rate; the rate of interest which an investor could obtain by putting money into a guaranteed investment which virtually cannot fail; in the United States the risk-free rate is generally regarded as today's yield on a three-month treasury bill (T-bill). The rate is widely published in the financial press daily, and readily obtainable from the Internet on demand. Here, the Bank of Canada publishes an interest rate called CORRA (the Canadian Overnight Repo Rate), which is usually very close indeed to the 3-month Canadian T-bill rate and is used as the risk-free rate for

Canadian calculations. To see daily CORRA and other treasury rates go to https://www.bankofcanada.ca/rates/interest-rates/.

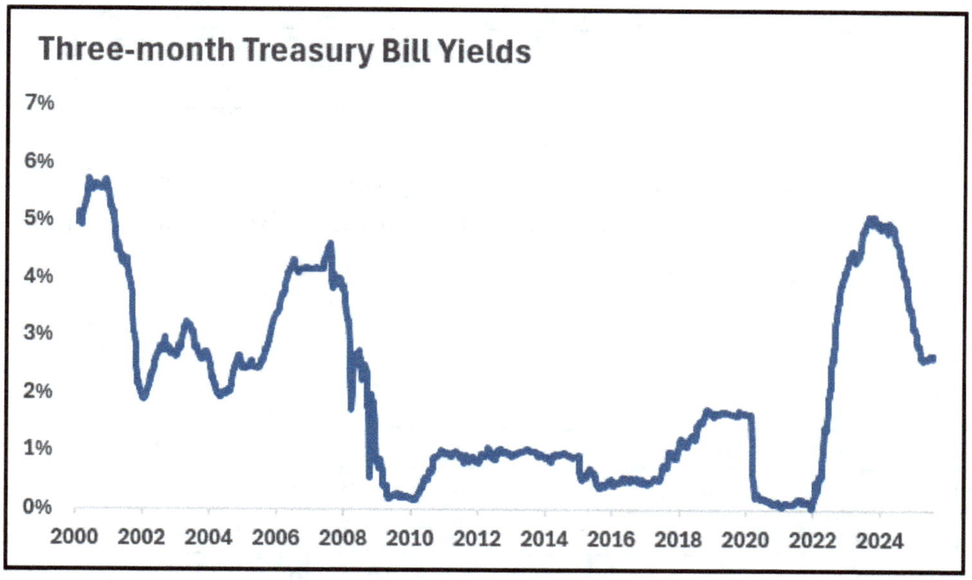

FIGURE 157: Three-month T-bill chart 2000-2025

β, the Greek letter named *beta*, is a little more complicated. It is the measure of the volatility of an individual stock or security, compared to the "market as a whole." The market as a whole usually refers to the S&P 500 in the United States, or the S&P/TSX Composite Index in Canada. We don't want to get too deeply into the math, the β of any given stock is usually available on-demand from the Internet. It's computed over time, and it indicates the relationship between the investment's excess return over the risk-free market and the benchmark's excess return over the same standard. The benchmark is the index to which the stock is compared, for example the S&P 500. A β above one indicates that the stock has a higher level of risk compared to the whole market, while a β below one indicates that it is systematically less risky than the market. Most companies will have a β in the range from 0.5 to 2, a few stocks carry much higher numbers. β is very rarely above 20.[26]

Rm – Rf calculates the difference between the rate of return achieved by the stock market as a whole and the risk-free rate.

It is quite straightforward to calculate CAPM once you have these external inputs. We have constructed a tiny Excel table to make it easier. You can build this yourself or download it. The file is called CAPM.xlsx. We have filled the fields to calculate CAPM for the Canadian Pacific Railway company.

---

[26] For a listing of Canadian stocks with very high betas, see Tradingview, n.d. You will see that very high beta stock listings are dominated by mining and scientific companies but can also include high-risk technology enterprises.

TABLE 31: Canadian Pacific CAPM

CAPM Calculation - Canadian Pacific - August 6, 2025

Rf	β	Rm	Result (Ke)
2.66%	1.05	5.40%	**5.537%**

Ke = rf + Beta(Rm-Rf)

The two optional elements CSRP and CRP are the *company specific risk premium* and *country risk premium.* A company specific premium is added if investors demand a higher rate of return due to some characteristic of the company. The following table shows the effect on CSRP of several factors.

TABLE 32: CSRP factors

Lower CSRP	Higher CSRP
Larger company	Smaller company
Dominant position in market	Lower position in market
High market concentration	Low market concentration
Low competition in market	Strong competition in market
High barriers to entry	Low barriers to entry
High profitability	Low profitability
High liquidity ratio	Low liquidity ratio

CRP is country risk, added if investors demand additional returns because the company is operating in a higher risk environment. Higher risk environment covers a multitude of possibilities, including an unstable government, difficult economic conditions such as high inflation or deflation, risk of default on government debt, unstable currency and rules/regulations which make business more difficult, such as currency controls. Interestingly many writers on this subject point to the U.S. as an example of a country with no country risk, yet the country ticks at least two of the five boxes.

CRP is usually calculated using one of two methods; a formula, or an estimate like β but found by comparing relative volatility of stock markets in the country of interest and those of a stable, developed country. Conveniently for valuers and other professionals who need to use CRPs, the Stern School of Business at NYU publishes a monthly table calculating the value for all countries (Damodaran, 2025). Not surprisingly, the countries with the highest premium (tied at 24.82% in July 2023) are those which figure frequently in the news with major problems—Belarus, Lebanon, Sudan, Syria and Venezuela. The United States and Canada both have CRPs of 0%.

Advanced finance courses sometimes require calculation of CSRP or CRP. In general statistics and data modeling courses they are usually given if required.[27]

Weighted Average Cost of Capital (WACC)

To calculate the overall cost of a company's capital, we tabulate its sources and their individual costs, then obtain the weighted average of those costs. We'll start with a simplified example then do an actual calculation for Canadian Pacific.

A company's financing structure may comprise ordinary (common) shares, preferred shares, bonds other borrowing arrangements. The last two require a little special treatment because interest paid on them is tax-deductible, so the real cost of them is reduced by the rate of company tax.

Our hypothetical company has issued $1 million of common shares, $2 million of 5% preferred shares, and corporate bonds of $3 million, yielding 3.5%. The tax rate is 27%. As a result, its overall capital sums to exactly $6 million. We've calculated its CAPM at 7.5%. We can now tabulate the capital structure as follows, allocating percentages to the various components. Note that the common shares are reckoned at their *book value*, not their market value.

TABLE 33: Hypo Company WACC

Security	Value	Percentage	CAPM/Yield	Tax Rate	Net Yield	Weighted Cost
Common Shares	1,000,000	0.167	7.50%	N/A	7.50%	1.25%
Pref Shares	2,000,000	0.333	5%	N/A	5.00%	1.67%
Bonds	3,000,000	0.500	3.50%	27%	2.555%	1.28%
Total Capital	6,000,000				WACC	4.19%

Hypo Company's WACC is 4.19%. This intuitively "feels" about right; the capital structure is dominated by the bonds, which are at the lower rate of 3.5%, while the ordinary shareholders hold the lowest component of the capital at 16.7% but influence the overall rate upwards with their demand for 7.5%. Let's do this once more with a real company.

[27] The formula for CRP is annualized standard deviation on equity index, divided by annualized standard deviation on bond index. It is highly qualified, however, by conditions including that government bonds must be denominated in a currency which has a default-free entity behind it, such as the Euro.

TABLE 34: Canadian Pacific WACC

Security	Value	Percentage	CAPM/Yield	Tax Rate	Net Yield	Weighted Cost
Common Shares	69,701,697,000	0.820	5.54%	N/A	5.54%	4.54%
Pref Shares		0.000		N/A	0.00%	0.00%
Bonds	15,304,639,500	0.180	3.14%	18%	2.566%	0.46%
Total Capital	85,006,336,500				WACC	5.00%

Canadian Pacific has no preferred shares outstanding. Thus, its WACC is calculated only with reference to its common shares and debt. The capital structure is heavily dominated by common shareholding with an RRR of 5.771%; bonds supply only 18% of the company's capital at a lower yield. As a result, the WACC is 5,19%, not far below the cost of the share capital.

Time Value of Money

The value of a business is largely dependent on its earning potential. A business is unlikely to have much value (apart from salvage value) if it is not expected to turn a profit in the years to come. Thus, valuation of a business today involves a calculation of the present value of what it is likely to earn in the future. For discussion here, we're going to assume two things that make life simpler; first, inflation is the normal situation, and second, profits are paid out and interest is earned on an annual basis.

Now a question. Assuming that earnable interest rates and inflation are both at 5%, would you rather have $1 now, or the promise of $1 in a year's time. You, like all investors, are going to prefer the $1 now, because you can invest it and have $1.05 in a year's time; meanwhile, the price of everything will have risen 5% and it will still be the same. If you wait a year to receive the dollar, everything will cost more, you will have earned no interest, and you will only be able to buy then something that costs 95.24 cents today. In other words, $1 a year from now is only worth 95.24 cents today. How did we arrive at that exact figure? The formula is to take that dollar and divide it by 1 plus the interest rate. If we want to make the same calculation for two years hence, we divide by (1 plus the interest rate)^2, and so on. A dollar five years from now is only worth $1/(1.05)^5$, or 78.35 cents. To check that this works, put 78.35 into your calculator or Excel, and add 5%, five times. It will come back to the $1 that is due in five years.

The process of calculating the present value of future cash flows is known as DCF analysis, *Discounted Cash Flows*. The percentage that is used may be referred to as the *discount rate.*

One last important fundamental concept. The time when you receive future money affects the exponent of the discount rate. If today is December 31, and you are going to receive money on December 31 each year for the next five years, the discount rate in the denominator of each year's calculation will be a whole number. However, if the money is to be received evenly throughout the year, that is on average halfway through the year, the exponent will be 0.5 in the first year, 1.5 in the second, and so on. Here are contrasting calculations.[28]

TABLE 35: Discounted cash flows

	31/12/2025	31/12/2026	31/12/2027	31/12/2028	31/12/2029
Payment	$100	$100	$100	$100	$100
Divided by	1.05	1.05^2	1.05^3	1.05^4	1.05^5
Value today	$95.24	$90.70	$86.38	$82.27	$78.35
		Total value on Dec 31, 2024			**$432.95**

	31/12/2025	31/12/2026	31/12/2027	31/12/2028	31/12/2029
Payment	$100	$100	$100	$100	$100
Divided by	1.05^0.5	1.05^1.5	1.05^2.5	1.05^3.5	1.05^4.5
Value today	$97.59	$92.94	$88.52	$84.30	$80.29
		Total value on Dec 31, 2024			**$443.64**

Today on these tables is December 31, 2024. We are promised $100 per year, for the next five years, and the discount rate is 5%. In the first example we are paid at the end of each year; in the second we are paid mid-year. The present value of the $500 we are to receive is $432.95 if the payments are made at the end of the year, but $443.64 if they are made mis-year. The assumption underlying these calculations is that once we have the money, we can invest it at the current discount rate.

Net Present Value

Net Present Value (NPV) is a concept which builds on the time value of money. NPV is used to evaluate equipment purchases, investments and even whole companies. To calculate NPV it is necessary to know the discount rate or cost of capital as discussed above.

In a situation where the discount rate is 5%, you could buy for $1,000, today, an asset which will last exactly one year and will produce an incoming cash flow of $1020 at the end of the year. There is no need to discount the $1,000, as it must be spent immediately. However, the income of $1,020 is divided by 1.05 to reflect its present value. The present value of $1,020 is $971.42; subtract from this, the initial investment of $1,000 and the result is a negative figure, ($28.57). A negative NPV indicates that the project should not be undertaken, as it will not produce the desired return.

---

[28] The file can be downloaded, it is named TVM.xlsx.

NPV calculations usually cover more than one year. A typical example is an asset purchased for $800,000 today, with a useful life of 5 years producing revenues of $175,000 at the end of each year and a salvage value at the end of $25,000.

TABLE 36: Net Present Value of income

	Income	Formula		
Purchase Price			$	(800,000)
Income Y1	175,000	=175000/1.05	$	166,667
Income Y2	175,000	=175000/1.05^2	$	158,730
Income Y3	175,000	=175000/1.05^3	$	151,172
Income Y4	175,000	=175000/1.05^4	$	143,973
Income Y5	175,000	=175000/1.05^5	$	137,117
Salvage	25,000	=25000/1.05^5	$	19,588
NET PRESENT VALUE			**$**	**(22,753)**

As the years pass, the value of each successive $175,000 diminishes. The salvage value, because it is only reclaimable at the end of five years, is also discounted. The investment is not worthwhile—it will not generate the required return on the investment.

Note that if the cash flows were not discounted, this might have looked like a good investment with an eventual return of $100,000.

Excel contains a function, NPV, which can be helpful in calculations. It is limited however in that it assumes the first value it is given is the income one period from now, and that the following numbers are the subsequent periods. We need to understand how complete NPV is calculated, before deploying the formula. In this instance it would be:

```
=NPV(5%,B3:B7)+D2+D8
```

This too is a somewhat simplified example. In Canada, when considering equipment purchases, we must take account also of the "tax shield." The Canada Revenue Agency (CRA) permits businesses to take an annual deduction (similar to depreciation) for the loss of value of assets purchased for use in the enterprise. Until relatively recently (November 2018), this was complicated by the fact that only half the permitted deduction could be taken if the asset was purchased part-way through the first year; today as we write businesses can take advantage of the *Accelerated Investment Incentive* which allows deduction of 2x the permitted allowance in the first year – which is half the full year rate. In effect, the permitted allowance is now the same in the first and subsequent years.[29] [30]

A more typical example of an NPV calculation in the real world might involve either the assessment of a potential investment, or the comparison of two competing acquisitions to serve the same purpose. We might be asked whether a client should make an investment in the following circumstances:

- Initial cost of machine: $800,000
- Income per year for 10 years: $180,000

---

[29] After identifying a specific asset which may be eligible for the accelerated deduction, it's important to check for special rules which may change the situation; for example, if the purchase was not at arm's length. In the case of certain "green" assets there may be eligibility for 100% deduction in the first year.

[30] To qualify assets must be available for use before 2028.

- Salvage Value: $60,000
- WACC 10%
- Tax rate: 27%
- CCA rate for equipment: 20%

The calculation of whether this is worthwhile can be answered quantitatively by calculating the NPV of the project. In stages:

Initial cash outlay is $800,000. No discounting is required as this will be paid up-front.

The 10 years' income can be calculated manually or using the Excel NPV function. However, it is the after-tax income that must be discounted—$131,400 for 10 years. This is worth $807,396.

The value of the CCA tax shield comes next. It is calculated in perpetuity (i.e., assuming the machine is never sold) using the formula:

```
(C*d*T / d + k)
```

Where C = Capital Cost, d = CCA percentage, T = Tax rate, k = WACC. This comes to $151,396.

The tax shield benefit is however lost after 10 years. This loss is quantified by the formula:

```
((C*d*T)/(d+k))*((1/(1+k))^t)
```

where t is the years of life of the machine before sale. This calculates to ($55,518).

Finally, there is the salvage value itself, $60,000 10 years from now = $60000/1.10^{10}$ = $23,133.

The sum of these elements is $119,011: a positive number. Therefore, the project is worthwhile.

If the company compares the relative values of two machines, with different costs and productivities, it should calculate NPV for each purchase and compare them. All other things being equal, it would select the machine with the higher NPV.

Terminal Value

Looking into the future for 3–5 years and predicting the income of a business is no easy task. However, when considering the purchase of a business and thus attempting to value it, some value must also be ascribed to earnings beyond the initial period. There are two methods in common use among valuators to calculate this "terminal value." Whichever is used, the first step is to determine the last year for which a reliable estimate can be made—typically the third or fifth year from now.

The *perpetual growth model* assumes that the business will generate income for ever. It is also known as the *Gordon growth model* (Gordon, 1959). The alternative is the *exit multiple method*, which operates on the assumption that the business will be sold.

The perpetual growth model uses the formula:

```
(FCF*(1+g))/(d-g)
```

FCF is the free cash flow for the last period in the initial forecast. g is the rate of growth expected in perpetuity, and d is the discount rate, normally the WACC. Valuators normally use a growth rate close or identical to the rate of inflation expected in the long term (thus, in Canada, often 2%), and do not allow it to exceed the GDP growth rate averaged over the last several years.

The exit multiple method looks outward to sales of similar companies that have happened relatively recently. It will use one metric from those companies, such as net profit or EBITDA, multiplied by a factor which is derived from looking at the selling price of those companies. If for example a grocery chain is being valued, and recent similar sales have been at prices of around 5x the last year's net profit, then 5x last year's net profit will be used for this company, too. There is no obligation created to sell the company at the end of the forecast period; rather, the value of the company today incorporates this number as part of the reckoning.

Generally, the Gordon growth model tends to produce higher valuations than the exit multiple. A common solution is to take terminal value as the average of the two. Terminal value can be negative, if a company is in trouble; this can be a serious indication of trouble ahead.

Valuation

All these individual calculations have value standing alone, but they are critical components of some methods of calculating the value of a business. Best practice for any business is to have a valuation on hand, and to have it updated each year. Why? Because stuff happens.

A key character with interest in the value of a business is the tax authority. Many transactions which happen in the life of a business attract tax, which may depend on its valuation.

As a business owner or part-owner, knowing the valuation is important for estate planning and sometimes for tax planning.

On the dark side, the business owner may die, triggering estate taxes, or become disabled and have to sell. Any change in the ownership of a business, including adding or removing a partner, or sale of the whole or part, will require valuation. On the brighter side, this also applies to unexpected opportunities to sell the business or part of it, or to merge with another business. Expansion of the business may also create a requirement for new investors or lenders; they will want to know the existing valuation.

Divorce, child support litigation and other negative family events frequently trigger disputes about the worth of a business, or the net worth of the owner(s). Larger scale disasters, affecting the existence or operations of a business, may trigger insurance claims which will be based on the value of the business before the event.

Many tax calculations, and some others, may require appraisal of the business at *fair market value*. This is a required standard, for example, of the IRS in the United States. An appraiser's report will specify the standard used; if it is fair market value, then this represents "the price something would sell for on the open market assuming that both buyer and seller are reasonably knowledgeable about the asset, are behaving in their own best interests, are free of undue pressure, and are given a reasonable time period for completing the transaction" (Chen & Boyle, 2025). FMV is virtually always expressed in cash.

The price for which anything, including a business, is sold will frequently be different to FMV. Among the many reasons for this are:

- Power disparity. The parties to the sale may have different bargaining strengths.
- Skill disparity. The parties to the sale may not be equals as negotiators.
- Human factors. Either party may make a mistake, or act for emotional reasons.
- Information disparity. Either or both parties may have incomplete information.
- Non-arm's-length. There may be a collateral relationship between the parties.
- Consideration disparity. The settlement may not be in cash; both sides of the bargain are then subject to differences of valuation.

In determining value, the appraiser will pick a specific point in time (usually "now") and look at the accumulated value of all anticipated future benefits. Several approaches may be used, with some either used to verify a main method, or with averaging applied across two or more.

Despite all the rationales and formulas employed, there will always be an element of subjectivity to valuation.

In approaching a valuation, the starting point is to choose the methodology or methodologies to be employed. A flow chart can be helpful:

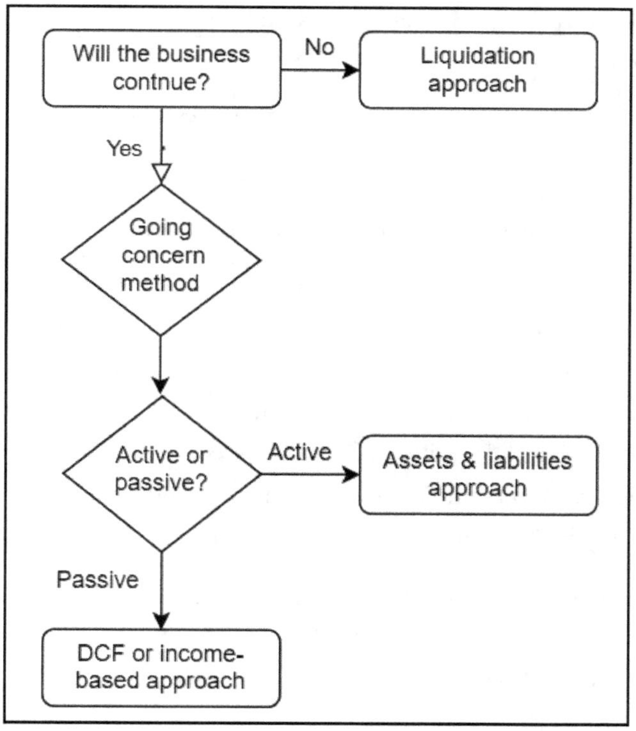

FIGURE 158: Selection tree for valuation approach

The following is a list of the main valuation methods with brief descriptions; there is no one which fits all situations. Some appear to be variations of similar methodologies. In practice most valuators will pick at least two methods that appear appropriate then average them.

Based on Income

- DISCOUNTED CASH FLOW—Forecasted profits, adjusted for cost of capital and inflation.
- TIMES REVENUE—Revenue, multiplied by a factor typical for the sector and economy.
- EXCESS EARNINGS—a hybrid method which is based on a rate of return on assets, and a rate applied to company goodwill.

Based on Assets

- BOOK VALUE—Balance sheet assets minus liabilities.
- REPLACEMENT—Amount the company would have to pay to replace all its assets at current FMV.
- LIQUIDATION—Amount of cash that would remain if all assets were sold on a distressed basis and liabilities paid.
- BREAKUP—Amount of cash or value of new shares owners would receive if all business units were sold off separately.
- ASSET-BASED—Amount of cash owners would receive if all assets were sold at FMV and liabilities paid.

Based on Markets

- CAPITALIZATION—Share price x Shares outstanding
- PRECEDENT TRANSACTIONS—value is derived by comparing the company to others in the industry which have been sold recently.

To bring this chapter to a close, we'll solve a typical exam type question using the DCF method.

THE QUESTION

The owners of X company have requested a valuation, and provided the following information:

X manufactures thermal control units for satellites. They are in high demand and X is the industry leading supplier. There are high barriers to entry in the market, so X does not fear new competitors. The number of satellites in production is constantly growing. Last year's sales were $15 million, spread evenly through the year, and an increase of 20% per year is expected for the next four years. This year, new manufacturing equipment will need to be purchased at a cost of $3 million. All existing equipment is fully depreciated. Manufacturing costs are 55% of revenue, general and administrative costs are 6% and selling expenses are 1%. Depreciation is kept equal to allowable CCA. The following key statistics also apply:

- CCA rate 20% (the accelerated investment incentive applies)
- Net federal and provincial taxes 27%
- Inflation is predicted to be 3% per annum for the foreseeable future; the risk-free rate is also 3%.
- Debt:equity ratio 0.25
- Pre-tax debt costs 10%.
- Cost of Equity is calculated using CAPM; equity risk premium is 3% and b 1.5. The specific premium is 5% but there is no country risk premium.

THE SOLUTION[31]

Before doing calculations, it's wise to look at the question and discard any unnecessary information; also to figure out if there are any gaps for which assumptions will be needed. Spoiler—there are no gaps, thus no assumptions needed, and all the distracting, unnecessary information was already colored red.[32]

We can incorporate the relevant information into a series of calculations.

TABLE 37: X Company valuation components

X Company - Valuation as at 1 January, Yr 1

CAPM - Cost of Equity	
Risk-Free Rate	3%
Equity Risk Premium	3%
ß	1.50
Specific Premium	5%
Cost of Equity	**12.5%**
(Rf + ß(Rm)+CSRP)	

Finance Components	
Debt:Equity Rat	0.25
Debt	20%
Equity	80%
(D/E / 1+D/E)	

Cost of Debt	
Pre-Tax	10%
Tax	27%
After-Tax	**7.3%**
(IR-(1-T))	

WACC	%age	Cost	Product
Debt	20%	7.3%	1.4600%
Equity	80%	12.5%	10.0000%
(SUMPRODUCT %age, cost)			**11.46%**

CAPEX

Class 8 CCA 20%	Yr 1	Yr2	Yr3	Yr4
3,000,000	900,000	420,000	336,000	268,800

---

[31] The full solution xcompany.xlsx is downloadable.

[32] X could be manufacturing anything, the process is the same. Talk of barriers to entry and competitors are distractors making you think about specific premium, but that is given. This is a cash-flow based calculation so how the company handles depreciation is irrelevant. There are no figures to inflate, all the growth rates are given and expenses are a percentage of revenues, however the predicted inflation rate will be needed for terminal value.

TABLE 38: Pro-Forma cash flows

CASH FLOW PRO-FORMA STATEMENT				
	Yr 1	Yr2	Yr3	Yr4
Sales (15M + 20% Yr 1)	18,000,000	21,600,000	25,920,000	31,104,000
COGS (55% of Sales)	9,900,000	11,880,000	14,256,000	17,107,200
Gross Margin	8,100,000	9,720,000	11,664,000	13,996,800
General and Admin Costs (6%)	1,080,000	1,296,000	1,555,200	1,866,240
Selling Costs (1%)	180,000	216,000	259,200	311,040
Net Profit before Tax	6,840,000	8,208,000	9,849,600	11,819,520
Income Tax (27%)	1,846,800	2,216,160	2,659,392	3,191,270
Net Cash Flow before Tax Shield	4,993,200	5,991,840	7,190,208	8,628,250
Tax Shield	243,000	113,400	90,720	72,576
Net Cash Flow after Tax Shield	5,236,200	6,105,240	7,280,928	8,700,826
Discounted Cash Flow b4 CAPEX	4,959,715	5,188,289	5,551,229	5,951,738
CAPEX	3,000,000			
TOTAL Discounted Cash Flows less initial CAPEX				**18,650,971**

TERMINAL VALUE	
FCF Y4	8,700,826
g	0.03
d (WACC)	11.46%
Terminal Value	105,932,037
PV of Terminal Value	**68,635,874**

VALUATION	
DCF	18,650,971
Terminal Value	68,635,874
VALUATION	**87,286,846**

All the formulas used to create the above Pro-Forma cash flow statement and ultimately the valuation can be found in the various sections above, we will not belabor them here.

Multiple Choice Questions for Chapter 8

1. The most suitable trendline for data which first increase or decrease, but then flatten, is
    a. logarithmic.
    b. polynomial.
    c. moving average.
2. Power curves are most often found in:
    a. business.
    b. engineering.
    c. Medicine.
3. Population growth is best modeled on a(n) ____ curve.
    a. linear
    b. power
    c. exponential
4. In Solver, an integer constraint
    a. forces Excel to calculate a number in every cell.
    b. forces Excel to answer questions with absolute values as answers.
    c. prohibits Excel from providing solutions with decimal places.
5. A profit maximization model in Solver requires the input of fixed costs.
    a. True.
    b. False.
6. In Solver, the shadow price:
    a. shows the increase in contribution margin obtained by obtaining one extra unit of a constrained resource.
    b. shows the price increase necessary to cover the increased cost of one extra unit of a constrained resource.
    c. Shows the loss which would be avoided by obtaining one extra unit of a constrained resource.
7. β (beta):
    a. is the ratio of the S&P 500 Index to the S&P/TSX Composite Index.
    b. is the ratio of the volatility of a stock or security compared to the market as a whole.
    c. Is the difference between the rate of return achieved on a stock and the risk-free rate.
8. In a deflationary economy, the present value of $100 will be ____ its value in one year.
    a. lower than
    b. higher than
    c. the same as
9. The selling price of a business may differ from FMV because of
    a. power disparity.
    b. market disparity.
    c. the time value of money.
10. Times revenue, book value and precedent transactions are all methods of:
    a. calculating WACC.
    b. calculating NPV.
    c. valuing a business.
    d. assessing the future of a not-for-profit

11. In practice, which approach do most professionals use to calculate the value of a business?
    a. The best single method according to the industry.
    b. The mean of two methods appropriate to the industry and reason.
    c. The average using all methods of evaluation.

9. REGRESSION ANALYSIS

Before commencing this chapter, please open Excel and click on the Data tab. Look to the far right of the ribbon in the *Analyze* group, for Data Analysis. If it is not there, please install the (free) Data Analysis ToolPak as follows: click *File* tab, *Options* from the bottom left of the screen, then *Add-ins* from the menu at the left. At the bottom of the dialog box select *Excel Add-ins* from the Manage menu, then *Go*. A pop-up box will show available add-ins—select Analysis ToolPak and *OK*. The ToolPak will install automatically.

Introduction

It is commonly stressed that "correlation does not imply causation." Understanding that two variables have some commonality, how should we explore relationships to know whether we can reliably predict one variable based on another, or others? Regression is the answer—it is the method used to quantify that reliability. It still does not complete our understanding of cause and effect.

After using regression to understand which variables do influence others, there is a bonus. The numerical analysis of the past can help with prediction of the future. If a farmer knows that June rainfall influences the July harvest, by June 30th they will be able to predict what will be taken from the fields in July.

Two types of data can be used for regression analysis:

- *Cross-sectional data* are a snapshot of statistics at or close to a point in time—how things *are;*
- *Time series data* capture the values of variables at several points in time, usually equally spaced. Time series data allow businesses to dig deeper into trends and patterns, allowing them to look for causes. They also support predictions for the future and can thus be employed in exercises like purchase planning, cash flow budgeting and the search for investment.

Correlation can provide guidance on where to look for relationships, and its strength can help understand the *linearity* of a relationship. *Autocorrelation,* however, is a complicating feature of time series data. Is there a relationship between the weather today and what it is most likely to be tomorrow? If interest rates went up in the last period, are they more likely to go up in the current period? If the answer to such a question is yes, then there is a degree of autocorrelation. It is measured by calculating the correlation between a set of time series data and themselves, lagged by one or more periods. Like with correlation, the possible values range from -1 to +1, with +1 indicating perfect autocorrelation. Autocorrelation is particularly important in capital markets analysis, because buy/sell decisions can be made more confidently with stocks exhibiting a high degree.

Terminology

In *simple regression,* we analyze the effect of one variable on another. The variable doing the affecting is known as the *independent variable* (also *predictor* or *explanatory variable),* while the one receiving the effects is the *dependent variable* (a.k.a. *response* or *target variable*).

In *multiple regression*, there is still one dependent variable but there are two or more independent variables.

Depending on the data, relationships may be linear or may take other forms such as exponential or logarithmic. Some non-linear data can be linearized by a mathematical process known as *transformation*; linear regression analysis may then be cautiously performed on it. Here, we'll cover only linear regression.

Looking For Relationships

Excel provides several methods of examining relationships between variables. CORREL function provides a value for correlation, with +1 being a perfectly positive relationship and -1 being perfectly negative. At 0, there is no relationship. Following is a table of salary data captured at the start of a new year for a small data processing company with 17 employees. The table can be quickly copied or downloaded (Annual Salary.xlsx).

TABLE 39: Salary Data

	A	B	C	D
1	Job Title	Yrs HE	Yrs w Co	Salary
2	Clerk	0	1	20,000
3	Clerk	0	2	21,000
4	Clerk	0	3	22,050
5	Clerk	0	4	23,153
6	Receptionist	0	1	22,000
7	Receptionist	0	2	23,100
8	Processor	2	1	24,000
9	Processor	2	2	25,200
10	Processor	2	3	26,460
11	Processor	2	4	27,783
12	Team Lead	3	1	40,000
13	Team Lead	3	2	42,000
14	Team Lead	3	3	44,100
15	C-Level	6	2	75,000
16	C-Level	6	3	80,000
17	C-Level	6	4	85,000
18	MD	7	4	250,000

The first question of interest is whether years of higher education (*i.e.* after High School) has any relationship to salary. With its organization by salary (lowest to highest), it is even visually clear from the table that there is some degree of inter-relationship.

`=CORREL(D2:D18,B2:B18)` returns the result 0.77477, which confirms there is a strong though not perfect positive relationship.

A second Excel tool to visualize the relationship is the Scatterplot available from the Charts group on the Insert ribbon. In its native form using these data it is not helpful, as the small numbers in the Years column appear indistinguishably on the baseline. There are various solutions; one is to add a column for Days of Higher Education and multiply the numbers in Column B by 365, then divide each of the annual salaries by 12 to produce monthly salaries.

Best practice is to put the independent variable on the X axis, and the dependent on the Y.

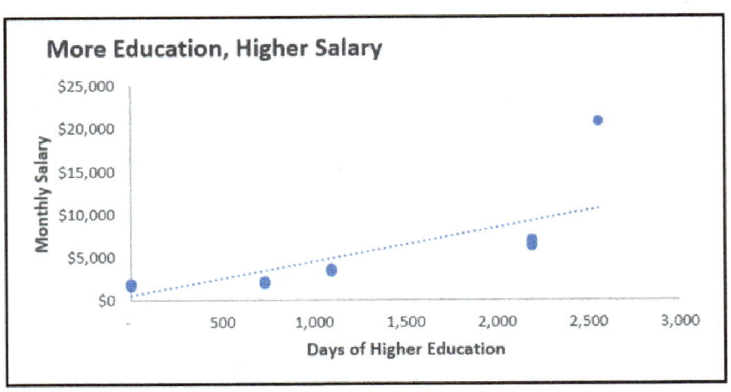

FIGURE 159: Salary scatterplot

The resultant chart (at left) illustrates what we already suspected—the more higher education is obtained, the higher the likely salary at this company. Notice that there is an *outlier* in these data—the salary of the Managing Director (MD) is so much higher than the other employees that the trendline is drawn unnaturally upwards.

Probably for most purposes, these data will be more useful without the outlier. If the outlier is clearly not a member of the population being studied, then it is best excluded. If it is unclear, best practice is to perform the analyses with and without the outlier and if necessary, report both results. Here, there is a good case for excluding the MD because the way their salary and benefits are calculated are likely to be very different from those of other employees.

CORREL and scatterplots can also guide to the conclusion that there is no discernable relationship. The next table shows passenger departures from a major port, and toy sales (in millions of $) at a major national chain. You would not expect much of a relationship here, except that perhaps cruise departures might be down at Christmas when toy sales are up. Exactly as would be expected, there is no discernable relationship on the chart, and the correlation is very weakly negative (-0.267), not worth pursuing.

Month	Port Passengers	Toy Sales
Apr	11,989	50,010
May	57,661	49,035
Jun	69,347	49,026
Jul	85,912	51,102
Aug	80,358	62,100
Sep	74,525	45,002
Oct	20,229	43,100
Nov	2,023	72,210

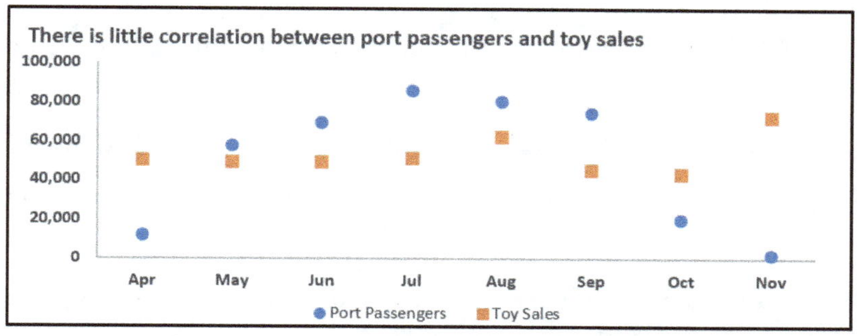

FIGURE 160: Monthly port passengers and toy sales

Covariance is yet another way of looking at relationships. It is a measure of the extent to which two variables change in the same way. For example, if the peak in variable A coincides with the peak in variable B, this is an indicator of strong positive co-variance (for instance, ice cream sales and pool drownings). As with correlation, covariance does not prove causation, but may point to a common cause (in the ice cream/drownings example, maybe hot weather). The COVARIANCE functions in Excel calculate sample and population covariance. There is a relationship between covariance and correlation, but they are different; covariance is not constrained to the range -1 to +1, but from -infinity to +infinity.

Linear Relationships

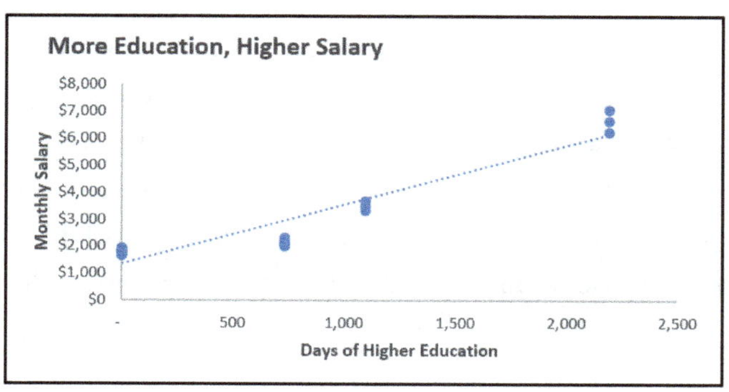

FIGURE 161: Linear relationship

Going back to the salary table the chart on the left now has the outlier removed. There is now an even stronger positive, linear relationship. A *trendline* is inserted to quantify the relationship; it shows at all points the predicted change in Y (salary) occasioned by a change in the value of X. It is known as the *least squares line*, which requires some explanation—and some new terminology.

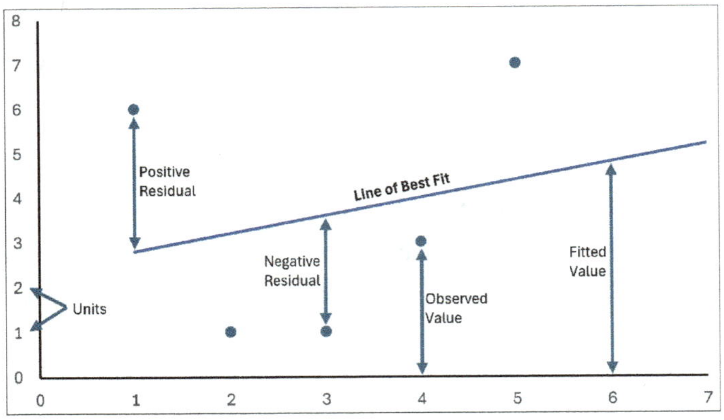

FIGURE 162: Line of best fit and relationship terms

With the line in place, some actual (observed) values will be above, and some below. The distance from the line to each value, vertically, is the *residual.* Some observed values may fall exactly on the line, but most will be to one side or the other. Imagine an observed value falling below the line. The distance up from the X axis to the value is the observed value, and the distance from there up to the line is the residual. It follows that

`observed value - residual = fitted value`

(the value where the line predicts the observed value would have been based on the relationship).[33] The *line of best fit* is the line with the smallest sum of squared residuals (which are all positive numbers), leading to the name.

Why not use the sum of the residuals, instead of the sum of their squares? If the line is correctly placed, the sum of the residuals will be exactly 0—the positives will cancel out the negatives. Mathematicians could—and sometimes do—use the sum of the absolute values of the residuals (*i.e.,* all the negatives are turned positive). Around the time of the First World War (1914–18) this was the subject of great debate between intellectual mathematicians, but it was finally accepted that in most cases, the sum of squares is a more efficient methodology than the sum of absolutes.

Simple Linear Regression

We repeat, correlation does not imply causation. Regression advances the enquiry, but it is not definitive. When an analysis shows a strong relationship, that goes some way towards suggesting causation, but it could still be that it is in the other direction—Y is causing X. Simple regression also does not eliminate the possibility of covariance, that a third variable is causing both datasets to respond in a similar fashion.

Vancouver traditionally has demand for more puppies than can be supplied by the local market. To meet the shortfall, charitable agencies fly in unwanted puppies from places with a surplus, such as Taiwan, Romania and Mexico. Imagine that in late 2020, arrivals of flights from Taipei, Bucharest and Mexico City were plotted against available puppies in Metro Vancouver. The data would show a high correlation—arrivals from those cities were at an all-time low, and there were virtually no puppies available anywhere in Vancouver. Did the lack of flights cause a shortage of puppies? Or was the shortage of puppies indicating that most demand had

---

[33] For complete clarity—residuals below the line are negative. Therefore, positive observed value, minus *minus residual* adds the two absolute values together to arrive at the fitted value. Re-formatting the equation—Fitted Value + residual (*which may be negative)* = observed value.

been fulfilled, so the normally planned flights didn't take place? Either allocation of X and Y would have shown a strong relationship.

But neither was the cause of the other. COVID19 was at its fullest extent, strong restriction on interaction between humans were in place, and air travel had dropped to an unimaginable low. Because of travel and entry restrictions, there was virtually no demand for passenger travel thus flights were few and far between. COVID19 also caused the puppy shortage—thousands of families with two working parents who had never had time or facilities for a puppy, were suddenly at home, with bored children, looking for new things to do. The shelters emptied because demand for puppies suddenly increased; when there were no more puppies, older dogs also found a home. Meanwhile, with no flights, there were no rescue dogs arriving to fill the gap.

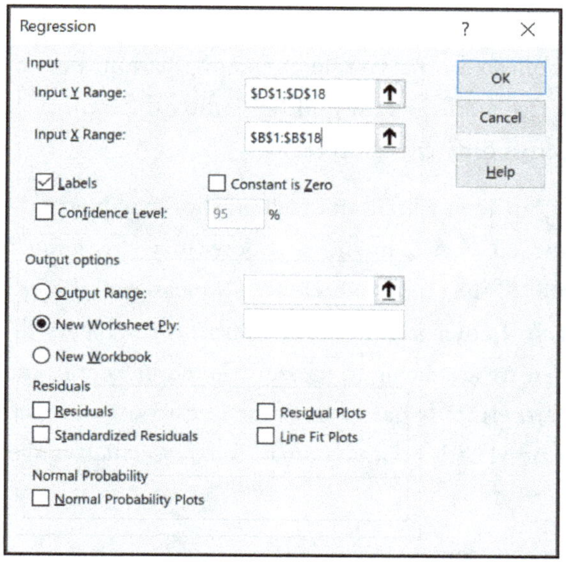

FIGURE 163: Linear regression dialog box

In the salary data which we started to analyze above, there are two obvious variables which might help to explain the salary discrepancies: days of higher education, and years with the company. If each is analyzed, the results will start to quantify the relationships. We'll start with higher education. With the table opened as shown above, select the *Data* tab, *Data Analysis*, select *Regression* from the dropdown list, and *OK*. For a simple linear regression analysis of each one, we need only input the two ranges (as shown—if they are filled by click and select they will absolutely reference the ranges by placing $ signs in them ($B$1:$B$18), fill the box for Labels, and OK. Excel will generate a Summary Output report, with lots statistical data.

The *Regression Statistics* appear first.

TABLE 40: Summary output

SUMMARY OUTPUT

Regression Statistics	
Multiple R	0.762436
R Square	0.581309
Adjusted R Square	0.553396
Standard Error	37372.48
Observations	17

The five statistics in this part of the output are the goodness of fit measures. They indicate how well the calculated line fits the observed data.

Multiple R is the coefficient of correlation. It is exactly the same number obtained if CORREL is applied to the two ranges.

R square is the coefficient of determination. It informs the extent to which variation around the Y axis is explained by the X variable. Here it is 58%, which is useful but not extremely strong. The better the linear fit, the closer R square is to 1.0 (or100%).

Adjusted R square is the R square, adjusted to reflect the number of independent variables used. It is not relevant in simple regression but is the more reliable in multiple regression. There, it will deal with a limitation of R square, which always increases when potential independent variables are added. Adjusted R square helps monitor whether extra variables are of value in the regression; when new variables are added, adjusted R square will be the place to look to see the effect.

Standard Error in this section—it will appear again later—is for the coefficients of the complete regression model. This includes the interceptor and the, or all the, independent variable(s). It is (more or less) the standard deviation sampling distribution. Standard errors and standard deviations are usually distributed around their mean (always 0 for residuals) in a similar fashion to most variable statistics; that is, approximately 95% of all observations will fall within two standard deviations of the mean.

The regression model will typically be calculated from data collected on a sample of the population, not the entire population. Therefore, if a different sample was used, the coefficients would be slightly different. The standard error tells us how much variation we might expect across different samples.

Think of a shooter in a practice range, firing towards a target. A person who is an excellent shot may pierce the target within a few inches of the center most times out of a hundred where a mediocre shooter may have a much broader distribution of the holes. If the distance from the center of the target to each hole is measured, that is a residual. The standard error measures the extent to which each shooter has missed the target—the bigger the number, the less reliable the shooter. The effect of X on Y, what we are trying to measure, is the shooter in this scenario. The question remains; what is a big or small standard error? It has to be compared to the numbers involved in the actual data; so in the above, a standard error of 3114 is relatively small for data which ranges from 20,000 to 80,000.

Observations counts the number of observations, or records, in the sample.

TABLE 41: ANOVA

ANOVA					
	df	*SS*	*MS*	*F*	*Significance F*
Regression	1	29087602327	29087602327	20.82591567	0.000373021
Residual	15	20950533067	1396702204		
Total	16	50038135394			

The second part of the report is rarely used, especially for simple regression. Entitled ANOVA (which is short for "Analysis of Variance," it breaks down the sum of squares calculation further.

- *df* indicates the degrees of freedom; this is calculated from sample size less the number of restrictions and is needed for some other calculations. Here with 17 records and one restriction there are 16 degrees of freedom.[34]
- *SS* is the sum of squares, as described above.
- *MS* is the SS (above) divided by the degrees of freedom.
- *F* is the result of an F test for the null hypothesis; standing alone it is complex to interpret, but it is a step along the way of calculating ...
- *Significance F*, which is the same thing as the P-value for the variable. P-value is explained in the next section.

TABLE 42: Intercept and coefficient

	Coefficients	*Standard Error*	*t Stat*	*P-value*	*Lower 95%*	*Upper 95%*	*Lower 95.0%*	*Upper 95.0%*
Intercept	7097.364303	13066.98094	0.543152572	0.595004771	-20754.24627	34948.97488	-20754.24627	34948.97488
Yrs HE	17385.4835	3809.646862	4.563542009	0.000373021	9265.413423	25505.55357	9265.413423	25505.55357

This section is the most useful for making predictions based on the data.

Coefficients give first the intercept, then a value for the X variable. Both of these will be necessary to create a linear regression equation for these data. The formula is:

```
Y = mx + b, or Y = (slope * x) + intercept
```

In this case, to calculate Y for any value of X, Y (monthly salary) would be estimated as 3.969 x days of higher education + 591.44.

Standard Error in this table is calculated for each individual independent variable. As with the earlier standard error, again it indicates how much we might expect each coefficient to vary, if we used different samples from the same population. In the above table, then, the coefficient for Days HE is approximately 4; if we had several samples from the same population, we might anticipate coefficients from 3.13 to 4.87. The standard error here can be mathematically treated as part of the T-test; as it is the denominator in the equation, the smaller it is in relation to the coefficient, the larger the t-statistic and the less the likelihood of a false conclusion.

T-stat(istic) is the result of the application of Student's T-test to calculate the ratio of the fitted value to its standard error[35] (similar to a z-score, but available when sample size is small, or standard deviation is not

[34] We have noticed that textbook explanations of degrees of freedom rarely go beyond explaining the mathematics. An example may help. Suppose you are a painter, and you are offered 7 colors of paint. You can choose one for each day of the week, *but no two colors can be the same (the restriction)*. On Monday you have a choice of 1 from 7, Tuesday 1 from the remaining 6, and so on. By Sunday, however, you have no choice. You had six choices with a degree of freedom, but on the 7th day no freedom. So, with 7 colors and 1 restriction, you had 6 degrees of freedom.

[35] Or the coefficient divided by the standard error.

available). The greater the T-statistic, the less the likelihood of incorrectly rejecting the null hypothesis. It is a mathematical step along the way to calculating ...

P-value. The most important figure. It tells us the likelihood of our results having happened randomly rather than as the result of a relationship; or said another way, the likelihood of falsely rejecting the null hypothesis (that there is no relationship). Typical analyses set 0.05, or 5%, as the standard allowable risk of error; here, we are at 0.03 of 1 percent, so we can conclude that rejection of the null hypothesis is reliable.

Upper and Lower 95% show the boundaries of the margin of error for the set level (95%).

Reading the report holistically, then, hours of higher education explain 58.1% of the variance in salary level, we have a formula for calculating estimated salaries, and there is a very small risk indeed of us falsely concluding that there is a relationship.

Now run the simple regression report again, but this time with Yrs w Co—Years with the Company—as the X variable. You should obtain an R Square value of 0.1895 (not very good) and a P-value of 0.08, or 8%, which is outside our tolerance. Clearly Days of Higher Education is a better indicator.

Multiple Regression

To determine whether we can improve our predictions, we can test the data using multiple regression. Here the power of Excel becomes evident, as calculations which would take hours or weeks manually are performed in less than a second. For multiple regression, X variables must be grouped together. The regression dialog box then looks as follows, with a multi-column range in the X range.

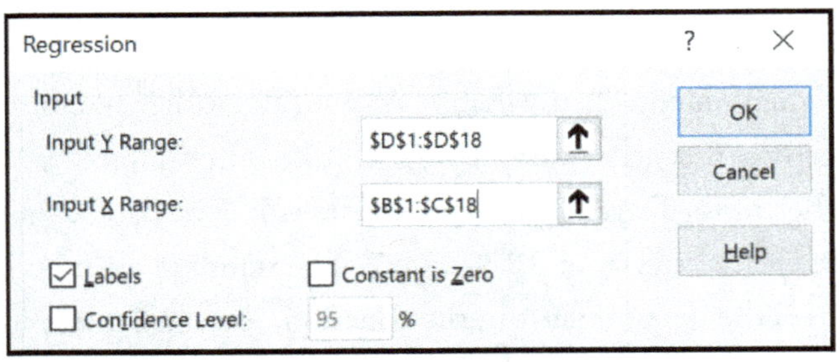

FIGURE 164: Multiple regression dialog box

The results of this analysis are not very impressive, Yrs w Co has a P-value of 0.3359 which is unacceptable, and the R Square improves only to 0.609. Instinctively, this doesn't feel quite right, compared to our initial impression that the relationships in the data were obvious.

Recall that there was an outlier in the data, the exceptionally large salary of the Managing Director. Run the multiple regression again with that position removed; remarkably, the Adjusted R square is at nearly 89% and the P-value for Days HE has dropped to a microscopic level. The formulas which could be drawn from this report are likely to be much more accurate for the range of lower-level positions than the analysis of all the data.

This brings us back to consideration whether to include Yrs w Co in the regression model. To answer this conundrum, run a single regression on the original data, with the outlier removed. R square actually improves by only a tiny fraction of a percentage, tending to support our view that Yrs w Co is not adding much value if any.

To summarize on the decision to include or exclude a variable:

- Look first at the P value. If it exceeds the acceptable level of risk (significance), it is a candidate for exclusion.
- Do not rely on correlation alone. A variable can easily have a high correlation with the dependent variable yet be of limited utility in the overall regression.
- In more complex multiple regressions, sometimes variables logically fit into related groups. It may be worthwhile to experiment with including or excluding all variables in such a group.
- There are no hard numerical rules about inclusion and exclusion of variables. At times two datasets may be similar—it could be beneficial to pool their data. A variable might have a p-value over 5%—but it might still be included because we know it is important.

The Regression Formula

The last table in the regression report contains all the data we need to construct the regression formula and make predictions based on it.

TABLE 43: Intercept and coefficients

	Coefficients	*Standard Error*	*t Stat*	*P-value*
Intercept	-932.8301658	1877.677746	-0.4968	0.6270401
Yrs w Co	742.1778228	744.7251818	0.9965795	0.3358826
Days HE	3.626251528	0.935601149	3.8758519	0.0016798

This is the table from the first multiple regression which we ran on the salary data, above. Let's try to predict monthly salary for an employee who has been with the company for 5 years and has 2 years (730 days) of higher education. We start with the intercept, then add the data that we have multiplied by their coefficients. In this example, the intercept is a negative figure. The intercept has no intrinsic meaning on its own—it is the point on the Y axis where the line of best fit would cross, where the values of all independent variables are 0.

```
Predicted salary = -932.83 + (742.18*5) + (3.626*730)
```

The answer is $5,425, and this is the fitted value for this potential employee. Look back at the original table—does it fit with what you might have predicted based on what you know? It seems rather high, because it is higher than any employee with three years' further education, and higher than any of the team leads, who each have three years. This is almost certainly the result of the disproportionate effect of the outlier. Using the regression equation with the outlier removed, it becomes 1088.72 + (141.85*5) + (2.134*730) = $3,355, very close to the salary of the team lead with the least time of service.

Standardized Coefficients

Where a model has many independent variables, it's useful to be able to filter out those that have little significance, even though their p-values are within range. The method of doing this is to look at the coefficients; but they are based on differing scales so first require standardization.

A deep dive into this is beyond our scope. It is enough to understand that thorough standardization involves converting the original data from measures into z scores, then performing regression on those results. There is also a post-analysis method which generally produces sufficient results: the standardized coefficient is calculated by multiplying the non-standardized coefficient by the standard deviation of y (the dependent variable) and dividing it by the standard deviation of x (the specific independent variable). Where this results in negative values, convert them to absolute values before ranking.

Stepwise Regression

Stepwise regression is a technique used in multiple regression to select or remove variables based on their significance. There is commercial software which will perform this iteratively; however, it can also be done by hand.

In *forward selection*, the model is first run with no variables. Each potential variable is then added to the model, keeping those that prove to be statistically significant, until the results are optimal.

In *backward elimination*, the full set of independent variables is first analyzed, then they are removed one at a time to see if they are statistically significant. Those that are not are left removed, while those that are, are replaced.

Dummy Variables

Sometimes a variable is potentially relevant to the regression analysis but cannot be used because it is categorical. There are two possibilities: a binary variable, such as male / female, or a variable with more than one type such as morning, afternoon, evening, night. Where there are three or more categories, multiple dummy variables must be created.

In the sample dataset Annual Salary.xlsx, we have (at line 31) added a new copy of the data then created two new columns. In column D we indicate the gender of the employee. In the next column "Dummy," contiguous to the data we are already using, we use an IF statement to produce either a 0 or a 1.

```
=IF(D32="F”,0,1)
```

TABLE 44: Employment table with numerical dummy variable to express gender

Job Title	Salary	Yrs HE	Gender	Dummy	Yrs w Co	Days HE	Salary/Mo
Clerk	20,000	0	F	0	1	0	1,667
Clerk	21,000	0	F	0	2	0	1,750
Clerk	22,050	0	F	0	3	0	1,838
Clerk	23,153	0	F	0	4	0	1,929
Receptionist	22,000	0	F	0	1	0	1,833
Receptionist	23,100	0	F	0	2	0	1,925
Processor	24,000	2	F	0	1	730	2,000
Processor	25,200	2	F	0	2	730	2,100
Processor	26,460	2	M	1	3	730	2,205
Processor	27,783	2	M	1	4	730	2,315
Team Lead	40,000	3	F	0	1	1,095	3,333
Team Lead	42,000	3	F	0	2	1,095	3,500
Team Lead	44,100	3	M	1	3	1,095	3,675
C-Level	75,000	6	F	0	2	2,190	6,250
C-Level	80,000	6	F	0	3	2,190	6,667
C-Level	85,000	6	M	1	4	2,190	7,083

Next, we create a pivot table to review average salaries according to gender (the outlier is removed).

TABLE 45: Average salaries

Row Labels	Average of Salary
F	34,792
M	45,836
Grand Total	**37,553**

Is gender discrimination a problem at this company? From this very preliminary analysis, it seems it might be. Multiple regression using the dummy variable which we created will help us look at the significance of factors other than gender.

Table 46: Coefficients with dummy variable

	Coefficients	*Standard Error*	*t Stat*	*P-value*
Intercept	837.8451783	409.5211376	2.045914365	0.063326716
Dummy	-659.0230386	442.6452157	-1.488829011	0.162336186
Yrs w Co	299.5105376	179.9074545	1.664803376	0.121823876
Days HE	2.185489409	0.19763856	11.05801119	1.19582E-07

With an Adjusted R square value of almost 90%, Days HE (Higher Education) still is the dominant factor; the P-value for Yrs w Co suggests at best a weak secondary influence (but not significant at 5% or even 10% level), and that gender is an unreliable third factor. Does this make sense when we look back at the numbers? In fact, it does; in each of the three higher categories of employment, the highest earners are male; they have similar educational levels to the females but more years with the company. Years with the company is a candidate for exclusion because of its high P-value; but sensibly, it should not be excluded from this particular analysis because it explains the lack of significance of another variable (gender).

Where the categorical options are more than two, we create multiple dummy variables. On a new sheet named "Beef," we've created a tiny table of farms and the quality of their beef.

TABLE 47: Canadian beef

Canadian Beef						
Farm	Grade	A	B	D	E
Appy Valley	Prime	0	0	0	0
Spread Man Ure	A	1	0	0	0
Sprawling Akers	B	0	1	0	0
Strawberry Fields	D	0	0	1	0
Benson Edges	E	0	0	0	0

Each farm produces a different quality of beef. (Canadian beef is graded into these five categories. When you see "AA" and "AAA" at the supermarket, these are sub-grades of A; all three A grades are slightly inferior to prime; the differences relate to the amount of marbling.) To incorporate these data into a regression table, one dummy column is created for each quality **except one**, then an IF statement is used to populate the correct cell with a 1, and the others in the record with a 0. Regression analysis will then include ALL four columns A to E. We have deliberately left out one category, Prime, as this is a requirement to avoid **multicollinearity**. That occurs when one independent variable in a group can be perfectly predicted from the others. Leaving out a **reference variable** in this manner avoids the complication.

In determining whether dummy variables are needed, be cautious of data that looks like numbers but is in fact categorical. For example, in England university degrees are awarded with levels of 1, 2.1, 2.2, 3.1 and 3.2. These, however, are categories, they could have been A, B, C, D and E with the same ranking. The numerical ranks need to be converted to dummy variables just as if they are letters.

Interaction Variables

Sometimes, we may believe that the effect of one independent variable on Y depends on the value of another independent variable. They are interactive. We cope with this by including an interaction variable; this is the product of the two independent variables that we believe to be interactive. In our sample employment data, we might believe that there is a relationship between years worked at the company and years of higher education (along the lines of, lesser qualified employees have higher turnover). At line 50 of the sample data, we have repeated once more the employment list, then created an interaction variable (YwC*DHE) and run multiple regression with all three variables. The result, an adjusted R square of 90.4%, is slightly better than the same regression without the interaction variable.

TABLE 48: Interaction variables

	Coefficients	*Standard Error*	*t Stat*	*P-value*
Intercept	1642.018931	484.9135654	3.386209519	0.005405746
Yrs w Co	-84.82664654	193.2603081	-0.438924306	0.668515221
Days HE	1.254473952	0.543938752	2.306277955	0.03974324
YwC*DHE	0.327446792	0.189830583	1.724942241	0.110173745

Cross-Validating the Model

After performing various regression analyses on a dataset and determining the optimal parameters, it's natural to want to evaluate the effectiveness of your model. One approach is to wait for future data, measure the independent (X) variables again, and compare the new outcomes to your predictions. However, this approach is time-consuming and can lead to disappointing results. Fortunately, there's no need to wait thanks to *cross-validation*.

Cross-validation is a technique used to assess the performance and generalizability of a regression model. It helps to determine how well the model will perform on unseen data by partitioning the original data into subsets, training the model on some of these, then checking its performance against the remaining data.

Manual versus machine cross-validation

Cross-Validation is commonly performed with the assistance of specialized software such as the scikit-learn library in Python, splitting the data into a minimum of three subsets. Here we will briefly describe the process, then demonstrate a manual procedure using a simpler split into two halves. Other software which performs similar analyses includes XGBoost (Python), caret (R), mlr3 (R), Matlab, Weka, and RapidMiner.

Steps in cross-validation

1. Data Splitting: The dataset is divided into k equally sized folds (subsets), where k is a number and each fold contains the number of records divided by k.
    - Model Training and Validation: For each of the k folds:
        - Use k - 1 folds to train the model.
        - Use the remaining fold to validate the model.

This process is repeated k times, with each fold being used exactly once as the validation data.

2. Evaluation: The performance metrics (*e.g.*, R square) are averaged over the k iterations to provide an overall estimate of the model's performance.

How much data to hold back

In k-fold cross-validation, the amount of data held back for validation depends on the value of k. For instance, in 5-fold cross-validation, 20% of the data are held back in each iteration. Similarly, in 10-fold cross-validation, 10% of the data are held back in each iteration. The choice of k can depend on the size of the dataset and the computational cost. For smaller data sets, higher k values (e.g., 10) can be useful while in larger data sets, lower k values (e.g., 5) can be more computationally efficient.

Cross-validation has the advantage of providing a more accurate estimate of model performance on unseen data and helps to identify overfitting since we can observe how generalizable the model is.

Manual demonstration with 2-fold validation

In the following section we will use a set of anonymous medical data to demonstrate cross-validation. If you wish to perform the analysis yourself, please download the dataset diabetes.xlsx. The data in this set are a survey of 20,000 random male subjects selected from a massive population.

Diabetes (full name "diabetes mellitus") is a disease in which the human body has difficulty handling sugar in the blood (glucose). Too much sugar can lead to serious illness including coma and death. It is a treatable condition and early intervention can have life-changing results. It is therefore of great interest to doctors to be able to predict the occurrence of diabetes from other factors.

These data contain columns for age, the presence or absence of hypertension (high blood pressure), presence or absence of heart disease, smoking history (0 for never, 1 for historically, 2 for now), Body Mass Index, blood glucose level and HbA1c. This last measurement is the subject's average blood glucose level over the last few months, a bit like a baseball or cricket player's batting average for a season. Multiple regression analysis can be used to see how well these factors predict the presence of diabetes.

For these 20,000 records, the independent variables have moderate predictive capability, with both R square and adjusted R square at 0.417 percent. Just under 42% of the predictability of diabetes is explained by the combination of these variables, with all except smoking having low P-values and HbA1c being the strongest. A perusal of other medical literature will quickly lead to the realization that another very important variable, family history, is missing from the list; however, it is not important for our purposes.

We want to know how well this regression model will generalize on similar datasets. To demonstrate, we will select a k of 2 and divide the data into two subsets of 10,000 records each.

Multiple regression is performed only on the first half. An adjusted R square of 0.42 is now obtained, slightly but not significantly better than for the whole dataset. Here are the intercept and coefficients for the first half.

TABLE 49: Coefficients for 50% of data

	Coefficients
Intercept	-1.159635564
Age	0.00226257
Hypertension	0.079009933
Heart Disease	0.085147731
Smoking	-0.005092509
BMI	0.005245202
HbA1c_level	0.110037945
Blood_Glucose	0.002892527

The data are split by inserting three blank rows after row 10001. Then, in row 10003, the coefficients are listed in order using the TRANSPOSE function (=TRANSPOSE(L18:L24)).

TABLE 50: TRANSPOSE coefficients

	A	B	C	D	E	F	G	H
10002		=TRANSPOSE(L18:L24)			(in cell B10003)			
10003		0.002263	0.07901	0.085148	-0.005093	0.005245	0.110038	0.002893

Then in column I, starting at Row 10005, a predicted value for Column A, presence or absence of diabetes, can be calculated using the independent variables multiplied by the coefficients, adding the intercept, from cell L17.

```
=$L$17+(SUMPRODUCT($B$10003:$H$10003,B10005:H10005))
```

Note that the intercept (in L17) and the coefficients are made absolute references. The resulting calculation is then copied down to all rows in the second half of the dataset.

The last step is to calculate the correlation between the predicted data in column I, and the data in column A, in the 10,000 records we held back. `=CORREL(A10005:A20004,I10005:I20004)`. The result is a positive correlation of 64.37%; squared, this is 0.4144, extremely close to the R square of our original dataset.

All these calculations are performed on the second tab "Split" of the downloaded dataset.

How should these results be interpreted? The correlation of over 64% is good though not exceptional, indicating that the regression statistics we have generated can be expected to perform reasonably well on other sets of data. We could gain further comfort from our model by switching the roles, performing an analysis on the second half of the data then using it to predict outcomes in the first half.

Early in this exercise, we noted that our multiple regression model explained about 42% of the patient outcomes. Aside from improving the dataset with the addition of other independent variables, we could go on to examine the residuals (the differences between actual and predicted values) to assess the randomness of their distribution. This would help us to see if there is any unexplained variance. Here, we have a strong indication that there is no overfitting due to the similarity between our new R square (from the cross validation) and the original, but in similar exercises, if we did, we might use some sophisticated techniques such as ridge (also known as Tikhonov) regression or lasso regression (least absolute shrinkage and selection operator). These procedures, outside the scope of this book, recalculate the coefficients to reduce their variance where there is significant multicollinearity, and make the model less sensitive to the collinear predictors.

Predicting Indigenous Family Incomes: A Test Case in Multiple Regression

At regular intervals, Indigenous Affairs Canada surveys First Nations communities across Canada and publishes a Well-Being Index, broken down by community. Please download the provided file CWB_2021.xlsx and read the following data dictionary. The data file is genuine, but we have abridged it to exclude communities of under 250 people, and communities with data missing.

TABLE 51: Data dictionary for Community Well-Being Index

CSD Name	The name of the Community Sub-Division
Income	**Median family income, rated on a scale of 1–100 compared to all family incomes in the survey.**
Education	**Median educational level, rated on a scale of 1–100 compared to all educational levels.**
Housing	**Median housing quality, rated on a scale of 1–100 compared to all housing qualities.**
Type	**InC = Inuit Community, FNC = First Nations Community, NIC = Non-Indigenous Community.**
CWB	**Overall Community Well-Being Index**

We are interested to know whether we can predict median family income accurately for these communities, using the other measured factors. Excluding CWB, which is calculated based on the other measurements, use Excel's multiple regression feature to discover how well Population, education, housing and community type can be used to predict median family income. Then answer these questions (answers are in the Key at the back of the book; there is also a step-by-step guide to complete the exercise, but please try to do the work yourself before following the steps).

1. What is the adjusted R Square value for the regression?
2. What is the intercept value?
3. Excluding FNC and NIC, which always have values of only 1 or 0, which factor has the most influence on family income level?
4. Which factor has the least influence?
5. Do any of the predictor variables have a P-value that should exclude them?
6. Is the regression a good, moderate, or poor predictor of family income level?

GUIDED STEPS

1. Delete or move away the column "CWB"
2. Create one extra column before "Type" so that two blank columns are available, immediately to the right of "Housing."
3. Create a dummy column for "FNC" in Column F, where 1 means the Type in Column H is FNC, and 0 means it is not.
4. Do the same for "NIC" in column G. (InC) will become the reference variable.
5. Insert four blank rows after row 2001, so that we have a primary group and a reference group for verification.
6. Perform multiple regression analysis on rows 1–2001
7. Use the results of the regression analysis to create a list of predicted Income levels for the remaining rows of data.
8. Compare the predicted results with the actual values and calculate the correlation.
9. Using the post-analysis method described above, standardize the coefficients and rank them.

Multiple Choice Questions for Chapter 9

1. Autocorrelation exists when
    a. what happened in the previous period has a relationship with what happens in the current period.
    b. there is strong correlation between two variables.
    c. Transformation is used to linearize data relationships.
2. The best visual indicator of a relationship is usually found in
    a. a bar chart.
    b. a scatterplot.
    c. A histogram.
    d. A table.
3. Squaring residuals
    a. produces absolute values.
    b. diminishes the ratios between values.
    c. brings all values to a range between -1 and +1.
4. The adjusted R square is more useful for
    a. simple regression.
    b. multiple regression.
    c. prediction than analysis.
5. ^, or hat, indicates
    a. a prediction.
    b. a correlation.
    c. a relationship.
6. Categorical variables to be included in regression analysis require
    a. dummy variables in all circumstances.
    b. dummy variables where there are more than two.
    c. multicollinearity.
7. The grading of Canadian beef into Prime, A, B, D and E is an example of
    a. interactivity.
    b. dummy variability.
    c. categorical variables.
8. Splitting data into two halves and testing a regression model from one half, on the other, is known as
    a. cross-validation
    b. bootstrapping
    c. correlation
    d. parallel regression.

10. AUDIT DATA ANALYTICS (ADAs)

We introduced ADAs in our earlier book *Information Systems for Accountants*. While not essential, it may be helpful to review that content before progressing into this chapter.

The word *audit* comes by a circuitous route from the Latin word *audire*, meaning to listen. An auditor is a person who listens. Audit alone means he/she/it hears. It is not immediately apparent why an auditor today would be listening—but historically, the practice was to have the person responsible for the accounts read them out to the accountants who reviewed them. This allowed the auditor(s) to observe the demeanor of the reader as part of the assessment of their honesty.

In parallel with the name, the purpose of audit has evolved. Until around 1700, only governing figures or bodies, and religious institutions, were audited for the purpose of preventing the misappropriation of assets. Since the industrial revolution, however, the development of company structures has increasingly called for professional services to attest to the quality of financial statements and the absence of fraud.

Risk Assessment

At the risk assessment stage of an audit, ADAs engage early with the quest to lower the risk of material misstatement in the financial statements. The range of procedures which may be deployed is continually increasing. Some current examples include:

Journal Entry Testing. Traditionally, auditors spent a large amount of billable time preparing samples, often limiting the journal entry data to certain columns. This has become impossible with the increasing complexity of ERP systems. Automated testing on the entire database has become possible, especially with AI-powered software. AI is able to learn, quickly, what is normal and what is not, thus producing targeted results from large data ranges. A particular ability that has emerged with AI-driven software is that of detecting deliberate activity intended to circumvent internal controls, such as breaking up a transaction across general ledgers.

Process Mapping. Auditors performing risk assessment, particularly for new clients, usually need to map out processes within the client's business model. A *process* is a series of steps, decisions, acts or tasks that starts with input(s) and ends with output(s). The process adds value between the start and end. Flowcharts are the traditional tool for process mapping; they may be produced in Microsoft PowerPoint, Visio, Lucidchart or several other applications.

Exception Analysis. An exception is an unexpected or unusual event, which does not fit within the normal range expected based on the available data. The term is used much more widely than just in auditing or accounting; thus, software for its detection (for example, in scientific data) is already very advanced. Exception handling is its own field of specialization in programming languages like C++ and Java.

Aging Analysis. Focusing on allowances for bad debt, manual audits tend to focus on unpaid accounts at year end, most frequently dividing them into 30, 60, 90 day and older receivables. The ability of big data tools to analyze all data allows auditors to gain a view on the speed of payment of all accounts in a period, and perform a more sophisticated analysis of the likelihood of non-payment of outstanding items.

Scanning for Attributes. ADAs can quickly establish normal ranges for data, thus pointing out unusual items, or look for duplication, omissions or incomplete data very quickly, generating reports on large datasets in a matter of seconds.

The Data Lifecycle

Different analysts point to differing numbers of stages in the data life cycle. It is referred to as a cycle because it is a continuous process—the results of one project typically feed into the next.

The Harvard Business Review lists eight stages. For audit data purposes, three of them (bolded) are more significant than the others and it is those upon which we will enlarge, along with two which we've inserted (in square brackets []).

Generation—*Collection—Processing*—[Usage]—*Storage*—Management—Analysis—Visualization—Interpretation—[Purging].

In the collection stage, data which become available to the organization are captured. They can come from a variety of sources including data entry at retail or shipping points, web forms, surveys or interviews. At this stage it is important for the organization to ensure that it collects all data that are available and relevant for its purposes, but also that it does not collect data which will never be used.

- Processing (a.k.a. maintenance) involves handling the data so that it can be used. Software and human processes may be invoked to detect or prevent incorrect processing, or to further trim down the data to their useful components.
- Usage occurs as the data are used to implement operations or pursue objectives. At this point, the data will be organized and structured in a way that enables the entity to be managed effectively.
- Storage, typically in a database, involves retention of useful data for future use. Archiving, an aspect of storage, involves movement of data which are no longer required out of active environments.
- Purging, usually of archived data that will never be used again, clears space and reduces cost. Our experience is that this function is the most frequently poorly performed, and the ever-decreasing cost of storage does not lend a powerful incentive to IT managers to devote resources to finding and deleting old data.

Automating Data Analytics

It follows from the above examples of automatable procedures that these receive the bulk of the investment of time and money in audit. Indeed, they are common to much of the field of data analytics. A key value in the planning process is to identify data, create process maps and develop treatments that can be applied to future data (thus, audits in future years) as well as the current project. Important decisions should be made early as to how often procedures will be run, what exactly they will cover, and how to handle exceptions.

A key differentiator between traditional audit and automated audit is the easy availability of continuous auditing. Whereas a traditional audit would be planned around year-end and be an annual event, automated procedures can maintain constant watchfulness over the processes they review and provide early alerts. This also streamlines the eventual annual procedures. An audit client with continuous auditing will typically point to its results as evidence of the effectiveness of internal controls.

Potential Issues

The design of continuous auditing software requires the ability for the auditor to set an appropriate level of sensitivity. The rules set for compliant operation will cause an alarm to be generated by every exception. Human intervention is required for each alarm, to determine whether the event is really worthy of attention (true positive) or a normal event, construed as an exception (false positive). The danger of too many alarms is that auditors may be overloaded with information/tasks, and be distracted from their core mission—evaluation of the system.[36]

Implementing Audit Data Analytics

The first step in planning automation is to define the purpose. There could be many different objectives, for example:

- Analyzing segregation of duties
- Identifying operational inefficiencies
- Identifying fake employees or suppliers
- Confirming compliance with legislation or regulation
- Testing account balances
- Identifying trends and patterns in the data
- Comparing data across periods, departments or companies
- Detection of fraud
- Assessment of expense claims

Next, the planner must undertake a comprehensive review of the data, and ensure they are in suitable form to allow automated analysis.

Suitable software must be selected. Though there are specialized packages, many ADA functions can be performed using generalized software (Excel) or generalized audit software like Caseware's IDEA.

The automated procedures are then performed. Just as there are many possible purposes, there are many possible tests.

---

[36] The problem of false positives is common to every area of life. The fable of "The Boy who Cried Wolf" is an apt illustration.

Descriptive analytics may for example perform age analyses, identify largest or smallest values, summarize data, execute unbiased sampling. **Data reduction** or **filtering** may be performed at this stage to identify the data most relevant to the exercise.

Diagnostic analytics might use z-scores to detect outliers, or Benford's law to look for atypical activity. Clustering, matching and stratification as described previously may identify characteristics or relationships that are hard to detect by other means.

Profiling is a valuable application of diagnosis. Patterns are identified from the larger dataset, then the characteristics of an individual customer can be compared to the general pattern. In a sales environment like Amazon, where all goods are shipped, it would be possible to predict the likelihood of a customer's product being delivered late, or lost, based on the wider analysis. Auditors can use profiling to look back at historical exceptions and assess their importance—thus, their candidacy for further examination.

Predictive analytics interpret the data to open a window into the future. In an earlier chapter we explored regression; classification of a record allows the attribution of likely characteristics based on past performance. If 40% of packages shipped to a particular postal code are never received by the end customer, it's a reasonable prediction that the next package shipped has a 40% chance of being lost also.

Probability metrics are a sophisticated add-on to classification models. They provide a single value (score) which can be used to compare different models, based on how well predicted probabilities match the expected probabilities for a classification. *Sentiment analysis* is used to evaluate text, such as emails, reviews or reports, for positive or negative expressions, enabling the user to predict the outcome of a future event.

Prescriptive analytics include:

- *what-if analysis*, which allows management to make decisions based on comparing outcomes.
- *applied statistics* which allow analysis of past data to identify needs and deficiencies, supporting planning.
- *artificial intelligence* learns from past actions to predict future actions in similar circumstances.

After performing analytic procedures, auditors will review the results and report back to management with a view to resolving as many issues as possible. Not only should the quality of the current audit be enhanced, but future audits should run more smoothly.

The results of ADAs will usually be included in the file of audit evidence and preserved for future reference and comparison. On an ongoing basis, detection and resolution of exceptions will be re-evaluated; this will be part of review of the ADAs for continuing effectiveness.

Many Excel-based statistical procedures and tests that are appropriate for ADAs have been described in more detail elsewhere in this book or in *Information Systems for accountants.* The following table summarizes some of the more common examples.

Table 52: Common ADA procedures

Test	Procedure
Aging Analysis	Create "days outstanding" column: =Aging_Date (eg y/e) – Order_Date Use IF statement to place value in appropriate column for calculating total aged receivables: =IF(Days_outstanding)<=30,amount,0
Sorting	Home, Format as Table, use drop-down menus
Relative size	=AVERAGE, =MEDIAN, =MIN, =MAX, =SUM
Random Sampling	Analysis Toolpak—Data Analysis, click Sampling and set parameters.
Benford's Law	Use =LEFT to isolate the first digit of each value; use =COUNTIF to calculate the total number of occurrences of each digit 1–9; rank the counts using the SORT function (Data ribbon); examine (visually) whether they rank 1–9; if necessary, import the Benford distribution, sort the counts 1–9 and use =CORREL to compare the two lists.
Z-score	Calculate average and standard deviation (=STDEV.P for population, =STDEV.S for sample); then z-score = (value – mean)/standard deviation.
Fuzzy matching	Download the fuzzy lookup add-in. Match tables and columns.[37]
Stratification	Charts: use different colors to distinguish data from different sources or in different groups; Pivot Tables: use pivot table field and areas to segregate data of interest.
Clustering	Scatter Charts—to visually identify possible clusters.

[37] Where the null hypothesis (no relationship) is rejected, but it is true, this is a false positive. This is a Type I Error. Where the null hypothesis is accepted, but it should not have been, this is Type II. An easy way to remember this is that in Type I, an innocent person is convicted, while in Type II, a guilty person is acquitted. Setting the tolerances too low in fuzzy matching will result in too many false positives; too high, and there will be more Type II errors.

Multiple Choice Questions for Chapter 10

1. Processing of data is also known as
   a. maintenance.
   b. usage.
   c. storage.
2. Purging of data is normally legally performed on
   a. archived data that will never be used again.
   b. data that are best hidden from the auditors.
   c. data that expose the company to liability.
3. Fuzzy matching of address or banking data may detect:
   a. fake suppliers.
   b. inflated expense claims.
   c. trends and patterns in the data.
   d. operational inefficiencies.
4. A company's policy requires two managers to sign all expense claims of $500 or above. The statistical law which might be employed to look for avoidance of this control is known as:
   a. Benford's law.
   b. Sod's law.
   c. Murphy's law.
   d. Newton's law.
5. Sentiment analysis reviews mainly:
   a. human generated text.
   b. machine generated text.
   c. statistical data.
   d. outcomes from the application of Benford's law.
6. Aging analysis typically involves application of a mathematical operator to:
   a. two dates.
   b. two products.
   c. two employees.
   d. two managers.
7. Random sampling functions in Excel are found in the
   a. data analysis ToolPak.
   b. Solver Add-on.
   c. Data ribbon.
   d. Formulas tab.
8. Setting the tolerances too low in fuzzy matching will result in:
   a. too many false positives.
   b. too many false negatives.
   c. a computer crash.
9. What kind of error has occurred when an innocent person is convicted?
   a. Type III.
   b. Type II.
   c. Type I.

PART III. FINANCIAL MODELING

11. FINANCIAL (BUSINESS) MODELING

Introduction

In this chapter, which many students find to be a very fulfilling capstone project, we will learn to use Excel to model outcomes for a business proposal. This requires consideration of many inputs, building formulas, and consequent decision-making. We will start with some relatively simple examples, the use of modeling to make a single operational decision. Then we will progress to a full demonstration of a complex business model.

Rounding Numbers

Budgeting and modeling often call for the use of round numbers, because decimal places don't make sense or are overkill.

You *can* buy 1.5 tons of steel, or 2.25 gallons of oil, but you can't buy or sell half a car, a third of a ship, or half of a resort.

For high value assets, justifiable selection of the correct rounding function—ROUNDDOWN, ROUND, or ROUNDUP, is heavily dependent on the exact circumstances of the exercise. The two critical factors are the purpose of your budget, and the risks to be addressed. When dealing with units of an indivisible item, the size and value of the item may also be important. For example, trucks might cost $200,000, so rounding up or down could have a massive financial impact, which compounds; but if you are selling hundreds of books for $19.99 each, the overall financial impact will be very small and you would normally address the issue of whole numbers with ROUNDDOWN.

ROUND, with a syntax like =ROUND(123.45,1) will round the number or formula first presented to the number of decimal places specified after the comma, following normal mathematical rounding rules (5 is rounded UP).

ROUNDDOWN rounds down to the required number of decimal places, while ROUNDUP rounds up to the required number of decimal places.

In all three cases, using a rounding function will mean that for subsequent calculations, Excel will ONLY use the numbers you see in the cell. If you use the display buttons to change what you see, Excel will still work with the decimal places it knows in background, which may not lead to the result you want.

ROUNDDOWN is used when you want to be conservative or frugal in your estimates. ROUNDDOWN rounds any value (typically from a formula) to a specified number of decimal places, downwards. `=ROUNDDOWN(123.579,0)` becomes 123, even though conventional rounding would have taken it up to 124. For example, if you know that you are working with a strict budget, and can't exceed it, but want to plan purchases of machines or units that can't be split (like cars, trucks or airplanes), then ROUNDDOWN is appropriate. If your calculations show that you can afford 8.7 trucks but you don't have the cash to buy 9 trucks, you must round down.

ROUND is used if your estimate is more general in nature, but you need whole numbers in your presentation. This will give you the closest whole number to the calculated result with unlimited decimals, and where there are no indications of a budget, your eventual result will be closest to reality.

ROUNDUP is most used when you are being cautious by building in a safety margin. ROUNDUP rounds up to the next number with the specified number of decimal places. `=ROUNDUP(123.123,0)` becomes 124. You might deliberately want to overestimate costs to build a worst-case scenario, or you might be dealing with a commodity where having exactly the estimated amount is not safe. For example, in a construction project you calculate that you will need 8.7 tons of concrete. This is an ESTIMATE—but you might need more. It could be disastrous if your estimate is off by 0.1 percent and you run out just before you finish. You round up to 9 tons.

Selecting the wrong rounding function can have profound financial implications, as we will see.

When you encounter exam questions that indicate rounding is desired, start by figuring out which of these situations you are in.

Example 1: ROUNDDOWN

eTrux will start in 2025 with 5 trucks but hopes to grow its fleet by 40% each year. Financing is tight, and the purchasing department cannot get extra money for cost over-runs.

TABLE 53: ROUNDDOWN Number of trucks

Year	2025	2026	2027	2028	2029
Number of Trucks	5	7	9	12	16

Example 2: ROUND

eTrux will start in 2025 with 5 trucks but hopes to increase its fleet by 40% each year. Remember you can't buy part of a truck. (In this example, there is no indication that conservatism is needed, so you need your best estimate of what is likely to happen). Because this is a disruptive *growth* model, you don't want to have insufficient trucks to meet the demand you expect.

TABLE 54: ROUND Number of trucks

Year	2025	2026	2027	2028	2029
Number of Trucks	5	7	10	14	20

Example 3: ROUNDUP

eTrux will start in 2025 with 5 trucks but will aggressively grow its fleet by 40% each year. Remember you can't buy part of a truck. (In this example, management is clearly pushing to maximize growth).

TABLE 55: ROUNDUP Number of trucks

Year	2025	2026	2027	2028	2029
Number of Trucks	5	7	10	14	20

You will see that the ROUND function produced an eventual number of 20 trucks, while no rounding took us to 16. The ROUNDUP function, however, produced a much smaller number because of the conservatism.

A Rounding Example for High Cost Assets

FIGURE 165: LNG tanker (OpenAI, 2025).

FLO Tankers, Inc., is based in Vancouver, Canada. It owns and manages a fleet of bulk carriers, and has extensive experience in delivering grain, oil and chemicals, by ship, around the globe.[38] All its business and accounting is conducted in US dollars. In the data presented here, "m" is used as an abbreviation for "million" as some of the numbers are very large; m^3 is however cubic meters.

Due to its excellent relationship with Saudi Aramco, the state-owned resource producer in Saudi Arabia, FLO has an opportunity to enter the business of delivering liquified natural gas—LNG. This requires specialized tankers which cannot be used for any other purpose. LNG is transferred into tankers at Ras Tanura, one of the largest oil and gas exporting ports in the world. The destination, Khalifa Bin Salman port in Bahrain, is 10 hours' sailing time away. It is a key distribution point for LNG used throughout that country. The tanker(s) will return "in ballast," that is, empty; due to the specifications of LNG tankers, they can only be used to carry LNG. Each round-trip will take exactly 24 hours.

[38] It's not relevant to the exercise, but FLO stands for Fleet, Logistics, Operations, and its ships are registered in the Marshall Islands. FLO tankers is fictitious—there is no such company.

FLO has determined that the best fit for its fleet is to acquire one or more Q-max tankers. Each ship has a capacity of 250,000 cubic meters of LNG. Aramco is offering a contract to deliver a fixed quantity of LNG on this route daily, 365 days a year, for five years. Here are the relevant prices and accounting considerations.

- Price of new Q-max tanker: $250m
- Useful life: 30 years; salvage value $20m
- Annual maintenance: $10m
- Insurance, annual: $1.5m
- Crew requirements: 35; annual crew costs (24/365) $3.5m
- Fuel: Round Trip $360,000
- Operational Expenses Round Trip: $40,000
- Port Fees $200,000 (average) per round trip
- Company Income Tax, The Marshall Islands: 0%
- Combined federal and provincial taxes, British Columbia: 27%
- Revenue per cubic meter delivered: $3.50

This is a competitive market, and FLO will not lose business if it cannot satisfy all the requirements of its customer. Saudi Aramco is interested in negotiating a contract for at least 250,000 cubic meters of LNG per day, up to 475,000, in increments of 25,000.

We can use straight-line depreciation; insurance and maintenance costs will be similar regardless of how much we use each tanker. Variable costs are only variable with the number of vessels—even if we use only 10% of capacity on a tanker, we will still need to pay full crew and trip costs. In this respect they behave rather like fixed costs.

As we consider this opportunity, the conflict between conventional wisdom and intuition is thrown into relief. If we think about contracting to deliver 275,000 cubic meters, the second lowest quantity suggested by the client, conventional business wisdom says "round up, if not you are leaving money on the table." Our intuition argues "round down, you don't want to have 90% of the fuel tanks empty." Assuming there are no limitations on our ability to raise finance to purchase the necessary ships, which is the better course of action?

Another instinctive reaction might be that simple rounding will provide the answer, based on the theory that FLO will have better net earnings if the second tanker is at least half full—thus, the point of indifference must be half-way between the payload of one tanker (250,000 m^3) and that of two (500,000 m^3). That would be 375,000, but this is not correct because the potential revenue from the deliveries pro-rates with the volumes, while fixed and variable costs do not.

Modeling the outcomes will provide us with a solution to this problem. It will also tell us the quantity at which FLO will be indifferent as to whether it purchases one tanker or two.

In this special-purpose model, we can disregard several items that would be essential if a full business plan was being developed. We can compare apples to apples without worrying about inflation, exchange rates, time value of money, cost of capital, deferred taxes, and contingencies.

Here is the simple pro-forma P&L for the opportunity, with the initial payload set at 250,000 m^3—the full capacity of a single ship. If FLO rounds down the number of ships required, and contracts to deliver just one shipload per day, it projects a profit of $320m, and this is the most money it can ever earn with just one ship. This is the result of the ROUNDDOWN function, and it appears to be a viable proposition. In this unique instance, ROUNDUP produces the same result, because exactly one tanker rounds up to 1.

TABLE 56: Flo Tankers rounding framework

FLO Tankers Inc.

Capital & Fixed Costs	
Modeling Years	5
New Tanker Cost	250,000,000
Useful Life	30
Salvage Value	20,000,000
Annual Depreciation	7,666,667
Insurance/yr	1,500,000
Capacity m^3	250,000
Variable Costs	
Days in Year	365
Crew costs/yr	3,500,000
Fuel/trip	360,000
OpEx/trip	40,000
Port Fees/trip	200,000
Total per trip	600,000
Regulatory	
Tax rate	27%

Decision Factors		
Revenue/m^3	3.50	
Payload	250,000	
	ROUNDDOWN	**ROUNDUP**
Vessels needed	1	1

Pro-Forma Profit & Loss Accounts

	ROUNDDOWN	**ROUNDUP**
Revenue	1,597,968,750	1,597,968,750
Fixed Costs		
Insurance	7,500,000	7,500,000
Depreciation	38,333,335	38,333,335
Variable Costs		
Crew Costs	17,500,000	17,500,000
Trip Costs	1,095,750,000	1,095,750,000
Profit Before Tax	438,885,415	438,885,415
Tax	(118,499,062)	(118,499,062)
Net Profit	**320,386,353**	**320,386,353**

TABLE 57: Financial consequences of rounding down and up

	ROUNDDOWN	ROUNDUP
	One Tanker	Two Tankers
Cubic Meters	Profit/Loss in $millions	
275,000	320	(560)
300,000	320	(401)
325,000	320	(240)
350,000	320	(81)
375,000	320	58
400,000	320	174
425,000	320	291
450,000	320	407
475,000	320	524

We can now manually adjust the decision factors, to add increments of LNG as required by the customer. Then, we can use the powerful What-If functions of Excel to answer all our questions. Try overwriting the Payload value with 275,000, 300,000 and so on up to 475,000. The ROUNDDOWN number of vessels will stay the same, but ROUNDUP will change to two, and we will instantly have an answer as to whether we would leave money on the table by *not* rounding up.

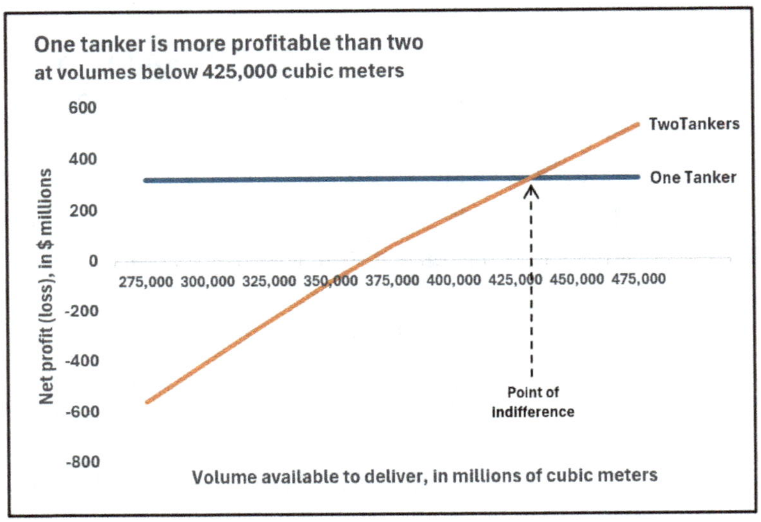

FIGURE 166: ROUNDUP line chart

The answer is clearly that for all volumes up to over 425,000 m^3, ROUNDDOWN was the smart choice; no money was left on the table, and we avoided losses or reduced profits. Our intuitive guess was right with the initial increments, *but the point of indifference was not at the halfway point.* It is somewhere between 425,000 and 450,000; using Excel's Goal-Seek function we can determine that it is 431,337. This quantity is not on the negotiating table; the nearest best option will be 450,000.

The business decision is now easy to make. If FLO has the finances and risk appetite[39] for two tankers, then it should contract to deliver 475,000 m^3 per day, and invest in two tankers to earn the maximum $524m. It follows that the highest profit will come from the largest volume, as each cubic meter is delivered at a profit over costs.

If, however, FLO is unsure of its financing or wants to put its first toe into these waters with limited risk, then it should contract for only 250,000 m^3 and let competitors the rest. The moment it heeds the notion that it should ROUNDUP at 275,000 because otherwise it is leaving money on the table, it incurs losses of $403m. All quantities above 250,000 and below 431,337 are a bad choice for FLO.

The model also allows us to look at different revenues for deliveries, and see what happens if more, or less, is paid per cubic meter delivered. The breakeven price in this simplified model, with one vessel carrying 250,000 m^3 is $2.54; with two ships, carrying 475,000 m^3, it is $2.66.

Note that in this exercise, we were given the units to be delivered and the price set by the customer. In real life, they are likely to be less knowable, particularly price. The model gives us valuable cost information (breakeven) for use in negotiations with the customer. For instance, if negotiation on price was stalled at $2.61, FLO would know that it can only agree to deliver 250,000 m^3 or 500,000 m^3. If FLO is required to tender for the contract, then it knows that its price offerings must be tied to volume considerations, with both specified in the offer.

In this exercise we have looked at a very specific use case, LNG tankers. However, the application of the theory is much broader—it could for example be used to analyze airline fleet operations, hotel and resort expansions, data center operation, renewable energy, cell telecommunications, or warehousing.

Full Business Modeling: Starting with an Idea

There's a saying in the airline industry, origins unknown, that the best way to make a small fortune is to start with a large one. It is also commonly applied to farming, winemaking, restaurant ownership and movie making. For airlines, cataclysmic events like 9/11 and the COVID Pandemic have taken their toll, and it seems like a monthly event that another airline files for bankruptcy. At least a dozen airlines filed for bankruptcy in 2023;[40] Canada boasts the distinction of hosting the first of the year, Cascadia Air, on January 11th.

Who could resist, though, the thrill, glamor, and romance of owning an airline? Undaunted by the widely held belief that it's an extremely difficult industry, we're going to explore the idea of starting our own. Sensibly, we

---

[39] Risk appetite is always a key consideration when scaling up is a possibility. In this instance, FLO may well want, before making the large investment and commitment, to learn more about the LNG business with just one tanker, even if more profit could be earned with two. LNG is a volatile business—fluctuating fuel prices, regional conflicts, government interference and other factors could all have profound effects on the outcome of this venture.

[40] Cascadia, Flybe, Flyr, Novair, Aeromar, Viva Air, Ultra Air, Niceair, GoFirst, Fly Gangwon, Air Moldova and Air Oradea.

are going to put our financial skills and our old friend Excel together to come up with some real numbers; we'll evaluate the likelihood of success or another dramatic failure.

FIGURE 167: Air Amlani Boeing jet (OpenAI, 2025)

The process of compiling financial numbers and formulas to evaluate various outcomes as part of the planning or evaluation process is known as **financial modeling**. It typically looks forward, though it can look back ("What if we had …?) and can be used to support **budgeting**. The subtle difference is that a **budget** is largely a target, a specific plan for revenues and expenses for a defined period. Bridging the gap is a **budget forecast**, a type of financial model built to create a budget. Financial models, in contrast, are built using inputs that can be changed to test various ideas and scenarios. Will Air Amlani ever take off? We'll use that question to demonstrate the process, tools and techniques of financial modeling.

Excel is not the only modeling tool in the market; indeed, there are more powerful apps that make it easier to handle highly complex propositions with many products, markets, and currencies. Oracle and IBM provide powerful examples. However, Excel is a first-class platform for the work. Here, we will assume that you have considerable familiarity with Excel but re-visit the most important functions to ensure they are fully understood. We will pay attention to the less familiar functions and add-ons that are most applicable to modeling (data tables, Goal Seek and Solver). Equally importantly, we'll cultivate techniques and best practices which help us build the best possible models for this purpose.

Before We Start Building: Inclusions and Exclusions

As accountants, there are several standard items we would expect to see in a financial model, particularly the model Statement of Financial Position, before addressing any unique features of the specific industry or proposal. It is necessary to consider those items at a very early stage and decide whether, and how, they should be reflected in the model. We can take certain liberties in a financial model which we would not take if we were actually preparing annual accounts; for example, if the purpose of the model is a **feasibility study**, we can disregard some very minor revenue streams or expenses which would definitely have to be included in annual financial statements.

Time frame, periodic calculations and sales growth are critical early considerations. Having established a five-year period for this demonstration, is it necessary to break any of the years into smaller portions? It is not unusual for the first year or two to require monthly cash budgeting, then revert to annual cash budgeting once the business is established. Is there seasonality to the product? At one extreme, if we were proposing to operate an ice cream truck in Ottawa, we might well find it viable only to operate for six months, with much larger sales in July and August. In this case we would need schedules and forecasts which break down by month. We might consider leasing out our truck to someone in Florida for the colder months. In this demonstration, we are going to confine ourselves to whole years.

Business growth is also important. In most business models, we would expect to build brand loyalty, experience and thus sales, over a five-year period. Rather uniquely, our business model here suggests that we are going to hit the ground running (perhaps an ironic phrase for an airline) with our target load factor achieved and stay at that level for the entire five years. The number of seats on an airplane is finite, and it is quite reasonable to propose that we would carefully manage pricing to optimize occupancy at this level from the very start.

The following table shows the principal Financial Position items with reasons for any unusual exclusion.

TABLE 58: Model inclusions and exclusions

Item	Decision	Rationale
Cash	INCLUDE	
Accounts Receivable	EXCLUDE	We are a passenger-only airline and sell all tickets online. We don't grant credit to anyone. Receipts from payment card processing have a 2-day time lag but we can treat this immaterial amount as cash
Inventory	EXCLUDE	Our business is designed NOT to carry inventory. Duty-free goods are on consignment; passenger meals are supplied on a just-in-time basis by an outside vendor; parts are carried at Boeing which is less than an hour's flight away.
Fixed Assets	INCLUDE	
Prepayments	INCLUDE	
Accounts Payable	INCLUDE	
Wages Payable	EXCLUDE	We have two pay periods per month, with the second on the last day. There are never wages payable holding over into a new period.
Government Remittances payable	EXCLUDE	In almost all jurisdictions, taxes and other payments are withheld from salaries. The amounts and remittance dates vary considerably. We will ignore these for our basic model, but later in the chapter discuss how they could have been handled without using specifics from any one jurisdiction
Unearned Revenue	INCLUDE	
Aircraft Mortgage	INCLUDE	
Bonds Issued	INCLUDE	
Share Capital	INCLUDE	
Dividends Payable	INCLUDE	
Retained Earnings	INCLUDE	

Understanding what is to be included and excluded from the model is important groundwork to ensure that the model serves its intended purpose.

Before We Start Building: Our Purpose

The principal consideration which must be undertaken first is to develop a clear understanding of the intended audience, and the purpose of the exercise. Financial models might be built as a feasibility study (will this business earn a profit?); an investment or banking pitch (will you put your money into this business?); as support for an Initial Public Offering (can we list on the Toronto Stock Exchange?); or for many other reasons. No one size fits all—the purpose will govern the exact content.

Here, the object is not to teach how to plan a business, nor is it to teach how to run an airline! The business proposition is a vehicle to teach financial modeling, and to create the knowledge which the student needs to show off their Excel and modeling skills. While the model must be realistic, we can simplify some real-world practices (such as deferred tax accounting) which would detract from the main purpose.

Stages

The modeling process has three stages.

Inputs are gathered; areas are created to hold them in the workbook. Inputs are somewhat fixed, certainly outside the control of the business. In our model, examples of inputs are fuel prices, landing fees and pilots' salaries. We say "somewhat" fixed because they are fixed by someone else; they are certainly not static, and our modeling will, in the advanced stages, need to incorporate uncertainty and predictions of things like inflation, exchange rates, interest rates and the actions of competitors. *Decision variables* are the values controlled by the business. For example, if (as we do) we have a flight route that takes 6.5 hours, a decision variable will be the number of flights per day. We could go there and back once a day, or we could fly three times, night-stopping the plane at the destination every second night. The choice between 2 and 3 flights a day will be a decision variable, with financial consequences such as hotel costs for flight crew.

Processing is the assembly and analysis of all relevant inputs. This includes the intermediate schedules and calculations which will inform the model financial statements.

Outputs are what users are looking for. They are the results of calculations based on the inputs and decision variables. A line-item output might be "Fuel expense"—the per-flight, monthly or annual cost of fuel based on the routes and frequencies flows. More complex, but still an output, would be the final determination of profitability for the entire operation.

In this chapter, we will concentrate on building good models and ensuring that our data and formulas are valid and correct. However, there is little point to building a great model if the results are difficult to communicate.

Structure, Content and Visual Aspects

The plan—we start out with some idea of the overall structure of the model. There is a logical flow, which we'll demonstrate, to the pages of the workbook. A typical structure might be eight or more pages in total: cover, Inputs, schedules (possibly several), cash budget, income statement, statement of financial position, statement of changes in shareholders' equity, and a page of references and sources. A time frame must be selected at an early stage; three or five years would be a very typical span. The greater the number of years, the less reliable estimates and projections will become. However, there are businesses (such as mining) which take a very long view indeed—sometimes as many as 25 or 35 years.

The look—it's also necessary to plan a consistent visual presentation for the spreadsheets themselves. Excel gives us an excellent set of options including fonts, colors, indents, ways to add text and graphics. Typically, the model will be presented to a diverse audience including non-financial professionals. Think about the eventual vehicle (*e.g.* PowerPoint, Excel, Word, Power BI); regardless, a cover sheet is necessary which captures the audience's attention and has a look consistent with the company's image. The cover sheet, or the second page, should contain an executive summary (some users will only read this far—get your key points made early!)

If it is planned or likely that the model will be printed, the physical parameters must be planned so that this is possible—no spreadsheets 50 columns wide, for example.

Color of text and shading is critically important; it would make life easier if there were universal agreement on what, exactly, colors mean. We will give detailed attention to this area below, but for now we simply stress that in the input and schedule areas, the most important use of color is to show what can be changed for experimentation, and what should never be changed because of the risk of breaking the model. Color must be deployed to distinguish inputs from calculations.

On the financial statements themselves, however, it is essential to have a logical and eye-pleasing scheme. There will never be inputs on the financial statements, they are all universally built from calculations referring to the inputs and schedules. The different audience, *i.e.* the end user, requires a simple and consistent look. We'll describe that when we discuss those pages.

The inner workings—invisible to the audience, but essential to the modeler—are the Excel functions and practices employed. The most important in our view are the cell/range naming facility, IF function and LOOKUP functions.

The Ground Rules

There are just three, with very different applications and implications.

Verify and document all sources.

When seeking out inputs, find the numbers in credible documents and reference them carefully. Depending on exactly what software is used to create the model, this can be done in various ways—a series of footnotes or endnotes (in Word), in-cell comments, hyperlinks, or endnotes (in Excel), and so on. Source documentation can be large and copious—it needs to be inconspicuous enough that it doesn't distract from the main message. For this reason, the best place for a reference is on its own page at the end.

No magic numbers.

The term "magic number" is a popular way of referring to a hard-coded value. It's worth spending a little more time on this concept, with an example. An unwary modeler might subconsciously think that there are 365 days in a year, and that there is no need to take account of leap years. Indeed, many accounting practices do disregard leap years for budgeting calculations or use 365.25 days for a four-year period.

In this model, a number is required in the Income Statement for annual fuel cost. Hypothetically,

- Fuel costs $2 per liter, an input in cell B1.
- A flight uses 5,000 liters of fuel, input in cell B2.
- There are two flights per day, decision variable in cell B3.

The formula for annual fuel cost might be keyed into the Income Statement as =B3*B2*B1*365. At several places throughout the model, similar calculations are keyed for other variable costs such as landing fees, crew costs and enroute airway charges. The 365 is a *magic number*, or hard-coded value.

This all seems logical enough until the unions decide, in a negotiation, that they will not agree to staff working on Christmas Day or New Year's Day. Suddenly there are 363 days in a year, and 364 in a leap year.[41] Now it would be necessary to search all over the model for all these instances of 365 and change them. If Days_in_year had been an input or decision variable at the outset, all that would be required would be to change 365 to 363 in *one place*, and all dependent calculations would automatically adjust.

Are dates magic numbers? Typically, the financial statements covering a period of years or months will have dates across the top. This, we would suggest, is the sole instance in which it might be permissible to hard code numbers, as they are really text strings and not numbers which would ever be treated as inputs in a formula. However, it is relatively simple on the inputs page to type the first year or month, then an increment in a separate cell. The dates shown in each sheet of the financial statements can then have the dates calculated from the first date and successive increments—then if the project is delayed or brought forward by a year, or the model is to be re-used at a different time for a different project, the dates can be changed accurately for all period and sheets simply by changing one input. Dates are best treated as magic numbers, for this reason.

Are zeroes (0) magic numbers? Absolutely they are, and they should never be hard coded into financial statements. They belong in the inputs along with all the other numbers and may legitimately be part of a table (for instance, cost of a supply based on number ordered).

It is tempting to think that certain decisions can be hard coded as zeroes. As an example, a new mining venture is certain that it will not produce anything of value for its first three years, and hard codes zeroes into its dividend line on the Cash Budget, Statement of Financial Position and statement of shareholders' equity. But what if the company makes a major discovery in its second year, and sells a property for an enormous profit? Suddenly a dividend is available where none was thought possible, and the modeler has to go searching for those zeroes. All

---

[41] In practice even days in the year can be very complex. In this example, imagine if our plane needs 2 days on the ground for servicing in years 1–4, but two weeks on the ground for a major overhaul in year 5. Add in the predicted days when we can't fly because of hurricanes or air traffic control strikes—it starts to get very messy. All this needs to be provided for at the input stage, without magic numbers.

this would have been avoided if dividends, even in forecast unproductive years, had been calculated on a payout ratio or by a formula, instead of being set at zero.

As a challenge, see if you can think of *any* input or decision variable that could be reliably hard-coded into the financial statements themselves, with no conceivable inconvenience. It may be an impossible task. In many financial modeling courses, assignments are given extra credit for absence of magic numbers, or marks are deducted if they are present.

No daisychaining

Having input the basic data and built schedules to handle complex preliminary calculations, it is very tempting to refer back, as we build the financial statements, to the last page where we referenced a number. This can work, and may save time on the first build, but can lead to complications later. For example:

In a relatively simple transaction, a business plans to subscribe to an internet service. The payment will be made once a month, on the first day of the month. The amount is placed on the inputs page, then that cell is referenced in the cash budget, under January. Then February references January, March references February, and so on. By December, we have built a daisy chain with 13 links. We go to the income statement and cross-reference the respective January cell to January in the cash budget. Then we repeat the daisy chain across the monthly income statement.

This all looks straightforward enough, until the internet provider changes its billing practices to quarterly. Now when we make the change to the cash budget, the income statement becomes incorrect. If all the cells had referred back to the source, we could change the formulas in the cash budget and nothing would change in the income statement.

Building the Model

The plan

We're going to build a five-year business model, starting in January 2024. We'll follow the basic structure already mentioned, with three pages of schedules, so our model will have ten sheets in one Excel workbook—Cover Page, Inputs, three Schedules, Cash Budgets, Income Statement, Statement of Financial Position, Statement of Changes in Shareholders' Equity, and References. As we progress, we may modify this structure to keep things elegant.

The business proposition

Our cover page will set the tone for the entire presentation. Some potential readers in a real-life scenario may never go beyond it. When preparing a model in an academic course, check the rubric carefully—typically there will be a requirement to add team name(s), student numbers, course identification and so on. In a corporate setting there will frequently be a requirement to include a company logo and copyright notice. The legal department, particularly in regulated or reporting environments, may require the inclusion of disclaimers (for example, indicating that the information may, or should not, be relied upon by potential investors).

The cover page should include a brief description of the proposed business and the reason for its selection; it should also include a summary of the conclusions of the model. This is referred to as the "executive summary." The first part should be composed *before* building the model, it is part of the early formative process. The conclusions, however, will be the last thing written, because they can only be comprehensively summarized from the model's outputs.

Capital considerations

As we plan to start a business, one of the most important sets of calculations needed will revolve around capital requirements. One of the main reasons many new businesses fail is that although the owners have sufficient money to start, they don't plan to have sufficient money to keep going until the business becomes profitable and has positive cash flow (Nobel, 2011, demonstrated that between 30 and 40 percent of high potential startups failed to establish themselves and ended in bankruptcy). For this reason, it is typical for banks and investors to ask for the first year's, or first two years', projections to be shown by month rather than by year (we have not done this here, it would significantly expand the model but is unnecessary in a demonstration—all the principles are the same).

Start-up capital refers to the money required to get the business up and running. At least a portion of the start-up capital will come from professional investors or lenders, including possibly venture capitalists. Start-up capital should be carefully distinguished from the more restrictive *seed capital*, which is usually a lower amount and is required for the promoters of the business to create a business plan of sufficient quality to attract investment.

Having enough start-up capital, however, does not guarantee survival. If, as is typical in early years, the business does not generate a profit or positive cash flow, it will need additional capital to cover its losses until cash flow turns positive. The key concept here is *working capital*—current assets minus current liabilities. Building a financial model for the proposed business should enable the reader to calculate both the start-up capital required, and the working capital needed to keep going in the difficult early months or years. The model Cash Budget will tell the reader what level of initial investment will be required both to start the business and keep it going—net cash should never become negative, or the company will shortly be unable to meet its liabilities.

Inputs

To start building the second page, Inputs, we need a basic idea of what the business is going to look like. In every case where we cite a number, cost or calculation that comes from a third-party source, we must document that source in a footnote. This is an essential best practice for building the model itself, and we will demonstrate a couple of ways to include the data in our workbook with the sources in this exercise. There may be a few places where a guess is needed—whenever this happens, it should also be noted.

Building the Inputs page will most often require the most research, thought and re-design. The modeler will return to this page many times to add or change content as the model evolves. At this stage, the business must be thought through, end-to-end, with a moderate level of detail applied to each input area. It will be important to distinguish between Inputs generally, and schedules.

There is a great deal of scholarship regarding color coding within financial models. There are no hard rules on this subject, though there are a few common practices. At an early stage, please decide how you will indicate what is an input or decision variable, and an output, so that they are easily distinguished and reviewed. Then create a color key and place it towards the top of the Inputs page, so that both modelers and users can refer to it. Here is an example:

Table 59: Color key

Hexadecimal	Color Key	Element
#AEEEEE	Black on pale blue	Inputs, generally, except decision variables—can be changed
#FFCCCB	Black on pale red	Decision variables—the things you want to "play" with
#000000	Black	calculations on data from same sheet—DO NOT CHANGE
#000000	**Bold Black**	**Scaffolding (sometimes with shaded background), and Important totals or summaries**
#218838	Green	Calculations from data in other sheets
#FF0000	Red	Negative numbers (usually with parentheses or minus signs)

The hexadecimal codes for each color are suggestions as to the exact shade to use in Excel. These codes, which consist of a hash and six characters, define the amount of red, green and blue in each component. To set up a background ("fill") in Excel, click on the cell(s) you want to fill, click on the fill color symbol in the Font menu, choose More Colors, click on the "Custom" tab if it's not already selected, then fill in the code is the Hex box. Excel will automatically convert the Hex code into an RGB (Red, Green, Black) color set and specify the components of each color. When you click OK, your cell will fill with the correct color. A similar procedure is followed to color text. Note that if you use "Automatic" text color, the default in Microsoft apps, #000000 gives different results depending on the background, for example turning white if the background is dark.

There is a set of principles which should go into the color scheme design, regardless of what exactly you choose.

General Rules

1. Don't overuse color, especially for fonts. Clear, readable text is most often black or at least dark gray.
2. Keep backgrounds light. Overly aggressive colors or deep dark backgrounds impair readability and may misplace emphasis.

The Specifics

1. Input cells need to be distinguishable from formula outputs, so that the user knows what they can change without breaking the model. This is most often accomplished with a light blue background.
2. Inputs (basic data) need to be distinguished from the key management decisions, such as price (if it's variable), investment amounts, margins, *etc.* We use a salmon background to draw clear attention to these "decision variables."
3. Cells which are output from formulas should be left untouched by users. These are typically left in black, with white backgrounds; however, the use of green to indicate calculations involving references to other sheets is very frequently seen in the investment banking community, and we adopt it here.

4. Headers and scaffolding need to be distinguishable. This is typically accomplished at least in part by their position, but you may use larger or bold fonts; a yellow background is sometimes employed.
5. Totals and summaries benefit from being slightly enlarged, bolded, or both. Sometimes a light gray or almost neutral background is added. Over-use of bolding will take away from the impact.
6. Many practitioners indicate that it's acceptable to use red for negative numbers, decreases and losses. Others say it should be avoided. We use it here (it can be coded in Excel), and for greater clarity minus signs or parentheses may be included.
7. Links and references can be colored and underlined in blue; Excel will often do this without being asked based on the format.

Corporate schemes and preferences will often dictate the choices of fonts and colors.

Schedules

The next group of pages, schedules, will contain granular detail of calculations flowing from the Inputs. As an example, depreciation of assets will feature in the non-cash expenditures of the business (but not on the cash flow page). In our case the major asset will be the plane; we will require inputs for purchase cost, annual depreciation, and residual value, exhibiting the choice of depreciation method. We will want the model to have the flexibility to accommodate a new plane at one cost or a used plane at a lower cost; we may also want the option to change type of plane altogether and use our work to evaluate an alternative manufacturer or type. Some detailed calculations will be required to calculate depreciation costs for inclusion on the Income Statement; however, we may not want the clutter on the Inputs page. In this instance we would place the depreciation schedule on page 3. Similar considerations may apply to inflation predictions, exchange rates, seasonal variation, and many other factors. It is a judgment call where to place these; if they are not complex, they can stay on the inputs page, but if they are complex and take up extensive space, they are best placed on their own schedule. In the Air Amlani model, we have separated out revenue calculations, cash expense outputs, and "other schedules"—the latter being projected increases in inflation, fuel prices, seniority and exchange rates, and the aircraft mortgage.

Financial statements

The four model financial statements—Cash Budget, Income Statement (Profit & Loss), Statement of Financial Position (Balance sheet), and Statement of Changes in Shareholders' Equity—will be familiar items to accountants. It is critical to understand that aside of the descriptive lines and headers (known as the **scaffolding** of the tables) NO numbers will be hard coded into these statements. Rather, we will build a framework, and ALL numbers, even dates will flow from formulas based on the Inputs and Schedules. It will be critical to ensure that changes to inputs or decision variables made anywhere in the model leave the three financial statements balanced.

The next three tables illustrate generation of calendar year titles using this concept. Named cells are created for First_Year and Interval.

Table 60: Timescale inputs

Timescales	
First Year of Ops	2025
Annual Interval	1

TABLE 61: Timescale formulas

	A	B	C	D	E	F
1			Air Amlani			
2			Model Statement of Financial Position (Canadian $)			
3			As at December 31			
4						
5		=First_Year	=First_Year+Interval	=C5+Interval	=D5+Interval	=E5+Interval

TABLE 62: Calendar year titles

	A	B	C	D	E	F
1			Air Amlani			
2			Model Statement of Financial Position (Canadian $)			
3			As at December 31			
4						
5		2025	2026	2027	2028	2029

In this example, two assumptions have been made—that the financial year will correspond to the calendar year, and that business will start on January 1 in the first year. If either of these are untrue, some more sophisticated formulas will be required.

The first year of business, 2024, is a management decision, thus a decision variable. 2024 is keyed into Cell A3 reflecting this decision. Another decision variable, annual interval, is typed as 1.[42]

On the Model Statement of Financial Position, rows 1–2 and column A are hard-coded (typed in) as part of the structure of the report. 2024, the first year of operation (for now) is retrieved by reference from the Inputs page. Then, cell B4 of the Statement of Financial Position refers back to the input—and cells C4–F4

[42] You might instinctively think that the annual interval would always be one. However, there will be cases when it is otherwise—consider modeling road tours for a rock band who plan to go out every two years to promote an album made at home in the previous. The annual interval would be two.

progressively add the chosen annual interval (1) from the Inputs page to the first year. The result: if the first year is changed on the Inputs page, all the years will correctly update on the Statement of Financial Position.

An almost rhetorical question—why did we not incorporate the first year to the Statement by reference, then add 1 to it in the subsequent years' formulas? Think about this before reading the footnote.[43]

A second more complex example relates to cash flow. Distilling to very basic calculations for now, let's imagine that the Inputs page and revenue schedule combine to contain the revenue per seat, percentage of seats occupied per flight, number of flights per day and number of operational days in the year. This is a combination of decision variables and inputs. With some multiplication we could arrive at an estimate of revenues from seat sales, which would be produced by a formula on the Income Statement. A variation on that same formula will go into Inflows on the Cash Budget. After a portion of that revenue has been spent on expenses, and an adjustment for unpaid supplier invoices, the remaining cash automatically updates on the Statement of Financial Position, and the income position, tax liability, retained earnings and possibly other items would update automatically. Everything must stay in balance.

Ratios, references and sources

The final pages in our workbook will be used to exhibit some key financial metrics, then store the references and sources we have used for our business proposition and data, so that they can be verified or updated by users. As it is unlikely anyone will ever read the reference page, it doesn't need to be pretty. It should however be complete and support easy reference by the curious reader. For students building a model as a class exercise, it is a chance to demonstrate the scope of work completed and show that appropriate external research has been conducted.

The Process, Start to Finish

In this section, we'll work all the way through building a financial model from start to finish. We have chosen quite a complex area, the airline industry, so to keep the focus on modeling skills we'll indulge in a lot of simplification. We are aiming to demonstrate the process, as opposed to the fine detail. We're going to do it all in Excel.

The cover page

We are going to cover three elements: formal requirements, business proposition and executive summary.

Formal requirements

In a business setting, we would pay heed to requirements set by the company for which we are modeling. There may be company colors, fonts, preferences, required inclusions and so on. In our academic setting we would

---

[43] Because that would have incorporated a magic number into the formula. Is it the case that you would never want to change the interval? No—you might want to change the model to cover two-year intervals, or half-year intervals. All this could be accomplished from the input page.

consult the rubric for directions. A typical set would be to include a team name, name of team members, student numbers, course identification and a title. That's all straightforward, we will show these when we get to a draft page.

Business proposition

The range of possible businesses we might choose is enormous. We might conceive of a global company. The original hub-and-spokes idea behind FedEx started with a college paper in 1965. There is a legend that the paper was given a failing grade by the professor teaching the course, but it is almost certainly false. Its author, FedEx founder Frederick Smith, cannot remember what grade he received; Professor Hall passed away in 1968 (Snopes, n.d.)· We might equally choose a much more modest proposition such as a local bicycle courier service for downtown Vancouver. We have observed that more than 50% of students tasked to come up with a business idea choose some type of restaurant or food service. Whatever you choose for this exercise, it's a good idea to keep it to a manageable size. Some type of justification for the choice will be required for the cover page.

Our business idea is to operate an airline that flies a single route, from Vancouver to San Salvador, the capital of El Salvador. We consider that the following factors suggest that it might be viable.

(1) Western Canada is home to thousands of Salvadoran emigrants and their families. Large influxes came in two waves in the 1980s, many as refugees but others as economic migrants. Hard-working and family-oriented, there is a strong market for flights visit the homeland now that the conditions that led to their original emigration have subsided under the new government. Among Latin Americans living in Canada, Salvadorans are the third largest group after Mexican and Colombian immigrants (Wikipedia contributors, n.d.).

(2) There are few direct flights from Canada to Central America in general, and none from Vancouver to San Salvador. However, again with security improvements, El Salvador has grown in attractiveness as a tourism destination (Lonely Planet, n.d.). We predict that with competitive pricing, there will be strong demand for seats on direct flights to San Salvador.

(3) Almost all flights with connections require a transit through United States airports. Connecting passengers in the USA require visas, which are difficult and expensive to obtain. Many Salvadorans living in Canada cannot obtain US visas or are reluctant to transit through American airports (Hinterland Travel, n.d.).

(4) San Salvador is a potential gateway airport for other Latin American destinations, with direct flights available to Santo Domingo, San Jose (Costa Rica), Panama City, Bogota (Colombia), Quito and Guayaquil (Ecuador) (FlightConnections, n.d.).

FIGURE 168: Boeing 737-900ER

The distance from Vancouver to San Salvador airport is 3137 miles, or 2730 nautical miles. This limits our choice of aircraft, but after considerable research we have concluded that the most suitable and economical choice for this route is the Boeing 737-900ER. There is considerable convenience in choosing a plane which is made in Seattle, only 3 hours' drive and less than an hour's flight from Vancouver. All our modeling will focus on this aircraft, though we will design our model so that an entirely different plane can be substituted if necessary.

We must condense this argument into a short, sharp, punchy paragraph for the cover page. In real life an investment of this size, involving over $100 million USD, would occasion lengthy research papers and consultancy. We'll assume we've got through all that and are ready to concentrate on the numbers.

Executive summary

This is the last thing we will write, so it is left blank for now. We've scaffolded the worksheet to contain the elements we've considered so far. We're ready to move on to Inputs, a large, time-consuming task, but one where careful design now will save huge amounts of time later.

TABLE 63: Scaffolded cover page

Course Ref:	BUSI 414
Course Name:	Data Visualization
Team:	The High Flyers
Students:	A Amlani 12345678
	R Davis 66676602
	S Rahmani 87654321
	M Mouse 12122121

DATA MODEL: AIR AMLANI

Business Proposition: We will operate a single aircraft, a Boeing 737-900ER, daily, on one route YVR-SAL-YVR. The route is not served by a direct flight with any other airline, and many Central American travellers do not want to connect through the U.S.A., which requires a transit visa (1). Canada has a large Salvadoran population. They, and Canadian tourists, are incentivized to visit El Salvador due to recent improvements in the security situation (2). SAL is also a potential hub for travel to several other Latin American destinations (3).

Copyright © 2025, A Amlani & R Paul Davis

IMPORTANT LEGAL NOTICE: This document has been prepared for internal use only and should NOT be relied upon by potential investors or lenders. A full prospectus will be issued in due course if the Directors determine that the business proposition is viable.

Inputs page

It's time to gather up all the key data which will form the basis of our financial model and lead us eventually to viable conclusions. The modeled Financial Statements which will eventually be produced form a guide to what data must be acquired—we will need sections for income, expenses (cash and non-cash), financing and shareholder capital. Some parts will require more detailed schedules, to be included on the following page. All this will be built in Excel, and there will be a high degree of interdependence between the elements.

Some of the terms used to describe aspects of this business may be unfamiliar. It would not be unreasonable to wonder if it's really necessary to learn the details of operating a particular business type; after all, this book is about analysis of financial data, not operating an airline. However, any new business for which you are asked to prepare models will be somewhat unfamiliar, and you will indeed need to learn not only the basic vocabulary but also considerable detail about its operation. To smooth the path, here are a few key definitions and explanations.

Aircrew describes pilots (flight crew) and flight attendants (cabin crew). All Boeing 737s require two pilots—a captain (left seat) and first officer (co-pilot)(right seat). Regulations typically require 1 cabin attendant for each 50 seats (not passengers).

Cycle describes a complete operation of the aircraft, from starting the engines through taking off, landing and shutting down. If the engines are started and stopped without a take-off, that is not a cycle.

Jet A1 (aka **Avtur**) is jet fuel. It is commonly priced in liters but consumed in kilograms. A liter of jet fuel weighs 0.81 kg.

Leg refers to one part of an aircraft's daily work, taking off from one destination and landing at another. It is subtly different from a cycle which can involve take-off and landing at the same airport; also, even more obscurely, if the plane must perform a touch-and-go where it puts its wheels on the runway but never comes to a stop, then returns to land again, the journey will comprise two cycles but only one leg.

Pax is a common abbreviation for "passenger(s)."

Load factor is the percentage of seats filled on an aircraft for a leg.

Naming cells and ranges

In the coming sections, naming cells and ranges will become very important. In this section explore options and mention some pitfalls to avoid.

Naming a cell is accomplished by selecting the cell, then clicking in the small box which displays the cell address (e.g. "A1") immediately above cell A1. The name can then be typed over the address. Throughout the entire workbook, the name can then be used to refer to the cell when creating formulas.

TABLE 64: Calendar data

Days_in_Year | fx 365.25

	A	B
13	Calendar Data	
14	Days in Year	365.25
15	Non Ops Days	2
16	Service Days	5
17	Act of God Days (4)	9
18	Legs Per Return	0.5

In this example, the input for Days in Year, 365.25, is highlighted. The cell is named by typing Days_in_Year into the box above A1.

There are some rules to observe.

- The cell name cannot start with a number or special character—only a letter or the underline symbol.
- It must also be one continuous group of characters, hence the placement of the underling between First and Seats in this example.
- Cell names must always be unique. If you try to type in one which you have already used, when you try to confirm the entry, the cursor will jump to the cell where you already used it, whether in the same sheet or another sheet of the same workbook.
- It is good practice, though not a rule, to keep the cell names close to the line item names to which they refer. This makes them easier to remember and understand when building or analyzing formulas later.

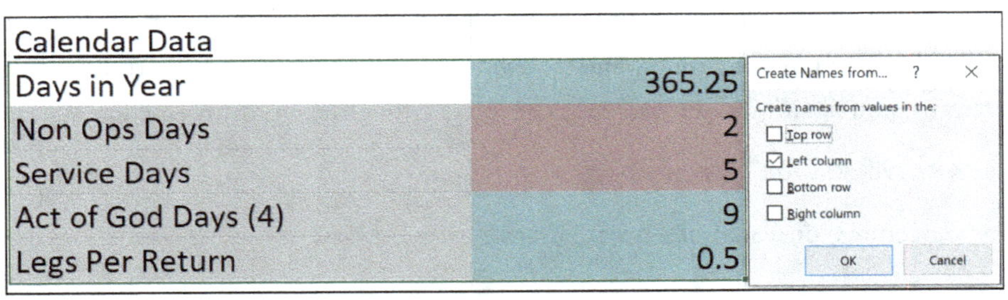

FIGURE 169: Create names from selection

Where there is a group of cells to be named, Excel provides a time-saver. In this example, we have selected the group of labels and columns, gone to the Formulas tab, and selected **Create from Selection** in the Defined Names group. The selection of Left column tells Excel to name the cells on the right using the names on the left; Excel inserts the underline symbol between words to conform the names to the rule above.

If the name in the source column starts with a number or special character, Excel inserts an underline symbol at the start of the name.

Anything which is enclosed in brackets, like (4), is not included by Excel when naming cells from a selection.

Excel does not permit the same name to be used for two cells or ranges. If the *Create from Selection* function is used and Excel detects a duplication, it will display a question as to whether the existing "definition," *i.e.* name, is to be changed. Selection of Yes will result in deletion of the name from the first cell, and any formulas which reference it will update to refer to the new cell.

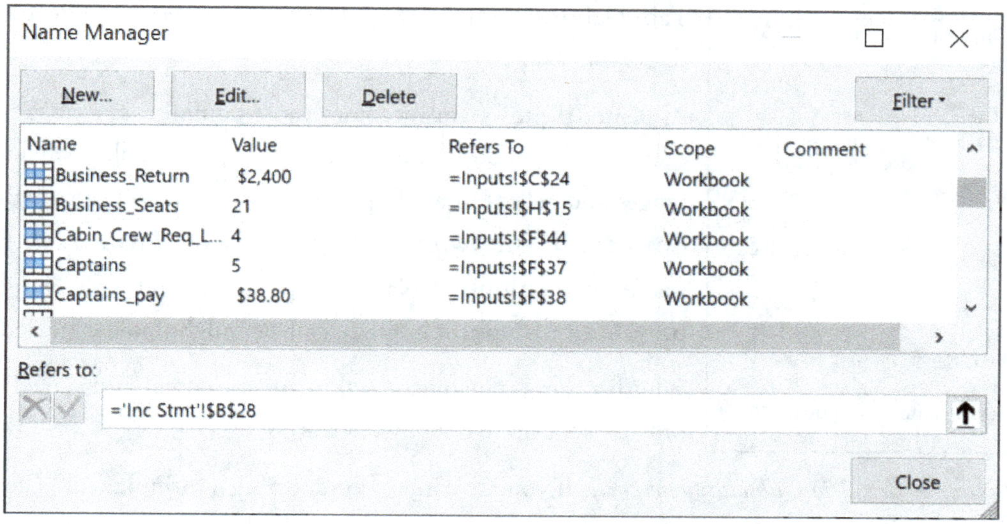

Figure 170: Name manager

If there is a mistake in a cell name, it is easy to correct. Either highlight the cell and make the correction in the box above A1 or invoke the *Name Manager*. To open the Name Manager, either press Ctrl+F3, or go to the Formulas tab, Defined Names group, and click on Name Manager. The pop-up box will display a list of all named cells and ranges *in the entire workbook*, with options to add, edit or delete names, or perform filters on what is displayed. Each line also displays the current value in each named cell or range, and its location.

Table 65: Catalog of named ranges

Acc_Y1	='Inc Stmt'!$B$28
Acc_Y2	='Inc Stmt'!$C$28
Acc_Y3	='Inc Stmt'!$D$28
Acc_Y4	='Inc Stmt'!$E$28
Acc_Y5	='Inc Stmt'!$F$28
Accounting_Ongoing	=Inputs!$H$47
Accounting_Start_up	=Inputs!$H$46
AccY4	='Inc Stmt'!$E$28
Act_of_God_Days	=Inputs!$C$17
Act_of_God_Days__4	=Inputs!$C$17
Air_Maint_Y1	='Inc Stmt'!$B$19
Air_Maint_Y2	='Inc Stmt'!$C$19
Air_Maint_Y3	='Inc Stmt'!$D$19
Air_Maint_Y4	='Inc Stmt'!$E$19
Air_Maint_Y5	='Inc Stmt'!$F$19
Aircraft_Fuel	=Inputs!$C$35
Aircraft_Fuel_Kg	=Inputs!$C$36
Aircraft_Main_PFH	=Inputs!$C$37
Aircraft_Mortage	=Inputs!$H$57
Aircraft_Mortgage_Rate	=Inputs!$H$58
Aircraft_Mortgage_Term	=Inputs!$H$59

Often when working with complex models, it will be useful to have a permanent display or print-out of all named cells. To create this click on an empty cell with sufficient space beside and below. Go to the Formulas Tab, Defined Names Group, select *Use in Formula,* select *Paste Names* then *Paste List.*

As a model grows and becomes more complex, and at the end of the exercise, it's a good idea to create a page just to hold a catalog of named ranges and cells. On an empty page, go to an empty cell. Press *F3* to open the *Paste Name* dialog, then click *Paste List.* Excel will paste two columns: Name of the range, and what it refers to. We provide an example of how such a page might look at the left.

This list is not dynamic. If cell names are added or changed, the list can only be kept up to date by re-creating it.

Named cells are, by definition, absolute references. If you are copying or dragging a formula with a cell reference, the cell reference will not change. In other words, in this model the named cell Economy_Seats is equivalent to $B$2. There will be times when this is undesirable, therefore cell address references will be used despite the existence of a cell name.

As we move forward, we will see just how useful the naming of cells is, especially when we need to cross-reference cells in different sheets. With cell addresses it is necessary to name the source sheet; cell names however are stored by Excel in an index which enables referring to any cell, in any sheet, just by its name.

Income (revenues)[44]

Incoming revenue streams are a logical place to start. We are going to present calculations on an annual basis, so we will need to include some temporal inputs which enable them. We will also need some performance statistics for our plan to calculate both revenue and expenses, so we can include them here. There will be some differences, according to how many flights we operate per day; they too must be provided for.

An important consideration for most new businesses is that they are likely to increase sales over at least the first few years of operation, as they gain customer loyalty and experience. We have made no provision for this in our operation, as "seats on an aircraft" are a finite number. We believe there is large pent-up demand for our service

[44] To keep this model manageable, we have ignored several likely income streams that are relatively small. In the real world we would likely allow related businesses to sell through links on our website, earning pay-per-click revenue or commission; we would sell travel insurance with our tickets, again earning commission; we might sell unused space in the hold for cargo. A review of other airlines' financials suggests that the revenue from "other" activities, *i.e.* those not in the mainstream business, tends to be quite similar to the "other" costs also incidental to the mainstream. When we address expenses, below, we'll similarly exclude some smaller outflows.

and our initial assumption is that we can fill an average of 90% of our seats. In a business which expected increasing demand, we would build a schedule for increases and incorporate it in our revenue and expense calculations for each year.

TABLE 66: Revenue inputs

11	**REVENUES**					
12						
13	Calendar Data		Operational Data		Service Data	
14	Days in Year	365.25	Distance YVR SAL (nm)	2726	Economy Seats	139
15	Non Ops Days	2	Airspeed (knots)	510	Business Seats	21
16	Service Days	5	Time per Leg (hr)	5.35	First Seats	20
17	Act of God Days (4)	9	Taxi Time	0.5	Total Seats	180
18	Legs Per Return	0.5	Leg Time (hr)	6.00	Load Factor	90%
19			Legs per day	2		
20						
21	Pricing Data		Add-On Revenues		Timescales	
22	Economy Return	$ 800	Duty Free per Pax	$ 40	First Year of Ops	2025
23	Business Factor (5)	3	Duty Free Factor (6)	4.38%	Annual Interval	1
24	Business Return	$ 2,400	Meal Service	$ 8		
25	First Factor (5)	8	Meal Factor	80%		
26	First Return	$ 6,400	Reserved Seats	$ 25		
27	First Ck Bag	$ 50	Res Factor	50%		
28	First Bag Factor	60%	Pet Fee	$ 200		
29	Second Ck Bag	$ 70	Pet Factor	2%		
30	Second Bag Factor	10%				

A few features of revenues merit explanation, and as some of the items may be unfamiliar, we'll walk through them.

The data are divided up logically into groups. Within the groups, the color coding which we selected earlier is deployed to indicate the input type of each number. Footnotes, in parentheses (for example (4)) document sources for industry data. We have also named each individual cell, using the exact same name as in the lists. Below the inputs is a section of outputs; this contains calculated data based on the inputs above, which might be useful for specific explorations but will not show in the Financial Statements.

There are several outputs built on these data which are going to be useful later. These are placed in the first schedule, the revenue schedule, to avoid cluttering the inputs page.

Table 67: Revenue outputs

	A	B	C	D	E	F
1	**REVENUE OUTPUTS**					
2						
3	Ops Days Yr	349.25	Legs per Yr	698.5		
4						
5	Revenues Per Leg					
6	**Economy**		**Business**		**First**	
7	Econ Pax Rev	$ 50,040	Busi Pax Rev	$22,680	First Pax Rev	$57,600
8	First Bag Rev	$ 3,753				
9	Second Bag Rev	$ 876				
10	Duty Free Rev	$ 219	Busi DF Rev	$ 33	First DF Rev	$ 32
11	Meal Rev	$ 801				
12	Res Seat Rev	$ 1,564				
13	Pet Rev	$ 500	Busi Pet Rev	$ 76	First Pet Rev	$ 72
14	**Econ Rev /Leg**	**$ 57,753**	**Busi Rev /Leg**	**$22,789**	**First Rev /Leg**	**$57,704**
15						
16	**Total Rev Leg**	**$ 138,245**				
17	**Total Rev Yr**	**$96,564,072**				

There are no magic numbers in these data. Some of the inclusions may seem unnecessary until this requirement is reconsidered. For example, it might seem obvious that a return flight between two airports contains two "legs." Yet in the temporal data, we have "Legs_Per_Return." Our tickets will all be return tickets; therefore, when we want to do calculations that involve legs, we will need to divide numbers by 2 (multiply them by 0.5).

Some specific explanations of concepts follow.

In *Calendar Data,* Service_Days are days when the plane will be grounded for scheduled servicing. Act_of_God_Days are days when we can't fly due to natural factors—we have selected 9 because that is the average number of days San Salvador airport is closed each year for hurricanes.

There are no separate calculations for Leap Years. When dealing with annual data, we typically have three options: ignore leap years (every fourth year will have an error of 1/365, which is insignificant); provide for them (this involves a series of complex IF statements to multiply everything by 366/365 in leap years, which is unwieldy); or use 365.25 days per year, which averages out the effect of leap years over each four year period. We have elected the third option, which greatly simplifies the model without losing veracity.

In *Operational Data,* Taxi_Time and Time_per_Leg are consolidated, and rounded, into Leg_Time. This will be useful in calculating crew remuneration.

In *Service Data,* the numbers of seats are fixed by the standard design of this aircraft. The load factor is the average percentage of seats (overall) which we expect to sell on each leg. There are different configurations, or even different aircraft available, so these numbers could be varied for experimentation.

In *Pricing Data,* we have calculated that the average price of a one-stop return ticket from Vancouver to San Salvador is around $775. We believe that we can charge a slight premium for a non-stop flight, thus have started out with $800. Also, we have reviewed many other airlines' pricing policies and noted that a business class ticket is typically about three times the price of economy, and First Class about eight times. Therefore, we have included the business and First Class tickets at these multiples of the economy price. We plan to charge for checked-in bags; $50 for the first, and $70 for the second. "Factors" refer to the percentage of passengers we expect to buy these extras—thus the industry average for medium-haul, 60%, is used for the first bag and 10% for the second.

In *Add-on Revenues*, we estimate revenues from duty-free sales on board, sales of meals to economy passengers, reserved seat fees and pet fees. While the revenues from these are modest, over the course of a year they will add up to substantial numbers. We do not know yet whether they will make the difference between a profit and a loss, but they could.

Unless there is a change to industry data, the only inputs we are going to play with among these data are the blue decision variable cells. It will be an easy matter to see the effect, for example, of changing from 2 legs per day (in which case the plane always returns to Vancouver), to the logical maximum of 3 legs per day (in which case it will overnight in El Salvador every second day).[45] We can play with the ticket prices, experiment with different load factors, or change the pricing on add-ons. We can see what would happen to revenues if we decided to fly on Christmas Day and New Year's Day (by changing Non_Ops_Days to 0).

We are not yet ready to calculate break even prices or operations. But we can already perform analyses using Goal Seek, for example, to determine what the economy ticket price would need to be to earn $100 million in revenues in a year, flying two legs per operational day.[46] Data tables could also be created based on this data. For example, we could already begin to explore the effect on revenue (but NOT profit) of different load factors which we think we could achieve at different prices. We could determine maximum possible revenue if we thought that we could achieve 95% at an economy ticket price of $700, 90% at $800 and 85% at $900, using a two-way data table. Later, however, we will perform more complex analyses aimed at *profit* maximization when we have included expenses and financing data.

Both Goal Seek and Data Tables are fully described in *Information Systems for accountants*, our companion for that course, so we will not repeat them at length here. The full model as built here is available; please download it and try making up your own questions to solve with these procedures.

At this point, we have created a static, single-year revenue model. As we are working on a five-year plan, the projection into the future is going to require further calculations based on possible changes such as inflation or exchange rates. Those more granular calculations will be achieved with the help of schedules which we will place on the next page. First, though we must deal with expenses and financing.

---

[45] Total revenues would jump from $97 million to $145 million; this is logical, if we fly 50% more than our revenues should increase by a similar amount, unless we over-supply the market; an over-supply would affect load factor which we could modify on the Key Inputs page to see the financial implications.

[46] The answer is $830, all other things remaining the same.

When we look at a table of inputs and consider using it to explore options, the value of the color-coding scheme is immediately apparent. No audience member should ever type anything into an output cell, and soft-coded inputs should only be changed to reflect an actual change in an externally provided price or quantity. For example, if the model were used to do the same calculations for a different destination, the distance cell would require a new number. The blue numbers which are decision variables invite experimentation as they are the numbers that can potentially be changed by management, largely consisting of prices and operational decisions such as legs per day.

Cash expenses

TABLE 68: Cash expenses[47]

32	CASH EXPENSES								
33									
34	Operational Data			Personnel Data			Admin Data		
35	Aircraft Fuel (lt)(7)(USD)	$	0.559	Fly Hrs Yr		900	Sales Dist Costs (18)		6%
36	Aircraft Fuel kg (USD)	$	0.69	Non Fly Factor (13)		2	Card Fees (19)		1.5%
37	Aircraft Maint PFH (8)(USD)	$	1,324	Captains		5	Website IT Costs (20)		4%
38	Airport Landing Fee	$	536.32	Captain pay (14)	$	38.80			
39	Airport Parking Fee	$	73.76	First Officers		5	Tax Data		
40	Airport Pax Fee	$	9.71	First Officer pay (15)	$	24.11	Federal Business Tax		15%
41				Senior Cabin Crew		5	Provincial Business Tax		12%
42	Nav Fees nm (10)	$	1.20	SCC pay (16)	$	42,133	Tax Base		-
43	Business Meal Cost (11)	$	35	Pax Factor Cabin Crew		50	Professional Data		
44	FC Meal Cost (11)	$	100	Cabin Crew Req/leg		4	Legal Start Up	$	1,000,000
45	Insurance (12)(USD)	$	165,000	Junior Cabin Crew Req		17	Legal Ongoing	$	200,000
46	Fuel Consumption (hr)(kg)(13)		2650	JCC pay (17)	$	41,287	Accounting Start Up	$	1,000,000
47	Kg per Liter		0.81	EI CPP Rate		15%	Accounting Ongoing	$	200,000

In *Operational Data*, we deal with the actual costs of operating our aircraft on the route. Fuel is typically priced by the liter, but consumption is measured in kilograms. The numbers to make the necessary conversions and calculate fuel costs per leg are shown. We have actual costs for Vancouver Airport (YVR), but as the San Salvador costs are not published, we have assumed that they are similar to those for Vancouver. This is conservative as in reality they are likely to be lower.

Navigation fees are charged by national Air Traffic Control authorities for overflight, typically on a per-nautical-mile basis. As there are several countries involved in our route, we've taken an average in Canadian dollars. Business and First Class passengers will be expecting quality food, which we will pay for; insurance is a must.

---

[47] To keep this model manageable, we've concentrated on the principal costs and ignored some smaller items that would occur in real life. For example, we have ignored the cost of diversions (when the aircraft must land at a different airport due to unexpected weather at the destination, lost or damaged baggage claims and occasional deep cleaning costs). We can make a reasonable assumption that these would be offset by the income streams which were ignored for simplicity in the revenue calculations.

Note that several of these costs are quoted in USD, which is typical for the industry. Again, in the Financial Statements we will convert them to Canadian dollars using numbers from the schedules.

In *Personnel Data* we have some complex calculations. Safety regulations restrict the number of hours aircrew may spend in the air, although pilots typically work three times that number of hours on planning, briefing, weather reports, training and testing. The industry standard (900) is shown, then the factor of 2x more. All this is taken into consideration and multiplied by typical labor rates sourced from recruiters for pilots, first officers and cabin crew.

To calculate the number of captains needed, the syntax is thus

```
=ROUNDUP((Leg_Time*Legs_per_Yr/Fly_Hrs_Yr),0)
```
[48]

That is, the time of each leg, multiplied by the number of legs per year, divided by the number of hours per year to be flown by each Captain. You can't have half a Captain; thus the ROUNDUP function is used. Then we can use some efficient logic; the plane needs a first officer in the right cockpit seat, so having calculated for Captain we can use the same number (=Captains) for the number of first officers, and again for the number of Senior_Cabin_Crew.

In building formulas like this, the value of naming cells and ranges starts to be demonstrated. As you type a formula using cell names instead of cell addresses, Excel as soon as you start to type a cell name will display a list of cells it might be and allow you to choose one instead of typing the whole name. This is a tremendous time saver and also reduces risk of error. It is even more effective when working on multiple sheets within the same workbook.

Regulation also requires one cabin crew member for every 50 seats (not passengers), so there will be four on board each of our flights. In the outputs section, annual costs for each category of employee are calculated, and a 15% premium on those costs is allowed for Employment Insurance and CPP premia which must be paid by the employer.

In *Admin* data we take some short-cuts to arrive at broad estimates, based on other airlines' performance. It would be overkill for us to dissect every office expense, furniture depreciation, agency commissions and the like; instead, we base a prediction of overall cost on revenue (at 6%), card processing fees (as most of our sales will be on the Internet) at 1.5% of revenues and website/IT costs at 4%.

In *Tax Data* we have generalized, assumed that we will not attract small business tax benefits, and calculated that our net federal tax is likely to be 15% of any profits, and provincial tax 12%.

Again, a few lines are devoted to producing interim outputs which we will manipulate when we create our financial statements.

---

[48] The 0 included in this formula is NOT a magic number. It is part of the formulaic instruction to Excel, thus will not be a "value" implicated in other calculations.

In *Professional Data* we have considered the likely legal and accounting fees we will pay for start-up costs, and on an ongoing basis. We are likely to need a great deal of professional advice as we negotiate contracts, consider taxation and asset protection regimes and engage with regulators. We should have asked several firms to quote for these services and incorporated their likely cost into our projections.

Again we have separated out the more complex computations based on these inputs into a schedule, named "Expense schedule."

TABLE 69: Cash expense outputs

	A	B	C	D	E	F
1	**CASH EXPENSE OUTPUTS**					
2						
3	Fuel cost per Leg (USD)	$ 10,973	Pay Captains Year	$ 523,800	Total Sales Dist	$ 5,793,844
4	Maint per Leg (USD)	$ 7,077	Pay FO Year	$ 325,485	Total Card Fees	$ 1,448,461
5	Nav Fees per Leg (USD)	$ 3,271	Pay SCC Year	$ 210,665	Total Web IT	$ 3,862,563
6	Catering per Leg	$ 2,535	Pay JCC Year	$ 701,879		
7	Total Airport Fees leg (9)	$ 2,183	EI CPP Year	$ 264,274		

Non-cash expenses[49]

TABLE 70: Non-cash expenses

49	**NON-CASH EXPENSES**				
50					
51	Aircraft New Cost USD (21)	$	112,600,000	Useful Life Years	20
52	Residual Value USD (22)	$	10,000,000	Annual Depreciation USD	$ 5,130,000
53	Depreciable Value	$	102,600,000		

Depreciation of commercial aircraft is no simple matter. While a single machine in a factory may have a calculable lifespan, whether in hours run or items produced, different parts of an aircraft depreciate at different rates and will not expire together. The fixtures and fittings inside (seats, luggage bins, *etc.*) typically last about 10 years; the engines will become unusable after running for a certain number of hours, while the airframe itself will have a life expressed in cycles. The airframe itself is likely to last longest; that is a good thing, because its seats and engines can be replaced with relative ease. Airliner airframes typically last between 40,000 and 110,000 cycles; in our proposition, even if we fly 3 cycles per day for 20 years, we will not exhaust the airframe. Sometimes the landing gear, or "undercarriage" does not last as long as the rest of the airframe.

For these reasons, different types of aircraft have vastly different lives. Hawaiian operators are famous for being among the few that exhaust airframes in less than 20 years, because they typically fly very short routes in relatively large aircraft. Operators in developed countries often like to replace aircraft within the first 20 years; operators in developing countries, however, often reduce expenses by purchasing used aircraft later in their life. There are a few early model Boeing 737s still in commercial use at 50 years of age; it is quite common to encounter a 747 that has been in service for more than 30 years.[50]

All this is much too complex for our model. We are going to use just three numbers: the price of our new plane, 20 years, and a tentative residual value of $10 million USD. Why tentative? There are very, very few used 737-900ERs on the market, thus it is difficult to gauge pricing. However, well-used 737s generally tend to sell around this price, we consider it conservative, and it will allow us to perform straight-line depreciation over 20 years and give us credible figures for the first five years in our model.

[49] We over-simplify again. In real life the purchase of a new aircraft in 2024 would result in a taxation advantage from the Accelerated Investment Incentive offered by the CRA to companies purchasing new equipment. We will disregard this complex calculation for the purposes of this model.

[50] There is an interesting fallacy about age of aircraft. Most members of the public, if asked, would prefer to fly on a newer plane. Statistically, though, a 40-year-old plane still flying has demonstrated that it can conduct tens of thousands of flights without a crash; a brand-new plane has no such safety record to point to!

The dollar values shown in the table are in USD. This is as far as we can go for now, because we have not yet built our schedule of exchange rates. We will calculate the conversions to Canadian dollars when we build the Statement of Income. It's worth noting at this stage that as we will acquire the purchase price of the aircraft (in USD) with Canadian dollars, its book value will become a CAD value and depreciation calculations can thus be performed without consideration of future exchange rates. The one value that is likely to be in USD is the eventual salvage cost, which is deducted from the new cost to arrive at depreciable value in CAD. Deploying straight-line depreciation, this will be the same CAD value every year.

Financing

Our final group of inputs relates mainly to the Shareholders' Equity section on the liabilities side of the Statement of Financial Position.

TABLE 71: Financing inputs

55	**FINANCING**						
56							
57	Share Capital Opening	$	-	Bond Issue	$ 50,000,000	Aircraft Mortgage	$ 100,000,000
58	Shares Issued	$	50,000,000	Bond Issue Costs	2%	Aircraft Mortgage Rate	5%
59	Share Issue Costs		5%	Bond Proceeds	$ 49,000,000	Aircraft Mortgage Term	20
60	Share Issue Proceeds	$	47,500,000	Bond Interest Rate	5%	Credit Terms	30
61	Dividend Payment Ratio		50%	Bond Term	5	Average Prepay	60
62	Dividend Base	$	-				

The first inputs regarding financial matters are likely to be little more than guesses. Until we start to see cash-flow results and profit or loss calculations, the numbers cannot be made more precise. Here we are beginning to see more evidence of the dialectic between inputs and the Financial Statements which depend on them. At this stage, we "eyeball" the numbers we can already see and make a rough estimate that we are likely to need $200 million Canadian dollars to start our operation. The largest up-front cost will be to purchase the aircraft, but as it can be used as security for borrowing, we can reduce cash needs by financing a large part of that purchase.

Mortgage Financing

We have decided to seek $100 million of mortgage financing on the aircraft, another $50 million from a bond issue, and whatever else is needed will be made up by share capital. Of these, the share capital is the most flexible, particularly if the operators of the business are going to put in some of their own money.

Financing Costs

We have also accounted for the cost of issuing debt and shares, using standard industry assumptions (2% and 5% respectively for the various administrative, legal and underwriting costs). And we've entered the interest rates which we feel will secure us the financing we need; 5% on the aircraft mortgage and 5% on the bonds. We can defer a decision on the life of the bonds until we've produced some cash flow statements—it may be that we will be in a position to redeem them after five years, or we may have no available cash and need to look at 10 years or even longer.

Share Issue

The share calculations require some special treatment. On the Inputs page, you'll see that we show both the cash inflow from the sale of shares—tentatively $50 million—and the share issue costs of $2.5 million, resulting in a new inflow of $47.5 million. This is a useful illustration of differing treatments in the financial statements. On the Cash Budget, we are going to show $50 million as a cash inflow, and the cost flowing out. The costs, however, are not expensed on the Income Statement; correspondingly, the Statement of Financial Position will show only a liability of $47.5 million, the actual proceeds of the share issue. Then, when we finally translate this to the statement of changes in shareholders' equity, the full picture is shown again with the share issue costs reduced from the equity to arrive at the net value.

The ordinary (common) shareholders will be hoping for some return on their capital. As a placeholder we have set up 50% of net income (after tax). This may well be reviewed once we see the ongoing cash flows of the business.

Bond Issue

Treatment of Bonds is more complex than share issue. At the outset, we have an option either to record the costs as a deferred charge, or to net them against bond proceeds. In the former case, the deferred charge becomes a non-current asset on the balance sheet and is amortized over the life of the bond. Here, we'll use the second method.

The initial journal entries will be:

DR Cash (actual funds received, net)

DR Discount on Bonds Payable

    CR Bonds payable (the full face value).

For accounting purposes, the discount on bonds payable is then amortized over the life of the bond. Again we have an option, to use effective interest, which is more accurate but more complex, or straight-line amortization. Straight line is sufficient for our purposes.

Correspondingly, the bond issue expense is debited to the Income Statement and credited to the Statement of Financial Position. The amortization is then accomplished by adding to interest expense on the Income Statement and crediting the discount on the Statement of Financial Position. In our model, with $1 million in bond issue costs and a five-year term. The last consideration is that all the numbers relating to the bond are variable inputs and must be accomplished by formulaic references to the Inputs Page. The full treatment is contained in the model: the Cash Budget shows both the inflow and outflow, while the amortization of the costs is an interest costs on the Income Statement and the Statement of Financial Position reflects the declining asset. Shareholders' equity is not affected.

Supplier Financing

The financing section concludes with a decision variable for credit terms and a soft coded input for paydays per year.[51] We have negotiated 30-day payment terms with our suppliers and will be paying our staff 24 times per year. Both create a form of financing for the company and are significant in cash flow calculations. However, because we use accrual accounting, they do not affect the Statement of Income.

It may seem cynical, unfair (and certainly not very British) for companies to hold off paying suppliers or staff as a form of financing. However, it is a pervasive practice, and some very well-known companies have poor reputations for paying as a result (Informal-Ask, 2020). It is also common for large companies to have supplier payment "runs"—one or two days a month when all invoices due are settled.

Before we move on

We have reached an important milestone in building our model; we may have completed the list of Inputs; after preparing a few schedules we can start to build financial statements. However, just before doing so, it's a really good idea to step back, look at the sheet, and ask "Have we missed anything?" As we build the financials, it will never be too late to go back and add or change something essential, but it is better to have the big picture covered at this stage.

For example, note that there is no executive compensation in our Inputs. This is a substantial start-up business and we have worked on the assumption that the principal investors, who will be putting money IN, will also populate the Board of Directors and benefit from dividends when profits are made. That might be an unwarranted assumption for many small businesses—for example, a family setting up a shop, restaurant or food truck will most probably need to take an income from the business from quite early in its life.

---

[51] The B.C. Paydays Act, in s.17(1), requires that there must be at least two paydays per month and wages must be paid within 8 days of the last day of the period being remunerated. Air Amlani has elected to pay on the 15th and last day of each month, in arrears. As a result, there will be no wages payable on the Financial Statements.

Other schedules

TABLE 72: Economic schedules

Air Amlani - YVR-SAL-YVR. Schedules

Projected	2025	2026	2027	2028	2029
Inflation Rate (A)	1.03	1.03	1.02	1.02	1.02
Fuel Price Increase	1.01	1.01	1.01	1.01	1.01
Seniority Increases	1.02	1.02	1.0175	1.0150	1.0125
USD Exchange rate	$ 1.39	$ 1.36	$ 1.27	$ 1.27	$ 1.26

(A) Based on consideration of several respected forecasts for example https://economics.td.com/ca-long-term-forecast

(B) Based on consideration of several non-government global forecasters for example https://thebalancemoney.com/oil-price-forecast

(C) Based on the expectation that we can negotiate with our staff to keep annual seniority increases at 2% above inflation. In the last three years new starts, at lower wage rates than staff with seniority, will ameliorate the effects of these increases.

(D) Based on consideration of several bank forecasts e.g. HSBC found at https://www.exchangerates.org.uk/

On the last Schedules page we've recorded variable, projected data which will affect the five-year forward-looking projections in the Financial Statements. This page also holds mortgage repayment calculations. If we had any, this would also be the place to put mortgage and amortization schedules for blended principal and interest payments. These items have in common that they would clutter the inputs page—this granular data are not necessary for the reader to review the big picture but do need to be present to support the calculations in the Financial Statements.

Note again that even the years (2024, 2025 *etc.*) are not directly typed into this sheet. They are created using the First_Year_of_Ops named cell from Inputs, with progressive additions of the Annual_Interval. In a heartbeat, we will be able to change the range of years by changing the first year on the Inputs page.

The projected rates for the various years are, as noted on the page, based on a review of informed authorities. They are at very best-informed guesses, and we may want to review and change them during the five-year period. In general, though, there will be no user inputs on the Schedules (or, indeed, on any of the subsequent pages). The projected rates and prices are externally supplied data; the decision variables for the mortgage are changeable on the Inputs page, with all the resultant calculations being outputs.

On the Other Schedules page, we name some cells. However, we may not always use those names in subsequent formulas: the reason is that when we create the Financial Statements, we want to be able to use Excel's Copy feature to calculate across rows, without needing to re-key every calculation (copy does not adjust source data when referring to named cells).

The rows with projections are the best candidates for naming: the inflation rates, for example, are named Inflation_Y1 through Inflation_Y5. This is a really good place to start thinking of the five years as Y1 to Y5—remember that the years may be changed but formulas will not need to be, as long as the year in the first column is thought of as Y1.

Another convenience applied to the Schedules page is the expression of percentages as multiples of 1—3% is expressed as 1.03, and so on. This makes all the formulas which incorporate them significantly less complicated and reduces risk of error.

TABLE 73: Mortgage table

19	**AIRCRAFT MORTAGE**					
20	***Annual, Blended Principal and Interest Payments at Year End***					
21	20 Years, Fixed Rate 5%					
22						
23	Year	**2025**	**2026**	**2027**	**2028**	**2029**
24	**Opening Balance**	$ 100,000,000	$ 95,000,000	$ 90,000,000	$ 85,000,000	$ 80,000,000
25	**Interest**	$ 5,000,000	$ 4,750,000	$ 4,500,000	$ 4,250,000	$ 4,000,000
26	**Principal**	$ 5,000,000	$ 5,000,000	$ 5,000,000	$ 5,000,000	$ 5,000,000
27	**Payment**	$ 10,000,000	$ 9,750,000	$ 9,500,000	$ 9,250,000	$ 9,000,000
28	**Balance**	$ 95,000,000	$ 90,000,000	$ 85,000,000	$ 80,000,000	$ 75,000,000

Scaffolding the financial statements

It's time to start building the three Financial Statements based on the data inputs. While they will be presented in a standard order (Cash Budget, Income, Financial Position), some elements of the cash flow statement will need to be drawn from the Income Statement (for example). It is therefore best practice at this stage to build the scaffolding—that is, create the headers and titles for all three Financial Statements. These can be changed and adapted as the model builds. The contents will reflect our understanding of how the business is accounted for and should fulfil the expectations of financial professionals who may review them.

Between Cash Budget and the Income Statement, there will be many similarities in the headings and titles; however, there will be important differences. Cash Budget will have investment money coming in and an outflow for the cost of the plane; the Income Statement will not. On the other hand, the Income Statement will include Depreciation Expense, but as this is non-cash it will not appear on the Cash Budget.

The next four tables show a typical scaffolding set-up for this business. The value of creating these at this stage will quickly be realized as we start to populate the pages.

TABLE 74: Scaffolding for the Cash budget

	A	B	C	D	E	F
1				**Air Amlani**		
2				**Model Cash Budget (Canadian $)**		
3				**For the Financial Years Ended December 31**		
4						
5		**2025**	**2026**	**2027**	**2028**	**2029**
6	**INFLOWS**					
7	**Start-Up**					
8	Share Capital					
9	Bond Issue					
10	Aircraft Mortgage					
11						
12	**Recurring**					
13	Passenger Revenue					
14						
15	TOTAL INFLOWS					
16						
17	**OUTFLOWS**					
18	**Start-Up**					
19	Share Issue Costs					
20	Bond Issue Costs					
21	Aircraft Purchase					
22	Legal					
23	Accounting					
24						
25	**Recurring**					
26	*Operational*					
27	Aircraft Fuel					
28	Aircraft Maintenance					
29	Airport Landing Fees					
30	Airport Parking Fees					
31	Airport Passenger Fees					
32	Catering Costs					
33	Crew Costs					
34	Insurance					
35	Navigation Fees					
36	***Administrative***					
37	Accounting Costs					
38	Banking Charges					
39	Legal Costs					
40	Sales and Distribution					
41	Website & IT					
42	***Financial***					
43	Mortgage Interest					
44	Mortgage Repayment					
45	Bond Interest					
46	***Taxation***					
47	Income Taxes					
48	***Shareholders***					
49	Dividends					
50	Bond Redemption					
51	**TOTAL OUTFLOWS**					
52						
53	**NET CASH FLOW**					
54						
55	CLOSING CASH POSITION					

Table 75: Scaffolding for the Statement of Income

	A	B	C	D	E	F
1			Air Amlani			
2			Model Income Statement (Canadian $)			
3			For the Financial Years Ended December 31			
4						
5		**2025**	**2026**	**2027**	**2028**	**2029**
6	**INCOME**					
7	Passenger Revenue					
8						
9	TOTAL INCOME					
10						
11	**EXPENSE**					
12	**Start-Up**					
13	Legal					
14	Accounting					
15						
16	**Recurring**					
17	***Operational***					
18	Aircraft Fuel					
19	Aircraft Maintenance					
20	Airport Landing Fees					
21	Airport Parking Fees					
22	Airport Passenger Fees					
23	Catering Costs					
24	Crew Costs					
25	Insurance					
26	Navigation Fees					
27	***Administrative***					
28	Accounting Costs					
29	Banking Charges					
30	Legal Costs					
31	Sales and Distribution					
32	Website & IT					
33	***Financial***					
34	Mortgage Interest					
35	Bond Interest					
36	**Depreciation and Amortization**					
37	Depreciation					
38	Amortization (interest)					
39						
40	TOTAL EXPENSE					
41						
42	NET PRE-TAX INCOME					
43						
44	***Taxation***					
45	Income Taxes					
46						
47	NET INCOME AFTER TAX					

TABLE 76: Scaffolding for the Statement of Financial Position

	A	B	C	D	E	F
1	**Air Amlani**					
2	**Model Statement of Financial Position (Canadian $)**					
3	**As at December 31**					
4						
5		**2025**	**2026**	**2027**	**2028**	**2029**
6	**ASSETS**					
7	***Current Assets***					
8	Cash					
9	Prepaid Insurance					
10	***Non-Current Assets***					
11	Aircraft					
12	Discount on Bonds Payable					
13	TOTAL ASSETS					
14						
15	**LIABILITIES**					
16	***Current Liabilities***					
17	Accounts Payable					
18	Unearned Revenue					
19	Income Taxes Payable					
20	***Long Term Liabilities***					
21	Aircraft Mortgage					
22	Bonds Issued					
23	***Shareholders' Equity***					
24	Share Capital					
25	Retained Earnings					
26	Dividends Payable					
27	TOTAL LIABILITIES					

Note the inclusion of a *Checksum* below the total liabilities line. This is a temporary measure, populated by a formula to deduct total liabilities from total assets for each year. This provides a very quick check to ensure that the Assets and Liabilities remain balanced as changes are made throughout the Statements; also, where there is a difference, the number which shows in the checksum is likely to give a valuable clue as to where the error might be.

TABLE 77: Scaffolding for the Statement of Changes in Shareholders' Equity

	A	B	C	D	E	F
1			Air Amlani			
2			Model Statement of Changes in Shareholders' Equity (Canadian $)			
3			As At December 31			
4						
5		2025	2026	2027	2028	2029
6	Ordinary Share Capital at Jan 1					
7	Add: Issue of Ordinary Shares			-		
8	Less: Share Issue Costs					
9	Net Share Capital at Dec 31					
10						
11	Retained Earnings at Jan 1					
12	Net Income					
13	Less: Dividends Declared					
14	Net Retained Earnings					
15	**Total Shareholders' Equity At Dec 31**					

We'll now begin to populate the financial statements, starting with the cash budget.

Cash budget

TABLE 78: Model Cash Budget

	A	B	C	D	E	F
1			**Air Amlani**			
2			**Model Cash Budget (Canadian $)**			
3			**For the Financial Years Ended December 31**			
4						
5		**2025**	**2026**	**2027**	**2028**	**2029**
6	**INFLOWS**					
7	**Start-Up**					
8	Share Capital	50,000,000				
9	Bond Issue	50,000,000				
10	Aircraft Mortgage	100,000,000				
11						
12	**Recurring**					
13	Passenger Revenue	112,902,634	99,951,151	102,781,399	104,837,027	106,933,767
14						
15	**TOTAL INFLOWS**	**312,902,634**	**99,951,151**	**102,781,399**	**104,837,027**	**106,933,767**
16						
17	**OUTFLOWS**					
18	**Start-Up**					
19	Share Issue Costs	2,500,000				
20	Bond Issue Costs	1,000,000				
21	Aircraft Purchase	156,514,000				
22	Legal	1,000,000				
23	Accounting	1,000,000				
24						
25	**Recurring**					
26	***Operational***					
27	Aircraft Fuel	9,778,758	10,538,439	9,978,865	10,020,857	10,047,858
28	Aircraft Maintenance	4,537,207	5,079,338	5,231,718	5,340,534	5,447,345
29	Airport Landing Fees	343,850	384,935	396,483	404,730	412,824
30	Airport Parking Fees	24,728	27,683	28,513	29,106	29,688
31	Airport Passenger Fees	1,008,508	1,129,010	1,162,880	1,187,067	1,210,808
32	Catering Costs	1,625,260	1,819,455	1,874,039	1,913,018	1,951,278
33	Crew Costs	2,026,103	2,128,624	2,236,333	2,320,978	2,402,908
34	Insurance	334,950	175,049	178,549	182,120	185,763
35	Navigation Fees	2,097,259	2,347,851	2,418,286	2,468,585	2,517,957
36	***Administrative***					
37	Accounting Costs		200,000	206,000	212,180	216,424
38	Banking Charges	1,693,540	1,499,267	1,541,721	1,572,555	1,604,007
39	Legal Costs	200,000	206,000	212,180	216,424	220,752
40	Sales and Distribution	5,317,964	5,953,383	6,131,985	6,259,526	6,384,717
41	Website & IT	3,545,309	3,968,922	4,087,990	4,173,017	4,256,478
42	***Financial***					
43	Mortgage Interest	5,000,000	4,750,000	4,500,000	4,250,000	4,000,000
44	Mortgage Repayment	5,000,000	5,000,000	5,000,000	5,000,000	5,000,000
45	Bond Interest	2,500,000	2,500,000	2,500,000	2,500,000	2,500,000
46	***Taxation***					
47	Income Taxes		24,105,244	14,613,710	14,975,739	15,042,467
48	***Shareholders***					
49	Dividends	-	16,293,359	26,171,145	19,134,723	19,734,955
50	Bond Redemption					50,000,000
51	**TOTAL OUTFLOWS**	**207,047,436**	**88,106,559**	**88,470,398**	**82,161,159**	**133,166,228**
52						
53	**NET CASH FLOW**	**105,855,198**	**11,844,592**	**14,311,001**	**22,675,868**	**(26,232,460)**
54						
55	CLOSING CASH POSITION	105,855,198	117,699,790	132,010,791	154,686,659	128,454,198

The *Cash Budget*, like all Financial Statements, is entirely generated by formulas from the data input on other pages. This is the first of three important predictive tools, because it will enable us to answer questions like how much money we need to get started, what cushion we might have for unexpected downturns, and how much money will be available for shareholders during the period. Some of the formulas used here are complex, and it will be instructive to look at a few in more detail.

Each "side" (Inflows and Outflows) of the Cash Flow is divided into two parts—one-time start-up flows, which usually occur only in the first year (though we could, for example, be planning to raise additional capital in a subsequent year),[52] and recurring flows which will happen each year throughout the life of the business.

Passenger Revenue, our sole source of operating income, was already calculated on an annual basis in the interim outputs on the Inputs page. On the Statement of Income, it is picked up from the Total_Rev_Yr cell on the Inputs page, then increased in line with inflation for the subsequent years. An important small detail is that most inflation rates are only used for FOUR years in a five-year plan; the 2024 rate, for example, is fully manifested by December and is thus applied to the 2025 income. The last inflation rate, however, is needed for calculations of unearned revenue. On average for Latin American routes, tickets are purchased 60 days in advance. At each Year End, we will have 60 days' worth of ticket prices already in our bank accounts, and an unearned revenue component for that amount in the Statement of Financial Position. If we complete the Statement of Income line for passenger revenues, we can use that to calculate the unearned revenue for each year; by placing that on the Statement of Financial Position we can then work back from those numbers to calculate the cash inflows for each year.

We'll jump to the Statement of Income and set up the Passenger Revenue line. The 2024 (Y1) income will be as calculated on the Inputs page; the subsequent years will build in the component of inflation with 2025, for example, being the 2024 income plus 2024 inflation:

```
=Total_Rev_Yr*Inflation_Y1
```

We will also name those cells (e.g. Pax_Revenue_Y1[53]), this will help avoid mistakes as we use them in other Statements.

On the Statement of Financial Position, we'll create first the liability row for Unearned Revenue, at Average_Prepay/Days_in_Year (from Inputs) * Pax_Rev_Y2 from the Income Statement. A similar operation will fill the cells for years 2–4, but in the last year we encounter the problem that we haven't calculated revenues for the sixth year. We will now need to do that integral to the formula:

```
=(Average_Prepay/Days_in_Year)*Pax_Rev_Y5*Inflation_Y5
```

---

[52] Things could become more complicated if we had a revolving line of credit from the bank; thankfully, we don't have to deal with that here.

[53] Don't make the mistake of including the year in the name—remember that years are generated from the Key Inputs page and can change.

You might wonder why we do not, at the same time, create the Cash line in the Statement of Financial Position and add in the offset for the unearned revenue. The reason is that the Cash line will be populated by referencing the net cash position from Cash Budget, and thus already incorporate the unearned revenue.

Back to the Cash Budget. For the Passenger Revenue in Y1, we can add the Passenger Revenues for that year (Pax_Rev_Y1) to the Unearned Revenue (Unearned_Rev_Y1). In the subsequent years, however, we cannot repeat this formula because we need to take out the previous year's unearned revenue (now earned). So Year 2 will be:

```
Pax_Rev_Y2+Unearned_Rev_Y2-Unearned_Rev_Y1 (and so on).
```

Aircraft Purchase, a single one-time outflow in Canadian dollars, is calculated from the product of the USD cost and the Y1 Exchange rate from the Schedules.

Things get more interesting, and complex, with some of the operating expenses, and again we will start off the calculations in the Income Statement.

Next we are going to deal with all the expense lines. Please note carefully that we are going to calculate each of these on the *Income Statement,* then work backwards to Cash Budget to consider their effects.

Aircraft fuel is our largest expense. We have a 2024 price, from which we can calculate an annual total in CAD using total consumption (a product of flying hours and consumption), the fuel price and a conversion from USD. There will be no inflation in the later year calculations, as that is already caught in the predicted fuel price. The syntax for the first year is:

```
=Fuel_cost_per_Leg*Legs_per_Yr*USDx_Y1
```

Then in subsequent years it becomes

```
=Fuel_cost_per_Leg*Legs_per_Yr*USDx_Y2*Fuel_Inc_Y1
```

Note that as with inflation, the increase element is referring back one year to capture the increased fuel price for the current year.

Although the *price* of fuel is presently estimated to rise at 1% each year in USD, dollar exchange rates are expected to become more favorable to Canadians over the last four years of our plan, meaning that fuel costs overall will go *down* in 2025 and never rise again to 2024 levels during this period.

We can now name the outputs for fuel costs on the Income Statement, Fuel_costs_Y1 etc.

As we make changes to decision variables, for example flying three legs per day instead of two, all these costs will automatically update.

Having calculated annual fuel costs in the Income Statement, it's possible to use those to show the effect on cash flows. Because we've negotiated 30-day payment terms for all suppliers, the last 30 days of supplies at the end of each year are going to be unpaid. 30/365.25 is, in Inputs terms, Credit_Terms/Days_in_Year. On the Cash Budget, the Aircraft Fuel entry for the first year will be

```
=Fuel_costs_Y1-(Fuel_costs_Y1*Credit_Terms/Days_in_Year)
```

In the four following years, the cash outflow for fuel will be 30/365.25 of the previous year's fuel costs, plus the current year's costs less 30/365.25 of that: so for the second year,

```
=(Fuel_costs_Y1*Credit-Terms/Days_in_Year)+(Fuel_costs_Y2-
        (Fuel_costs_Y2*Credit_Terms/Days_in_Year))
```

Aircraft Maintenance, Landing, Parking and Passenger Fees are all calculated based on activity, and assumed to increase at the projected rate of inflation, Navigation Fees and Catering Costs, Sales and Distribution costs, and Website & IT costs, will all receive similar treatment. There is no need to belabor the calculations here. Note however that for years 2–5 inflation will be added to the current year cost.

Accounting is a special case. We will assume that external accounting and audit work will be done close to, or after, Year End. Accounting charges will therefore be paid wholly in the following year but be accrued in the current year. The current year charges will become an account payable at the end of each year. *Legal Fees* on the other hand get different treatment; law firms like to be paid by retainer, in advance, so we will assume that all legal fees will be settled in the year incurred.

Insurance also gets special treatment. In most businesses, annual insurance costs are paid at some point in the year and will comprise a mixture of current year costs and prepaid costs for the following year. In our example, insurance runs for the calendar year so the following year's premium will be paid just before year end. The first year's cash flow for insurance will consist of the current year's premium plus next year's, the latter being shown as an asset on the Statement of Financial Position.

Banking charges relate to the costs of processing card payments. They are deducted from settlements by the card processor, so are contemporaneous with the income. We will calculate these at the set percentage of passenger revenue. They should not be calculated on the Income Statement and referenced on the Cash Budget, or *vice versa*, they must be re-calculated in both places.

Crew Costs are subtly more complex. We have to cope with inflation, but also with seniority increases as some of our pilots and cabin crew stay with us. We have made an assumption that we can agree on seniority increases of 2% over inflation; however, by the third year some staff will be leaving and cheaper, new staff will join so the inflation + 2% calculation is not static. This is all taken care of in the schedules; in these calculations we have taken care of the Income Statement figures, and as we will have paid wages up to date to the end of the month on December 31st, there will be no wages payable on the Statement of Financial Position. In this instance, the Cash Budget will exactly match the Income Statement but again, we will use original calculations.

At this point, having calculated annual expenses on the Income Statement then worked out their impacts on cash flow, we can return to the Cash Budget to work out the financial cash flows, but will need to refer to the Income Statement once more to deal with taxes and dividends.

The *Financial Cash Flows* respecting borrowing are taken directly from the principal and interest figures on the Inputs page, or in the case of the mortgage from the mortgage schedule. They are relatively straightforward as they are required to be paid on the dates they fall due, conveniently at Year End.

Income Taxes theoretically could, but should not, be calculated only with reference to the previous pages. The tax rates are on the Inputs page, but on the next page, the Income Statement, we are going to calculate net profits. Tax will be a function of those profits, so we can make a placeholder formula to refer forwards to the Income Statement and take the tax from there. Then the tax cashflow will adjust automatically every time any change is made to a decision variable.

However, that is not the end of the work on income tax in the Cash Budget. We have to take account of the rules under which tax is paid and remitted. In Canada, there are differing tax rates for difference levels of income, and two taxation authorities to consider (federal and provincial). We have assumed for the purpose of this model that there will be one net tax rate equal to the sum of theoretical rates of 15 and 12 percent—a total of 27%.

In the first year of a new operation, if there is a profit, a tax liability will be incurred. But that tax will not be paid until the second year. This condition will be drawn from an IF statement in the Income Statement. Then, however, we also have to consider instalments. If a business actually pays tax in any one year, it must pay advance remittances of tax in the following year equivalent to the previous. Importantly, these instalments are equal to the tax actually paid, not the liability incurred on profit in the previous year.

Instalments are payments made during the current year in anticipation of the tax which will become due for the year once profits are calculated. Although the amount of instalments required is the same as last year's tax, it doesn't mean that the business is paying double tax. It is paying the amount due for the previous year, then advance payments towards the current year's tax liability. When it eventually pays the current year's tax, it will deduct the instalments already paid during the year.

That sounds complicated, and it is. An example may help.

Suppose that a business makes the following profits and losses:

Year 1: ($100,000)

Year 2: $100,000

In the first year, the business would have no tax liability and no payment.

In the second year, the business would incur a tax liability (27%) of $27,000 but offset against this would be an identical reduction for the loss in the first year. So, it would pay nothing to the governments. What instalments should it pay in the third year?

The answer, simplified, is that it should pay no instalments, because its tax payment for the previous year was based on $0. It is the tax liability for the year after taking account of previous losses if they are carried forward, not the payment respecting just that year, that determines the amount of instalments.

There is an inherent risk, however. If a business has moved from losses to growing profits, its instalments will be insufficient to meet the eventual tax liability, and it will be penalized for underpayments. CRA allows businesses to adjust their remittances using the "current year method," but this requires accurate forecasting which is not always a realistic expectation. We won't adopt that method here.

Coming back to how to treat this in the Cash Budget, we can see that conditional =IF formulas will be required. Although we might expect a profit, or loss, the modeling requirement is that both be provided for. The formulas will change slightly over the years.

In the Cash Budget, the outflow for income taxes will be blank, unless the company elects to pay instalments under the current year method.

To determine outflow for tax in the second year, we will first take the tax liability for the first year from the Income Statement, then add instalment payments of an equivalent amount. The instalments paid in the second year, if any, will then affect the taxes payable at the end of the second year on the Statement of Financial Position.

In the third year, instalments will be based on the actual tax liability in the second year (that is, the amount for tax liability (previous year) without taking any account of remittances. Going forward, the tax liability for the previous year paid on Income Statement will determine the instalments for the next period; meanwhile, the taxes actually paid in each year will be reduced by the amount of instalments already paid.

We'll come back to taxes when discussing the Income Statement, to complete this picture. Here, though, are some examples of the formulas in the Cash Budget.

Year 2: `=IT_Y1 + IT_Y1`. The reference is to the income taxes payable on the Income Statement, and it's doubled to take account of instalment remittances. If there was no profit in Y1, then this would be zero.

Year 3: `=IT_Y2 - IT_Y1+IT_Y2`. The tax liability for Y2, less the instalments paid in advance during that year, plus instalments equal to the actual tax paid in Y2 (taking account of any past losses).

In subsequent years the Year 3 formula will be repeated adding one to each integer.

Dividends, like taxes, are going to depend on figures which will first be calculated on the Income Statement. On the Inputs page, we set up a decision variable of 50% (of net income after tax) for dividend distribution, so the formula is built to calculate that number for cash flow. Dividends will only be paid if there is a profit, so an IF statement is required to set dividends to 0 in the event of a loss. The syntax for the first year for example is

```
=IF(Net_Income_Y1>Dividend_Base,Net_Income_Y1*Dividend_Rate,Net_Income_Y1-
Net_Income_Y1)
```

where Net_Income_Y1 on the Income Statement is net income after tax.

The best place to work through this calculation is on the Statement of Financial Position. The result will make two appearances—as Dividends Payable for the year in which they are earned, and as a reduction of Retained Earnings for that same year. We then pull the first four years' dividends back into the Cash Flow statement as they will actually be paid in the year following.

What is Dividend_Base? This is a decision variable, set up on the Inputs page, which governs the minimum amount of income which must be made before a dividend is calculated and paid. Why have we set it up this way? Think about this before reading the footnote.[54] And the option if there is no net income, Net_Income_Y1-Net_Income_Y1? This will produce zero (for example, -1,000 minus -1,000)—we have again avoided the temptation to key in a magic number of 0.

Dividends are going to be declared after Year End. They will therefore affect Cash Budget only in the following year, but on the Statement of Financial Position they will be deducted from Retained Earnings, and show up as a dividend payable. In the Cash Budget, we can take them directly from the Income Statement, offset by one year.

After performing the many calculations on the Income Statement, and before starting to write the formulas which will produce their effects on Cash Budget, it will be useful to name the output sells on the Income Statement. As you decide which cells to name, think about which ones will be the subject of cross references on other pages of the Financial Statements.

Bond Redemption makes a solo appearance in 2029, because we want to evaluate the period for which we might originally need to issue bonds. Including the full value of our bond issue as a disbursement in 2029 must not result in a closing negative cash position. We will shortly see that this *is* going to be possible with the numbers presently included in the Inputs page.

Filling in the subsequent years 2025–2028 is in large part going to be easy, for most of the cells we will be able to calculate based on the 2024 numbers adjusting for inflation or other relevant factors in the schedules. Then we will earn a huge bonus: while the Cash Flow statement is not the same as the Income Statement, many of the line items are the same and we will be able to move quickly through the Income Statement, repeating the formulas, as a result.

The final lines to be added to the Cash Budget are the net for each year, and a cumulative line which tells us the amount of cash left (or the shortage thereof) at the end of each year.

---

[54] Because, if we wrote the formula with 0, to ensure dividends were paid whenever there is a profit, we would have incorporated a magic number. We might not always want to pay dividends on everything over 0, so that number is changeable on the Key Inputs page.

Income statement

TABLE 79: Model Statement of Income

	A	B	C	D	E	F
1			Air Amlani			
2			Model Income Statement (Canadian $)			
3			For the Financial Years Ended December 31			
4						
5		**2025**	**2026**	**2027**	**2028**	**2029**
6	**INCOME**					
7	Passenger Revenue	96,564,072	99,460,995	102,444,824	104,493,721	106,583,595
8						
9	TOTAL INCOME	**96,564,072**	**99,460,995**	**102,444,824**	**104,493,721**	**106,583,595**
10						
11	**EXPENSE**					
12	**Start-Up**					
13	Legal	1,000,000				
14	Accounting	1,000,000				
15						
16	**Recurring**					
17	***Operational***					
18	Aircraft Fuel	10,653,814	10,528,115	9,929,715	10,029,012	10,049,544
19	Aircraft Maintenance	4,943,221	5,091,518	5,244,264	5,349,149	5,456,132
20	Airport Landing Fees	374,620	385,858	397,434	405,383	413,490
21	Airport Parking Fees	26,941	27,749	28,582	29,153	29,736
22	Airport Passenger Fees	1,098,754	1,131,717	1,165,669	1,188,982	1,212,762
23	Catering Costs	1,770,698	1,823,818	1,878,533	1,916,104	1,954,426
24	Crew Costs	2,026,103	2,128,624	2,236,333	2,320,978	2,402,908
25	Insurance	165,000	169,950	175,049	178,549	182,120
26	Navigation Fees	2,284,933	2,353,481	2,424,086	2,472,567	2,522,019
27	***Administrative***					
28	Accounting Costs	200,000	206,000	212,180	216,424	220,752
29	Banking Charges	1,693,540	1,499,267	1,541,721	1,572,555	1,604,007
30	Legal Costs	200,000	206,000	212,180	216,424	220,752
31	Sales and Distribution	5,793,844	5,967,660	6,146,689	6,269,623	6,395,016
32	Website & IT	3,862,563	3,978,440	4,097,793	4,179,749	4,263,344
33	***Financial***					
34	Mortgage Interest	5,000,000	4,750,000	4,500,000	4,250,000	4,000,000
35	Bond Interest	2,500,000	2,500,000	2,500,000	2,500,000	2,500,000
36	**Depreciation and Amortization**					
37	Depreciation	$ 7,130,700	$ 7,130,700	$ 7,130,700	$ 7,130,700	$ 7,130,700
38	Amortization (interest)	$ 200,000	$ 200,000	$ 200,000	$ 200,000	$ 200,000
39						
40	TOTAL EXPENSE	$ 51,924,731	$ 50,078,898	$ 50,020,926	$ 50,425,352	$ 50,757,707
41						
42	NET PRE-TAX INCOME	$ 44,639,341	$ 49,382,097	$ 52,423,898	$ 54,068,369	$ 55,825,888
43						
44	***Taxation***					
45	Income Taxes	12,052,622	13,333,166	14,154,453	14,598,460	15,072,990
46						
47	**NET INCOME AFTER TAX**	**$ 32,586,719**	**$ 36,048,931**	**$ 38,269,446**	**$ 39,469,909**	**$ 40,752,898**

The Model Income Statement tells us whether we can expect our business to be profitable. Most of the line entries we already calculated to incorporate the relevant amounts into Cash Budget. We have to include our financing and start-up *costs* but not financed income here in the first year; the most important differences are just three items.

Start-Up Expenses

In the first year of the Income Statement there is a special section for Start-Up Expenses. One might be forgiven for thinking, after the complex treatments of share issue and bond costs, that professional fees associated with the launch should also be capitalized and amortized. Situations in which this is required are however extremely rare; in both US GAAP and IFRS accounting, these fees are normally required to be expensed in the period in which they are incurred, that is, in the first year in our model. For transparency, however, they are separated out so that users of the financial statements can see their effect as being one-time costs associated with commencement.

Depreciation

We have to *include* depreciation, which is our only non-cash expense. That will affect our profitability, and in turn will complete the computation of income taxes, which we can then refer back into the Cash Budget statement. The calculation of net income after tax will also determine the amount of shareholder dividends to flow out of cash.

Income Taxes

The Income Statement includes a vitally important calculation of tax liability in the current year, and its progressively more complicated formulas must be set up to encompass the possibility of profit or loss in any year. It is not sufficient simply to show tax payable if there is a profit. It's important to remember that the income tax expense on the Income Statement is a reflection of tax payable *for each year,* not tax payable on the profits *of that year.*

The first year's calculation is straightforward: if there is a profit, tax will be payable. If net pre-tax income is positive, that income multiplied by the tax rate.

```
=IF(Net_Income_BT_Y1>Tax_Base,Net_Income_BT_Y1*(Federal_Business_Tax+Provinci
                          al_Business_Tax),Tax_Base)
```

In the second year, however, this will not be sufficient. We must take account of the possibility of a loss in the first year, reducing tax liability in the second. The tax liability is based on the cumulative total net income, which may be 0 or less than 0, less any taxes attributed to previous years. To avoid using a magic number of 0 in the financial statements, there is a Tax_Base figure, set at 0, in the Inputs page.

For subsequent years, the formula grows in coverage as it looks at cumulative net pre-tax income over a longer period each year and reduces any resultant liability by taxes previously assessed. The complex formula required are exhibited in the model; they are significantly easier to review in context than if they were repeated here.

With these calculations done and our potential profits and taxes established, we can return to the Cash Budget and refer to the Income Statement for the missing numbers. Based on the numbers we have worked with so far, we can see positive cash flow from 2024 onwards, and a healthy reserve steadily building over the following years.

Statement of financial position

TABLE 80: Model Statement of Financial Position

	A	B	C	D	E	F
1				Air Amlani		
2				Model Statement of Financial Position (Canadian $)		
3				As at December 31		
4						
5		**2025**	**2026**	**2027**	**2028**	**2029**
6	**ASSETS**					
7	***Current Assets***					
8	Cash	105,855,198	117,699,790	132,010,791	154,686,659	128,454,198
9	Prepaid Insurance	169,950	175,049	178,549	182,120	185,763
10	***Non-Current Assets***					
11	Aircraft	149,383,300	142,252,600	135,121,900	127,991,200	120,860,500
12	Discount on Bonds Payable	800,000	600,000	400,000	200,000	-
13	**TOTAL ASSETS**	**256,208,448**	**260,727,438**	**267,711,241**	**283,059,979**	**249,500,461**
14						
15	**LIABILITIES**					
16	***Current Liabilities***					
17	Accounts Payable	2,730,545	2,775,886	2,784,070	2,831,596	2,873,439
18	Unearned Revenue	16,338,562	16,828,719	17,165,293	17,508,599	17,858,771
19	Income Taxes Payable	12,052,622	1,280,544	821,286	444,007	474,530
20	***Long Term Liabilities***					
21	Aircraft Mortgage	95,000,000	90,000,000	85,000,000	80,000,000	75,000,000
22	Bonds Issued	50,000,000	50,000,000	50,000,000	50,000,000	-
23	***Shareholders' Equity***					
24	Share Capital	47,500,000	47,500,000	47,500,000	47,500,000	47,500,000
25	Retained Earnings	16,293,359	26,171,145	45,305,868	65,040,823	86,058,766
26	Dividends Payable	16,293,359	26,171,145	19,134,723	19,734,955	19,734,955
27	**TOTAL LIABILITIES**	**256,208,448**	**260,727,438**	**267,711,241**	**283,059,979**	**249,500,461**
28	*Checksum*	-	-	-	-	-

Despite the complexity of our business, the Statement of Financial Position is the simplest and quickest document to compile.

Cash, our sole current asset, is taken directly from the cumulative position on the Cash Budget.

Our only fixed asset is our aircraft. Its value is in 2024 taken from the purchase price less that year's depreciation; subsequently, each year's depreciation is taken off the previous year's value.

Prepaid Insurance is the value of insurance for the following year. This can be taken directly (remembering to stagger the years) from the Income Statement; however, we will need one additional calculation for prepaid insurance in Year 5, the Y5 insurance cost plus Y5 inflation.

We will have a lot more fun with the liabilities side.

Accounts Payable will usually be the most complex calculation. We must arrive at a total for all those payments to suppliers that were deferred in the last 30 days of the year, to the following year. We are going to demonstrate this in a single formula; however, it would be quite acceptable also to tabulate the expenses on the Schedules page and draw in the payable amounts, arriving at a total to transfer to the Statement of Financial Position. We'll start with Accounts Payable for Year 1.

Placing the cursor in the accounts payable row under the first year, we'll first add together all the expense categories that are subject to 30-day payment terms, cross-referencing back to the Income Statement. Start with two opening parentheses so that we can apply the Credit_Terms/Days_in_Year multiplication. The only category to add to the total will be the *whole* of the accounting fees, which we plan to pay after year end.

=((Fuel_costs_Y1+Air_Maint_Y1+Landing_Fees_Y1+Parking_Fees_Y1+Pax_Fees+Y1+Nav_Fees_Y1+Caterin g_Y1+SD_Y1+WIT_Y1)*Payment_Terms/Days_in_Year)+Acc_Y1

It's not particularly difficult to type this out, but you don't need to. After typing the = sign in the cell on the Statement of Financial Position, you can then go to the Income Statement and click on each relevant cell.

Now another neat trick—which you may already have discovered. We can't just copy that formula across the years, because named cells are absolute. But because our naming has been completely consistent, we can copy it across then change the numerical digits in each formula, rather than re-creating it for every column. Copy the Accounts Payable cell for the first year into the other four, then work through them changing the 1s into 2s for the second year, and so on.

The *Unearned Revenue* we calculated earlier when working on the Cash Budget.

Income Taxes Payable we can pull from the Income Statement (careful, not from Cash Budget!)

The *Aircraft Mortgage* liability is taken from the Mortgage Schedule. If we were preparing statements for an annual report, we would separate the current portion of long term debt. This is unnecessary here as we are interested only in the value of total liabilities. The Cash Budget has assessed our ability to meet liabilities as they fall due.

Bonds Issued are taken from the Inputs page, noting that with the current intention of redemption at the end of the fifth year there is a 0 entry in the relevant cell.

The *share capital* continues unchanged throughout.

Finally, we need to insert *Retained Earnings.* The best place to calculate these, after dividends are ascertained, is in the statement of changes in shareholders' equity. We can reference forward to that statement and take them from there.

Now the acid test! Do the Total Assets, each year, reconcile exactly with the Total Liabilities? Thankfully they do, and this gives us considerable confidence in the content of our model. However, this is not the last time we will check this—after making any change to any decision variable, we should always go back to the Statement of Financial Position and ensure that it remains balanced. The key to this wonderful result, we cannot stress enough, is *no magic numbers*. If everything is correctly referenced to an input cell, then a balanced situation on the first pass is highly likely to replicate no matter what inputs we change subsequently.

Statement of changes in shareholders' equity

TABLE 81: Model Statement of Changes in Shareholders' Equity

	A	B	C	D	E	F
1			Air Amlani			
2			Model Statement of Changes in Shareholders' Equity (Canadian $)			
3			As At December 31			
4						
5		2025	2026	2027	2028	2029
6	Ordinary Share Capital at Jan 1	-	47,500,000	47,500,000	47,500,000	47,500,000
7	Add: Issue of Ordinary Shares	50,000,000				
8	Less: Share Issue Costs	2,500,000				
9	Net Share Capital at Dec 31	47,500,000	47,500,000	47,500,000	47,500,000	47,500,000
10						
11	Retained Earnings at Jan 1	-	16,293,359	26,171,145	45,305,868	65,040,823
12	Net Income	32,586,719	36,048,931	38,269,446	39,469,909	40,752,898
13	Less: Dividends Declared	16,293,359	26,171,145	19,134,723	19,734,955	19,734,955
14	Net Retained Earnings	16,293,359	26,171,145	45,305,868	65,040,823	86,058,766
15	**Total Shareholders' Equity At Dec 31**	**63,793,359**	**73,671,145**	**92,805,868**	**112,540,823**	**133,558,766**

This valuable statement consists largely of amounts drawn directly from other statements. In the share capital section are captured the transactions that result from issue of shares, including disclosure of the netting of costs.

The statement starts with a zero balance in retained earnings, drawn from Dividend_Base on the Inputs page. Net Income is drawn from the Income Statement. Retained Earnings is a matter of deducting any dividends paid from the previous retained earnings plus net income. The one crucial function within this statement is the calculation of dividends, which has an interesting condition.

First, dividends are only going to be paid, in the normal course of events, if the company has made a income in the relevant year. But more than this, dividends can only be paid if retained earnings prior to their payment are positive, *and* in sufficient quantity to pay the dividends. Therefore, a conditional formula needs to be worked out to ensure that both preconditions are satisfied.

In the first year, this is straightforward. The retained earnings before dividends will be the same as net income, therefore the formula simply compared net income to 0 (Dividend_Base) and if the former is greater, the dividend declared is the income, multiplied by the Dividend Payment Ratio, If the loss (negative income) is less than 0, then there will be no dividend.

```
=IF(Net_Income_Y1>Dividend_Base,Dividend_Payment_Ratio*Net_Income_Y1,Dividend_Base)
```

When we come to subsequent years, an AND calculation is required to ensure both that there is a profit in the current year, and that retained earnings before the dividend are more than the amount that is proposed to be paid. It is not enough to ensure that cumulative retained earnings are more than 0, because of the risk that a large loss in Y1 is covered by profits in Y2, but not sufficiently to permit the full 50% dividend. Instead, the formula needs to check that the available amount of retained earnings is sufficient to pay the dividend and keep the retained earnings at or above 0, and that the proposed dividend is only half of the cumulative retained earnings, not of the whole amount for the year. This is the most complex formula we will encounter in this entire exercise, let's state it then analyze it. This is the formula to calculate the dividend in Y2; for the subsequent years, simply add 1 to all the integers in the formula and it will correctly calculate for subsequent years.

```
=IF(AND(Net_Income_Y2>Dividend_Base,Net_RE_Y1+Net_Income_Y2>Dividend_Base,Net
_RE_Y1>Net_Income_Y2*Dividend_Payment_Ratio),(Net_Income_Y2*Dividend_Payment_
Ratio),MAX(Dividend_Base,(Net_RE_Y1+Net_Income_Y2)*Dividend_Payment_Ratio))
```

The =IF(AND tells Excel that conditions are about to be listed. They are that there is a profit in Y2, and that the net retained earnings plus second year net earnings are greater than 0, So there is some money available to pay a dividend if both of these are satisfied. What is that dividend to be? It's the dividend payment ratio multiplied by the net income for the current year. If the conditions aren't satisfied, then it's half of the cumulative retained earnings, if there are any, but 0 if that number is still negative (the latter choice being accomplished by using MAX). Said differently, this last part is 0 if the net earnings are still in a loss position, but half of the net earnings over the two-year period if the losses from the first year have been more than covered in the second.

Cash management

Once the model is built and populated, we can look back at the figures and consider our original estimates regarding financing, as well as any actions that might be taken based on the results. Often the most important of these is cash management. In the case of our model, while we know that airlines need a big cash buffer to survive in the event of major changes or negative events, one matter likely to draw attention is the large cash position at the end of each year. At a minimum most of this cash should be invested to produce extra income; however, the best investment of it would be to reduce debt. We are paying 5% interest on the bond and the aircraft mortgage, but the closing cash positions for any year have never fallen below $100 million. Did we need to issue the bond at all? We would need to look at a monthly Cash Budget for the first year to answer that question definitively, but it seems likely that we didn't need that money. When we take it out, a major expense (bond interest) of $2.5 million per year will disappear; the remaining cash will not fall by the entire $50 million, and we will be better off by $12.5 million at the end of Year 5. Did we need the entire $100 million mortgage on the aircraft? Again, perhaps not; we can't pay it all off, but what if we reduced it by $20 or $30 million, thereby further reducing our interest costs?

Our shareholders are going to be looking at management's performance. Do these plans reflect wise management of the company's assets? If the company is going to do as well as we predict, should we not be scaling in Y2 or perhaps Y3, adding an aircraft, a route, or other income-generating activities? It seems that by Y4 we might be able to carry no debt; or, more enterprisingly, to grow the operation to service another route or two. The shareholders will not be happy to see the company accumulate a vast amount of cash which sits idle. If debt is not to be reduced, then perhaps their dividends should be increased.

Ratios

TABLE 82: Ratios

	A	B	C	D	E	F	G
1	**Air Amlani**						
2	**Key Financial Ratios**						
3	**As At December 31**						
4							
5		**2025**	**2026**	**2027**	**2028**	**2029**	
6	**Liquidity**						
7	Current Ratio	3.41	5.64	6.36	7.45	6.07	Current Assets/Current Liabilities
8	**Profitability**						
9	Gross Margin	0.76	0.76	0.77	0.77	0.77	Gross Profit/Revenue
10	Operating Margin	0.62	0.64	0.65	0.65	0.65	Operating Income/Revenue
11	Net Margin	0.34	0.33	0.32	0.31	0.31	Net Income/Revenue
12	Return on Assets	0.13	0.12	0.12	0.12	0.13	Net Income/Total Assets
13	Return on Equity	0.51	0.44	0.35	0.29	0.24	Net Income/Shareholders' Equity
14	**Solvency**						
15	Debt to Equity	2.76	2.18	1.68	1.34	0.72	Total Debt/Shareholders' Equity
16	Interest Coverage	1.67	1.76	1.85	1.95	2.06	EBIT/Interest Expense
17	Debt Ratio	0.69	0.62	0.58	0.53	0.39	Total Debt/Total Assets

Calculation of key financial ratios is an added value for users of the model. This can be accomplished by building formulas which reference the relevant parts of the model.

Relevant ratios will differ by type of business. Business types with inventories will benefit from the addition of a quick ratio in the Liquidity area, along with Efficiency Ratios such as inventory turnover, AR turnover and asset turnover. Publicly listed companies (those with shares traded on a recognized exchange) will be interested in *some* of the standard ratios such as EPS, earnings per share; however, it is virtually impossible to predict share prices in a start-up model so ratios like Price to Earnings and Price to Book, which rely on market prices, cannot be reliably predicted.

References

TABLE 83: References

References	
(1)	https://www.hinterlandtravel.com/el-salvador/destinations/usa
(2)	https://www.lonelyplanet.com/el-salvador
(3)	https://www.flightconnections.com/flights-from-san-salvador-sal
(4)	https://www.worlddata.info/america/el-salvador/hurricanes.php#
(5)	Based on averaging many comparative prices at skyscanner.net
(6)	https://www.statista.com/statistics/1270410/duty-free-shops-footfall-rate-us/ Approximately 60% of passengers buy from duty-free, but only 7.3% on board The average profit from each on-board sale is $40
(7)	https://jet-a1-fuel.com/price/canada
(8)	https://app.aircraftcostcalculator.com/content/emailreports/2f6a642e-1542-4f2a-9427-977bb175917d.htm
(9)	https://www.yvr.ca/en/business/fees-and-charges
(10)	http://www1.navcanada.ca/OnlineForms/FeeCalculator/FeeCalculatorIntro_en.asp
(11)	https://www.vox.com/the-goods/2020/2/10/21117507/airplane-food-explained
(12)	https://app.aircraftcostcalculator.com/content/emailreports/2f6a642e-1542-4f2a-9427-977bb175917d.htm
(13)	Regulations limit a typical airline pilot to about 900 hrs per year "in the air" but typically they work, train and test 2 hours for every hour in the air. https://www.flyingmag.com/guides/how-many-hours-do-pilots-work/
(14)	https://ca.indeed.com/career/captain/salaries
(15)	https://ca.indeed.com/career/first-officer/salaries
(16)	https://www.glassdoor.ca/Salaries/senior-cabin-crew-salary-SRCH_KO0,17.htm
(17)	https://www.glassdoor.com/Salaries/canada-cabin-crew-salary-SRCH_IL.0,6_IN3_KO7,17.htm
(18)	Difficult to estimate, but Air Canada's are 5.6% and British Airways 5.9%, both based on the latest annual reports.
(19)	Large volume card processors such as Global Payments typically quote just under 1% for processing Canadian card transactions, and approximately 2.2% for foreign cards. We anticipate a 50/50 split therefore 1.5% is a fair estimate
(20)	Air Canada's web and IT costs are 3.29% based on last annual report. We believe 4% of revenue is conservative.
(21)	https://www.statista.com/statistics/273941/prices-of-boeing-aircraft-by-type/
(22)	https://www.controller.com/listings/for-sale/boeing/737/jet-aircraft/3

We've copiously maintained a list of sources and assumptions. The reference page will look somewhat like this (nobody ever reads it as such!).

The executive summary

When we compiled the Cover Page for this model, we commented that the last thing to be written was the executive summary. We have reached that point! It's going to be a succinct summary of the findings we have made by building the model. To generate relevant content, we need to think about the kinds of questions our intended audience will have. This will demonstrate the power of the model. Let's think about the business and pose some of those questions, then consider how to answer them.

(1) Is the business plan viable as it exists? *We look at the Cash Budget and Income Statement, and conclude "yes."*

(2) The plane we have chosen has the standard configuration of 139 economy, 21 business and 20 first class seats. There are other configurations available, for example 189 all economy seats. We are not confident that we can sell premium seats on this route—what will happen if we take the alternative configuration? *On the Inputs page, we change the Service Data for seats to 189-0-0 and compare cash flows and net profits. Our range of profits for the five years was $30.2 million to $37.9 million; with the new configuration it drops to $4.6 to $10.9 million. That's a pretty hefty drop which highlights our dependence on selling premium seats to keep profits high.* Quick check—did the Statement of Financial Position remain balanced when we made the change? Yes!

(3) We have an opportunity to add freight revenues. How would we account for that? *We'd add a section for freight operations on the Inputs page, plug in the estimated numbers then flow them through to the Cash Budget and Financial Statements. It would merely be an extension of what we've already done. We would have to consider the effects of adding this freight operation on all aspects of the business and ensure that it increases net profits.*

(4) We don't think the Load Factor of 90% is realistic. All other things being equal, what is the lowest load factor at which we could break even in the first year and start to see profits in the second? *Here we would use Goal Seek. Setting a target of 0 for Net Income in 2024, we would address decision variable cell Load_Factor on the Inputs page. The answer is 45%.* Wow, all other things being equal that's a huge margin to play with! Quick checks: with this result, are we still OK for cash flows (yes); does the Statement of Financial Position still balance (yes!).

(5) We think we'd have a better chance of selling 90% of the Business and First-Class seats if the factors were 2x economy and 3x economy. What would this do to our profits? *Change the Business_Factor and First-Factor cells on the Inputs page to 2 and 3 and review the profits. Again, check cash flows and make sure the Statement of Financial Position is still balanced.* We'd still make a profit every year, and there would be enough cash flow to redeem all the bonds at the end of 2029. The Financial Position still balances.

(6) In order to break more effectively into the market, we'd like to lower ticket prices. What is the lowest economy ticket price we can offer to break even in 2024 and make a profit after that? *Goal Seek to the rescue again. Set net income after tax to 0 and change Economy_Return on the Inputs page.* The answer is $388. Wow! At that price we'd probably achieve a 99% load factor!

(7) We would be more competitive if we didn't charge for baggage or reserved seats? What would happen if we eliminated those charges? *Go to the Inputs page and re-set these decision variables to 0. Everything you want to know will calculate immediately.*

(8) Global warming is a huge problem in the tropics. What if there are 20 days of hurricanes next year instead of the usual 9? *Go to the Inputs page and change Act_of_God_Days to 20. Everything will recalculate automatically.*

(9) It looks like we will have a strong cash position even in the first year. Do we really need the bond issue? *Go to the Inputs page and reset the Bond_Issue cell to 0 (that will take care of the redemption, too). Then review Cash Budget and the other Financial Statements.* We will still have positive cash, though only $12 million, at the end of 2024. We perhaps could consider lowering each of the financing components to reduce overall investment by about $30 million.

(10) We decide that we don't like Boeings so much. What difference would it make if we bought an Airbus? *Well, we don't have to start all over again. We need to gather up all the data for the Inputs page and key it into the relevant cells. All the calculations and results will still be valid!*

And so on, and so on. Our colleagues in marketing, sales, advertising, finance and of course the bean counters and external consultants will all have their own ideas to insert; given appropriate instructions they are welcome to play with the model and see the effects of the changes they would like to see. Meanwhile, our last task is to write that executive summary. Using our model and the above experiments, here is the Cover page with the summary now included.

TABLE 84: Cover page with Executive Summary

Course Ref:	BUSI 414
Course Name:	Data Visualization
Team:	The High Flyers
Students:	A Amlani 12345678
	R Davis 66676602
	S Rahmani 87654321
	M Mouse 12122121

DATA MODEL: AIR AMLANI

Business Proposition: We will operate a single aircraft, a Boeing 737-900ER, daily, on one route YVR-SAL-YVR. The route is not served by a direct flight with any other airline, and many Central American travellers do not want to connect through the U.S.A., which requires a transit visa (1). Canada has a large Salvadoran population. They, and Canadian tourists, are incentivized to visit El Salvador due to recent improvements in the security situation (2). SAL is also a potential hub for travel to several other Latin American destinations (3).

Executive Summary: The business plan appears viable. Using the specified aircraft and pricing economy seats at $800 return, just a shade over the average price for a journey with connections inside the USA, we will need approximately $170 million of financing which can be achieved from a combination of share capital, bond issue and a mortgage on the aircraft. Our initial projections indicate a return on investment of approximately 16% can be achieved overall, rising to 21% in the fifth year. There is considerable latitude in our calculations; break-even could be achieved with tickets at half the price charged by Air Canada, Delta or AeroMexico; there is scope to increase revenues by adding freight carriage. Should we fail to sell sufficient premium seats, there is considerable room to decrease their prices by half or more while remaining profitable.

Copyright © 2025, A Amlani & R Paul Davis

IMPORTANT LEGAL NOTICE: This document has been prepared for internal use only and should NOT be relied upon by potential investors or lenders. A full prospectus will be issued in due course if the Directors determine that the business proposition is viable.

Other things we could do

Accountants and investors like projections, predictions, analyses, and many other mathematical products. All the basic data are here in this workbook to produce those on demand—the only limit is our imagination.

The mathematical part of our task is done. Depending on the intended audience we may now want to spice up our report with some carefully chosen visualizations to make it more interesting, in the earlier chapters of this book you learned some ways to do that using familiar tools.

What to do when your balance sheet doesn't

You've worked hard, scaffolded your financial model in Microsoft Excel, input all the figures. You've checked and double-checked your formulas and reached that magic moment when the final cells are completed in Excel. You add a checksum (total assets minus total liabilities) to the Balance Sheet. You hope to see a row of zeroes across the years. No – no – no! There are values in the checksums that shouldn't be there. What do you do now? Don't be disheartened, most complex models require some corrections before they work flawlessly.

Here is a logical series of steps and tricks to track down the error(s) and arrive at a set of zero differences which will survive stress-testing.

1. *Make a backup copy of your work.*

   As you proceed through these steps, we are going to try many changes. Make a backup copy first, so that you can revert to your original if you lose track of what you've done.

2. *Force Recalculation (F9).*

   Before you do anything else, use F9 to force Excel to recalculate all the values in your work. Occasionally a stale calculation will remain and mess with later calculations. This is rare, but it takes just a second to do.

3. *Understand the beast.*

   Look at the checksums as they progress through the three or five years of your model. There are three typical scenarios:

TABLE 85: Imbalances

a) Imbalance increases at a constant rate

	2025	2025	2027	2028	2029
Checksum	20	40	60	80	100

b) Imbalance stays the same across years

	2025	2025	2027	2028	2029
Checksum	-	20	20	20	20

c) No discernable relationship between imbalances

	2025	2025	2027	2028	2029
Checksum	20	30	35	140	197

If you see type a, a constant increase in the imbalance amount, you are going to be searching for an error which is repeated year after year. Type b, a constant amount, is the easiest, because you can pin the error down to the first year that it happens, and when you correct that, the others will also correct. Type c means there are multiple errors, there will be more work to do.

4. *Check all financial statements for magic numbers.*

   Magic numbers are hard-coded numbers within any of the financial statements. Including zeroes. There shouldn't be any! In Excel, click on the Formulas tab then select Show Formulas. Look carefully for any numbers which appear in your formulas. If there are any, correct them with references to the input pages or schedules.

5. *Run a search for the checksum number.*

   Use Excel's search facility to run through all your sheets for instances of the checksum number. Search first on Values, then on Formulas. If you find any matches, consider carefully whether they could be implicated in the final imbalance. This works particularly well with highly detailed values such as 100.97, less well with round numbers.

6. *Run a search for double the checksum number, and half of it.*

   Often an imbalance is created by a wrong treatment (a minus sign that should be a plus sign, a debit that should be a credit) of a number. If this has happened the imbalance may be half, or twice, the erroneous number.

7. *Apply the rule of 9.*

   Divide the checksum number by 9. If the result is a whole number, with no remainder, this is an indication that there may be a transposition error in your data. For example, if in one place you typed 46 where 64 was the right number, the imbalance will be 18 (divided by 9 = 2).

8. *Try changing numbers in your inputs and schedules.*

   Before you start this test, use the New Window feature on the View tab to see your balance sheet in a separate pop-up. Change one input. If the checksum (imbalance) stays the same, that input likely isn't implicated in the problem. Re-set it to the original value and change the next. Work through them all, and if changing one changes the imbalance, investigate all uses of that input to see if there's an error.

9. *Use Excel's audit tools.*

   On the formula tab, there are two functions to trace precedents and dependents. Use these to check that formulas correctly refer to the intended source cells.

10. *Recreate your most complex formulas.*

    Identify the formulas that have many arguments or which gave you serious intellectual challenges, such as income tax calculations. Re-build these from scratch and compare to your original.

11. *Check for circular references.*

    Excel has built-in checks to identify circular references and other errors, they are available on the Formulas tab.

    If none of these techniques locate errors, the last step is to go back to the beginning and carefully check all your work, step by step. If you find one error, correct it, and the checksums still don't balance, consider what you learned from the first one before continuing – it may be that the same error is repeated and now easier to find.

Conclusion

The essential principles for financial modeling are careful planning, robust structure and the deployment of good techniques to ensure accuracy. Following the steps outlined above you can create financial models which address immediate needs and provide insights for decision-making.

Multiple Choice Questions for Chapter 11

1. The three elements of financial modeling are:
    a. inputs, decision variables and financial statements.
    b. inputs, processing and outputs.
    c. inputs, schedules and decision variables.
2. A magic number is:
    a. a hard-coded value in financial statements.
    b. a number which updates automatically with changed conditions.
    c. a number which is generated from other numbers.
3. ___ capital is required to produce a business plan, while ___ capital is required to get the business up and running.
    a. Seed; working
    b. Start-up; working
    c. Seed; start-up
4. According to the Harvard Business School, ____ percent of high potential start-ups end in bankruptcy.
    a. 20–30
    b. 30–40
    c. 40–50
5. In Microsoft Excel, named cells:
    a. cannot be referred to on different worksheets.
    b. cannot be used in what-if formulas.
    c. are absolute references.
6. Depreciation is:
    a. a non-cash expense.
    b. necessarily included in cash flow statements.
    c. deductible from taxable income for tax purposes in Canada.
7. The B.C. *PayDays Act* requires:
    a. all salaries to be paid by the end of each month.
    b. at least one payday per month.
    c. at least two paydays per month.
8. Scaffolding refers to:
    a. the formulas and calculations included in a financial model;
    b. the visible structural elements of a financial model;
    c. the program used to create a financial model (*e.g.* Excel).
9. Bond redemption:
    a. is amortized over the life of the bond
    b. is a non-cash expense
    c. is included in the cash flow statement at full value when it occurs.
10. In a financial model, the last thing written is:
    a. the executive summary.
    b. the balance sheet.
    c. the cash flow statement.

11. Why is it important to use a consistent color key in a financial model? Choose the best answer.
    a. The final presentation must be aesthetically pleasing to the viewer.
    b. The financial industry recognizes specific color conventions which modelers are expected to follow.
    c. Color codes inform the user what they can change for what-if questions without breaking the model, and indicate the sources of inputs and outputs.
    d. Color codes indicate the reliability of the data used.

APPENDIX: LIMITATIONS OF SOLVER

To follow through this demonstration, please download the file Animal Medication.xlsx. This worksheet was built to demonstrate optimization concepts in Chapter 4, but we will now develop it using Solver in a failed attempt to find the optimal mix of cost price.

As a prelude, please name a couple of cells. Name the Gross Profit cell J82 GP, the Optimal Sales total in J79 Optimal_Sales, and the Order quantity in D85 Max_Sales. Go up to D50 and name it Test_Value. With this done, go to the Data tab and select Solver from the Analyze group. The usual dialog box will appear:

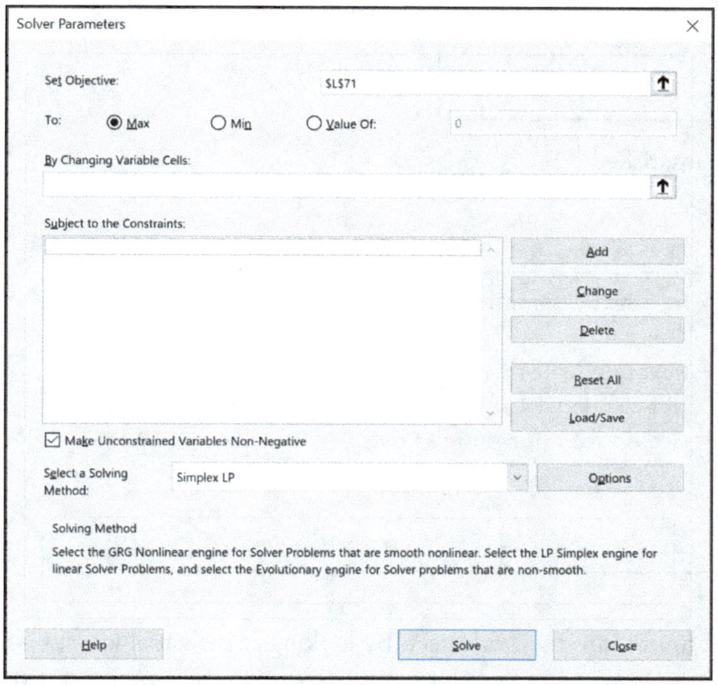

FIGURE 171: Solver dialog box

Unlike with many dialog boxes, this one can be kept on screen while you move around the underlying worksheet. For the objective, ensure the Max button is selected, then click in the Set Objective box and click on the Gross Profit in the Income Statement or just type GP, the name of the cell (J82).

Next select the variable cell to be changed: it is the test value cell which we've used throughout this model, D50 or Test_Value.

For constraints, we cannot sell more than 100 books because of the number of students enrolled; therefore, next to the constraints box click on Add. A small dialog box will appear in which you can set the cell reference to J79 (Optimum_Sales), the operator as <= (must be equal to or less than), and the constraint as D85, Max_Sales.

Clicking OK will bring back the large dialog box, with the constraint listed; for the solving method, select Simplex LP. Now click on Solve.

In a fraction of a second, Solver reports that it has found a problem through a new dialog box.

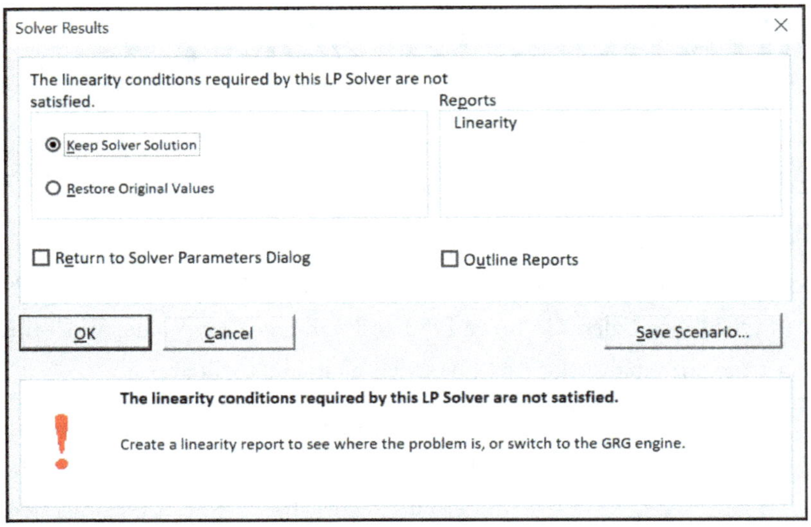

FIGURE 172: Solver conditions unsatisfied

Solver's linearity conditions are not satisfied by this model. It suggests the solution—to switch to the GRG method of solution. Click on Solver again, all the previous entries are saved but now switch the Solver method to GRG Nonlinear. Click Solve again, and in an instant Solver delivers a result.

To see it, click OK.

TABLE 86: Solver's incorrect solution

Variable Costs Table	
Order	**Cost**
1	$25
20	$ 23
40	$ 21
60	$ 19
80	$ 17
100	$ 15

Income Statement	
Revenue (Sales * Price)	$ 3,061
Net cost (cost * sales)	$ 1,092
Gross Profit (Revenue - Cost)	$ 1,969

Solver has substituted the optimal values that it found into the worksheet. By looking at the variable cell C48, we see that the apparent optimal price is $59, this will produce 52 sales at a cost of $21 per book, and the maximized profit of $1969.

As you might have guessed, this is not the correct result. Go back to the original exercise now and look at the manually produced optimization—49 books sold at a price of $61, for a profit of $2,058. Close, as the saying goes, "but no cigar."

ANSWER KEY FOR MULTIPLE CHOICE QUESTIONS

Chapter 1

1 d; 2 d; 3 a; 4 b; 5 b; 6 b; 7 a; 8 d; 9 d; 10 c; 11 a; 12 a; 13 c; 14 a; 15 c; 16 c.

Chapter 2

1 a; 2 a; 3 a; 4 d; 5 d; 6 d; 7 a; 8 a; 9 b; 10 b; 11 b; 12 a; 13 a.

Chapter 3

1 b; 2 b; 3 b; 4 c; 5 a; 6 a; 7 d; 8 c; 9 c; 10 a; 11 a.

Chapter 4

1 a; 2 d; 3 c; 4 c; 5 c; 6 c; 7 c; 8 c; 9 c; 10 b; 11 c; 12 c; 13 c.

Chapter 5

1 a; 2 c; 3 c; 4 c; 5 c; 6 a; 7 d.

Chapter 6

1 a; 2 c; 3 a; 4 b; 5 b; 6 b; 7 a; 8 b; 9 c; 10 a..

Chapter 7

1 b; 2 c; 3 a; 4 b; 5 b; 6 b; 7 a; 8 a; 9 a; 10 b.

Chapter 8

1 a; 2 b; 3 c; 4 c; 5b; 6 a; 7 b; 8 a; 9 a; 10 c; 11 b.

Chapter 9: Regression Exercise

1. 0.670565; 2. 40.211166; 3. Education; 4. Census Population; 5. Yes—Census Population (0.4900347); 6. Moderate

Chapter 9

1 a; 2 b; 3 a; 4 b; 5 a; 6 b; 7 c; 8 a.

Chapter 10

1 a; 2 a; 3 a; 4 a; 5 a; 6 a; 7 a; 8 b; 9 c.

Chapter 11

1 b; 2 a; 3 c; 4 b; 5 c; 6 a; 7 c; 8 b; 9 c; 10 a; 11 c..

TABLE OF ABBREVIATIONS

Abbreviation	Full Form
AI	Artificial or Augmented Intelligence
AII	Accelerated Investment Incentive
Avtur	Aviation Turbine Fuel
BBC	British Broadcasting Corporation
BI	Business Intelligence
CAPEX	Capital Expenditure
CAPM	Capital Asset Pricing Model
CCA	Capital Cost Allowance
CORRA	Canadian Overnight Repo Rate
CPA	Certified Public Accountant
CRA	Canada Revenue Agency
CRAAP	Currency, Relevance, Authority, Accuracy, Purpose
CRP	Country Risk Premium
CSRP	Company Specific Risk Premium
DAX	Data Analysis Expressions
DCF	Discounted Cash Flows
EBITDA	Earnings before Interest, Taxes, Depreciation and Amortization
FBA	Fellow of the British Academy
FIFA	Federation Internationale de Football Association
FMV	Fair Market Value
GDP	Gross Domestic Product
GPS	Global Positioning System
GRG	Generalized Reduced Gradient
IDEA	Interactive Data Extraction and Analysis
IPO	Initial Public Offering
IQR	Interquartile Range
LL.D.	Doctor of Laws
LNG	Liquified Natural Gas
LP	Linear Programming
MAPE	Mean Absolute Percentage Error
MBE	Most Excellent Order of the British Empire
MAE	Mean Absolute Error
NV	Net Present Value
PC	Personal Computer
PDF	Portable Document Format
Ph.D.	Doctor of Philosophy
RMSE	Root Mean Squared Error

RRR	Required Rate of Return
S&P	Standard & Poor's
SEO	Search Engine Optimization
TSX	Toronto Stock Exchange
UBC	University of British Columbia
WACC	Weighted Average Cost of Capital

REFERENCES

Acampora, J. (2023, November 2). When to use pie charts—Best practices. *Excel Campus*. Retrieved July 12, 2025, from https://www.excelcampus.com/charts/pie-charts-best-practices/

Aeropay Ltd & Anor v Bentolila, https://www.casemine.com/judgement/uk/5b46f1ff2c94e0775e7efa08

Ambady, N., & Rosenthal, R. (1993). Half a minute: Predicting teacher evaluations from thin slices of nonverbal behavior and physical attractiveness. *Journal of Personality and Social Psychology, 64*(3), 431–441. https://doi.org/10.1037/0022-3514.64.3.431

Anscombe, F. J. (1973). Graphs in statistical analysis. The American Statistician, 27(1), 17–21. https://doi.org/10.1080/00031305.1973.10478966

Associated Press. (2021, May 27). Syria's Assad wins a fourth term in a predictable landslide. https://www.yahoo.com/news/syrias-assad-wins-fourth-term-204335016.html

BC Transplant. (n.d.). *Organ Donor Registry*. BC Transplant. https://register.transplant.bc.ca/

Bendix, A., & Carman, J. (2022, May 23). Map: Monkeypox confirmed in 16 countries. *NBC News*. Retrieved July 12, 2025, from https://www.nbcnews.com/health/health-news/map-countries-confirmed-monkeypox-cases-2022-outbreak-rcna30124

Berger, V. (2007). Selection bias and covariate imbalances in randomized clinical trials (Statistics in practice). Wiley.

Bergstrom, C. & West, D. (2020). Calling bullshit: The art of skepticism in a data-driven world. Random House.

Bergstrom, C. & West, D. (2020). Calling bullshit: The art of skepticism in a data-driven world. Random House.

Bergstrom, C. & West, D. (2016). The principle of proportional ink. http://callingbullshit.org/tools/tools_proportional_ink.html.

Berinato, S. (2016, June). Visualizations that really work. *Harvard Business Review*. https://hbr.org/2016/06/visualizations-that-really-work

Blakeslee, Sarah (2004). The CRAAP test. LOEX Quarterly. 31 (3).

Blanchar, J. C. (2016). *Familiarity bias: Examining a cognitive-affective mechanism underlying ideological support for the status quo* (Doctoral dissertation). University of Arkansas. ScholarWorks@UARK. https://scholarworks.uark.edu/etd/1758

British Columbia Coroners Service. (n.d.). *Winter activity: Statistical report*. Government of British Columbia. https://www2.gov.bc.ca/assets/gov/birth-adoption-death-marriage-and-divorce/deaths/coroners-service/statistical/winter-activity.pdf

British Columbia Government. (2022, April 13). Motor Cycle Safety—the rider and the gear. https://www2.gov.bc.ca/gov/content/transportation/driving-and-cycling/road-safety-rules-and-consequences/motorcycle-safety

Bruno, G. (2022, December 1). Sexual health: 5 neutraceutical ingredients to watch. https://www.linkedin.com/pulse/sexual-health-5-nutraceutical-ingredients-watch-gene-bruno/

Bryman, A. (2016). *Social research methods* (5th ed.). Oxford University Press.

Cannon, B. (2024, May 6). 20 surprising historical connections that are mind-blowing. Retrieved July 12, 2025, from https://www.rd.com/list/mind-blowing-historical-connections/

CIKS Anaadi. (2024, October 8). Stories as a way of preserving Indigenous knowledge. Center for Indigenous Knowledge Systems. https://www.ciks.anaadi.org/post/stories-as-a-way-of-preserving-Indigenous-knowledge

Cleave, P. (2021, May 28). How to reduce social desirability bias. SmartSurvey. https://www.smartsurvey.com/blog/how-to-reduce-social-desirability-bias

Cleveland, W. S., & McGill, R. (1984). Graphical perception: Theory, experimentation, and application to the development of graphical methods. *Journal of the American Statistical Association, 79*(387), 531–554.

Cooper, H., Gibbons-Neff, T., Schmitt, E., & Barnes, J.E. (2023, February 2). Russia and Ukraine have lost a staggering 200,000 troops killed or wounded, officials say. The New York Times. https://www.nytimes.com/2023/02/02/us/politics/ukraine-russia-casualties.html

Creswell, J. W., & Creswell, J. D. (2018). *Research design: Qualitative, quantitative, and mixed methods approaches* (5th ed.). SAGE Publications.

Croizet, J.-C. (2012) *The racism of intelligence: How mental testing practices have constituted an institutionalized form of group domination*. In Bobo, L.D. et al. (2012) *The Oxford handbook of African American citizenship, 1865–present*. Oxford University Press.

Damodaran, A. (2025, January 9). *Country default spreads and risk premiums* [Webpage]. NYU Stern.

Darley, J. M., & Gross, P. H. (1983). A hypothesis-confirming bias in labeling effects. Journal of Personality and Social Psychology, 44 (1), 20–33.

Dignen, B. (2011). *Communicating across cultures*. Cambridge University Press.

History.com. (2025, May 28). Why did the dinosaurs die out? https://www.history.com/topics/pre-history/why-did-the-dinosaurs-die-out-1

Tufte, E. (1983). *The Visual Display of Quantitative Information*. Graphics Press.

eforebrahim. (2022, June 11). *Data Visualization Cheat Sheet by Dr. Andrew Abela* [Reddit post]. r/learnmachinelearning. Reddit. https://www.reddit.com/r/learnmachinelearning/comments/va2omm/data_visualization_cheat_sheet_by_dr_andrew_abela/

Elder, L., & Paul, R. (2012). The thinker's guide to intellectual standards: The words that name them and the criteria that define them. Foundation for Critical Thinking Press.

Elections BC. (2024, November 8). 2024 General Election results. https://electionsbcenr.blob.core.windows.net/electionsbcenr/Results_7097_GE-2024-10-19_Party.html

Ellis, A. (1962). *Reason and emotion in psychotherapy*. Lyle Stuart.

Elmore, S. A., & Weston, E. H. (2020, June). Predatory journals: What they are and how to avoid them. *Toxicologic Pathology, 48*(4), 607–610. https://doi.org/10.1177/0192623320920209

Encyclopaedia Britannica. (n.d.). *Dodo*. In *Britannica.com*. https://www.britannica.com/animal/dodo-extinct-bird

Engaging Data. (2023, January 14). US County Electoral Map – Land Area vs Population. Engaging Data. https://engaging-data.com/county-electoral-map-land-vs-population/

EPA. (2024, August 30). Learn about Volkswagen violations. https://www.epa.gov/vw/learn-about-volkswagen-violations

Evans, N. (2012, April 9). Ben Hur bloopers: Can you spot the mistakes in the ancient Roman epic? https://www.mirror.co.uk/news/uk-news/ben-hur-bloopers-can-you-784963

Festinger, L. (1957). *A theory of cognitive dissonance.* Stanford University Press.

Few, S. (2004). Show me the numbers: Designing tables and graphs to enlighten (1st ed.). Analytics Press.

Few, S. (2009). Now you see it: Simple visualization techniques for quantitative analysis. Analytics Press.

Few, S. (2018). The data loom: Weaving understanding by thinking critically and scientifically. Analytics Press.

FlightConnections. (n.d.). *Direct flights from San Salvador (SAL)* [Webpage]. FlightConnections. https://www.flightconnections.com/flights-from-san-salvador-sal

Fractalytics. (n.d.). *Bubble chart with D3.js* [Webpage]. Fractalytics. https://fractalytics.io/bubble-chart-with-d3js

Francis, A. (n.d.). Case study of Apple Inc: "Think Different" Branding Campaign. https://www.mbaknol.com/management-case-studies/case-study-of-apple-inc-think-different/

Gallo, C. (2024, February 27). Scientists pinpoint the exact moment people lose interest in a presentation. *Inc.*. https://www.inc.com/carmine-gallo/scientists-pinpoint-exact-moment-people-lose-interest-in-a-presentation.html

Galton, F. (1885). Regression towards mediocrity in hereditary stature. *The Journal of the Anthropological Institute of Great Britain and Ireland, 15*, 246–263.

Gonzalez, G. (2018, October 10). How Amazon accidentally invented a sexist hiring algorithm. https://www.inc.com/guadalupe-gonzalez/amazon-artificial-intelligence-ai-hiring-tool-hr.html

Gordon, M. J. (1959). *Dividends, earnings, and stock prices. The Review of Economics and Statistics, 41*(2), 99–105. https://doi.org/10.2307/1927792

Grass FactCheck. (2023, February 7). Fake News. Retrieved July 12, 2025, from https://factcheck.ge/en/story/41613-disinformation-according-to-the-data-of-israeli-intelligence-russia-killed-157-000-ukrainian-troops-and-over-1-500-nato-military-personnel-in-ukraine

Groves, R. M., et al. (2009). *Survey methodology* (2nd ed.). Wiley.

Groves, R., Singer, E., & Corning, A. (2000, February). Leverage-saliency theory of survey participation: Description and an illustration. Public Opinion Quarterly 64(3): 299–308.

Handwerk, B. (2023, December 20). *What are the Pyramids of Giza—and who built them? National Geographic.* https://www.nationalgeographic.com/history/article/giza-pyramids

Harris, G. (2008, March 26). Cigarette company paid for lung cancer study. https://www.nytimes.com/2008/03/26/health/research/26lung.html

Harvard Business School. Why companies fail—and how their owners can bounce back. https:///hbswk.hbs.edu/item/6591.html

Hennig, C. (2019, May 21). Motorcyclist deaths in B.C. spike 50% in a year. https://www.cbc.ca/news/canada/british-columbia/motorcyclist-deaths-spike-2018-1.5142877

Hickey, W. (2013, June 17). The worst chart in the world. https://www.businessinsider.com/pie-charts-are-the-worst-2013-6

Hinterland Travel. (n.d.). *US visa requirements for El Salvador citizens.* https://www.hinterlandtravel.com/el-salvador/destinations/usa

Holmes, O. W. (1861). *Currents and counter-currents in medical science: With other addresses and essays.* Boston: Ticknor and Fields.

http://campusphere.de/datensicht/files/EdwardR.Tufte.%20Tufte

IBM. (n.d.). *Data visualization.* https://www.ibm.com/topics/data-visualization

Informal-Ask. (2020, September 14). Costco ruined my business (warning and rant) [Reddit post]. r/Costco. Reddit. https://www.reddit.com/r/Costco/comments/istmpc/costco_ruined_my_business_warning_and_rant/

Inhofe, J. (2012). The greatest hoax: How the global warming conspiracy threatens your future. WorldNetDaily Books.

Kahneman D., & Tversky A. (1972). Subjective probability: A judgement of representativeness. *Cognit. Psychol.* 3 430–454.

Kahneman, D., & Tversky, A. (1972). Subjective probability: A judgment of representativeness. *Cognitive Psychology, 3*(3), 430–454. https://doi.org/10.1016/0010-0285(72)90016-3

Kahneman, D., & Tversky, A. (1973). On the psychology of prediction. *Psychological Review, 80*(4), 237–251. https://doi.org/10.1037/h0034747

Kahneman, D., Knetsch, J. L., & Thaler, R. H. (1991). Anomalies: The endowment effect, loss aversion, and status quo bias. *Journal of Economic Perspectives*, 5(1), 193–206. https://doi.org/10.1257/jep.5.1.193

Kenny, D.T. (2015, March 22). Music to die for: how genre affects popular musicians' life expectancy. https://theconversation.com/music-to-die-for-how-genre-affects-popular-musicians-life-expectancy-36660

Knaflic, C. N. (2015). Storytelling with data. Wiley.

Knaflic, C. N. (2015, p.61). Storytelling with data. Wiley.

Kosara, R. (2019). *Circular part-to-whole charts using the area visual cue.* Proceedings of the EuroVis 2019 Conference. https://media.eagereyes.org/papers/2019/Kosara-EuroVis-2019a.pdf

Kuhn, G. (2019). Experiencing the Impossible: The science of magic. Chicago University Press.

Kuhn, G., Amlani, A. A., & Rensink, R. A. (2008). Towards a science of magic. *Trends in Cognitive Sciences*, 12(9), 349–354.

Leber, R. (2018, February 26). 3 years ago, we all laughed at James Inhofe's snowball. The joke was on us. https://www.motherjones.com/environment/2018/02/3-years-ago-we-all-laughed-at-james-inhofes-snowball-the-joke-was-on-us/

Levin, D. T., & Simons, D. J. (2000). Perceiving stability in a changing world: Combining shots and integrating views in motion pictures and the real world. *Media Psychology*, 2(4), 357–380.

Loftus, E. F., & Palmer, J. C. (1974). Reconstruction of automobile destruction: An example of the interaction between language and memory. *Journal of Verbal Learning & Verbal Behavior, 13*(5), 585–589.

Lonely Planet. (n.d.). *El Salvador.* https://www.lonelyplanet.com/el-salvador

Luellen, E. (2018, October 22). Why averages are often wrong, Towards Data Science, October 22, 2018.

Maishman, E., & Lukiv, J. Ukraine war: Zelensky aide reveals up to 13,000 war dead. (2022, December 1). https://www.bbc.com/news/world-europe-63829973

MarcRummy. (n.d.). *Tweets* [Twitter profile]. X (formerly Twitter). https://twitter.com/MarcRummy

McDermott, R. (1980). Profile: Ray L. Birdwhistell. *The Kinesics Report.* 2 (3): 1–16.

Mehrabian, A. **(1971)**. *Silent messages.* Wadsworth.

Microsoft. (n.d.). Present your data in a doughnut chart. *Microsoft Support.* https://support.microsoft.com/en-us/office/present-your-data-in-a-doughnut-chart-0ac0efde-34e2-4dc6-9b7f-ac93d1783353

Morgan, N. (2014, May 14). Decisions Don't Start with Data. Harvard Business Review.

Treacy, M. (n.d.) *Interactive Excel Dashboards.* https://www.youtube.com/watch?v=K74_FNnlIF8&list=PLmd91OWgLVSLy87GfZCR74BG1nhO7ER0s&index=1

National Safety Council. (2018). *Distracted driving: A deadly epidemic.* https://www.amljia.org/wp-content/uploads/NOV_Distracted-Driving.pdf

National Safety Council. (2020). Just drive: Understanding distracted driving and inattention blindness.

Newbold, P., Carlson, W. L., & Thorne, B. (2013). *Statistics for business and economics* (8th ed.). Pearson Education.

NHS Blood and Transplant. (n.d.). *Do not donate.* NHS Organ Donation. https://www.organdonation.nhs.uk/register-your-decision/do-not-donate/

O'Neil, C. (2016). *Weapons of math destruction: How big data increases inequality and threatens democracy.* Crown Publishing Group.

Pearl, J and Mackenzie, D. 2018. The book of why. Basic Books.

Phillips, A. (2017, June 16). 'They're rapists': President Trump's campaign launch speech two years later, annotated. *The Washington Post.* https://www.washingtonpost.com/news/the-fix/wp/2017/06/16/theyre-rapists-presidents-trump-campaign-launch-speech-two-years-later-annotated/

Rasiel, E.M. (1999). The McKinsey Way. McGraw Hill.

Redman, T.C. (2015, October 29). Can your data be trusted? Harvard Business Review. https://hbr.org/2015/10/can-your-data-be-trusted

Redman, T.C. (2023). People and data: Uniting to transform your business. Kogan Page, Limited.

Rensink, R. A., O'Regan, J. K., & Clark, J. J. (1997). To see or not to see: The need for attention to perceive changes in scenes. *Psychological Science*, 8(5), 368–373.

Reputation Builder. (n.d.). Why are Angry Customers More Likely to Post a Bad Review? https://www.onlinereputationmanagement.us/angry-customers-likely-post-bad-review-happy-customers-good-one/

Reuters. (2021, May 27). Syria's President Bashar al-Assad wins fourth term in office with 95.1% of votes. Reuters. https://www.reuters.com/world/middle-east/syrias-president-bashar-al-assad-wins-fourth-term-office-with-951-votes-live-2021-05-27/

Reuters. (2022, September 21). Russia calls up 300,000 reservists, says 6,000 soldiers killedin Ukraine. https://www.reuters.com/world/europe/russias-partial-mobilisation-will-see-300000-drafted-defence-minister-2022-09-21/

Ricks, E. (2021, May 17). What is a bubble chart? Storytelling With Data. https://www.storytellingwithdata.com/blog/2021/5/11/what-is-a-bubble-chart

RoadSafetyBC (2020). *Motor vehicle related crashes, injuries and fatalities. 10-year statistics for British Columbia, 2010–2019.* Ministry of Public Safety and Solicitor General.

Roch, S., Fowler, J., Smith, B., & Bourgeois, D. (2022). *5.5 Data hierarchy.* In S. Roch, J. Fowler, B. Smith, & D. Bourgeois (Eds.), *Information systems for business and beyond* (Chapter 5). eCampusOntario Pressbooks. https://ecampusontario.pressbooks.pub/informationsystemscdn/chapter/5-5-data-hierarchy/

Rosling, H. (2010, March 20). *200 countries, 200 years, 4 minutes – The joy of stats – BBC Four* [Video]. YouTube. https://www.youtube.com/watch?v=jbkSRLYSojo

Rothstein, H. R., Sutton, A. J., & Borenstein, M. (2005). *Publication bias in meta-analysis: Prevention, assessment, and adjustments.* Wiley.

Samuelson, W., & Zekhauser, R. (1988). Status quo bias in decision making. Journal of Risk and Uncertainty, 1, 1, pp.7–59.

Schmälzle, R., Lim, S., Du, Y., & Bente, G. (2025, April 15). *The art of audience engagement: LLM-based thin-slicing of scientific talks* [Preprint]. *arXiv.* https://doi.org/10.48550/arXiv.2504.10768

Schneider, S. V., Krieglstein, F., Beege, M., & Rey, G. D. (2022). The impact of video lecturers' nonverbal communication on learning: An experiment on gestures and facial expressions of pedagogical agents. *Computers & Education, 176*, Article 104350. https://doi.org/10.1016/j.compedu.2021.104350

Simons, D. J. (2010, November 3). *Selective attention test* [Video]. YouTube. https://www.youtube.com/watch?v=vJG698U2Mvo

Smylie, J., & Firestone, M. (2016, January 18). Back to the basics: Identifying and addressing underlying challenges in achieving high quality and relevant health statistics for Indigenous populations in Canada. Canadian Institutes of Health Research. Stat. J. JAOS 2015:31(1): 67–87.

Snopes. (n.d.). *The origins of FedEx* [Fact-check]. Snopes. https://www.snopes.com/fact-check/term-paper-goods/

Tableau. (n.d.). *Tree maps* [Data insights reference library page]. Tableau. https://www.tableau.com/data-insights/reference-library/visual-analytics/charts/treemaps

Thaler, R. H., & Sunstein, C. R. (2008). *Nudge: Improving decisions about health, wealth, and happiness.* Yale University Press.

The Associated Press. (2023, July 10). New data suggests 50,000 Russian deaths during Ukraine war. https://www.aljazeera.com/news/2023/7/10/new-data-uncovers-50000-russian-deaths-during-the-ukraine-war

The Observatory of Economic Complexity. (2021). *What does Algeria export?* https://oec.world/en/visualize/tree_map/hs92/export/dza/all/show/2021/

TradingView. (n.d.). *Canadian stocks with high beta* [Webpage]. TradingView. https://www.tradingview.com/markets/stocks-canada/market-movers-high-beta/

Tversky, A., & Kahneman, D. (1974). Judgment under uncertainty: Heuristics and biases. *Science*, 185(4157), 1124–1131.

Van Putten, M., Zeelenberg, M., & van Dijk, E. (2010). Who throws good money after bad? Action vs. state orientation moderates the sunk cost fallacy. *Judgment and Decision Making, 5*(1), 33–36. https://doi.org/10.1017/S1930297500002011

3Blue1Brown. (2015, April 15). *Bayes theorem, the geometry of changing beliefs* [Video]. *YouTube.* https://www.youtube.com/watch?v=HZGCoVF3YvM

Warwick, K.W. (2020, January 8). Is margarine more healthful than butter? MedicalNewsToday. https://www.medicalnewstoday.com/articles/304283

Wason, P. C. (1960). On the failure to eliminate hypotheses in a conceptual task. *Quarterly Journal of Experimental Psychology, 12*(3), 129–140. https://doi.org/10.1080/17470216008416717

Welton, M. (n.d.). Pekingese: What's good about 'em, what's bad about 'em. https://www.yourpurebredpuppy.com/reviews/pekingese.html

Wheelan, C. (2013). *Naked statistics: Stripping the dread from the data.* W. W. Norton & Company.

Wikipedia contributors. (n.d.). *Latin American Canadians*. Wikipedia. https://en.wikipedia.org/wiki/Latin_American_Canadians

Willis, J., & Todorov, A. (2006). First impressions: Making up your mind after a 100-ms exposure to a face. *Psychological Science, 17*(7), 592–598. https://doi.org/10.1111/j.1467-9280.2006.01750.x

Wu, J., Silva, D., & Chiwaya, N. (2024, April 2). MAP: See the states where marijuana is legal. NBC News. https://www.nbcnews.com/news/us-news/map-see-if-marijuana-legal-your-state-n938426

Wyton, M. (2023, June 1). Rise in motorcyclist deaths prompts calls for enhanced safety training. https://www.cbc.ca/news/canada/british-columbia/motorcycle-safety-road-design-bc-solutions-1.6861489

Wyton, M. (2023, May 29). String of motorcycle deaths in B.C. spurs calls for improved road repairs, safety standards. https://www.cbc.ca/news/canada/british-columbia/motorcycle-deaths-bc-spring-2023-1.6857691

Yuanhe. (n.d.). *Yuanhe Deluxe Roulette Wheel Set – 20-inch casino-grade glossy roulette game set* [Product page]. Amazon.ca. https://www.amazon.ca/Yuanhe-Casino-Deluxe-Glossy-Roulette/dp/B09KZGC3LQ/

Zendesk. (2013, April). *Customer service and business results: A survey of customer service from mid-size companies*. Dimensional Research.

INDEX